THE FATHERS
OF THE CHURCH

A NEW TRANSLATION

VOLUME 93

THE FATHERS OF THE CHURCH

A NEW TRANSLATION

EDITORIAL BOARD

Thomas P. Halton
The Catholic University of America
Editorial Director

Elizabeth Clark
Duke University

Robert D. Sider
Dickinson College

Robert B. Eno, S.S.
The Catholic University of America

Michael Slusser
Duquesne University

Frank A. C. Mantello
The Catholic University of America

Cynthia Kahn White
The University of Arizona

Kathleen McVey
Princeton Theological Seminary

Robin Darling Young
The Catholic University of America

David J. McGonagle
Director
The Catholic University of America Press

FORMER EDITORIAL DIRECTORS

Ludwig Schopp, Roy J. Deferrari, Bernard M. Peebles,
Hermigild Dressler, O.F.M.

Laszlo G. Szijarto
Staff Editor

ST. LEO THE GREAT
SERMONS

Translated by
JANE PATRICIA FREELAND, C.S.J.B.
AGNES JOSEPHINE CONWAY, S.S.J.

THE CATHOLIC UNIVERSITY OF AMERICA PRESS
Washington, D.C.

Copyright © 1996
THE CATHOLIC UNIVERSITY OF AMERICA PRESS
All rights reserved
Printed in the United States of America

The paper used in this publication meets the minimum requirements of American National Standards for Information Science—Permanence of Paper for Printed Library materials, ANSI Z39.48-1984.
∞

LIBRARY OF CONGRESS CATALOGING-IN-PUBLICATION DATA

Leo I, Pope, d. 461.
   [Selections. English. 1995]
   Sermons / St. Leo the Great ; translated by Jane Patricia Freeland, Agnes Josephine Conway.
      p. cm. — (The Fathers of the church ; v. 93)
   Includes bibliographical references and index.
   1. Sermons, Latin—Translations into English. 2. Catholic Church—
Sermons. I. Jane Patricia, Sister, 1910– . II. Conway, Agnes Josephine, 1921– . III. Title. IV. Series.
BR60.F3L42 1995
[BR65.L42]
252'.014—dc20
95-23000
ISBN 0-8132-0093-8
ISBN 978-0-8132-2827-9 (pbk.)

CONTENTS

Abbreviations	vii
Bibliography	ix
Introduction	3
His Elevation to the See of Peter	17
Annual Collections	34
Days of Fast in December	49
Christmas	76
Epiphany	132
Days of Fast in Lent	166
Lenten Sermon on the Transfiguration	218
Passion of the Lord	225
Ascension	322
Pentecost	330
Feast of Sts. Peter and Paul	352
Commemorating Alaric's Invasion of Rome	360
Martyrdom of the Maccabees	362
Feast of St. Lawrence	365
Days of Fast in September	368
On the Beatitudes	394
Against Eutyches	401
General Index	407
Scriptural Index	427

ABBREVIATIONS

CCL Corpus Christianorum Series Latina. Vol. 138–138A. *Sancti Leonis Magni Romani Pontificis: Tractatus Septem et Nonaginta.* Ed. Antonius Chavasse. Turnhout: Brepols, 1973.
CMH *Cambridge Medieval History.* Ed. G. M. Gwatkin and J. P. Whitney. Vol. 1: *The Christian Roman Empire and the Foundation of the Teutonic Kingdoms.* Cambridge: Cambridge University Press, 1967.
DSp *Dictionnaire de Spiritualité, Ascétique et Mystique, Doctrine et Histoire.* Ed. M. Viller; F. Cavallera; and J. de Guibert, S.J. Fasc. 59–60. Paris: G. Beauchesne et ses fils, 1975.
DThC *Dictionnaire de Théologie Catholique.* Ed. A. Vacant, E. Mangenot, and E. Amann. Vol. 9. Paris: Letouzey et Ané, 1926.
EDR *Encyclopedic Dictionary of Religion.* Ed. Paul Meagher, O.P.; Thomas C. O'Brien; and Consuelo Maria Aherne, S.S.J. Washington, DC: Corpus Publications, 1979.
ER *Encyclopedia of Religion.* Ed. Mircea Eliade. New York: Macmillan, 1987.
FOTC *The Fathers of the Church.* New York: Cima Publishing Co., 1947–1949; New York: FOTC, Inc., 1949–1960; Washington, DC: The Catholic University of America Press, 1960–.
JBC *The Jerome Biblical Commentary.* Ed. R. Brown, J. Fitzmyer, and R. Murphy. Englewood Cliffs, NJ: Prentice-Hall, 1968.
NCE *The New Catholic Encyclopedia.* Prepared by an editorial staff at the Catholic University of America (Washington, DC). New York: McGraw-Hill, 1967.
NPNF *A Select Library of the Nicene and Post-Nicene Fathers of the Christian Church.* Ed. Philip Schaff and Henry Wace. 2nd series. Vol. 12: *The Letters and Sermons of Leo the Great, Bishop of Rome.* Trans. Charles L. Feltoe. New York: The Christian Literature Company, 1895.
PL Patrologiae Cursus Completus: Series Latina. Ed. J.-P. Migne. Vol. 54–56: *Sancti Leonis Magni Romani Pontificis Omnia Opera.* Ed. P. and H. Bellardinus. Paris: Migne, 1846.
PLS Patrologiae Latinae Supplementum. Vol. 3. Ed. Adalbertus Hamman. Paris: Éd. Garnier Frères, 1963.
SC Sources Chrétiennes. Ed. H. de Lubac, S.J.; and J. Daniélou, S.J. *Léon le Grand: Sermons.* Trans. Dom René Dolle. Paris: Éditions du Cerf, 1964, 1969, 1971, 1973. (SC 22, 49, 74, 200).

SELECT BIBLIOGRAPHY

For more complete coverage, see B. Studer in Quasten's *Patrologia* (Institutum Patristicum Augustinum. Turin: Marietti, 1967–78).

General Studies on Leo

Battifol, P. "Léon I." In DThC, 9:218–301.
Bonwetsch, N. "Leo I, called the Great." In *New Schaff-Herzog Encyclopedia of Religious Knowledge*, 6:448–450. New York: Funk and Wagnalls Co., 1910.
Camelot, P. Th. "Léon Ier (Saint) (440–461)." *Catholicisme* (1975), 7:312–317.
Dekkers, E. and A. Goar, ed. *Clavis Patrum Latinorum*. Steenbrugis: in Abbatia Sancti Petri, 1961.
Hudon, G. "Léon le Grand (Saint)." In DSp, 597–610.
Hunt, E., C.S.C. *St. Leo the Great: An Introductory Study*. New York: Sheed and Ward, 1934.
Jalland, T. G. *The Life and Times of St. Leo the Great*. London: Society for the Promotion of Christian Knowledge, 1941.
Kelly, J. N. D. "Leo I, Saint." In *The Oxford Dictionary of Popes*, 43–45. Oxford: Oxford University Press, 1986.
Murphy, F. X. "Leo I, Pope, Saint." In NCE, 8:637–639.
O'Brien, T. C. "Leo I, Saint." In EDR, 2:2095.
Stockmeier, P. "Leo 1. der Grosse." In *Gestalten der Kirchengeschichte*, 11:56–70. Stuttgart: Kohlhammer, 1984.
Studer, B. "Leo I, der Grosse, Papst (440–461)." *Theologische Realenkyklopädie*, 20:737–741. Ed. Berlin: 1990.

Bibles

Biblia Sacra: iuxta Vulgatam Clementinam: nova editio logicis partitionibus aliisque subsidiis. 3rd ed. Ed. R. P. A. Colunga, O.P., and L. Turrado. Biblioteca des autores cristianos 14. Madrid: Editorial Catolica, 1959.
The Jerusalem Bible. Ed. A. Jones. New York: Doubleday and Co., 1966.
The Catholic Biblical Encyclopedia: Old and New Testaments. Ed. J. E. Steinmüller and K. Sullivan. New York: Joseph F. Wagner, 1955–56.
The New American Bible. Trans. Members of the Catholic Biblical Association of America. St. Joseph Edition. New York: Catholic Book Publishing, 1970–1987.
The New World Dictionary-Concordance to the New American Bible. New York: World Bible Publishers, 1970.

SELECT BIBLIOGRAPHY

Texts

Bellardinus, P. and H. *Sancti Leonis Magni Romani Pontificis Omnia Opera*. PL.
Chavasse, A., ed. *Sancti Leonis Magni Romani Pontificis: Tractatus Septem et Nonaginta*. CCL.
Eddy, G., et al. *Leo Magnus: Tractatus*. Corpus Christianorum Instrumenta Lexicologica Latina Series B, 40. Turnhout: Brepols, 1987.
Hamman, A., ed. PLS.

Translations

C. L. Feltoe, trans. NPNF.
Garrido Bonafio, M. B[iblioteca des] A[utores] C[ristianos] 291 (1969).
Huyg, A. *Sint Leo de Groote: Over de Menscwording van Leerstellige brieven en preeken*. Amsterdam: 1941.
Mariucci, T. *Omilei e Lettere di S. Leo Magno*. Classici delle Religioni. Turin: 1969.
Saenz, A. *San Leon Magno y los Misterios de Cristo*. Paraná: 1984.
Steeger, T. *Leo der Grosse: Reden zu den Mysterien des Kirchenjahres*. Schriften der Kirchenväter 9. Munich: 1984.
Valeriano, E. *Il mistero Pasquale, Il mistero del Natale*. Alba-Rome: 1965, 1967.

Translations: Sermons

Dolle, R. "Les sermons en double édition de S. Léon le Grand." *Recherches de théologie ancienne et médiévale* 45 (1978), 5–33.
Magne, J. "La prière de consécration des vierges *Deus castorum corporum*: Étude du texte." *Ephemerides Liturgicae* 72 (1958), 245–267.
Steeger, T., ed. *Sämtliche Predigten aus dem lateinischen übersetzt und mit Einleitung und Inhaltsangaben*. Bibliothek der Kirchenväter 54–55. Munich: J. Kösel und F. Pustet, 1927.
Studer, B. "Die Einflüsse der Exegese Augustins auf die Predigten Leos des Grossen." In *Forma Futuri: Studi in onore del Cardinale Michele Pellegrino*, 917–930. Turin: Bottega d'Erasmo, 1975.
Vromen, F. *Leo de Grote: Preken voor het liturgischjaar* Oosterhout 4.

Studies on the Sermons

Capelle, B. "Une messe de s. Léon pour l'Ascension." *Ephemerides Liturgicae* 67 (1953), 201–209.
———. "Valeur spirituelle du Carême d'après s. Léon." *Orientalia Lovaniensia Periodica* 35 (1954), 104–114.
Carton, I. "Note sur l'emploi du mot *observantia* dans les homélies de s. Léon." *Vigiliae Christianae* 8 (1954), 104–114.
Chavasse, A. "Dans sa prédication S. Léon le Grand a-t-il utilisé des sources liturgiques?" In *Mélanges liturgiques offerts au R. P. dom Bernard Botte à l'occasion du cinquantième anniversaire de son ordination sacerdotale (4 juin 1972)*, 71–74. Louvain: Abbaye du Mont César, 1972.
———. "Le sermon prononcé par Léon le Grand pour l'anniversaire d'une dédicace." *Revue Bénédictine* 91 (1981), 46–104.
———. "Les fériés de Careme célébrées aux temps de s. Léon le Grand (440–

461)." In *Miscellanea liturgica in onore di sua eminenza il Cardinale Giacomo Lercaro, arcieviscovo di Bologna, presidente del "Consilium" per l'applicazione della costituzione sulla sacra liturgia,* 551–557. Rome: Desclée, 1966–67.

———. "Le sermon III de s. Léon et la date de la célébration des Quatre-Temps de septembre." *Revue des sciences religieuses* 44 (1970), 77–84.

Dolle, R. "Un docteur de l'aumône, s. Léon le Grand." *La Vie spirituelle* 96 (1957), 266–287.

———. "Les idées morales de saint Léon le Grand." *Mélanges de science religieuse* 15 (1958), 49–84.

Faraoni, V. "Primato della sede di Pietro nei *Sermones* di S. Leone Magno." *Palestra del Clero* 51 (1972), 727–734.

Ferrua, A. "Della festa dei SS. Maccabei e di un antico sermone in loro onore." *La Civiltà Cattolica* 89.3 (1938), 234–237 and 318–327.

Fischer, B. *Die Messe in der Glaubensverkündigung.* Freiburg: Herder, 1953.

Guillaume, A. *Jeune et charité dans l'Église latine des origines au XII siècle en particulier chez s. Léon le Grand.* Paris: Laboureur, 1954.

Hofmann, F. "Die Osterbotschaft in den Predigten Papst Leos des Grossen." In *Paschatis Sollemnia: Studien zu Osterfeier und Osterfrömmigkeit.* Ed. B. Fischer and J. Wagner. Freiburg: Herder (1959), 76–86.

Holten, D. R. "The Sacramental Language of Leo the Great: A Study of the Words *Munus* and *Oblata.*" *Ephemerides Liturgicae* 92 (1978), 115–165.

Hudon, G. *La perfection chrétienne d'après les sermons de s. Léon.* Lex Orandi 26. Paris: Éditions du Cerf, 1959.

Lang, A. P. "Anklänge an Orationen der Ostervigil in Sermonen Leos des Grossen." *Sacris Erudiri* 27 (1984), 129–149.

Mikat, P. "Die Lehre vom Almosen in den Kollektenpredigten Papst Leos des Grossen." In *Perennitas: Beiträge zur christlichen Archäologie und Kunst, zur Geschichte der Literatur, der Liturgie und des Mönchtums sowie zur Philosophie des Rechts und zur politischen Philosophie,* 2:46–64. Ed. H. Rahner, T. A. Michels, and E. von Severus. Beiträge zur Geschichte des alten Mönchtums und des Benediktinerordens. Münster: Aschendorff, 1963.

Pellegrino, M. "L'influsso di S. Agostino su S. Leone Magno nei sermoni sul Natale e sull' Epifania." *Annali del Pontifical Istitute Super de Scienze e Lettere "S. Chiara"* 11 (1961), 101–132.

———. "Temi dominanti nei sermoni natalizi di S. Leone Magno." In *Miscel. C. Figini,* 97–115. Milan: 1964.

Pepka, E. P. *The Theology of St. Peter's Presence in His Successors According to St. Leo the Great.* Ph.D. Dissertation. Washington, D.C.: Catholic University of America, 1986.

Polato, D. "Aspetti di una teologia della carita nei sermoni di s. Leone Magno." Dissertation. Padua, 1969.

Rosa, V. de. "Il digiuno liturgico nei sermoni di s. Leone Magno." *Annali del Pontifical Istitute Super di Scienze e Lettere "S. Chiara"* 11 (1961), 19–91.

Sieger, J. D. "Visual Metaphor as Theology: Leo the Great's Sermons on the Incarnation and the Arch Mosaics at S. Maria Maggiore." *Gesta* 26(1987), 83–91.

Testard, M. "Le *sacramentum* dans les sermons de s. Léon le Grand." Dissertation. Paris, 1948.

SELECT BIBLIOGRAPHY

Literary and Stylistic Aspects

Halliwell, W. J. *The Style of Pope St. Leo the Great.* The Catholic University of America Patristic Studies 59. Washington, DC: The Catholic University of America Press, 1939.

Mueller, M. *The Vocabulary of Pope St. Leo the Great.* The Catholic University of America Patristic Studies 67. Washington, DC: The Catholic University of America Press, 1943.

Pschmadt, M. "Leo der Grosse als Prediger." Dissertation. Bonn, 1912 (reprinted Wuppertaler Aktien Druckerei).

Steeger, T. "Die Klauseltechnik Leos des Grossen in seinen Sermonen: Untersuchungen zur rhythmik der lateinischen Kunstprosa im 5. Jahrhundert nach Christus." Dissertation. Munich, 1908.

Leo and the Roman Liturgy

Borella, P. "S. Leone Magno e il Communicantes." *Ephemerides Liturgicae* 60 (1946), 93–101.

Callewaert, C. "S. Léon et les textes du léonien." *Sacris Erudiri* 1 (1948), 35–123.

———. "S. Léon et le Communicantes et le *Nobis quoque peccatoribus.*" *Sacris Erudiri* 1 (1948), 123–164.

Coebergh, C. "S. Léon le Grand auteur de la grande formule *Ad virgines sacras* du sacramentaire léonien." *Sacris Erudiri* 6 (1954), 282–326.

Cross, F. L. "Pre-Leonine Elements in the Proper of the Roman Mass." *Journal of Theological Studies* 50 (1949), 191–197.

Dekkers, E. "Autour de l'oeuvre liturgique de saint Léon le Grand." *Sacris Erudiri* 10 (1958), 363–398.

Dolle, R. [Écritures Saintes] "S. Léon." In DSp 4 (1960), 158ff.

Duval, Y.-M. "*Sacramentum* et *mysterium* chez saint Léon le Grand." Dissertation. Lille, 1959.

———. "S. Léon et la Tradition." *Recherches de science religieuse* 48 (1960), 166–184.

Harrison, O. "The Formula *Ad virgines sacras*: A Study of the Sources." *Ephemerides Liturgicae* 66 (1952), 252–273, 352–366.

Jossua, J.-P. *Le Salut: Incarnation ou mystère pascal chez les Pères de l'Église de s. Irénée à s. Léon le Grand.* Cogitatio Fidei 28. Paris: Editions du Cerf, 1968.

Lauras, A. "S. Léon le Grand e l'Écriture Sainte." *Studia Patristica* 6 (1962) = *Texte und Untersuchungen* 8.1, 127–140. Berlin: 1962.

Lepelley, C. "Les mystères chrétiens chez s. <Léon> le Grand." Dissertation. Paris, 1955.

INTRODUCTION

INTRODUCTION

Life and Times of Pope Leo the Great
Before Leo's Pontificate

History records very few details about the early life of Pope Leo, the first of only two popes referred to as "the Great." He was born—probably sometime during the 390's—into a family of Tuscan origin[1] that had settled at Rome. We can judge from the quality and style of his writings that Leo had a solid classical and Christian education. Although in expressing his thoughts he uses all the elements of classical style and vocabulary, he (like St. Cyprian) does not anywhere in the *Sermons* mention names from classical literature. At the same time, his sermons are replete with quotations from and references to both the Old and the New Testaments. He grew to love Rome, in spite of its many and serious defects, claiming it for his "patria" (*Letter* 31.4). Leo (like Cicero) referred to Rome simply as "The City," and his praise of Christian Rome was ardent and eloquent (*Serm.* 82.1).

St. Augustine (*Letter* 191.1) mentions an "acolyte Leo" carrying a message about the Pelagian heresy from Pope Zosimus to the Bishop of Carthage in 418. If this can be identified with our Leo, we see that he was already involved as a young man about twenty years of age in the service of the Church. He was probably beginning to develop that wide vision and courageous spirit which would later allow him as Archdeacon of Rome to exercise considerable influence in ecclesiastical deliberations.

Leo's foresight benefited Pope Celestine by alerting him to various difficulties presented in the ideas of Nestorius, Patriarch of Constantinople.[2] Christological questions prompted

---

1. *Liber Pontificalis* I.218
2. Nestorius, Patriarch of Constantinople, whose objection to Mary's title "Mother of God" (with its christological implications) occasioned the General Council of Ephesus in 431.

Leo to ask John Cassian[3] for a clear summation of the Church's doctrine on the Incarnation. During the next pontificate, Leo strengthened Pope Sixtus III (432–440) against machinations by Julian of Eclanum who was trying to recover his bishopric.[4]

In 439 Leo traveled to Gaul on a mission to make peace between two generals, Aëtius (a government adviser) and Albinus (later the Praetorian Prefect of Rome). This dispute threatened the fragile security of those times. While still in Gaul, Leo learned about the death of Pope Sixtus and his own election as successor to the Chair of Peter. He had been chosen unanimously.

These few examples show how both civil and ecclesiastical authorities valued the vision and courage of their archdeacon. His considerable talents for administration, his clarity of intellect, and his spiritual leadership would often be put to the test during the next twenty-one years.

Leo's Pontificate (440–461)

During the 5th century, a time of transition and upheaval, the once-powerful Roman Empire slowly disintegrated as its people gradually blended with migrating Vandals, Goths, Franks, and Burgundians—an amalgamation that actually took several centuries. Although the turbulence, the disruption, and the destruction were intermittent, they troubled the whole Mediterranean and European areas at various times. There were periods of horror, but there were also periods of relative calm—when simply getting used to new neighbors and unfamiliar customs could be sufficiently trying for those accustomed to the old Roman ways. Tensions existed not only in the West, but in the East as well; not only in the military, economic, and civic spheres, but also in the Church. Religious crises interfaced with civic and military ones. Moral values and cultural supports were bruised.

---

3. John Cassian, a monk (founder of a monastery in Marseilles), wrote this treatise on the Incarnation as well as a series of conferences on the discipline and spiritual life of monks.

4. Bishop Julian of Eclanum supported the teachings of Pelagius and wrote against Augustine. He was deprived of his office by the Pope.

Into this turmoil came the Church's contribution to the defense of Western civilization, to the outcome of that struggle which provided a continuity of values from classical civilization—a contribution in the person of Leo the Great, pope from 440 to 461. He would emerge as the one individual who—while civic leaders were weakening—kept contact from his pivotal center at Rome with the world (Africa, Spain, Gaul, Italy, Illyria, and Alexandria). He was at once the clear and logical thinker, the authoritative and courageous leader, as well as the humble and prayerful shepherd of Christ's flock.

While trying to maintain civic equilibrium, Leo remained faithful to his primary duty, his care for the Church. His letters to people all around the Mediterranean area show us the innumerable ways in which he counseled bishops, strengthened unity in faith and in practices, disciplined the rebellious, encouraged the weak, and inveighed against those who were harming the faith. He demonstrated his courage when he accosted the barbarians in 452 and 455, and also when he asserted his authoritative teaching power in response to heretics (an equally great threat in those perilous times).

One factor which contributed to a widespread confusion about and hazy presentation of some dogmas was the use of the two different languages in the East and the West, Greek and Latin respectively. Then, within each one of these languages, there was an unstable employment of terminology, i.e., for words like "nature," "person," and "essence," which vacillated between their ordinary meanings and specifically philosophical ones.[5]

In addition to undertaking civic and diplomatic missions, Leo worked to bring church and state into a harmony of ideals and practices. For this end, and as a result of his dealings with the "Robber Council," he instituted the office of Papal Legate at Constantinople.

He sought to establish the correct date for Easter, so that—for the sake of unity—the whole Church would celebrate it at the same time. Leo fostered literature and the arts, particularly

---

5. cf. SC I.10.

in rebuilding and refurbishing churches destroyed by the barbarian looting. Many of the prayers and prefaces of the Leonine Sacramentary show the influence of his compositions in thought, style, and the allusions made to contemporary affairs.

Leo died on 10 November 461 and was buried at the shrine of St. Peter, Prince of the Apostles, whose "embattled constancy" Leo faithfully emulated while ruling from the Chair of Peter. Today, his feast is kept both in the West (10 November) and in the Byzantine liturgy (18 February), a fact which testifies to his efforts for the cause of unity.

History witnesses to Leo's brilliance, his clarity of intellect, and his unyielding zeal in defending the doctrines of the Church that had been handed down by the Fathers. The *Sermons* are replete with his wisdom, his holiness, and his compassion for the flock (present and yet to come). Well-deserved was the praise given him by Pope Benedict XIV in 1754 when he named Pope Leo the Great a "Doctor of the Church":

> It was due to his excelling virtue, his teaching, and his most vigilant zeal as shepherd of his people, that he won from our forefathers the title "Great." In expounding the deeper mysteries of our faith and vindicating it against the errors that assail it, in imparting disciplinary rules and moral precepts, the excellence of his teaching is so radiant with the majestic richness of priestly eloquence and has so won the admiration of the world and the enthusiasm alike of Councils, Fathers and writers of the Church, that the fame and reputation of this wisest of Popes can hardly be rivaled by any other of the Church's holy doctors.[6]

Chronological Outline of Events Surrounding Leo's Pontificate

408–10   Alaric and his Visigoths enter Italy. Stilicho (Commander of the Roman army in the West) killed. Rome sacked by Alaric. This last event so disturbed the people

---

6. An excerpt from the Apostolic Constitution of Pope Benedict XIV, "Militantis Ecclesiae," (12 October 754), quoted in Pope John XXIII's Encyclical "Aeterna Dei Sapientia," commemorating the fifteenth centenary of the death of Pope Leo the Great, 11 November, 1961; as found in *The Pope Speaks* Vol. 8, No. I, 7–22 (p. 12). In this Encyclical, John XXIII also refers to Pope Leo the Great as "Doctor of the Church's Unity."

GENERAL INTRODUCTION

	that St. Augustine began his *De Civitate Dei* to disprove the allegation that Christianity had caused this disaster.
412	Pelagianism condemned by the Synod of Carthage. Death of Alaric.
429–39	Roman Africa conquered by Gaiseric and his Vandals. Violence and terror abound.
430	Death of St. Augustine.
431	Council of Ephesus called to deal with the christological ideas of Nestorius.
438	Law Code promulgated by Theodosius II.
440	Death of Pope Sixtus III and Election of Leo I.
439–42	Vandals conquer Africa and terrorize the whole Mediterranean area, causing hardship through the depletion of food and money normally provided by Roman Africa.
441–42	Roman army withdraws from Britain in an effort to protect the mainland. Saxons begin to take over England. Attila and his Asiatic tribes harass the Eastern Empire.
449	"Robber Council" convened at Ephesus. Supporters of Eutyches manipulate its outcome.
450	Death of Theodosius II (Emperor in the East). Accession of his sister Pulcheria (along with her husband Marcian).
451	Attila and his Huns invade Gaul. Council held at Chalcedon (influenced by Leo's "Tome") condemns the Eutychian and Monophysite heresies.
452	Attila, the "Scourge of God," invades northern Italy, proceeds toward Rome. Beleaguered by setbacks and hardships, he retreats when confronted by Leo.
454	Death of Attila. Valentinian III murders Aëtius, the able commander-in-chief of the Roman army and the most important military man in the West. Power of the Huns weakens.
455	Valentinian III himself murdered by two of Aëtius' officers. During this turmoil, the Vandals (under Gaiseric) pillage Rome and perpetrate terrible atrocities. They loot and sack Rome for fourteen days. Maximus, the successor of Valentinian, killed while fleeing the city. Eudoxia (the widow of Valentinian) and their two daughters are taken back to Africa as captives.
457	Bishop Proterius murdered in Alexandria. Timothy Aelurus usurps his see. Leo urges the Emperor Marcian to

	redress the wrong done to the Church by this usurpation.
461	Death of Pope Leo.
472	Ricimer, a German general (successor to Stilicho and Aëtius), overcomes Rome. These three non-Romans were the most powerful military men in the government during this century.
476	Deposition of Romulus Augustulus and the takeover of Rome by Odoacer, first barbarian ruler of Italy.

Outline of Heresies Referred to in the Sermons

Basilides (*Serm.* 16.3): an early second century Gnostic with Docetistic leanings.

Docetism (*Serms.* 28.4 and 30.2): from apostolic times onward, the idea that Christ's humanity was only an appearance (not reality), and that, consequently, his suffering was not real.

Marcion (*Serm.* 16.3): a dangerous heretic of the second century who taught that there was a definite break between the Old and the New Testaments, between Judaism and Christianity, between Law and Grace; and that there are two gods.

Arianism (*Serms.* 16.3, 23.2, 24.5, 28.4, and 75.4): a fourth century heresy whose founder Arius declared ". . . the *Logos* is not eternal, nor co-eternal with the Father, nor uncreated like the Father, for it is from the Father that he has received life and being."[7]

Sabellianism (*Serms.* 16.3, 24.5, and 28.4): a third century Trinitarian heresy which claimed that God is one (the Son and the Holy Spirit being merely aspects of God and not Persons).

Macedonianism (*Serms.* 24.5, 28.4, and 75.4): a fourth century heresy which held that the Holy Spirit was not of the same substance as the Father and the Son (and was therefore a creature).

Photinianism (*Serms.* 16.3, 24.5, 28.4, 30.2, and 96.2): a fourth century heresy which held that there are not three Persons in God, i.e., that the Word is not the second Person.

Apollinarianism (*Serms.* 24.5, 28.4, 30.2, 47.2, and 96.2): a fourth century heresy which held that Christ did not have a rational human soul, but that the Word assumed its place.

7. Daniélou and Marrou (p. 250 and n.1).

Eunomianism (*Serm.* 16.3): a fourth century heresy which held that God cannot be begotten, therefore the Son is not God.

Nestorianism (*Serms.* 28.5 and 91.2): a fifth century heresy which held that Mary is not the Mother of God, "Mary bore a man, the vehicle of divinity but not God."

Manichaeism (*Serms.* 9.4, 16.4, 24.4–6, 34.4, 42.5, 47.2, 76.6, and 96.2): originally a pagan sect which imitated some Christian ideas but followed complicated and immoral practices with regard to food, clothing, and marriage.

According to Leo, "[Manichaeans] gainsay the prophets and the Holy Spirit. They have dared to suppress with a damnable impiety the Psalms of David which are chanted with all reverence throughout the Universal Church. They deny the Birth of Christ according to the flesh. They say that his Passion and Resurrection were merely appearances and not reality. They strip from the Baptism of regeneration any power of grace whatsoever. With them, nothing remains holy, nothing intact, nothing true" (*Serm.* 9.4).

Arian Vandals invading Africa persecuted all who were not Arians, and so Manichaeans fled from Africa. Many emigrated to Italy where Leo constantly publicized their errors and warned his people to avoid them. He cooperated with Valentinian III, who in 445 promulgated laws against their immoral practices, harmful as they were to the civic body.

Eutychianism (*Serms.* 28.5, 91.2, and 96.3): a fifth century heresy that was developed in opposition to the Nestorians. Eutyches, an aged monk not too well educated in theology, held that before the Incarnation there were two natures (divine and human) but after the Incarnation there was only one nature, for the divine absorbed the human. To deny the reality of Christ's human nature is to deny the efficacy of Christ's Passion (*passim* throughout Leo's *Sermons*). Eutyches' theory about the nature of Christ becomes a branch of Monophysitism.

Flavian, the Patriarch of Constantinople, called Eutyches to account before his synod of bishops at Constantinople. After a long delay, Eutyches finally appeared. When he did so, he stated his belief that, though Christ was born of Mary, his humanity (not of the same substance as ours) was absorbed into the divinity. Consequently, Christ had no real human nature. When the synod excommunicated him, he tried to have the decision overturned by an appeal to the pope.

Emperor Theodosius II called for a General Council at Ephesus in 449 to settle the matter. Leo was invited to the Council, but the distress and turmoil in Italy (due to a threat of invasion by Attila and the Huns) required his presence at Rome. He sent three legates: Bishop Julius of Puteoli, Renatus (a priest), and Hilary (a deacon). They carried a message (*Letter* 28) to Flavian. Flavian in turn was supposed to read it before the Council Fathers.

This famous letter (referred to as the "Tome") summarized with great precision and clarity the Church's teaching about the Incarnation. Nonetheless, it was not even read to the assembled clergy, many of whom were supporters of Eutyches. Dioscorus (who presided over the assembly) also favored Eutyches. Consequently, he delayed and finally refused to have the letter presented. Dioscorus summoned Eutyches, heard his unchanged declaration of faith in the one nature of Christ, and abolished his excommunication. He then charged Flavian and Eusebius of Dorylaeum with changing the teachings of Nicaea and Ephesus, and called for their deposition. Many of the participants tried to dissuade him from this position, but Dioscorus was inflexible. Flavian died a short time later, and the bishops who had opposed Dioscorus were deposed.

Hilary managed to escape and finally to reach Rome. His report distressed Leo, who then called a Synod at Rome, reported these disgraceful manipulations, and annulled the decisions of that Council (which he termed the "Robber Council"). His next step was to raise a protest over these injustices to Emperor Theodosius II. Demanding a new Council, he enlisted the help of Valentinian III (Emperor of the West) and his wife—who happened to be Theodosius' daughter—in influencing Theodosius. Refusing to accept Flavian's successor (an Anatolius) until he accepted the *Tome*, Leo sent four legates to Constantinople.

At this juncture (July 450), Theodosius II died as a result of injuries due to a fall from his horse. Pulcheria (his older sister) took the throne as Empress and married Marcian (who became her consort). Together they supported Leo. Eutyches lost his patron and was forced to remain in a monastery.

Finally, the requested Council (much larger than that earlier one) opened in Chalcedon on 8 October 451. It lasted for about three weeks. As legates from the pope presided over it, the former Council was reviewed. Dioscorus was deposed for refusing to accept Leo's *Tome* as well for his leadership in manipulating the Council. Then a commission was formed to draw up a statement. This doctrinal decree on the Incarnation included the Creed of Nicaea (as the foundation of Christian faith), the Creed of Constantinople I (as an interpretation of the Nicene Creed), the Council of Ephesus I along with the synodal letters of Cyril, and the *Tome* of Leo.

Several disciplinary matters were then taken up by the Council as well. Of these, only Canon 28 was rejected by Rome. It would have given precedence over the Apostolic Sees of Antioch and Alexandria to the See of Constantinople, thereby nearly equating its powers with the those of Rome. Leo refused to compromise the primacy of Peter. Later (in 453) he accepted the Council's dogmatic decree, but not the disciplinary canons.

Most Christians in the West were satisfied by the Council of Chalcedon, but some in the East continued to battle over its outcome. In 457 a group of such dissenters murdered Bishop Proterius while he was officiating at the Holy Thursday liturgy in the Basilica at Alexandria. Timothy Aelurus (a prominent member of the group) became the next bishop. Emperor Marcian punished the assassins, but accepted the usurper. Leo, however, quickly admonished Marcian about his duty to protect the good order of Church and state (*Letter* 156). Timothy was replaced by a lawful successor as Marcian again became a supporter of Leo. After the death of Leo in 461, Eutychianism, Nestorianism, and Monophysitism continued in various areas of the East.

Works of Pope Leo the Great

St. Leo left a body of letters and sermons which were of great benefit to his contemporaries, and—especially when it comes to the sermons—stand us in good stead even today. One hundred and forty-three letters present the Pontiff in his role of administrator, conscious of his obligations as Chief Pastor of the Church and of his authority in the Chair of Peter. These letters—which contain explanations of dogma, answers to questions, remedies for difficulties and abuses, and some congratulatory greetings—are addressed to civic leaders, as well as to bishops, priests, and abbots of the East and the West.

In his sermons, Leo the shepherd devotes all of his abilities to the task of teaching his flock. By word and example he represents a "blend of justice and mercy, of strength and gentleness."[8] His sermons encompass the whole content of Christian

---

8. Pope John XXIII's Encyclical "Aeterna Dei Sapientia," *op. cit.* p. 148.

life: strong faith in the message of Jesus and adherence to the Church he had founded to proclaim this message. Throughout Leo encourages the avoidance (at all costs) of everyone who distorts or disbelieves this message.

We have followed the text from CCL (138 and 138A) and consulted the SC edition as well for this translation. CCL arranges the *Sermons* as follows:

Volume 138:
  Introduction
  1–5   His Elevation to the See of Peter
  6–11 Annual Collections
  12–20 Days of Fast in December
  21–30 Christmas
  31–38 Epiphany

Volume 138A
  39–50 Days of Fast in Lent
  51   Lenten Sermon on the Transfiguration
  52–72 Passion of the Lord
  73–74 Ascension
  75–81 Pentecost
  82–83 Feast of Sts. Peter and Paul
  84   Commemorating Alaric's Invasion of Rome
  84B   Martyrdom of the Maccabees
  85   Feast of St. Lawrence
  86–94 Days of Fast in September
  95   On the Beatitudes
  96   Against Eutyches

Style of Leo's *Sermons*

Leo's language and style reveal something of his own character—thoroughly old Roman (not effusive, not full of imagery, but basic, solid, traditional, and logical). While this characterization might sound unappealing, Leo employed many of the rhetorical techniques used by Cicero. Latin utilizes them with great effect, but they can be rather difficult (if not impossible) to translate effectively. Sermons, however, should not be read as if they had been intended for the written page. It helps in the appreciation of Leo's talent to visualize the gestures and the bearing of the Pontiff, to imagine his intonation, emphases, and verbal skills.[9]

Leo constructed his sermons very carefully—with an introduction, a theme with examples, and a definite conclusion. Content and structure form an admirable, logical whole—a fact to which the numerous copiers and imitators of later centuries give ample witness.[10]

As a teacher, Leo had a gift for clarity and practicality. He did not know Greek (with its subtleties), but he did have an ability to craft his native Latin into an effective tool for elucidating doctrines handed down from the time of Christ and his apostles; for taking on the aberrations and downright falsehood of heresies, for peeling off their errors one by one; for making sure that even the newest of those "reborn in Christ" knew the tenets of their faith. Love of God and love of neighbor, articles of the Creed, the "Way" exemplified in the life of Christ, peace, unity, humility, forgiveness, courage, generosity, unremitting fidelity to the will of God, the need for appraising the deepest recesses of the heart, mortification, and daily prayer—all supported by the words of the Old and the New Testaments—find a place in his message.

Delivered at liturgical functions, the sermons had for an audience—among others—bishops, priests, civic leaders, and the men and women who were trying to keep the economic and political capital of the world functioning somehow amid the turbulence.

---

9. Fuller investigation into the style of Pope St. Leo can be found in Halliwell (*The Style of Pope St. Leo the Great*). See Bibliography.
10. Cf. CCL Introduction.

SERMONS

HIS ELEVATION TO THE SEE OF PETER

At the time of his election to the See of Peter on 29 September 440, Leo expressed his gratitude for the trust placed in him by God and by God's Church (*Serm.* 1). For some years thereafter he gave special sermons on the anniversary of his election, four of which have come down to us: *Serms.* 2 (441), 3 (443), 4 (444), and 5 (after 445?). The same general themes reverberate throughout the sermons: gratitude for the trust placed in him; humility resulting from his feelings of unworthiness and weakness, accompanied by a request for prayers that he prove competent; an appreciation for the magnitude of the work and the frequent occasions for stumbling presented by it; gratitude for the goodness, the unity, and the peace of his flock.

Fundamental to these sermons and to those on the feasts of Sts. Peter and Paul (*Serms.* 82 and 83) is his praise of St. Peter, his belief in the primacy of Peter, and his reliance on Peter who continues to rule the Church through his own weakness. This same dependence on Peter is found at the conclusion of all his Lenten sermons, in his sermons on the fasts of September and December, and in his sermon on the Transfiguration (*Serm.* 51). "Just as what Peter believed in Christ remains, so there remains what Christ instituted in Peter" (*Serm.* 3.2).

This strong affirmation of the primacy held by the Bishop of Rome (made from the very beginning of his reign) underlines Leo's conviction that Christ intended Peter and his successors to be a unifying principle in the Church. In recognition of this, Pope John XXIII considered Leo to be "Doctor of the Church's Unity."[1] "You are Peter and upon this rock I will build my Church, and the gates of hell will not prevail against it" (Mt 16.18). *Serms.* 4 and 83 contain his meditations on the words exchanged between Christ and St. Peter (Mt 16.16–19). It so happened that, during the fifth century when the fabric of Roman civilization was disintegrating, Peter's successor Leo was also the unifying principle of the world.

1. Encyclical Letter *Aeterna Dei Sapientia* (11 November 1961) as found in *The Pope Speaks* Vol. 8 (No. 1) 7–22.

Sermon 1

29 September 440

ET MY MOUTH UTTER praise of the Lord," and let my soul and my spirit, my flesh and my tongue "bless his holy name."[2] Silence about benefits received from God betrays an attitude not of modesty but of ingratitude. It is entirely proper to inaugurate the service of a consecrated bishop with "sacrifices of praise"[3] to the Lord, "since the Lord remembered us in our abjection and blessed us,"[4] since "he alone has done great marvels."[5] As a result, your holy affection made me seem present to you when a long journey had forced me to be away.[6]

I give thanks then to our God, and shall always do so "for everything he has given me."[7] I also celebrate your favorable judgment with the gratitude I owe upon seeing proof of how much reverence, love, and faith your devoted charity is capable of lavishing upon me. I yearn with pastoral solicitude for the salvation of your souls. You have passed so holy a judgment on me without my having done anything beforehand to deserve it.

2. "I beg you," therefore, "by the mercy of the Lord,"[8] help with your prayers the one for whom you have voted with your desires. Pray that the "Spirit" of grace "might remain in me,"[9] and that you might not begin to reconsider your decision. May the one who has instilled in you an eager longing for agreement provide for us all the shared benefit of peace. I could then be made fit for serving Almighty God and for surrendering myself to you for the rest of my life, entreating the Lord with confidence, "Holy Father, keep in your name the ones you have given me."[10]

While you continually make progress toward salvation, "my soul could" then "proclaim the greatness of the Lord."[11] In the compensation of the judgment that is to come, the reckoning of my priesthood could take its stand before the just Judge in

---

2. Cf. Ps 144(145).21.
3. Cf. Pss 49(50).14 and 106(107).22.
4. Pss 135(136).23 and 113.20.
5. Ps 135.4.
6. On a mission to make peace between two generals in Gaul.
7. Cf. Ps 115(116).12.
8. Cf. Rom 12.1.
9. Cf. 1 Jn 3.24.
10. Jn 17.11.
11. Lk 1.46.

such a way that, through your good works, "you" might be "a joy" to me, and "you a crown."[12] You have already given sincere testimony about the present life by your good will. Through Christ our Lord.

Sermon 2

29 September 441

God has seen fit to honor me this day, dearly beloved. In raising my lowliness to the highest rank, he has furnished proof that he scorns none of his own. It is an act of devotion, therefore, to take joy in receiving the gift, even though one cannot help but tremble for lack of deserving it. For, the same one who bestows the honor[13] also helps in the exercise of it; the same one who has conferred the dignity will give strength as well, to keep the weak from giving out under the weight of grace.

Now that the day on which the Lord willed that I first hold episcopal office has come back in due course, I have true cause to rejoice for the glory of God. "He has pardoned much" so that "he might be loved much" by me.[14] In order to make his grace marvelous, God has bestowed his gifts on one in whom he found no endorsement of merits.

What does the Lord suggest to our hearts by this? What does he recommend except that no one should presume upon his own justice and no one distrust God's mercy, this mercy which comes out all the more clearly in relief when the sinner is sanctified and the lowly one raised up? Heavenly gifts are not in proportion with the quality of our works. In this world, where "all life is a test,"[15] not everyone receives the compensation they deserve. Here, "if the Lord were to take note of iniquities," no one "would be able to bear" his judgment.[16]

2. Therefore, "proclaim the greatness of the Lord with me," dearly beloved, "and let us extol his name together."[17] That way, the whole reason for today's celebration may be referred

---

12. Cf. Phil 4.1 and 1 Thes 2.19–20.
13. Honor and dignity (*honor* and *dignitas*) in Latin are practically synonymous with and inseparable from holding office.
14. Cf. Lk 7.47. 15. Cf. Jb 7.1(LXX).
16. Cf. Ps 129(130).3. 17. Ps 33(34).4.

back to the praise of its source. As regards my own personal feelings, I confess that I rejoice most of all in your devotion. When I see this most splendid assembly of my esteemed fellow priests, I feel that in the midst of so many saints the hosts of angels are among us. I have no doubt that we are visited more abundantly today by the grace of divine presence, since here at hand, together at the same time and shining with one light, are so many very beautiful tabernacles of God, so many very outstanding members of Christ's body.

Neither, I am sure, does the most blessed apostle Peter withhold his holy approval and faithful love from this gathering. Nor has he himself forsaken your devotion, since it is reverence for him that has brought you together. He too rejoices in your affection. He embraces the observance instituted by our Lord among those who have a share in his honor. He approves the very well-ordered charity of the entire Church, which receives as Peter the one who occupies his see and which does not grow lukewarm in its love for so great a shepherd, not even in the person of so inferior an heir.

3. Therefore, dearly beloved, let this homage that all of you show toward my lowliness bring to fruition its zeal. Humbly beg the most merciful clemency of our God. May he "overcome those fighting against" us.[18] May he strengthen faith, increase love, and spread peace. May he see fit to make me, his humble servant, equal to so great a task and useful for your edification, since it is he who willed that I preside over the government of his Church "in order to manifest the riches of his grace."[19] May he see fit to prolong the time of our service, so that the added period might be profitable for devotion. Through Christ our Lord.

Sermon 3

29 September 443

Every time that God in his mercy sees fit to bring back the day of his gifts, dearly beloved, there is just and reasonable

---

18. Cf. Ps 34.1.   19. Cf. Eph 2.7.

cause for us to rejoice, provided that the origin of our having received the office be referred to the praise of its source. I realize that this observance, appropriate as it is for all priests, is especially incumbent upon me.

When I compare the impoverishment of my insufficiency with the greatness of the gift I have received, I too should cry out in those words of the prophet: "Lord, I have heard your word and was afraid; I have considered your works and trembled."[20] What indeed could instill as much anxiety and fear as labor for the frail, elevation for the lowly, dignity for the undeserving? Yet we do not despair or give up, since we do not depend on ourselves but on the one "who works in us."[21] So we have chanted with one voice the psalm of David, dearly beloved, not for our own exaltation but for the glory of Christ the Lord.

He it is also of whom it was said in prophetic manner: "You are a priest forever according to the order of Melchisedech,"[22] that is to say, "not according to the order of Aaron,"[23] whose priesthood passed down through the descent of his offspring and was a temporary ministry that ceased with the law of the Old Testament, but "according to the order of Melchisedech,"[24] in whom the office of eternal High Priest was prefigured. Since there is no mention of the parents he came from, he must be understood as standing for the one "whose genealogy cannot be told."[25]

Finally, since the mystery of this divine Priesthood also extends to its implementation by men, it does not pass down through the course of generations. It is not what flesh and blood have created that is chosen. Rather, the privileges of paternity give way and the social positions of families are disregarded, as the Church accepts for her rulers those whom the Holy Spirit has prepared. Among the people of God's adoption, which is priestly and kingly when taken as a whole,[26] the prerogative of earthly lineage does not obtain the anointing.

20. Hb 3.2.
21. Cf. 1 Cor 12.6, Eph 3.20, and Phil 2.13.
22. Ps 109(110).4 and Heb 5.6.   23. Heb 7.11.
24. Heb 6.20 and 7.11.   25. Is 53.8.
26. Cf. 1 Pt 2.9.

Instead, it is the approval of heavenly grace that engenders the prelate.

2. Therefore, dearly beloved, though we be found weak and slothful in carrying out the duties of our office—even if we want to accomplish something devoutly and energetically, we are slowed down by the very frailty of our condition—still, we have the constant propitiation of the omnipotent and perpetual Priest. Being at once like unto us and equal with the Father, he lowered his divinity to the human state and lifted his humanity up to the divine.

We rightly and piously rejoice in his arrangement because, although he has delegated the care of his sheep to many shepherds, he himself has not relinquished custody of his beloved flock. From his eternal protection derives the reinforcement of apostolic help that we have received. This never stops working either, and the stability of the foundation on which the height of the entire Church has been built up does not show any signs of straining, no matter how large the weight of the temple pressing down upon it. For the sturdiness of that faith which was praised in the leader of the apostles endures. Just as what Peter believed in Christ remains, there likewise remains what Christ instituted in Peter.

When—as it was unfolded in the Gospel reading—the Lord had asked the disciples whom they believed him to be, since there were many different opinions, and when the blessed apostle Peter had answered, saying, "You are Christ, Son of the living God," the Lord said, "Blessed are you, Simon, son of Jonah, because flesh and blood have not revealed this to you, but my Father who is in heaven. And I say to you that you are Peter and upon this rock I will build my Church, and the gates of hell will not prevail against it. And I shall give you the keys to the kingdom of heaven. And whatever you bind on earth, it will be bound also in heaven, and whatever you loose on earth, it will be loosed also in heaven."[27]

3. This pattern of truth remains. Persevering in the fortitude he received, blessed Peter does not relinquish his government

---

27. Mt 16.16–19.

of the Church. He was ordained before the others so that, when he is called rock, declared foundation, installed as doorkeeper for the kingdom of heaven, appointed arbiter of binding and loosing (with his definitive judgments retaining force even in heaven), we might know through the very mysteries of these appellations what sort of fellowship he had with Christ. He now manages the things entrusted to him more completely and more effectively. He carries out every aspect of his duties and responsibilities in him and with him through whom he has been glorified.

So, if we do anything correctly or judge anything correctly, if we obtain anything at all from the mercy of God through daily supplications, it comes about as a result of his works and merits. In this see his power lives on and his authority reigns supreme. This, dearly beloved, is what that confession has obtained. Since it was inspired by God the Father in the apostle's heart, it has risen above all the uncertainties of human thinking and has received the strength of a rock that cannot be shaken by any pounding.

In the universal Church, Peter says every day, "You are Christ, Son of the living God."[28] "Every tongue" that "confesses the Lord"[29] has been imbued with the teaching of this utterance. This faith binds the devil and loosens the chains of his captives. It ushers the outcasts of this world into heaven, and the gates of hell cannot prevail against it. So great is the firmness with which it has been divinely fortified that no heretical depravity can ever corrupt it and no pagan faithlessness overcome it.

4. Under these conditions then, dearly beloved, the celebration of today's feast involves a submission that conforms to reason. Regard him as present in the lowliness of my person. Honor him. In him continues to reside the responsibility for all shepherds, along with the protection of those sheep entrusted to them. His dignity does not fade even in an unworthy heir.

On that account, the presence of my venerable brothers and

---

28. Mt 16.16.
29. Cf. Rom 14.11.

fellow priests—though I have longed for it indeed and thought it something to be honored—has all the more sacred and devout a character if they redirect the reverence of this service, at which they have seen fit to be present, to the one whom they know to be not only the ruler of this see but the primate of all bishops.

When we present our exhortations to your holy ears, consider that you are being addressed by the one in place of whom we exercise this function. It is with his affection that we admonish you. We preach to you nothing other than what he taught, imploring that you "gird the loins of your minds," that you lead "a pure and sober" life "in the fear" of God,[30] and that your mind not consent to its concupiscences while forgetting its own primacy [over the body]. Brief and fading are the joys of earthly pleasures which try to divert those who are called to eternity away from the path of life.

(2) Let your faithful and devout minds conceive a passionate desire for heavenly things and lift themselves up, with eagerness for the divine promises, to love of the incorruptible good and to hope for the true light. Be assured, dearly beloved, that the labor by which you resist vices and repel carnal desires is pleasing in the sight of God and precious. It will be of benefit before the mercy of God not only to yourselves but to me also. It is from the progress of the Lord's flock that the shepherd's guardianship receives glory. "For you are my crown," as the Apostle said, "and my joy,"[31] if "your faith," which was preached "in the whole world"[32] from the beginning of the Gospel, "will have persevered in love and holiness."[33]

Though all the Churches throughout the entire world ought to blossom with every virtue, it is especially fitting that you should stand out among other peoples in the merits of loyalty. You have been firmly planted in the very citadel of the apostolic rock. Our Lord Jesus Christ redeemed you along with all the rest, but the blessed apostle Peter instructed you before all others. Through Christ our Lord.

---

30. Cf. 1 Pt 1.13 and 3.2.
31. Cf. Phil 4.1 and 1 Thes 2.19–20.
32. Cf. Rom 1.8.
33. Cf. 1 Tim 2.15.

Sermon 4

29 September 444

I rejoice, dearly beloved, in the pious affection that arises from your devotion. I thank God that I can sense a dedication to Christian unity among you. To judge from your assembly here, you clearly realize that the recurrence of this day has a bearing upon our collective jubilation and that the annual feasts of the shepherd celebrate the honor of the entire flock.

Although the Church of God as a whole has a hierarchical structure, so that the completeness of the sacred body consists in a diversity of members, "we are," nevertheless, as the Apostle says, "one in Christ."[34] No one functions so independently of another that even the lowliest part does not have some relationship with the Head to which it is connected. In the unity of faith and Baptism, we have an undifferentiated fellowship, dearly beloved, and a uniform dignity.

So proclaims the most blessed apostle Peter when he says with these most sacred words: "And you yourselves should be built up like living stones into spiritual dwellings, a holy priesthood, offering spiritual sacrifices acceptable to God through Jesus Christ."[35] And later on he says: "You, however, are a chosen race, a royal priesthood, a holy nation, a people set apart."[36] All who have been regenerated in Christ are made kings by the sign of the cross and consecrated priests by the anointing of the Holy Spirit.

Apart from the particular service that our ministry entails, all Christians who live spiritual lives according to reason recognize that they have a part in the royal race and the priestly office. What could be more royal than the soul in subjection to God ruling over its own body? What could be more priestly than dedicating a pure conscience to the Lord and offering spotless sacrifices of devotion from the altar of the heart?

Since this has been given to everyone alike through the grace of God, it is a devout and praiseworthy thing for you to take

---

34. Gal 3.28.   35. 1 Pt 2.5.
36. 1 Pt 2.9.

joy in the day of our elevation as if in your own honor. Let the episcopacy be celebrated in the entire body of the Church as one single mystery. When the oil of benediction has been poured out, the mystery flows, though more abundantly onto the higher parts, yet not ungenerously down to the lower ones as well.

2. Dearly beloved, our joint participation in this gift provides ample occasion for rejoicing together. Yet we will have a more genuine and more sublime cause for joy if you do not linger over the consideration of our lowliness. It would be far more useful and worthwhile to direct your attention higher, toward contemplating the glory of the most blessed apostle Peter. It would be far more useful and worthwhile to celebrate this day by venerating him first and foremost. He was inundated with such abundant channels of grace that, while he received many things by himself, nothing at all was transmitted to anyone else without his taking part.

At that time "the Word made flesh was" already "dwelling among us,"[37] and Christ had spent himself entirely in restoring the human race. Nothing was disorderly for his wisdom, nothing difficult for his power. Elements served him, spirits ministered to him, angels waited on him. No mystery performed by both the Unity and the Trinity of his Godhead together could possibly fail to have its effect. Yet out of the whole world Peter alone has been chosen to be put in charge of the universal convocation of peoples as well as of every apostle and all the Fathers of the Church. Although there are many priests and many shepherds among the people of God, it is Peter who properly rules each one of those whom Christ also rules principally. Great and wonderful a share in his power did God see fit to bestow upon this man, dearly beloved. If he wanted other leaders to share something with him, whatever he did not refuse entirely to these others he never gave unless it was through him.

All the apostles were asked by the Lord what people thought of him. Everyone gave the same answer as long as the uncer-

---

37. Jn 1.14.

tainty of human understanding was being displayed. But, when the Lord wanted to know what the disciples felt, the first in dignity among the apostles was the first to confess the Lord. When he had said, "You are Christ, Son of the living God,"[38] Jesus replied to him, "Blessed are you, Simon, son of John, since flesh and blood have not revealed this to you, but my Father who is in heaven,"[39] that is to say, for this reason are you blessed, since my Father taught you; since earthly opinion did not deceive you, but heavenly inspiration instructed you; since neither flesh nor blood but he, whose only Son am I, made me known to you. "And I," he said, "tell you,"[40] that is to say, just as my Father has manifested my divinity to you, so I make known to you your own prominence. "That you are Peter,"[41] that is to say, although I am the indestructible rock, I "the cornerstone who make both things one,"[42] I "the foundation on which no one can lay another,"[43] you also are rock because you are made firm in my strength. What belongs properly to my own power you share with me by participation. "And on this rock I will build my Church, and the gates of hell will not prevail against it."[44] "On this" strength, he means, I will raise up an eternal temple, and the loftiness of my Church, piercing into heaven, will rise up on the firmness of this faith.

3. This confession will not be restrained by the gates of hell. It will not be bound by the chains of death. For that declaration is indeed a declaration of life. While it lifts those who confess it up to heaven, no less does it sink down to hell those who deny it. It was with this in view that the most blessed Peter was told: "I shall give you the keys to the kingdom of heaven. Whatever you bind on earth will be bound also in heaven, and whatever you loose on earth will be loosed also in heaven."[45]

Certainly, the right to use this power was conveyed to the other apostles as well. What was laid down by this decree went for all the leaders of the Church. Yet not without purpose is it handed over to one, though made known to all. It is entrusted

---

38. Mt 16.16.
39. Mt 16.17.
40. Mt 16.18.
41. Mt 16.18.
42. Cf. Eph 2.20 and 14.
43. 1 Cor 3.11.
44. Mt 16.18.
45. Mt 16.19.

in a unique way to Peter because the figure of Peter is set before all the rulers of the Church.

Therefore, this privilege of Peter resides wherever judgment has been passed in accordance with his fairness. There cannot be too much severity or too much lenience where nothing is bound or loosed outside of that which blessed Peter has loosed or bound.

When the Passion of the Lord was drawing near, an event that was going to shake the constancy of his disciples, he said: "Simon, Simon. Behold, Satan has obtained his request to sift you (all) like wheat. I, however, have begged for you that your faith not fail. Once you have converted, strengthen your brethren, lest you (all) enter into temptation."[46] Each apostle encountered the same danger through temptation from fear. All equally needed the help of divine protection, since the devil wanted to harass them all and to crush them all. Still, the Lord took special care of Peter and prayed especially for Peter. It was as if the condition of the others would be more secure if the mind of their leader were not overcome.

In Peter, therefore, the fortitude of all is reinforced, for the aid of divine grace is ordered in such a way that the firmness given to Peter through Christ is conferred upon the apostles through Peter.

4. Therefore, dearly beloved, since we see that so great a protection has been divinely instituted for us, it is reasonable and just for us to rejoice in the merits and the dignity of our leader. We give thanks to the eternal king, the Lord Jesus Christ our Redeemer, for having given so great a power to the one whom he made leader of the entire Church. Even in our own times, if through us anything is done correctly or anything managed correctly, it must be attributed to his works, to his guidance.

To him was it said: "Once you have converted, strengthen your brethren."[47] To him did the Lord after his Resurrection say by a mystical suggestion (three times in answer to his threefold profession of unending love): "Feed my sheep."[48] Doubtless he now does that. As a dedicated shepherd, he carries out

---

46. Lk 22.31–32 and 40.
48. Jn 21.17.

47. Lk 22.32.

the mandate from the Lord. He strengthens us with his exhortations and never stops praying for us that we might not be overcome by any trial.

If, moreover, he extends this devoted concern to all the people of God everywhere—as indeed it has to be believed—how much more is he willing to lavish his assistance upon us, his adopted children? Among us does he rest on the sacred bed of blessed sleep, with the same flesh in which he presided [over the Church]. Let us, then, attribute this day on which our service was born, let us attribute this feast to him. It is under his patronage that we have merited to have a part in his see. Helping us through everything is the grace of our Lord Jesus Christ, who lives and reigns with God the Father and with the Holy Spirit for ever and ever. Amen.

Sermon 5

29 September (after 445?)

In the same way that the dignity of a father brings honor upon his son, so the joy of a priest gives happiness to his people. [This joy] comes from the generosity of God. As it has been written, "Every best present and every perfect gift comes from above, descending from the Father of lights."[49] We should therefore give thanks to the source of all good things. Whether in natural endowments or in moral standards, "it is he who made us and not we who made ourselves."[50]

When we confess this with devotion and faith, "boasting" not in ourselves but "in the Lord,"[51] the renewal of our intentions as time goes by bears fruit. We justly take joy in religious feasts when we show ourselves neither ungrateful (by keeping silent about gifts) nor proud (by presuming upon merits).

(2) Let us then, dearly beloved, refer every cause and every reason for today's solemnity to its Origin and Head. Let us render the thanks that is due. Let us praise the one who holds in his hand both the ranks of office and the moments of time.

---

49. Jas 1.17. 50. Cf. Ps 99(100).3.
51. Cf. 1 Cor. 1.31 and 2 Cor 10.17.

If we look at ourselves and at our own resources, we can barely find anything that we deserve to be happy about. "Enclosed"[52] in mortal flesh and subject to the frailty of corruption, we never enjoy so much freedom as not to be pounded by some assault. Nor can we obtain so complete a victory in this struggle that renewed conflicts cannot arise even after the triumphs. As a result, no bishop can attain to such a degree of perfection, no prelate remain so untarnished, that "he ought to offer the sacrifice of propitiation for the failings of his people" only, and not also "for his own sins."[53]

2. If this condition has a hold on every priest in general, how much more does it burden us and put pressure on us? In our case, the very greatness of the task at hand provides frequent occasions for stumbling. Every single pastor guides his flock with a special responsibility, knowing that he will have to "render an account" for the sheep entrusted to him.[54] We, on the other hand, have a joint responsibility with all of them. No one's ministry falls outside the scope of our work.

Our Lord enjoined upon Peter a love for the entire Church. As the whole world throngs to the see of the blessed apostle and demands the very same love to be doled out by us as well, we feel the burden weighing upon us to the extent that we are beholden to all. This gives occasion to fear. What assurance could we have of discharging our service except if he "who guards Israel were not to become tired or fall sleep"?[55] For he said to his disciples, "Know that I am with you all days, even to the consummation of the world."[56] What assurance could we have unless he were willing to be not only the guardian of the sheep, but the shepherd of their shepherds as well?

Bodily vision sees him not, but the spiritual heart beholds. Though absent in the flesh through which he could be seen [while on earth], he remains present in the divinity through which he is always and entirely ubiquitous. For "the just live by faith,"[57] and the justice of believers rests in this, that they accept

---

52. Cf. Heb 5.2.
53. Cf. Heb 7.27 and 5.3.
54. Cf. Heb 13.17.
55. Ps 120(121).3–4.
56. Mt 28.20.
57. Cf. Hb 2.4, Rom 1.17, Gal 3.11, and Heb 10.38.

with their minds what they do not perceive with their vision. "Ascending on high, the Lord took captivity captive and gave gifts to human beings,"[58] namely, faith, hope, and love. These gifts are great, are mighty, are precious, all because a marvelous inclination of the mind believes in, hopes for, and loves what eyes of the flesh do not make contact with.

3. We therefore confess, dearly beloved, not rashly but with faith, that the Lord Jesus Christ is present in the midst of believers. Although he "sits at the right hand" of God the Father "until he makes of his enemies a footstool,"[59] the High Priest has not left the assembly of his priests.

Fittingly[60] does this chant rise up to him from the mouth of the whole Church and from that of all priests: "The Lord has given his word, and he will not regret it; you are a priest forever according to the order of Melchisedech."[61] He himself is the true and eternal Bishop whose ministry can neither change nor end. He is the one prefigured by the high priest Melchisedech.

Melchisedech did not offer to God the Jewish victims. He presented the sacrifice of that Sacrament which our Redeemer sanctified in his body and blood. He it is whose priesthood the Father instituted, "not according to the order of Aaron"[62] (to pass away with the era of the law), but "according to the order of Melchisedech"[63] (to be recognized forever with the support of an indissoluble oath).

Attached to oaths among human beings are certain conditions that have been made irrevocable by permanent guarantees. Surety for the divine oath can therefore be found in promises that have been fixed by immutable decrees. Since regret implies a change of will, God does not regret what, according to his eternal good pleasure, he cannot want to be otherwise than how he has wanted it.

4. Mindful of God's generosity, dearly beloved, we honor the day on which we assumed the priesthood. It is not presumptuous for us to keep this feast, so long as we devoutly and honestly

---

58. Ps 67(68).19 and Eph 4.8.
60. Cf. Heb 7.
62. Cf. Heb 7.11.
59. Ps 109(110).1.
61. Ps 109(110).4.
63. Heb 6.20 and 7.11.

confess that Christ performs the work of our ministry whenever we do anything right, so long as we do not boast in ourselves, who "are able to do nothing without him,"[64] but in him who is our ability.

Giving further reason to our solemnity is not merely the apostolic but also the episcopal dignity of most blessed Peter. He does not cease to preside over his see but unfailingly maintains that fellowship which he has with the eternal Priest. That stability which he received from Christ the rock (by having himself been made "rock"[65]) has poured over onto his heirs as well. Whenever there is any show of firmness, it is undoubtedly the shepherd's fortitude that appears.

Nearly all the martyrs in every place have been granted—as a reward for enduring the sufferings they underwent and in order to make known their merits—the ability to help those in danger, to drive away sicknesses, to expel unclean spirits, and to cure infirmities without number. Who then will be so unacquainted with the glory of blessed Peter or so begrudging in their estimation [of it] as to believe any segments of the Church not guided by his watchful concern or endowed with his help? That love for God and for human beings which has not succumbed under fear to any prison walls, any chains, any rioting mobs, or any potentate's threats flourishes indeed and lives on in the leader of the apostles. So does the unconquerable faith that has not ceased to do battle and has not grown lukewarm in victory.

5. In our times, when sorrows turn to joy, labors to rest, dissensions to peace, we acknowledge being helped by the merits and prayers of our protector. We experience first hand in many situations how he presides with salutary advice, he with fair judgments. Since the right to bind and to loose remains in our possession, through the guidance of blessed Peter the condemned can be led to penance and the reconciled to pardon.

Therefore, dearly beloved, whatever honor you have con-

64. Cf. Jn 15.5.
65. Cf. Mt 16.18.

ferred upon us today, whether with the respect of brothers or the devotion of sons, know that you—as well as I myself—have in truth lavished it with more devotion upon him. We are glad not so much to preside over his see as to serve it. We hope that through his prayers the God of mercies might look benignly upon the days of our ministry and might be always willing to guard and to feed the shepherd of his sheep.

ANNUAL COLLECTIONS

Known together as the *De Collectis* (*Concerning the Collections*), *Sermons* 6–11 deal with the annual collection of alms taken up for the sick and the poor of Rome. Leo identifies the practice as "established by the Holy Fathers with most salutary effect" (*Serm.* 7.1), insisting that "the things that have been laid down by tradition from the apostles" should be preserved "with lasting dedication" (*Serm.* 8.1 and cf. 9.3, 10.1, *et al.*).

Each sermon mentions a different day of the week on which the offerings were to be made.[1] Although the particular time of year is not mentioned, many historians believe that the collections took place after the Feast of Saints Peter and Paul (29 June) to counter the pagan festival *Ludi Apollinares* held from 6–13 July.[2] Leo spoke rather harshly about pagan activities[3] that had provided the impetus for beginning this apostolic institution (Cf. *Serm.* 8.1 *et al.*).

It is now thought, however, that this public work of mercy was actually directed against the *Ludi Plebeii* and held annually in November.[4] For one thing, most manuscript holdings place the *Collection* sermons immediately after the *Elevation* sermons delivered at the end of September. Furthermore, in *Serm.* 9.4 (443) Leo urges his people to expose any concealed Manichaeans. By the time of *Serm.* 16 (datable to

---

1. Sunday: *Serm.* 6.2; Monday: *Serm.* 7.1; Tuesday: *Serm.* 8.1; Wednesday: *Serm.* 9.1; Saturday: *Serm.* 11.2.

2. *Ludi Apollinares*, inaugurated in 212 B.C. during a crisis of the second Punic War, were celebrated in honor of the god Apollo. They included plays and games held in the Circus.

3. "Since, at that time, the people who had once been pagan were ministering to demons with heightened superstition, the most holy sacrificial offering of our alms would be practiced in order to counter those ungodly victims" (*Serm.* 9.3). "It was, therefore, in an attempt to dismantle the snares of the ancient enemy that the collection was first established in the Church (quite deliberately) on the very day that the ungodly were ministering to the devil under the guise of their idols" (*Serm.* 8.2). "Whenever the blindness of pagans becomes more intently focused on its own superstitions, then especially should the people of God apply themselves with energy to prayer and pious works" (*Serm.* 8.1).

4. *Ludi Plebeii*, taking place—until the fourth century A.D.—from 12–16 November, consisted in processions with statues of the gods, feasts, plays, and chariot races.

12 December 443), he indicates that the crisis has been resolved. *Serm.* 9 on the Collections would therefore most likely have been delivered between October and early December of 443. Given that the *Ludi Plebeii* were held in November, moreover, that seems to be the most likely time.[5]

Although some sermons (6, 7, and 11) are shorter than others, the basic message is the same throughout: Give as generously as you can to the poor, because in so doing you are actually giving to Christ who will reward you (*passim*). "How marvelous this considerate goodness of the Creator! He wanted there to be assistance for two in a single act" (*Serm.* 6.1). "Almsgiving is a work of love, and we know that 'love covers a multitude of sins'" (*Serm.* 7.1).

Sermon 6

November 440

WE ARE TAUGHT by many examples from the divine Scriptures how great a merit there is in almsgiving and how great a power. Certainly all of us "benefit our own souls"[6] every time our compassion lends aid to the need of another. Our generosity should be ready and "willing,"[7] dearly beloved, if we believe that all give to themselves what they provide for the needy. Those who "feed" Christ in the poor store up their "treasure in heaven."[8]

Realize with what kindness the thoughtfulness of God has arranged things in this regard. He willed that you should have an abundance so that through you another might not be wanting. He willed, through the instrumentality of your work, "to free" the poor from the burden of need and you "from the multitude of your sins."[9] How marvelous this considerate goodness of the Creator! He wanted there to be assistance for two in a single act.

2. Next Sunday, then, is going to be the day of the collections. I encourage and advise each and every one of you in your holiness to take into consideration both the poor and yourselves. You should "recognize" Christ "in the needy"[10] to the extent

---

5. Cf. CCL 138.clxxxiv–vii.
6. Prv 11.17.
7. Cf. 1 Tm 6.18.
8. Cf. Mt 6.20, 19.21, 25.37 and 40.
9. Cf. 1 Pt 4.8 and Tb 4.11.
10. Ps 40(41).2.

that your resources "allow."[11] Christ our Lord gives testimony to the fact that he is the one whom we clothe, support, and feed in them.[12] That is how strongly he has recommended the poor to us.

Sermon 7

November 441

Well known and familiar to you is the injunction that we preach with the encouragement of a pastor, namely, that you endeavor to be dedicated in the work of mercy. But even if you never shirk the responsibility entirely, you should still be more inclined and more generous now in carrying it out. For this day of the collections, as it was first established by the Holy Fathers with most salutary effect, requires that all contribute from their means something to be used for supporting the poor, in so far as they are "able" and "willing."[13]

You know that—apart from the Baptism of regeneration in which all stain of sin has been washed away—this remedy has been granted by God to human weakness. If someone contracts any guilt while living on this earth, almsgiving wipes it away. Almsgiving is a work of love, and we know that "love covers a multitude of sins."[14]

2. As a result, dearly beloved, prepare your "free-will"[15] offerings carefully for next Monday, keeping in mind that whatever you distribute from your temporal possessions you will get back "many fold"[16] in eternal compensation.

Sermon 8

November 442

It is a matter of Christian duty, dearly beloved, to preserve with lasting dedication the things that have been laid down by tradition from the apostles. Those most blessed disciples of

---

11. Cf. Tb 4.8.   12. Cf. Mt 25.35–40.
13. Cf. 1 Cor 16.2, 2 Cor 9.7, and Tb 4.8.
14. 1 Pt 4.8 and Prv 10.12.   15. Cf. 1 Cor 16.2.
16. Cf. Mt 19.29.

SERMON 8

truth have—with a teaching inspired by God—made the following enjoinder upon us. Whenever the blindness of pagans becomes more intently focused on its own superstitions, then especially should the people of God apply themselves with energy to prayer and pious works. As much as unclean spirits delight in the error of infidels, they are no less crushed by the observance of true religion. Increases in righteousness sear the author of iniquity.

To prevent his impious and sacrilegious devices from bringing any defilement upon hearts consecrated to the true God, the blessed teacher of the Gentiles warned in the words of an apostle: "Do not yoke yourselves with unbelievers. What does righteousness have in common with iniquity? Or what fellowship does light have with darkness?"[17] Then he goes on to add some words in the spirit of a prophet: "Go out, go out from their midst and separate yourselves, says the Lord. Do not touch what is unclean."[18]

2. It was, therefore, in an attempt to dismantle the snares of the ancient enemy that the collection was first established in the Church (quite deliberately) on the very day that the ungodly were ministering to the devil under the guise of their idols. We want you then to gather in love, bringing "free-will" offerings of alms, at all the churches throughout your districts on Tuesday.[19]

In this undertaking, even if not everyone has the same means, there ought to be equal devotion all around, since the generosity of the faithful does not depend on the value of the gift but on the amount of "good will" involved.[20] Let the poor make some profit as well in this economy of mercy by setting aside from whatever possessions they have a sum that they can afford to part with to support those in need.[21] While the rich should be more bountiful with gifts, the poor should not be outdone in the spirit of giving.

Generally speaking, a more abundant harvest might be ex-

17. 2 Cor 6.14.
18. 2 Cor 6.17 and Is 52.11.
19. Cf. 1 Cor 16.2.
20. Cf. 2 Cor 8.11–12.
21. Cf. Tb 4.9.

pected from a larger amount of seed. But when it comes to righteousness, a plentiful crop can sprout up from a meager planting. We have a "fair and honest judge" who does not cheat anyone of the wages that have been earned.[22] Christ our Lord wants us to care about the poor so that, on the day when payment will be portioned out, he might lavish upon the "merciful" the "mercy" that he has promised.[23]

Sermon 9
November 443

God in his mercy and justice, dearly beloved, has set out before us the plans for his recompense—just as they had been laid down since the foundation of the world—explaining them by an act of the greatest kindness through the teaching of our Lord Jesus Christ. [He did this] so that, in receiving through symbols the things that we believe are going to take place, we might get to know them as if having already transpired.

Our Redeemer and Savior knew what great errors the devil had sown throughout the entire world by deception and with how many superstitions he had subjugated to himself the greatest part of the human race. But he did not want that the creature formed "to the image of God"[24] should any longer be driven onto the precipice of eternal death through ignorance of the truth. So he planted within the pages of the Gospel the manner of his judgment—which was such as to call back every person from the snares of this most cunning enemy, since no one would any longer be ignorant of the rewards to be hoped for by the good and the punishments to be feared by the wicked.

Because that instigator and author of sin whom "pride" first caused to fall and then "envy" to do harm,[25] "did not stand fast in the truth," he has put all his effort into "falsehood."[26] He has manufactured from this most poisonous fountain of his craft every manner of deception. His aim is to shut off any hope that

---

22. Cf. Pss 7(8).12 and 85(86).15.
23. Cf. Mt 5.7.
24. Cf. Gn 1.27.
25. Cf. Wis 2.24.
26. Jn 8.44.

human beings might have of attaining through devotion to that good which he himself had forfeited by self-exaltation. He would like to draw them into a partnership with himself in condemnation, since he himself cannot have access to that reconciliation which could be theirs.

Accordingly, whatever there has been on the part of human beings to offend God with any sort of impiety, it has been imparted to them through his deceits and the cause of its depravity has been his own iniquity. It was easy for him to launch into all kinds of shameful things those whom he had deceived in the question of religion.

Well aware of the fact that it is possible "to deny" God "through actions" as well as words,[27] he snatched love away from many of those whose faith he could not carry off. Since he had not deprived them of the confession made with lips, he robbed their works of fruit by causing avarice to take root in the soil of their hearts.

2. Because the ancient enemy makes use of these wiles, dearly beloved, Christ in his ineffable kindness wanted us to know what were to be the criteria for judging all humanity on the day of recompense. That way, while in this lifetime there is still available the medicine of legitimate remedies, while rehabilitation has not yet been denied to those who have been shattered, and while those who had long been sterile can still become fruitful before it is all over, the condemnation due in justice might be headed off and the reflection of God's criteria in judgment might never be removed from the eyes of our heart.

For the Lord "will come in the glory of his majesty,"[28] as he himself foretold. Hosts "of angels" beyond number, glimmering in their array, will be there "with him." Before the throne of his power "will be gathered up" the people "of all nations." Whoever has been born of human beings throughout all ages and around the entire world will stand before the Judge. Just "will be separated" from unjust and innocent from guilty. When the children of devotion have taken possession of the "kingdom

27. Cf. Ti 1.16.
28. Cf. Mt 25.31–46.

prepared" for them after their works of mercy have been reviewed, a charge of barrenness (resulting from a hard heart) will be brought against the unjust. Since "those on the left" have nothing to do with "those on the right," they will—by sentence of the Almighty Judge—be cast into the fire devised for tormenting "the devil and his angels"—to have a partnership in punishment with the one whose will they chose to follow. Who, then, would not tremble to think about that destiny of eternal tortures? Who would not fear ills that never come to an end?

(2) But this harshness has been disclosed so that mercy might be sought. We must therefore live this present life with an abundance of mercy. It might then be possible for someone returning to works of compassion after a perilous neglect of them to be absolved from this sentence. This is what the power of the Judge, this is what the grace of the Savior does. It offers the ungodly an opportunity to "abandon their ways" and sinners to withdraw from their habitual acquaintance with iniquity.[29]

Let those who want Christ to spare them have compassion for the poor. Let those who desire a bond with the fellowship of the blessed be "readily disposed" toward nourishing the wretched.[30] No human being should be considered worthless by another. That nature which the Creator of the universe made his own should not be looked down upon in anyone. Is it permitted for any of the hired hands to refuse that payment which the Lord declares to have been given him? Your fellow servant receives assistance, and the Lord returns thanks. Food for someone in need is the cost of purchasing the kingdom of heaven, and the one who is generous with temporal things is made heir of the eternal.

What brings it about that those paltry outlays should have deserved to be assessed at so high an appraisal? It could only have been that the values of charitable works are figured into the balance. When human beings love what God himself cherishes, they deserve to ascend into his kingdom since they have already passed over into his heart.

3. Established by the apostles, this day invites us to be occu-

---

29. Cf. Is 55.7.   30. Cf. 1 Tm 6.18.

pied with these works in a special way, dearly beloved. For it was on this day that the first collections were taken up. They had been deliberately planned by the Fathers with a practical aim. Since, at that time, the people who had once been pagan were ministering to demons with heightened superstition, the most holy "sacrificial offering of" our "alms" would be practiced in order to counter those ungodly victims.[31]

(2) So we encourage you in your holiness to assemble on Wednesday in the churches throughout your district and to make a contribution from your means to the expenses of mercy—in the amount that "ability" and "desire" suggest to you.[32] In this way might you be able to earn that happiness in which the one "who has regard for the needy and the poor" will delight without end.[33]

We must stay alert with a restless compassion in order to "have regard" for such a one. It might then be possible to seek out those whom bashfulness conceals and shame holds back. There are some who are ashamed to ask openly for what they need. They prefer to endure the misery of poverty rather than be embarrassed by making a request in public. We must therefore "have regard for" such as these and relieve them of their hidden need.[34] This would give them all the more joy since consideration would have been shown both to their poverty and to their self-respect.

Rightly indeed do we see the person of our Lord Jesus Christ in the poor and needy. "Although he was rich," as the blessed Apostle said, "he became poor so that he might make us rich by his own poverty."[35] So that his presence would not seem removed from us, he ordained the mystery of his glory and humility in such a way that we might nourish in his poor the very same one whom we worship as King and Lord in the majesty of the Father. Thereby are we "to be freed" from eternal condemnation "on that terrible day."[36] It is in return for our care of the poor so "regarded" that we are to be admitted into fellowship with the kingdom of heaven.

31. Cf. Sir 35.4.
33. Ps 40(41).2.
35. 2 Cor 8.9.
32. Cf. Tb 4.8 and 1 Cor 16.2.
34. Cf. Ps 40(41).2.
36. Ps 40(41).2.

4. So that your dedication might be pleasing to the Lord in all things, we encourage you to take up as well the following effort. Expose to your priests any Manichaeans—wherever they might be hiding. It would be a great act of loyalty to betray the hiding places of the ungodly and to vanquish in them the devil whom they serve. Against such as these, dearly beloved, it befits the whole world and the entire Church everywhere to take up the armor of faith. But your dedication in this work ought to stand out, since in your ancestors you have learned the Gospel about the Cross of Christ directly from the mouths of the blessed apostles Peter and Paul.

Let them not be allowed to hide who believe that the law given through Moses should not be accepted, the law which shows God to be the Creator of the universe. They gainsay the prophets and the Holy Spirit. They have dared to suppress with a damnable impiety the Psalms of David which are chanted with all reverence throughout the universal Church. They deny the Birth of Christ according to the flesh. They say that his Passion and Resurrection were merely appearances and not reality. They strip from the Baptism of regeneration any power of grace whatsoever. With them, nothing remains holy, nothing intact, nothing true. We must beware of them lest they do anyone harm. We must expose them, lest they gain a foothold in any part of our city. This cause that I declare, this request that I make, dearly beloved, will be to your advantage before the tribunal of the Lord. It is fitting that the palm of this work should be joined to the "sacrifice of alms."[37] Helping you through everything is the grace of our Lord Jesus Christ, who lives and reigns with God the Father and with the Holy Spirit for ever and ever. Amen.

Sermon 10

November 444

In keeping with things that have been laid down by tradition from the apostles, we encourage you with pastoral concern.

---

37. Cf. Sir 35.4.

They sanctified this day through works of mercy by cleansing it of the superstition practiced among the ungodly. Let us then celebrate it with the devotion due a religious custom. Let us show that the authority of the Fathers still lives among us and that their teaching endures in our obedience.

So great an ordinance was not intended to be useful for holiness in the past only, but in our times as well. What served them for uprooting empty superstitions can profit us with increases in virtue. What could be more suited to faith, what more helpful to compassion, than assuaging the poverty of those in need, undertaking care of the sick, succoring needs of the brethren, and recalling our own condition in the distress of others.

In this undertaking, he alone can truly ascertain how much anyone can and cannot do,[38] who knows what he has bestowed and upon whom he has bestowed it. Not only are spiritual provisions and heavenly gifts received through the bounty of God, but even earthly and bodily resources issue from his largess. He will have every right to ask for an accounting of these things, since he gave them more by way of entrusting them to be spent rather than of handing them over to be kept.[39] We must therefore use the gifts of God with justice and prudence so that the opportunity for a good work does not become an occasion of sin.

Riches in and of themselves are good. They offer many advantages to human society when they are in the possession of generous benefactors—but not when some extravagant person makes a show of them or some miser hides them away. When hoarded, they go to waste no less than if they had been foolishly spent.

(2) It would indeed be praiseworthy to flee intemperance and to avoid the losses that would result from base desires. Many munificent souls find it repugnant to hide their resources and, as they overflow with abundance, recoil from abject and sordid parsimony. Yet an abundance of such things cannot be considered prosperous nor frugality commended if their re-

---

38. Cf. Tb 4.8.
39. Acts 20.35.

sources are at the service of themselves alone, if no poor are assisted by their goods, if no sick are taken care of, if from the abundance of their means no captive sees ransom, no stranger comfort, no exile assistance.

Rich people like these are poorer than any of the poor. They forfeit those eternal revenues that are within their power to obtain. Resting upon a short-lived and not always unencumbered enjoyment of their possessions, they fail to nourish themselves at all on the savory food of justice and mercy. They are dazzling on the outside but murky within. Abounding in temporal things, they are impoverished of things eternal. Those who from what they have consigned to earthly storehouses have put nothing into the heavenly coffers afflict their own souls with hunger and put them to shame with nakedness.

2. But suppose that there are some rich people who, though they are not in the habit of helping the poor in the Church with their largess, keep at any rate the commandments of God and figure that from among the various meritorious activities of faith they are lacking but one virtue—and it is therefore a slight fault. Yet this one virtue happens to be so important that without it the others cannot be of any avail.

Be any full of faith, chaste, sober, and adorned with other noteworthy habits, yet if they are not merciful, they do not deserve mercy. For the Lord says, "Blessed are the merciful, for God will have mercy on them."[40] When the Son of Man will come in his majesty and sit on the throne of his glory, when all nations have been gathered together, the good and the bad will be separated. What will those who are destined to stand on the right be praised for if not the benevolent works and charitable services that Jesus Christ will consider as rendered unto himself?[41] That is because in making human nature his own he has not dissociated himself from any aspect of human lowliness. What accusations will be made against those on the left if not neglect of love, inhuman hardness, and denying compassion to the poor?

40. Mt 5.7.
41. Cf. Mt 25.31–46.

SERMON 10

As if those on the right would not have other virtues, those on the left other offenses! But at that great and ultimate judgment, the kindness of generosity or the ungodliness of avarice receives an extremely high value. Despite perpetrating all manner of the greatest crimes, some are accepted into heaven on account of that one good. Despite possessing the fullness of all virtues, others are cast into eternal fire on account of that one evil.

3. Let none then, dearly beloved, flatter themselves about any merits due to living a good life if they lack charitable works. Nor should any be complacent about the purity of their bodies if they have not "been cleansed" at all by the purification "of alms."[42] "Alms" wipe away "sins," do away with "death," and extinguish the punishment of eternal fire.[43] But those who will have been found empty of its fruit will be strangers to lenience from the one who gives recompense—as Solomon says: "Whoever stop up their ears so as not to hear the enfeebled will themselves call upon the Lord and likewise find no one to hear them."[44] So Tobias as well, instructing his son in the demands of religion, says: "Give alms from your possessions and do not turn your face away from any of the poor. That way, the face of God will not be turned away from you either."[45]

This virtue causes all other virtues to be worth something. It gives life even to faith itself—"by which the just live"[46] and which is called "dead without works"[47]—by mingling with it. While faith provides the basis for works, the strength of faith comes out only in works. "While we have time, then, let us perform good works for everyone, but especially for those who belong to the household of faith," as the Apostle says.[48] "Let us not grow weary of doing good, for in due time we shall reap."[49] And so this present life is a time for sowing, and the day of

---

42. Cf. Lk 11.41.
43. Cf. Tb 4.11 and 12.9; Sir 3.33; Dn 4.24; Prv 10.12, 15.27, and 16.6; and 1 Pt 4.8.
44. Prv 21.13.   45. Tb 4.7.
46. Cf. Rom 1.17, Gal 3.11, Heb 10.38, and Hb 2.4.
47. Cf. Jas 2.17, 20, and 26.   48. Gal 6.10.
49. Gal 6.9.

judgment the time for gathering,⁵⁰ when all will receive the yield of their seeds in proportion to the amount they have sown.⁵¹ Let no one get the wrong impression about this crop. At that time, what will be assessed is not so much the value of outlays as that of the heart in giving. Meager amounts given from meager resources will bring in as much revenue as great amounts given from great resources.⁵²

Let us therefore live up to these things that have been established by the apostles. Since that day will be the anniversary of the first collection, all of you should be prepared to make a "free-will"⁵³ donation so that all might have a part in this most holy oblation according to their means. Both "the alms themselves will pray for you"⁵⁴ as well as those who receive assistance from your gifts, so that you might always be prepared "for every good work,"⁵⁵ in Christ Jesus our Lord who lives and reigns for ever and ever without end. Amen.

Sermon 11

November 445

We have learned from divine precepts, dearly beloved, as well as from things laid down by the apostles, that every human being situated among the hazards of this life must seek the mercy of God by being merciful. What hope would lift up the fallen, what medicine heal the wounded, if almsgiving did not remit faults, and needs of the poor did not become remedies for sin? So by saying "Blessed are the merciful, for God will have mercy on them,"⁵⁶ the Lord made it clear that the entire scale on which he is going to judge the whole world when he appears in his majesty would be tilted while hanging from the following balance: Only the quality of good works directed toward the destitute would determine the sentence (for the ungodly to burn with the devil, for the generous to reign with Christ).

---

50. Cf. Mt 13.30 and 39. 51. Cf. 2 Cor 9.6.
52. Cf. Tb 4.9. Cf. 2 Cor 8.15 and 9.6.
53. Cf. 1 Cor 16.2. 54. Sir 29.15.
55. Cf. 2 Cor 9.8. 56. Mt 5.7.

SERMON 11

What deeds will not be brought out at that time? What hidden things will not be disclosed? What consciences will not lie open? No one then "will glory in having a pure heart or in being unstained by sin."[57] But since "mercy will be exalted over condemnation"[58] and the gifts of clemency will surpass any just compensation, all the lives led by mortals and all different kinds of actions will be appraised under the aspect of a single rule. No charges at all would be brought up where, in the acknowledgment of the Creator, works of compassion have been found.

As for those on the left, this is not the only thing they have done that will be brought against them. No, the fact that it will be shown that they have been strangers to human feeling does not mean that they will be found alien to other sins. Rather, though standing accused on many grounds, they will be condemned primarily on this count, that they have not "redeemed" their crimes "with" any "alms."[59]

Since only the hardest heart would fail to be moved by any misery at all among those in distress, and since someone who has the means but does not help the afflicted must be considered as unjust as the one who crushes the weak, what hope remains for sinners who do not even show mercy "for the sake of obtaining it themselves"?[60]

(2) In the first place, therefore, dearly beloved, those who are not good to others are bad to themselves, and those who do not come to the aid of others as best they can do harm to their own souls. Rich and poor have one and the same nature. Among other aspects of human frailty belongs the fact that no boon of well-being remains safe, since everyone ought to fear what anyone at all is capable of falling into.

All human beings, regardless of who they happen to be, should come to terms with the fact that they have a mortal nature subject to change—and usually for the worse. In view of this shared condition, let them have sympathy toward their own race. "Let them weep with those who weep,"[61] and let them

57. Prv 20.9.
59. Cf. Dn 4.24.
61. Cf. Rom 12.15.

58. Cf. Jas 2.13.
60. Cf. Mt 5.7.

sigh along with the sighs of those who mourn. Let them share their provisions with the needy. Through the ministry of a healthy body, let them bend down to those laid low by illness. Let them mark out a portion of their food for the hungry. Let them feel cold in the pale nakedness of those who shiver. Those who relieve the temporal misery of people in distress escape the eternal punishment due sinners.

2. As a result, dearly beloved, the holy Fathers—from a sense of duty—thoughtfully arranged that there should be certain days at various times to rouse up the dedication of the believing populace for a public collection. Since everyone who seeks aid has recourse especially to the Church, there would be a holy free-will collection from the resources of many to take care of needed expenses at the discretion of administrators.

Close at hand is the day that summons you to the fruit of this work—which we believe you desire. We add our encouragement. You should bring the gifts of mercy to the churches of your districts next Saturday. Since "God loves a cheerful giver,"[62] none should lay aside more than their possessions allow. Let all be equitable judges between themselves and the poor. May a joyful and worry-free pity dispel hesitation. Let those who come to the aid of the poor realize that they are actually spending this donation on God.

(2) From any amount of possessions whatsoever—and certainly these vary—there can be equal merit, provided that among the differing resources of those making donations compassion does not fall short of ability. God, "with whom there is no consideration of persons,"[63] receives in like manner the gift of rich and poor, since he knows what he has given to each individual and what he has not given. On the day of recompense, it is not the measure of finances but the disposition of intentions that will be judged. Through Christ our Lord.

62. 2 Cor 9.7.
63. Cf. Eph 6.9 and Col 3.25.

DAYS OF FAST IN DECEMBER

Leo extols the benefits of fasting (prescribed by both the Old and the New Testaments) in a number of his sermons. In *Serm.* 19.2 he refers to the spring fast of Lent, the summer fast after Pentecost, the autumn fast in the seventh month (September) and the winter fast in the tenth month (December). Leo upholds the necessity of bodily and spiritual fasts, stressing that abstinence from food must be completed with prayer and almsgiving.

He also enumerates works of mercy which must accompany fasting: defending widows, taking care of orphans, consoling mourners, making peace between factions, welcoming travelers, relieving the oppressed, clothing the naked, tending to the sick (*Serms.* 13.1(2) and 16.1). These public fasts derive a great beauty from the strength communicated to individuals when all pursue a common goal.

In *Serm.* 9 from the November *Collections* of 443, Leo asks his flock to reveal any hidden Manichaeans. Here, in *Serm.* 16.1 from the December Fast of 443, he warns his people to beware of heretics, naming Basilides, Sabellius, Photinus, Arius, and Eunomius. He mentions that Manichaeans had been investigated and brought to trial (*Serm.* 16.4).

Sermon 12

17 December 450

IF WE REFLECT upon the beginning of our creation with faith and wisdom, dearly beloved, we shall come to the realization that human beings have been formed according to the image of God precisely with a view that they might imitate their Designer. Our race has this dignity of nature, so long as the figure of divine goodness continues to be reflected in us as in a kind of mirror.

Indeed, the Savior's grace re-fashions us to this image on a daily basis. What fell in the first Adam has been raised up in the second. But our being re-fashioned has no other cause than the mercy of God. We would not love him but for the fact that "he has loved us first"[1] and has dispelled the darkness of our ignorance with the light of his truth.

Foretelling this through holy Isaiah, the Lord says: "I shall lead the blind onto a road they did not know about, and I shall have them tread upon paths they were not acquainted with. I shall turn darkness into light and crooked ways into straight. What I have just said, I shall accomplish. I shall not forsake them."[2] At another point [in Isaiah], he says: "I have been found by those not looking for me and have appeared out in the open to those who were not seeking after me."[3] How this was fulfilled, the apostle John demonstrates when he says: "We know that the Son of God came and has given us discernment so that we might recognize the true [God] and be in his true Son."[4] On another occasion, he says: "Let us love, therefore, since God has loved us first."[5]

It is by loving that God re-fashions us to his image. That he might find in us the image of his goodness, he gives us the very means by which we can perform the works that we do—by lighting the lamps of our minds and inflaming us with the fire of his love, so that we might love not only him but also whatever he loves.

If, in the final analysis, only that friendship among human beings has stability which a likeness of character holds together—though a similarity of wills may often incline toward degenerate passions—how much ought we to desire and to struggle that we might in no way strike a discordance with the things that have pleased God! Concerning this the prophet says: "Because there is wrath in his indignation and life in his will."[6] There will be no other way for us to possess any grandeur of divine majesty within us except by imitating his will.

2. So the Lord says: "You shall love the Lord your God with all your heart and with all your soul, and you shall love your neighbor as yourself."[7] Let the faithful soul take upon itself the unfading love of its Maker and Ruler. Let it subject itself

---

1. 1 Jn 4.10.
2. Is 42.16.
3. Cf. Is 65.1.
4. 1 Jn 5.20.
5. 1 Jn 4.19.
6. Cf. Ps 29(30).6.
7. Cf. Mt 22.37 and 39.

entirely to his will. In the works and judgments of God, nothing exists devoid of true justice and compassionate mercy. Even if some should be worn out by great labors and many trials, there is good reason for undergoing these when they know that they are being either corrected or proven by adversities.

Yet the filial devotion that comes from this love cannot be perfected without love of neighbor. By the term "neighbor" are to be understood not only those who are joined to us by friendship or kinship, but all people with whom we have a common nature, be they enemies or allies, free or slave. One Creator fashioned us all, one Maker breathed life into us all. We all enjoy the same sky and air, the same days and nights. Although some are good and others bad, some just and others unjust, God nevertheless shows generosity toward all, kindness toward all—as the apostles Paul and Barnabas said to the Lycaonians concerning the providence of God: "During generations past he gave leave for all nations to embark upon their own ways. Yet he did not allow himself to be left without witness, doing good to them, giving rain and fruitful seasons from heaven, filling our hearts with food and with delight."[8]

Instead, the broad scope of Christian grace has given us greater reasons for loving our neighbor. It extends to every part of the whole earth, despairing of no one and teaching that no one must be left out. How rightly does it command us to "love" our "enemies" and pray for our "persecutors,"[9] since he "grafts" the branch of "wild olive" onto the sacred branches of his own olive tree on a daily basis,[10] reconciling enemies, adopting the children of others, and making the godless just—so that "every knee should bend of those in heaven, on earth, and under the earth, and every tongue confess that the Lord Jesus is in the glory of God the Father."[11]

3. Since, therefore, God wants us to be good (because he is good), none of his judgments ought to displease us. Not to give him thanks in all things, what else does this mean than implicitly to find fault with him to some extent? Human beings in

---

8. Cf. Acts 14.15–16.
9. Cf. Mt 5.44.
10. Cf. Rom 11.17.
11. Phil 2.10–11.

their foolishness often dare to murmur against their Creator—not only about lacking something but even about having an abundance. When something is wanting, they complain. When there is plenty, they are ungrateful.

Lords with great harvests have disparaged the large amounts in their barns and groaned about the large quantities of overflowing vines. They were not content with the quantity of their produce but complained about its low quality. Yet, if the soil would have been less productive with the planted seed, and if the vines and olive trees would have issued forth a more restrained yield, the year would be blamed, the elements would be accused, nor would either air or sky be let off the hook.

Nothing recommends and strengthens faithful and loyal disciples of the truth more than a persevering and untiring praise of God. As the Apostle says, "Rejoice always. Pray without ceasing. Give thanks in all things. For this is the will of God in Christ Jesus for you all."[12] How great a part could we have in this kind of devotion unless vicissitudes exercise our steadfastness of mind? Only that way can love directed toward God not take pride in success nor give up in failure.

What pleases God should also please us. Let us rejoice no matter how much he sends us. Let the one who has made good use of many things make good use also of more modest supplies. Both abundance and scarcity serve our interests equally. When it comes to spiritual gains, we shall not be weighed down by a meagerness of produce if the fruitfulness of our hearts does not dry up. Let what the earth has not issued forth rise up from the soil of the heart. Those who have any good will left always find something to give.

In all works of compassion, dearly beloved, let every year profit us, regardless of its quality. Lack of resources in this world should not fetter Christian benevolence. Our Lord knows how to fill those "vessels of the hospitable widow" that had been "emptied" for her work of "compassion."[13] He knows how to change water into wine.[14] He knows how to satisfy thou-

---

12. 1 Thes 5.16–18.
13. Cf. *Serm.* 42.2 and 1 Kgs 17.9–16.
14. Cf. Jn 2.9.

sands of hungry people with just very few loaves.[15] He—nourished in his own—can multiply by taking away what he could have increased by giving.[16]

4. Three things especially pertain to acts of religion: "prayer, fasting and almsgiving."[17] We take every opportunity to practice these. On this occasion, however, they must be observed with greater zeal still. We have received from the apostles a time set aside for this purpose. December brings back a custom established of old,[18] namely, that we should carry out those aforementioned three things with greater diligence. Propitiation of God is sought by prayer, concupiscence of the flesh is extinguished by fasting, and "sins are redeemed by almsgiving."[19] Through all of them at the same time, the image of God is renewed in us—provided we are always ready to praise him, concerned about our purification without respite, and constantly intent upon supporting our neighbor.

This three-fold observance, dearly beloved, encompasses the effects of all virtues. It brings us to the image and likeness of God and makes us inseparable from the Holy Spirit. Prayer sustains a correct faith, fasting an innocent life, and almsgiving a kind disposition. On Wednesday and Friday, therefore, let us fast. On Saturday, however, let us keep vigil with the blessed apostle Peter. He will see fit to help our prayers, our fasting, and our almsgiving with his own entreaties. Through our Lord Jesus Christ who, with the Father and the Holy Spirit, lives and reigns forever and ever. Amen.

Sermon 13

15 December 440

Since the time has come to do as our devout custom suggests, dearly beloved, we preach to you with pastoral concern that the fast of December is to be observed. Thereby, in exchange for completing the reception of all fruits, a libation of self-denial

15. Cf. Jn 6.9.
16. Cf. Mt 25.37.
17. Cf. Tb 12.8.
18. Cf. Zec 8.19.
19. Cf. Dn 4.24.

is offered most fittingly to God who bestows them. What can be more efficacious than fasting? By its observance we draw near to God. Resisting the devil in this manner, we overcome seductive vices. Fasting has always been food for virtue. In short, from abstinence come forth chaste thoughts, movements of the will in conformity with reason, and wholesome suggestions. Through voluntary affliction, the flesh dies to concupiscence while the spirit is renewed with virtues.

(2) But, since our souls do not attain to salvation by fasting alone, let us supplement our fasting with acts of mercy toward the poor. Let us spend on virtue what we withhold from pleasure. Let abstinence on the part of someone fasting become nourishment for the poor. Let us put our efforts to the defense of widows, the advantage of orphans, the consolation of mourners, the reconciliation of rivals. Take in the stranger, relieve the oppressed, clothe the naked, care for the sick—in such a way that, whoever of us will offer from honest labor a "sacrifice" of compassion[20] to God the Maker of all good things, they might deserve to receive from him as a reward the kingdom of heaven.

On Wednesday and Friday, therefore, let us fast. On Saturday, however, let us keep vigil together with blessed Peter the apostle, that through the intercession of his merits we might be able to obtain what we ask for, through Christ our Lord.

Sermon 14

14 December 441

In the field of the Lord, whose workers we are, dearly beloved, we ought to practice cultivation of the soul with untiring prudence. That way, attending with constant exertion to what the law requires at this time, we might take delight in the fruit of holy works. If we neglect these works as a result of slothful leisure and lazy inactivity, our soil will not bear generous seed. On the contrary, laden with brambles and thistles, it will not produce things to be stored away in the barns, but things that will have to be burned with flames.

---

20. Cf. Sir 35.4

With the grace of God "showering down from above,"[21] that field comes to be protected through faith, gets plowed through fasting, receives seed through almsgiving, and becomes fruitful through prayers. If we plant and water it in this manner, no bitter root will sprout, nor will any harmful shoots grow up. When every seed of vice has been wiped out, the blessed crop of virtues will become strong. Indeed, compassion encourages us to make this effort all the time. During these days, however, set apart in a more special way for this work, a greater liveliness and more fervent concern must be aroused, lest, what compassion would have us do even without public notice, impiety might neglect even after such notice had been given.

2. We encourage you, therefore, with regard to the fast of December. We know that your love has been prepared for it with dedicated resolution. Let us together, with the help of Christ, have a single heart in celebrating it. We advise everyone to shine in good works to the extent that they have received from God the ability to do so. Our enemies, tormented by our sanctification, rage more violently and scheme with a keener shrewdness during these days, knowing that this time period has been arranged for us to show greater observance. They want to draw as many as possible away from a share in this devotion by instilling in some a fear of penury resulting from the outlays of generosity, by suggesting to others the discomfort arising from the hardship of fasting. Let the focus of a dedicated heart keep alert against these temptations, dearly beloved, and let thoughts of reluctance be driven out from the minds of Christians.

(2) What does not mean a lot for us can be enough for the poor. Neither their food nor their clothing represents anything of a burden. What they hunger for costs little. What they thirst for costs little. That nakedness of theirs which needs our help does not ask to be decked out elaborately. Still, the Lord judges our work with such compassion and appraises it so kindly that he would give a reward for just a cup of cold water. Because he scrutinizes hearts so justly, he will requite not only the actual

21. Cf. Is 45.8.

expenditure involved in the work, but the intentions of the one who performed it as well.

Sermon 15

13 December 442

With confidence, dearly beloved, do we encourage you to works of compassion, for we know from experience that you gladly undertake what we advise. You know, and you come to learn with God as your teacher, that the observance of divine commandments will profit to your eternal joy. Because human frailty very often grows weary and falters in many people on account of the instability arising from its own weakness, the merciful and compassionate Lord has given us remedies and helps whereby we might obtain forgiveness. Who would be able to escape so many allurements of the world, so many snares of the devil, in short, so many dangers of their own unsteadiness, if the clemency of our eternal King did not prefer to restore us rather than to throw us away?

Even those who have already been redeemed, already reborn, already made children of light, cannot pass through these days without temptation, so long as they are detained in this world which "has been placed completely in the power of the evil one,"[22] so long as corruptible and temporal things titillate the weakness of flesh. Nor can anyone easily attain to so unbloody a victory as to remain unwounded amid the many enemies and frequent conflicts—even if death has been avoided.

Consequently, the medicine of three remedies in particular must be applied for tending to the injuries often incurred by those who clash with an invisible enemy: persistence in prayer, in the mortification of fasting, and in the generosity of almsgiving. When these are practiced together, God becomes propitiated, fault gets wiped out, and the tempter finds himself expelled. Souls of the faithful should always be surrounded with these fortifications, but they ought to be even more carefully

---

22. 1 Jn 5.19.

SERMON 15

prepared during these days which have been established by custom specifically for these duties of compassion.

2. To this group of days belongs also the solemn fast of this December. We must not neglect it simply because it has been taken over from the observance of the old law—as if this were among the number of those things which have ceased, such as distinctions between food, different kinds of baptism, and sacrifices of birds and livestock. Those things which bore the figures of what was to come ended when what they signified reached fulfillment. Grace, which came with the New Testament, has not done away with the usefulness of fasting. By the dedicated observance of fasting, grace acquires that self-restraint which always benefits both body and soul.

Certainly, the following endure in the Christian understanding, namely, "You shall adore the Lord your God and him alone shall you serve,"[23] "You shall love the Lord your God with your whole heart," "You shall love your neighbor as yourself,"[24] and other such commandments. Likewise, the directions which have been given in the same books about the sanctifying and salubrious benefits of fasting have not been made void by any standard.

At any time and during all the days of life in this world, fasting makes us stronger against sins, overcomes concupiscences, repels temptations, makes pride bow down, mitigates wrath, and rears all the inclinations of good will up to the maturity of complete virtue. Yet this only happens if it takes up into partnership with itself the benevolence of love and exercises itself prudently in works of mercy. Fasting without alms does not so much cleanse the soul as afflict the flesh. It must rather be ascribed to avarice than to self-restraint when someone refrains from food in such a way as also to be fasting from compassion.

Let our fasting, therefore, dearly beloved, abound in the fruits of generosity. Let it be fertile with gifts of kindness for the poor of Christ. Let those who happen to be less well off not

23. Mt 4.10.
24. Mt 22.37 and 39.

lag behind in this work thinking they have little to contribute from their means. Our Lord knows the powers of all, and the fair Investigator understands from what quantity each one gives. Of course different resources cannot support the same expenditures, but what varies in outlay often becomes supplemented by merit, for the heart can be equal even where the amounts are not.

So that, God helping us, these things might be attended to with dedicated compassion, let us fast on Wednesday and Friday. On Saturday, however, let us celebrate the vigil with blessed Peter the apostle. Aided by his prayers, may we deserve the mercy of God in all things.

Sermon 16

12 December 443

Indeed, dearly beloved, the grace of God brings it about daily in the hearts of Christians that every desire of ours should be transferred from earthly things to heavenly. Yet we lead even this present life through the Creator's help and have it sustained by his providence, for the same one who promises eternal things also bestows the temporal. Consequently, just as we ought to give thanks to God for the hope of future happiness—to which we are running through faith because we are elevated to the understanding of such a great preparation—likewise must we honor and praise God for those conveniences also which we obtain at the return of each single year. From the very beginning God endowed the earth with fruitfulness and arranged the laws of producing fruit in each and every shoot and seed—all in such a way as never to forsake his own establishments.

On the contrary, the benign management of the Maker continues in all the things that have been made. Whatever the crops, the vines, the olive trees have produced for the use of human beings, all of this has issued forth from the generosity of divine goodness. Since the elements tend to be unpredictable, this generosity compassionately helps out the uncertain labors of farmers so that wind and rain, cold and heat, days and nights are all at our service. Human planning would not suffice for bringing to fruition its own work were the Lord not to supply the growth for our usual planting and watering.

Consequently, full compassion and full justice require that we too should help others from the things which the heavenly Father has mercifully bestowed upon us. Very many have no portion in fields, none in vines, none in olive trees. We must attend to their scarcity from that plenty which God has given. That way they too can bless God along with us for the fruitfulness of the earth. They too can rejoice that these things had been given to those who possess them because these latter had shared them with the poor and with wayfarers.

Happy that barn and most worthy of having all its fruits multiplied, that barn from which the hunger of the needy and the infirm has been satisfied, from which the needs of the wayfarer have been relieved, from which the wants of the infirm have been tended to. God in his justice has allowed them to suffer affliction through various discomforts in order to crown both the miserable for their resignation and the merciful for their benevolence.

2. Though all times are opportune for this work, dearly beloved, this one now is especially fitting and appropriate. Inspired by God, our Fathers gave sanction to this fast of December so that, when the entire harvest had been gathered, abstinence might reasonably be dedicated to God. That way, all might remember to make use of their plenty in such a way as to be both more restrained toward themselves and more lavish toward the poor.

Entreaty for sins has the greatest efficacy when accompanied by alms and fasting. Prayer rises up quickly to the ears of God when lifted up by the recommendation of these. Since, as it has been written, "the merciful man benefits his own soul,"[25] nothing belongs to each individual more than what has been spent on one's neighbor. Part of those physical resources which are used to help the poor become transformed into eternal riches. Born from this generosity are funds which will not be

---

25. Prv 11.17.

able to be diminished through use nor damaged through decay. "Blessed are the merciful, for God will have mercy on them."[26] He who constitutes the very exemplar of this precept will also be the sum of their reward.

3. There is no doubt, dearly beloved, but that our enemy, skilled in and eager for causing harm, has been stirred on by sharper goads of ill will through these works of compassion which recommend us more and more to God. If he has not been permitted to attack some with open and bloody persecutions, he corrupts them by drawing them into a false profession of the Christian name. He has heretics for his lackeys in this work. Once they had strayed from the Catholic Faith, he made them fight on his side and under his command—beneath the standards of various errors.

Just as, to deceive the first human beings, he had taken up the serpent as his tool,[27] so, to seduce the hearts of orthodox [Christians], he armed the tongues of these with the poison of his falsehood. With pastoral care, however, we oppose these snares, dearly beloved, to the extent that the Lord helps us. To prevent any of the holy flock from perishing, we advise you with fatherly admonitions to turn away from "wicked lips and treacherous tongue," from which the prophet asks that his soul "be kept free,"[28] since "their talk crawls like a crab,"[29] as the blessed Apostle said. They creep in low to the ground, take hold softly, squeeze gently, and kill undetected.

"They come," just as the Savior foretold, "in the clothing of sheep, but within they are ravenous wolves"[30]—who would not be able to deceive the true and simple sheep unless they covered their beastly madness with the name of Christ. Working in all of these is the one who, though an enemy of the enlightenment, "changes himself into an angel of light."[31] By his skill does Basilides becomes clever, and by his talent Marcion. Sabellius gets driven along under his leadership, Photinus rushes ahead under his direction. Arius serves his power, Eunomius

---

26. Mt 5.7.
27. Cf. Gn 3.1.
28. Ps 119(120). 2.
29. Cf. 2 Tm 2.17.
30. Mt 7.15.
31. Cf. 2 Cor 11.14.

waits on his spirit. That entire troop of such beasts withdrew from the Church's unity with him in charge and deserted the truth with him for their teacher.

4. Although he exercises a chameleonic leadership in every kind of distortion, he has nevertheless built his stronghold on the insanity of Manichaeans, finding among them the most spacious courtyard in which to vaunt himself the more arrogantly. Among them he holds sway over not merely one kind of depravity, but over an amalgamation of every error and godlessness lumped together. Whatever profanity exists among pagans, whatever blindness among carnal Jews, whatever illicitness in the occult arts of magic, in short, whatever sacrilege and blasphemy exists among all heresies combined, it has all flooded together into them as if into a kind of sewer where all filth collects.

Consequently, it would take too long to describe all their godlessness and foulness, for the great number of their crimes overwhelms the supply of words. It suffices to point out just a few of these, so that, from the ones you have heard, you can get a pretty good idea about those we pass over for being too ashamed to talk about them. When it comes to their ceremonies, however, which among them are as obscene as they are loathsome, we shall not remain silent about what the Lord has willed to be brought to light through investigation on our part, so that no one might think that we have been naively given over to dubious reports and questionable speculation about this matter.

As bishops and presbyters sat here with me, while Christian men and nobles were gathered together in the same assembly, we commanded their "Elect Men" and "Elect Women" to present themselves. When they had disclosed many things about the twistedness of their doctrine and the practices at their festivals, they proceeded to bring out that crime which is too shameful to utter. So carefully had it been investigated that no doubt could remain even for those who were less inclined to believe it or for those who cast aspersions [upon the allegations]. Every person who had been involved in perpetrating that unspeakable crime was present, namely, the ten-year-old girl, the two women who had raised her and prepared her for the disgrace, as well as the young man who violated the girl and the bishop who directed them in this despicable crime. All these made a single, consistent confession as that execrable thing which our ears could scarcely bear was brought out into the open. Lest we offend pure ears by speaking about this more openly, the records of these deeds suffice to demonstrate without any shadow of a doubt that no modesty, no honor, no chastity at all has been found in this sect where falsehood constitutes their law, the devil their religion, and turpitude their sacrifice.

5. Consequently, dearest friends, renounce your acquaintances with these people, execrable and pernicious in everything, people whom disturbances in other regions have brought upon us in greater numbers. Ladies, you especially should refrain from getting to know and conversing with such as these, lest as your unguarded ears begin to perk up at their fantastic stories you should fall into the devil's snares. He knows how he led the first man astray by the words of a woman and how he cast all human beings from the happiness of Paradise through the credulousness of woman. Now too he schemes against your sex with a more confident shrewdness, trying to despoil of both faith and honor those whom he can allure to himself through purveyors of his falsehood.

Please, dearest friends, take this advice as well. If it should become known to any of you where they live, where they teach, whom they meet, and in what company they take their recreation, you should faithfully make it known to us who are so concerned [with this problem]. It benefits you little not to be taken in by them yourself through the protection of God's Spirit if you fail to be stirred when you notice others being taken in. Everyone ought to exhibit the same vigilance against our common enemy for the public welfare—to prevent other members from being corrupted through the festering wound of any one member. Do not think that such as these ought not to be exposed, lest you be found guilty of silence in the judgment of Christ even if you have not been defiled by actual complicity.

6. So take up the loyal zeal of a devout concern. Let the caring

of all believers rise up against these most savage enemies of souls. God in his mercy has exposed to us a certain number of these baneful people so that a diligent caution might be awakened once the danger had been brought to light. What has already been done should not be enough, but let the same investigation continue. May it obtain the result not only that the orthodox might remain unharmed but also that many who have been deceived through the devil's seduction might be recalled from their error. Your prayers, your alms, and your fasts will be offered in a more holy way to the merciful God through that very dedication if this work of faith should have been added to all the duties of compassion.

7. Let us fast, therefore, on Wednesday and Friday. On Saturday, however, let us celebrate the vigil with blessed Peter the apostle here present. He—as we both believe and have found out from experience—never ceases to extend his pastoral watchfulness to the sheep entrusted to him by the Lord. He will obtain by his entreaties that the Church of God, which had been established through his preaching, should be free from all error. Through Christ our Lord.

Sermon 17

17 December 444

What the law taught, dearly beloved, provides much of use to what has been sanctioned by the Gospel. Certain things pass over from those old precepts to this new observance. We see from the very devotion of the Church that the Lord Jesus "did not come to destroy the law but to fulfill it."[32] Those signs have ceased by which the coming of our Savior had been announced. Those figures have been brought to completion which the actual presence of truth removed. Those things which the order of devotion established either for the regulation of our customs or for the sincere worship of God, these continue with us in the same form in which they had been established. The things which coincide between the two Testaments are not changed by any alteration.

32. Cf. Mt 5.17.

Among these is the solemn fast of December, which we must celebrate in our yearly custom because it is entirely just and devout that we should give thanks to the divine generosity for the fruits the ground has produced to be used by human beings according to the measure of his supreme providence. In order to show that we are acting with a willing heart, it is necessary that we take on not only the self-restraint of the fast but also the duty of almsgiving. That way, from the ground of our heart also the seed of virtue and the fruit of charity might spring up.

By having mercy on his poor we might deserve the mercy of God. The most effective prayer to make requests of God is that which is supported by the works of mercy, since those who do not turn away their hearts from poverty quickly turn the Lord's ear to themselves,[33] as the Lord says: "Be compassionate just as your Father is compassionate,"[34] and "pardon and you will be pardoned."[35] What is kindlier than this justice? What is more merciful than this reciprocity where the decision of the one to judge is placed in the power of the one to be judged? "Give and it will be given to you,"[36] he said. How quickly hesitant anxiety and delaying avarice are cut off so that a confident compassion might give away what the Truth has promised to give back to us!

2. Be steady then, Christian giver. Give what you receive, sow what you reap, scatter what you collect. Do not fear the cost, do not long after a dubious income. Your property increases by being well spent. Long for the lawful reward of mercy, and pursue the business of the eternal profit. Your benefactor wants you to be beneficent, and he who gives so that you might have, entrusts it so that you might distribute it, saying: "Give and it will be given to you."[37]

You must embrace the condition of this promise and show your gratitude. Although you have nothing "except what you have received,"[38] you cannot, nevertheless, not have what you have given. Consequently, those who love money and hope to increase their wealth with immoderate growth, let them

33. Cf. Tb 4.7.
34. Lk 6.36.
35. Lk 6.37.
36. Lk 6.38.
37. Lk 6.38.
38. Cf. 1 Cor 4.7.

rather practice this holy investment and grow rich by this art of usury, that they should not lay hold of the necessities of laboring men or fall into the traps of impossible debts through deceitful benefits. Let them instead be the creditors and the money-lenders of someone who said: "Give and it will be given to you,"[39] and "the measure with which you measure, the same will be measured back to you."[40]

Those are unfaithful and even unjust to themselves who do not want to have forever what they thought ought to be loved. However much they add, however much they collect and accumulate, they will leave this world helpless and needy, as David the prophet said: "For when they die they will not take any of their things, nor will the glory of their house go down with them."[41] If any would be benefactors to their own souls, they should entrust their goods to that one who is a suitable trustee of the poor and a most generous payer of interest. But an unjust and shameless avarice which, while deceiving, says it is offering a benefit, does not believe God who promises truly but at the same time believes human beings who bargain confusedly. While they think the present is more sure than the future, they often and deservedly run into the situation in which the desire of unjust gain is for them the cause of a not unjust loss.

3. Whatever the outcome, the system of usury is always evil where both to diminish the money and to increase it is a sin. Either people are unhappy in losing what they gave, or they are more unhappy in receiving what they did not give. Therefore the evil of usury must be shunned, and the profit that lacks all human kindness must be avoided. The means for unjust and grievous gain is increased, but the essence of the soul is worn down, since usury in money is the ruin of the soul. The holy prophet David showed what God thinks about people of this kind when he says: "Lord, who will dwell in your tent, or who will rest on your holy mountain?"[42] Those are taught by the reply of the divine voice, and those know

39. Lk 6.38.
41. Cf. Ps 48(49).17–18.
40. Lk 6.38.
42. Ps 14(15).1.

that they have a part in eternal rest if, among other rules of a holy life, "they do not give their own money at usury."[43] They are shown to be strangers to the "tent" of God and foreign to his "holy mountain"[44] if they seize a deceitful profit for their money by usury, and, while they want to be rich through another's loss, they are worthy to be punished by eternal penury.

4. But you, dearly beloved, who have believed the promises of the Lord with your whole heart, flee the foul leprosy of avarice and make a holy and wise use of God's gifts. Since you enjoy his generosity, take care that you may be able to have companions of your joy. The things that are supplied to you are lacking to many, and in their need the material has been given to you for imitating the divine goodness, so that through you the divine goodness might pass over to others. As you give out your temporal goods well, you are acquiring eternal.

5. On Wednesday and Friday, therefore, let us fast. On Saturday, however, let us keep vigil with the blessed apostle Peter. By his prayers, may the divine protection be obtained for us in all things, through Christ our Lord.

Sermon 18

16 December 451

Protections for the sanctification of our souls and bodies have been established by God, dearly beloved, for the reason that, when they are being renewed without cessation by the course of days and seasons, the very medicine for our weaknesses might warn us. Nature indeed is changeable and mortal because of the stain of sin, even though now redeemed and now renewed in holy Baptism. In so far as it is able to suffer, it inclines to degradation. Nature will be corrupted by bodily desire unless fortified with spiritual help, for, as there is nothing lacking to make human beings fall, so there is always pres-

---

43. Ps 14(15).5.
44. Cf. Ps 14(15).1.

ent help to support them, as the Apostle says: "God is faithful, who will not allow you to suffer beyond that which you are able, but he will make issue that you might be able to sustain it."[45]

Even though the Lord protects warriors and he who is "mighty in battle"[46] encourages his own soldiers, saying, "Do not be afraid, because I have overcome the world,"[47] still we should know, dearly beloved, that even with this incentive the fear is lifted, not the struggle. After the sharp point of terror has been made dull, the cause of the struggle remains, a struggle which is stirred up terribly by the crafty enemy in the fury of persecution, but brought in all the more harmfully by the appearance of peace. When the battles are out in the open, the crowns are also evident. This, too, nourishes and inflames the strength of patience, that, when disaster is nearest, the promise is also at hand. After the public attacks of the wicked ones cease and the devil restrains himself from the slaughter and torture of the faithful, lest by the intensity of his cruelties there be a manifold increase of our triumphs, the raging adversary turns his bloodthirsty hatred to quiet treachery, and those he could not overcome with hunger and cold, with sword and fire, he will wear out with an easy life, he will snare with willfulness, inflame with ambition, and corrupt with luxury.

2. The Christian battle line, when the Spirit of Truth draws up his own soldiers, has powerful defenses and invincible arms for destroying these and all others, as long as gentleness abolishes anger, generosity abolishes greed, and kindness abolishes envy. When the "right hand of the Most High changes"[48] many hearts, the old human being is made new, and from servants to wickedness those hearts become ministers of justice. Restraint has subdued luxury, humility has cast out arrogance, and those who were soiled in shame now shine in purity.

To these conversions, dearly beloved, through the providence of God's grace, are added the holy fasts which, on certain days, demand the devotion of a general observance by the whole Church. Although it is admirable and praiseworthy that

---

45. Cf. 1 Cor 10.13.
46. Ps 23(24).8.
47. Jn 16.33.
48. Cf. Ps 76(77).11.

each separate member of the body of Christ should be adorned with their own services, it is a still more excellent act and a more holy virtue when the hearts of devout people come together for one purpose. Then that one, for whom our holiness is a torment, is overcome not by a part but by the undivided whole.

To this work now, dearly beloved, December is dedicated, warning us in its own way, in conformity with the quality of the season, that no one should be lethargic in the chill of infidelity but should rather gain strength by the spirit of charity. We receive the meaning of the divine will through the very elements of this world as well as through books open to all, and the heavenly instruction never ceases even when we are instructed by the things which serve us.

3. In addition to that expression of the Apostle in which people who "lack the fruit" of devotion are compared to barren "trees,"[49] we must beware of that fig tree also as an example of unfruitfulness which the Lord Jesus condemned to eternal sterility, as the Gospel says, because it had nothing he could take when he was hungry.[50] We should understand how those who do not feed the hungry deny food to the one who said that what is given to the poor is bestowed on him. There will be trees under this curse to which the judge will say: "Depart from me, you cursed, into everlasting fire which my Father has prepared for the devil and his angels. For I was hungry and you gave me no food, I was thirsty and you gave me no drink," etc.[51] Each of these is recalled for this reason, that we might know that none will be beyond mercy if they have followed even a part of this duty. But a soul who helps no one will be a tree that has no fruit,[52] since it will be found to be a stranger to all mercy.

(2) The fast of December, which is in winter, calls us to a mystical agriculture in which the growth of the crops and branches and trees by which human weakness is upheld, might be cultivated in spiritual effort, so that the field of the Lord might be enriched at its outlay, and what he never intended to be without fruit might be even more productive in its own

49. Jude 1.12.
51. Mt 25.41–42.
50. Cf. Mt 21.19.
52. Cf. Mt 21.19.

abundance. Your devotion understands that this refers to the progress of the whole Church whose seed is faith, whose growth is in hope, and whose maturing is in charity. Discipline of the body and constancy in prayer obtain a true purity when they depend on the sanctification of alms, as the Lord says: "Give alms, and behold all things are clean for you."[53]

Let us fast, therefore, on Wednesday and Friday of this week. On Saturday, however, we must celebrate the vigil of the blessed apostle Peter, with the support and help of the one who lives and reigns with the Father and the Holy Spirit for ever and ever. Amen.

Sermon 19

14 December 452

When the Savior was instructing his disciples about the coming of the kingdom of God and the end of the temporal world, he was also teaching his whole Church in the apostles. He said, "Be on guard, lest perchance your hearts will be bloated with indulgence and drunkenness and worldly cares."[54] We know that this command pertains more especially to us, dearly beloved, who have been forewarned of that day, which even if it is a secret is certain to be near. It is necessary for every person to be prepared for its coming, lest it should find any either given over to their stomachs or tangled up in the cares of this world.

It has been proven daily by experience, dearly beloved, that the keenness of the mind is dulled by the satisfaction of the flesh, and the vigor of the heart is blunted by a superfluity of food. The delight of eating is contrary to the health of the body unless a rational temperance resists the pleasure and withdraws from its desire what is going to be a burden. Even if the flesh desires nothing without the soul, and it receives sensation from the same source whence it also assumes its motions, yet it is a quality of the soul to deny to itself some things of counter-

---

53. Lk 11.41.
54. Lk 21.34.

feit substance, and by an interior judgment to rein in the exterior things away from those which are improper.

The soul is more often free from bodily desires and can devote itself to divine wisdom in the palace of the spirit where, when all noise of earthly care is silent, it may rejoice in holy meditations and in eternal delights. Even though in this life it is difficult to sustain this, it can often be undertaken that we are occupied in spiritual matters more often and longer than in bodily matters, and while we spend longer time on better concerns, even temporal actions pass into incorruptible riches.

2. The usefulness of this observance, dearly beloved, is established especially in the Church's fasts, which, by the teaching of the Holy Spirit, are so distributed throughout the whole year that the law of abstinence is assigned to all seasons. So we celebrate the spring fast in Lent, the summer fast after Pentecost, and the autumn fast in September, but the winter in this month, December, knowing that there is nothing lacking in the divine precepts, and that all nature serves the Word of God for our instruction. Through all the turning points of the year, as if through the four Gospels, we learn from the unceasing trumpet both what we should preach and what we should do. The prophet said, "The heavens declare the glory of God, the firmament proclaims his handiwork, day pours out the word to day, night imparts knowledge to night."[55] What is there through which the truth does not speak to us? Its voice is heard in the day, it is heard in the night, and the beauty of all things, established by the work of one God, does not cease to put into the ears of our hearts a ruling order, to let us see the "invisible things of God through those which have been made intelligible to us,"[56] and it is subject not to the creatures but to the Creator of all things. When all faults are destroyed through self-restraint, and when whatever avarice thirsts for, whatever pride aspires to, whatever luxury longs for, is overcome by the firmness of this virtue, who does not understand how great a protection is brought us by fasting?

55. Ps 18(19).2–3.
56. Cf. Rom 1.20.

In these things it is shown that temperance covers not only food but all bodily desires. Otherwise it is useless to undertake hunger without putting aside an unjust will; to suffer a lack of food without withdrawing from a sin undertaken. It is a bodily fast, not a spiritual one, when there is no restraint for the body alone, but we remain in all those delights which are more harmful. What profit is it to a soul to act the mistress outwardly and inwardly to serve as a slave, to govern the body and lose the right of its own liberty? It often suffers justly from the rebellious servant which does not render its due service to the Lord. Then, fasting in your body from food, let your spirit fast from sin, and let it judge the earthly cares and desires by the law of its ruler.

3. Let the soul remember that she owes her first love to God and her second to neighbor, and that all her affections must be directed by this rule, that she should not withdraw from the worship of the Lord nor from usefulness to the fellow servant. How is God worshipped unless what pleases him pleases us also, and unless our affections never resist his rule? If we want what he wants, our weakness will take strength from the one from whom we receive our very willpower. As the Apostle says, "For it is God who, in his good will toward you, causes you both to will and to act."[57] Human beings will not be inflated by pride nor broken by despair if they use the goods divinely given them for the glory of the Giver, and recall their desires from those things they know to be harmful. Abstaining from the malignity of hatred, from the laxity of indulgence, from the disturbance of anger, from the desire for vengeance, they will be purified by the sanctification of the true fast, and will feed on the pleasures of incorruptible delights. Through spiritual practice they will know how to transform even earthly wealth into heavenly possessions, not by hiding for themselves what they receive, but by multiplying more and more what they give out.

4. For this reason, with the affection of paternal charity, we encourage you in your love to make the fast of the December fruitful for yourselves by the generosity of your alms, rejoicing

---

57. Phil 2.13.

that through you the Lord feeds and clothes his poor. Certainly to them he could dispense these resources that he has given you, unless in his ineffable mercy he would sanctify them in their patient labor and you in your work of charity.

Let us fast, therefore, on Wednesday and Friday. On Saturday, however, let us celebrate the vigil with the blessed apostle Peter. He is willing to help our entreaties and fasts and alms with his prayers, with the aid of our Lord Jesus Christ, who lives and reigns with the Father and with the Holy Spirit forever and ever. Amen.

Sermon 20

After 445?

The dispensation of God's mercy, which our Savior undertook for the restoration of the human race, has been divinely ordered, dearly beloved, in such a way that the Gospel of grace lifts the veil of the law, but does not destroy its purpose. We must guard this intention of the Lord in which he said that he "came not to destroy the law but to fulfill it,"[58] so that we too, as far as we can with God's help, might keep this rule. We know that nothing of the precepts of the Old Testament may be neglected if we are earnestly zealous to know what, there veiled by a shadow, is to pass away, and what has been founded in a process remaining to the end. Decisions about food and sacrifices, the circumcision of flesh, the diversity of baptisms and the ceremonies of baptism, are to be handled no longer under the symbolic signs which have also been fulfilled by those very things they signified. Yet the commandments and moral precepts continue as they were given, because they mean nothing other than what they say.

In Christian devotion they increase by doing, but do not cease by not being observed. To love God and neighbor, to honor father and mother, not to worship others' gods, and the remaining things which are either forcefully forbidden or wholesomely commanded, we respect in the same way from

---

58. Mt 5.17.

SERMON 20

legal institutes as from the Gospel decrees. Although many things have been added because of the newness of grace, nevertheless nothing has been diminished from the former justice. The regulations of the apostles were right in directing that the use of the ancient fasts should remain, and, although the custom of the Church taught us to exercise ourselves in long abstinences, nevertheless, it embraced the sanctification of moderation coming from the law. To those to whom it was given to be able to do the greater, it was improper not to observe what was less.

2. Clearly instructed by this reasoning, dearly beloved, we join in the fast of December by the Church's rule, and we call this to your devout attention, as is the custom. It is a matter full of mercy and full of justice that, when the harvest of the fruits of the earth is gathered, we should give thanks to God and pay our "sacrifice of mercy" to him[59] with the offering of the fast. Let all rejoice in their own abundance and let them be glad that they have brought much into their barns, but only so that the poor might also be glad in their wealth. Let the overflow of souls imitate the abundance of crops, the spreading of vines, the fruit of trees. What the earth has given, let our hearts give, so that we can say with the prophet: "Our earth has yielded its fruit."[60]

For God the true and supreme Farmer gives not only bodily fruits but spiritual ones as well, and he knows how to raise both seeds and plants in two-fold cultivation. He gives to fields the issue of seeds, he gives to souls the growth of virtues, which, as they have taken their origin from one Provider, so they call for the culmination of one work. Human beings, made "in the image and likeness of God,"[61] have nothing in the dignity of their nature so especially their own as that they can match the goodness of their Creator, who as he is a merciful donor of his own gifts, so he is a just creditor, willing for us to be companions in his work. Although we have no power to create nature, we can still use the material received from the grace of God, be-

---

59. Cf. Sir 35.4.
60. Ps 66(67).7.
61. Cf. Gn 1.26.

cause the earthly goods are not so collected for our own use that they should serve the satisfaction and pleasure of our bodily senses only. Otherwise we would be no different than sheep, no different than beasts, who do not know how to provide for the necessities of others, and can only care for themselves and their own offspring.

3. Animals, lacking intellect, are instructed in no commandments. They who have received no power of reason have received no law. Where there is the light of reason, however, there is the discipline of mercy, which owes love to God and to neighbor. Just so do human beings prove that they love themselves, when it is evident that they love the Maker of their nature above themselves, and the sharer of their nature as themselves. Rightly "on these two commandments depend the whole law and the prophets."[62] Rightly should the extent of all debate be expressed in the brevity of a few words to full advantage. We must love God, we must love our neighbor, in such a way that we take the form of love to our neighbor from that love with which God loves us, who is good even to the wicked and supports not only his worshippers with the gifts of his kindness, but even his antagonists. We must love our neighbors, we must love strangers, and what is owing to friends must be paid over and above to enemies.

Although the malice of some people does not grow gentle with any kindness, nevertheless, the works of mercy are not without fruit, and kindness never loses what is offered to the ungrateful. May none, dearly beloved, make themselves strangers to good works. Let none plead their penury as if it scarcely sufficed for themselves and they could not help another. What is offered from a little is great, and in the scale of divine justice not the quantity of gifts is measured but the constancy of souls. The "widow" in the Gospel put two coins into the "treasury," and this surpassed the gifts of all the rich.[63] No mercy is worthless before God, no compassion is fruitless. He has given different resources to human beings, but he does not ask different affections.

62. Mt 22.40.
63. Cf. Mk 12.41–44 and Lk 21.2–4.

(2) Let all take account of their possessions, and let those give more who have received more. Let the abstinence of the faithful be the food of the poor, and let what all deny themselves be a benefit to the needy, for although the medicine of frugality produces much for both soul and body, these fasts will still be of little use unless they are sanctified by the intention of mercy. A certain power of baptism is set in almsgiving because "just as water quenches a fire, so alms atone for sins."[64] It has also been said through the same Spirit, "Wash yourselves, be clean,"[65] and "Give alms and all will be clean for you."[66] Let no one be hesitant, no one doubt that the brightness of regeneration will be restored, even after many sins, for the one who is eager to be cleansed by the purification of almsgiving.

64. Sir 3.33.
65. Is 1.16.
66. Lk 11.41

CHRISTMAS

Leo wrote these Christmas sermons in the years 440–444 and 450–454. As he states in *Serm.* 28.4, ". . . practically no one has gone astray who did not disbelieve the reality of two natures in Christ while at the same time acknowledging a single Person." Consequently, from the very first years of his pontificate, he emphasized—in the discharge of his episcopal duty to preach—the reality and the wonder of (in short, the "Good News" about) the Incarnation of the Word. One phase of his preaching stresses the key points of the different heresies that had broken out in various parts of the world.[1] Instruction was vital if his flock was to recognize and avoid the deadly errors.

Teachers from East and West were spreading false ideas regarding the Church's doctrine about Christ. These ideas were due, in some measure, to differences in language. Even in the same language, one word could have different meanings for different people.[2] In his explanations of doctrine, Leo shows himself to be a master of delineation, discernment, and clarity. His statements about the divine and the human natures in Christ are repeated over and over, in almost every possible way, and from every angle: e.g., "Remaining what he was and taking on what he was not . . ." (*Serm.* 21.2); "As a result, so strong a bond of unity has been made between the two natures that, though each retains its own proper characteristics, whatever belongs to God cannot be separated from the man, while whatever belongs to the man cannot be disjoined from the divinity" (*Serm.* 28.1).

Not a speculative theologian, Leo did not intend to teach anything new, but simply to preserve ". . . the Christ of the Gospels and the Apostolic Age for the faith of posterity . . . ,"[3] all the while realizing that ". . . the Birth of our Lord Jesus Christ exceeds all understanding and goes beyond any precedent" (*Serm.* 30.4).

Another aspect of Leo's Christmas instruction stems from his endeavor to highlight for his people the joy attendant on this "Good News": ". . . our lowliness realizes how great a value its Creator has placed upon it . . ." (*Serm.* 24.2); "Peace was the first thing proclaimed by the angelic choir at the Lord's Nativity. It is peace which gives birth

---

1. "Even the history of the heresies of this period still requires intensive investigation" (Grillmeier, *Christ in Christian Tradition*, 492).
2. A list of such words in Greek and in Latin can be found in *ibid.* 516–517.
3. *ibid.* 492.

to children of God. Peace nurses love, engenders unity, gives repose to the blessed, and provides a home to eternity" (*Serm.* 26.3). Again, as always, the message of Christ in its fullness, so deeply ingrained in Leo's mind and spirit, speaks to the heart of everyone who heard his words—or who now reads them.

Sermon 21

25 December 440

UR SAVIOR, dearly beloved, was born this day. Let us rejoice. No, there cannot rightly be any room for sorrow in a place where life has been born. By dispelling fear of death, life fills us with joy about the promised eternity. No one has been cut off from a share in this excitement. All share together a single rationale for joy. Our Lord, finding no one free of guilt, has come to liberate all. Let saints exult, for the palm [of victory] lies within their reach. Let sinners rejoice, for they have been called to pardon. Let heathens take heart, for they have been summoned to life.

(2) God's Son (in the "fullness of time"[4] which the "inscrutable depths of divine wisdom"[5] had ordained) took on human nature to reconcile it to its Maker. In that way, "the devil" who invented "death"[6] might be overcome through that very thing which he had overcome. In the conflict undertaken on our behalf, battle was joined on the most remarkably fair terms. Omnipotent Lord engages this extremely savage enemy, not in his own majesty but in our lowliness, bringing against him the very same form and the very same nature [that had been overcome], partaker indeed in our mortality but wholly without sin. What is read about birth in general does not apply to this one: "No one is clean from stain, not even an infant, had his life on earth but lasted a single day."[7]

Into this unique birth, then, nothing has passed over from the concupiscence of flesh, nothing flowed from the law of sin. Chosen is a royal virgin from the shoot of David. Destined to become pregnant with the sacred fruit, she conceives an off-

---

4. Cf. Gal 4.4 and Eph 1.10.
5. Cf. Rom 11.33.
6. Cf. Wis 2.24.
7. Cf. Jb 14.4–5.

spring (both divine and human) in her spirit—before she does so in her body. So that she might not, in being uninformed about the divine plan, become frightened by its unusual effects, she learns from conversation with an angel what work was to be accomplished in her by the Holy Spirit.

She did not believe that her honor would be compromised, she who would soon be the Mother of God. Why indeed would she have any misgivings about the Conception on account of its unusual nature? She has been promised its accomplishment through the power of the Most High. That faith upon which her confidence rested finds reinforcement through the testimony of a miracle that had come as a precursor. Elizabeth has been endowed with an unhoped-for fruitfulness. For the one who had given conception to a sterile woman could undoubtedly give it to a virgin as well.

2. Consequently, the Word of God, God the Son of God, who "in the beginning was with God, through whom all things were made and without whom was made nothing,"[8] to free human beings from eternal death was himself made human. He condescended to take up our lowliness without diminishing his majesty. Remaining what he was and taking on what he was not, he united the true "form of a servant" with the "form"[9] in which he is equal to God the Father. He grafted together both natures in such a union that glorification should not overwhelm the lower nor humbling diminish the higher.

When, therefore, the identity of each substance is preserved and they join in a single Person, majesty takes up humility, strength takes up weakness, eternity takes up mortality. To pay the debt of our condition, his inviolable nature pours forth into a vulnerable one. True God and true man are combined into the unity of the Lord. So, as suited our healing, "one" and the same "Mediator between God and human beings"[10] was able both to die (by reason of one state) and to rise again (by that of the other). Appropriately, this birth of salvation brought no corruption whatsoever to the Virgin's integrity, for the issuing forth of truth served as guardian over her honor.

8. Cf. Jn 1.1–3. 9. Cf. Phil 2.6–7.
10. Cf. 1 Tm 2.5.

(2) Such, then, dearly beloved, was the Nativity that befit Christ, "the power of God and the wisdom of God."[11] By it he both conforms to us through humanity and rises above us through divinity. Were he not indeed true God, he could apply no remedy. Were he not indeed true man, he could not show example. Exulting angels sing at the Lord's Birth, "Glory to God in the highest," and proclaim, "On earth, peace to people of good will."[12] They indeed see the heavenly Jerusalem being constructed from all the nations of the world. How much should the lowliness of human beings rejoice over this indescribable work of divine pity when the sublimity of angels so delights in it?

3. As a result, dearly beloved, let us give "thanks to God the Father"[13] through his Son, in the Holy Spirit. "Because of that great love of his with which he loved us," he took pity on us, "and, when we were dead through our sins, he brought us to life through Christ,"[14] so that we might be a "new creature"[15] in him, a new handiwork. "Let us therefore put aside the old human being along with its actions."[16] Since we have become sharers in the Birth of Christ, let us renounce "works of the flesh."[17]

Realize, o Christian, your dignity. Once made a "partaker in the divine nature,"[18] do not return to your former baseness by a life unworthy [of that dignity]. Remember whose head it is and whose body of which you constitute a "member."[19] Recall how you had been wrested "from the power of darkness and brought into the light and the kingdom" of God.[20] Through the Sacrament of Baptism you were made "a temple of the Holy Spirit."[21] Do not drive away such a dweller by your wicked actions and subject yourself again to servitude under the devil, because your "price"[22] is the very blood of Christ, because he "will judge" you "in truth"[23] who has redeemed you in mercy, Christ our Lord. Amen.

11. Cf. 1 Cor 1.24.
12. Cf. Lk 2.14.
13. Cf. Col 1.12.
14. Cf. Eph 2.4–5.
15. Cf. 2 Cor 5.17 and Gal 6.15.
16. Col 3.8–9.
17. Cf. Gal 5.19.
18. Cf. 2 Pt 1.4.
19. Cf. 1 Cor 6.15.
20. Cf. Col 1.13.
21. Cf. 1 Cor 6.19.
22. Cf. 1 Cor 6.20 and 7.23.
23. Cf. Ps 95(96).13.

Sermon 22

25 December 441 (Recension A)[24]

Let us exult in the Lord, dearly beloved, and let us be gladdened with spiritual delight, for a day of new redemption has dawned for us, a day prepared from antiquity, a day of eternal blessedness. Made present to us on its anniversary is the mystery of salvation, promised from the beginning, fulfilled in the end, to remain without end. "It is fitting for us to adore the divine mystery" in this "with hearts raised upwards, so that, what God accomplishes through a great gift, the Church might celebrate with great rejoicing."[25]

(2) No sooner had the devil's malice put us to death with the poison of his envy than the almighty and merciful God immediately foreshadowed the remedy of his care. God (whose nature is goodness, whose will is power, whose work is mercy) foreshadowed a remedy **prepared** *predestined* at the very beginning of the world for the restoration of humanity. He announced to the serpent that the "seed of a woman" would, through his power, "crush" the arrogance of its poisonous "head"[26]—meaning "Christ," of course, God and man "in flesh."[27] Born of a virgin, he would condemn with his undefiled Birth that polluter of the human race.

For the devil was gloating over the fact that human beings, deceived by his craft, went without the divine gifts, and that, with the endowment of immortality stripped off, they were subject to the harsh sentence "of death."[28] He reveled in having found a certain comfort among his own evils from his compan-

---

24. This sermon comes down to us in two recensions. Recension A had been composed in 441. Recension B appears to represent a revision made by Leo himself at some later date. Material found in both recensions will appear in normal text. Material found only in Recension A will appear in **bold**. Material found only in Recension B will appear in *italics*. Some material found in both recensions but in a different order will be reproduced in both bold and italics in their proper order. Some material that does not coincide between the two versions of the Latin text but does not affect the English translation (such as word order or certain syntactical variants) will not be indicated.

25. Cf. Gelasianum 14. 26. Cf. Gn 3.15.
27. Cf. 1 Jn 4.2. 28. Cf. Gn 2.17 and 3.19.

ionship with the one who had gone astray. He also relished the fact that God, at the demands of strict justice, had changed his assessment of human beings, whom he had created in such honor. As a result, **dearly beloved**, it was necessary (by the designs of a secret plan) for the immutable God (whose will cannot be severed from his goodness) to complete by a deeper mystery the first intentions of his love. It was necessary that human beings, tricked into sin by the devil's wickedness, should not perish in opposition to God's plan.[29]

2. *When that time came, dearly beloved, which had been prearranged for the redemption of humanity, Jesus Christ,* the Son of God, comes into these nether regions of the world. Descending from his heavenly throne (yet without leaving his Father's glory), he was brought forth in an unusual manner, through a new [kind of] birth.

He was brought forth in an unusual manner because, though invisible in his own nature, he has been made visible in ours; because, though incomprehensible, he willed to be comprehended; because, though already existing before time, he came into being at a certain point in time; because the Lord of the universe, drawing a cloud over the dignity of his majesty, took on "the form of a servant"[30]; and because God, though incapable of suffering, did not think it beneath himself to suffer as man and to subject himself to the laws of death as a mortal.

He was brought forth through a new [kind of] birth, conceived by a virgin, born from a virgin, without the concupiscence of a father's flesh, without harm to the mother's integrity—because this kind of beginning was appropriate for the one who would be the Savior of humanity. He had in himself the essence of human nature yet knew not the depravities of human flesh. God acts as Maker for God born in the flesh—as the archangel verifies to the Blessed Virgin Mary: "The Holy Spirit will come down upon you, and the power of the Most High will overshadow you. Wherefore, the holy offspring to be born from you will be called the Son of God."[31]

(2) *Although his origin is different, his nature is the same. For a*

29. Cf. Ez 18.22–23 and 33.11. Cf. 2 Pt 3.9.
30. Cf. Phil 2.7.   31. Lk 1.35.

virgin to conceive, for a virgin to give birth, and for her to remain a virgin (which we believe), falls outside the realm of normal human experience. But it relies upon divine power. Here it is not the condition of the one who gave birth that will be considered, but the discretion of the one who was born. He was born a human being exactly as he willed and exactly as he had in his power to effect. If you look for the truth of his nature, consider the human material. If you examine the reason for his origin, confess the divine power.

For the Lord Jesus Christ came so that he might take away our pollution, not endure it; not succumb to our vices but heal them. He came so that he might attend to every infirmity of corruption and all the sores of unclean souls. For this reason, it needs be that he who brought a new grace of undefiled purity to human bodies should have been born in a new manner; that Incorruptibility, in being born, should guard the original virginity of his mother; and that the "power" of the divine "Spirit" poured into her[32] *should preserve the shelter of chastity and the guest-chamber of holiness that had pleased him so.*

That power had decided to raise up what had been cast down, to shore up what had broken down, and to give increased power to chastity for overcoming the enticements of flesh. In this way, the virginity which in others was not able to be preserved in giving birth could even in those others be imitated in being reborn.

3. That Christ chose to be born of a virgin, dearly beloved, does this not seem to be eminently reasonable? Indeed, the devil would not realize that salvation had been born for the human race. Since this conception (taking place through the Spirit) remained hidden from him, he would not suspect that the one whom he saw to be no different from others had been born in a different way than they? Noticing in him a nature like that of all others, he assumed that it had the same source as theirs. Nor did [the devil] gather that he was free from the chains of sin, since he found him not unacquainted with the weakness of mortality.

How "truthful" is "the mercy" of God![33] *There were many means available to him in a mysterious fashion for restoring the human race. Yet he chose this way in particular for seeing to it. He would not use the force of power to destroy the "devil's work,"*[34] *but the reasonableness of justice.*

32. Cf. Lk 1.35.
33. Cf. Ps 85(86).15.
34. Cf. 1 Jn 3.8.

SERMON 22

(2) *It was not unjust for the pride of this ancient enemy to arrogate for himself a tyrannical rule over all people. Nor was that dominion unwarranted beneath which he crushed them. After all, he had induced them to come over of their own accord from the law of God to obeying his will. In all justice, the slavery of this race could not rightly be taken away from him once it had surrendered—unless the very race which he had brought into subjection should overcome him.*

That this should happen, Christ was brought forth without the seed of man—from a virgin whom no human intercourse had made fruitful but the Holy Spirit. Although no conception takes place in mothers, as a rule, without the stain of sin, this mother derived cleansing from the very source that gave her to conceive. Where the transfer of a father's seed has not penetrated, the very first onset of sin has not been introduced.

(3) *Her untouched virginity did not know concupiscence, but provided substance.*[35] *It was nature that was assumed from the Lord's mother, not guilt. Created was the "form of a servant"*[36]*—without the condition of servitude. In such a way was the new man distilled from old that he took on himself the full essence of the race while shutting out the defect of that oldness.*

(3) **He was brought forth in a new [kind of] birth, because her untouched virginity did not know concupiscence of the flesh but provided its substance. It was nature that was assumed from the Lord's mother, not guilt. Created was the "form of a servant"**[37]**—without the condition of servitude. In such a way was the new man distilled from old that he took on himself the full essence of the race while shutting out the defect of that oldness.**

How "truthful" is "the mercy" of God![38] **There were many means available to him in a mysterious fashion for restoring the human race. Yet he chose this way in particular for seeing**

---

35. This sentence makes much more sense as it appears in Recension A (down below): **Her untouched virginity did not know concupiscence of the flesh but provided its substance.** In light of what follows, this passage means that Mary provided the complete essence of human nature without the defect of concupiscence (which does not belong to that essence but represents an accidental accretion)—an observation made repeatedly by Leo.

36. Cf. Phil 2.7.   37. Cf. Phil 2.7.

38. Cf. Ps 85(86).15.

to it. He would not use the force of power to destroy the "devil's work,"[39] but the reasonableness of justice.

It was not unjust for the pride of this ancient enemy to arrogate for himself a tyrannical rule over all people. Nor was that dominion unwarranted beneath which he crushed them. After all, he had induced them to come over of their own accord from the law of God to obeying his will. In all justice, the slavery of this race could not rightly be taken away from him once it had surrendered—unless the very race which he had brought into subjection should overcome him.

4. Accordingly, the merciful and omnipotent Savior controlled the process through which he first took on human nature in such a way as to veil under our weakness the divinity that was inseparable from his humanity. As a result, the shrewdness of that complacent enemy had been circumvented. He thought the birth of this boy (begotten for the salvation of the human race) to be no less subject to himself than that of anyone else who happens to be born. For the devil saw him whimper and cry. He saw him "wrapped in swaddling clothes,"[40] presented for "circumcision,"[41] and fulfilling the oblation of "sacrifice according to the law."[42] He noticed in addition the usual "growth of boyhood,"[43] and right up through manhood did not have any doubts about natural developments.

In spite of all this, he inflicted outrages; multiplied injuries; brought curses, insults, blasphemies, and reproaches against him. In short, he poured out onto him all the violence of his rage, exhausted every kind of trial. Knowing the poison that he had injected into human nature, in no way did he believe him free from *original* sin, since he had ascertained his mortality from so many indications of it. Consequently, this wicked plunderer and greedy collector held out against someone who of himself had done nothing by way of rebellion. In following up on the presumption of a corrupt origin, he uproots the

39. Cf. 1 Jn 3.8.
40. Cf. Lk 2.12.
41. Cf. Lk 2.21.
42. Cf. Lk 2.22–24.
43. Cf. Lk 2.40 and 52.

"decree" upon which he was relying.[44] He exacts a penalty for iniquity from him—someone in whom he did not find any fault.

(2) As a result, the ill-advising document of that death treaty gets revoked. *By virtue of his going after more than what justice allowed, the sum of the entire debt is canceled.* That "strong" one becomes tied up in his own chains. *Every contraption of the evil one gets turned back upon his own head.* "Once the prince of this world has been bound," the "fetters" of captivity are "removed."[45] Purged from the ancient contagion, nature returns to its dignity, death is dispelled by death, birth restored by birth. All at once, redemption takes away slavery, regeneration changes the beginning, and "faith justifies" the sinner.[46]

5. Whoever of you, therefore, takes pride (with devotion and faith) in the name of Christian, ponder by an accurate judgment the grace of this reconciliation. To you once "cast aside," to you driven out from the thrones of "Paradise,"[47] to you dying from long exiles, to you scattered into "dust" and ashes,[48] who had no longer any hope of living—to you has "power"[49] been given through the Incarnation of the Word. With it, you can "return from far away"[50] to your Maker, can recognize your Father, can become free from slavery, can be made again a child rather than an outsider. With this power, you who were born of flesh that is subject to decay can be "born again from the Spirit"[51] of God and can obtain through grace what you do not have through nature.

If you acknowledge yourself to be a "child" of God through the "spirit of adoption," you may dare to claim God as your "Father."[52] *Absolved from the guilt of "a bad conscience,"*[53] *you may sigh for the heavenly kingdoms. Supported by divine aid, you can "do the will of God."*[54] *You can imitate the angels above the earth. You can feed on the strength of an immortal substance. You can struggle with assurance on behalf of*

---

44. Cf. Col 2.14.
45. Cf. Mt 12.29 and Jn 12.31.
46. Cf. Rom 1.17, Gal 3.11, Heb 10.38, and Hb 2.4.
47. Cf. Gn 3.23–24.
48. Cf. Gn 3.19.
49. Cf. Jn 1.12.
50. Cf. Lk 15.13 and 17.
51. Cf. Jn 3.5.
52. Cf. Rom 8.15.
53. Cf. Heb 10.22.
54. Cf. Heb 10.36.

devotion against temptations of the enemy.[55] *If you keep the vows of a heavenly soldier, you do not have to doubt that you will be crowned for your victory in the triumphal camp of the Eternal King—when the resurrection prepared for the just receives you to be promoted into fellowship in the heavenly kingdom.*

6. "Since we have the confidence of so great a hope,"[56] dearly beloved, "remain steadfast in the faith where you have been grounded"[57]—lest that same tempter, whose domination Christ has *now* lifted from you, should lead you astray once more with any of his traps, lest he should ruin these joys of today with the cleverness of his trickery. He makes sport of the more naive souls through the pernicious conviction of those for whom this day of our celebration seems honorable not so much for the Birth of Christ as for the rising of the new—as they say—sun. Their hearts have been enshrouded with empty darkness, entirely cut off from any entry of true light. They are still dragged along by the most foolish errors of paganism. *Because they cannot raise the focus of their minds beyond what they see through eyes of flesh,* they revere with honor due to God the lights that serve as instruments for this world. *Far from Christian souls should be this wicked superstition and prodigious lie. Temporal things should be kept separate beyond all measure from the eternal, corporeal from incorporeal, subordinate things from their Master.* Although these things have a beauty that is to be admired, they have no divinity that can be adored.

(2) That power, therefore, that wisdom, that majesty must be worshipped which created the entire universe "from nothing."[58] He brought forth earthly and heavenly substance with his all-powerful ordering into whatever shapes and sizes he wished. May the sun, the moon, and the stars be well-suited for those using them, beautiful for those looking at them—but only so that their charms might be referred from them back to their Maker. Let God who made them be adored, not the creature who serves him.

(3) Praise **the Lord** *God*, therefore, dearly beloved, in all his

55. Cf. Eph 6.11.
57. Cf. Col 1.23.
56. Cf. 2 Cor 3.12.
58. Cf. 2 Mc 7.28.

works and judgments. May there be in you an unwavering belief in the Virgin's integrity through childbearing. Honor the sacred and divine mystery of human restoration with holy and genuine service. Embrace Christ, born in our flesh, **so that we may deserve to see him as the God of glory reigning in his majesty.** *so that we may deserve to see this same God of glory reigning in his majesty, who with the Father and with the Holy Spirit remains in the unity of divinity forever and ever. Amen.*

Sermon 23

25 *December 442*

Certainly, the things which pertain to the mystery of today's solemnity are well known to you, dearly beloved, and you have heard about them often. Just as this visible light brings pleasure to uninjured eyes, so the Birth of our Savior gives eternal joy to hearts that are well. We must never remain silent about it, even though we cannot explain it as is proper. We believe that the saying, "Who will recount his generation?",[59] pertains not only to that mystery by which the Son of God is co-eternal with the Father, but also to this beginning by which "The Word was made flesh."[60]

(2) And so, God the Son of God, equal to and of the same nature as the Father (from the Father and with the Father), Creator and Lord of the universe, wholly present everywhere and wholly surpassing all things, himself chose this day in the passage of time (which moves according to his own arrangement) to be born for the salvation of the world from blessed Mary, who keeps her honor unsullied through all the stages of procreation. As her virginity was not violated in giving birth, so it had not been defiled in conception. As the Evangelist said, "To fulfill what was said by the Lord through the prophet Isaiah: 'Behold a virgin will conceive in her womb and will give birth to a son, and his name will be called Emmanuel, which means "God-with-us." ' "[61]

---

59. Is 53.8 (LXX). 60. Jn 1.14.
61. Mt 1.22–23 and Is 7.14.

This wonderful giving birth by the holy Virgin brought forth together in a single offspring a truly human and truly divine nature, because neither substance held its properties in such a way that there could be in them a distinction of persons. Nor was the creature taken up into union with its Creator in such a way that the Creator and the creature should be related to one another as inhabitant and inhabitation respectively. Rather, one nature was connected with the other.

Although there is one nature which is received and another which does the receiving, still the diversity of both comes together into so great a unity that there is one and the same Son—who says that he is inferior to the Father in so far as he is true man,[62] and declares that he is equal to the Father in so far as he is true God.[63]

2. This unity, dearly beloved, by which the creature is joined to the Creator, is what blindness of Arianism could not see with the eyes of understanding. Not believing the Only-Begotten of God to have the same glory and substance as the Father, they fabricated for themselves a lesser divinity of the Son from those things which must be referred to the "form of a servant."[64] In order to show that this form did not belong to a distinct or other person within him, the Son of God also predicated about one and the same Person both of the following: "The Father is greater than I,"[65] as well as, "I and the Father are one."[66]

(2) "In the form of a servant, which he took on at the end of the ages" for the sake of our restoration, he "is less than the Father;" "but in the form of God, in which he was" before the ages, "he is equal to the Father."[67] In human lowliness was he "made from a woman, made under the law;"[68] but, remaining in the divine majesty, he is God "the Word, through whom all things were made."[69] Therefore he who, in the form of God, made man, in the form of a servant was himself made man, but

---

62. Cf. Jn 14.28.
63. Cf. Jn 10.30.
64. Cf. Phil 2.7.
65. Jn 14.28.
66. Jn 10.30.
67. Cf. Phil 2.7, 1 Cor 10.11, and Phil 2.6.
68. Gal 4.4.
69. Jn 1.3.

each is God from the power of that taking on, each is man from the lowliness of that taken on.

Each nature holds on to its own properties without any deficiency. Even as the form of God does not delete the form of a servant, so the form of a servant does not diminish the form of God. Therefore, the mystery of power united with frailty (because of this joint "nature" of the God-man) allows the Son to be called less than the Father. Yet the divinity—which is one in the Trinity of the Father, the Son, and the Holy Spirit—rules out any notion of inequality. Its eternity has nothing temporal, its nature has nothing unlike itself. There is one will in it, the same substance, equal power—and not three gods but one God—because the unity is true and indivisible, wherein there can be no differentiation.

In the whole and perfect nature of true man, therefore, true God was born, complete in divine attributes, complete in human ones. In speaking about "human ones," we mean those which the Creator put into us from the beginning, the same ones that he took on to be restored. Whatever the deceiver introduced and humanity in being deceived allowed, these things do not have even a trace in the Savior. Simply because he submitted to a share in human infirmities, he did not on that account become party to our sins. He assumed the "form of a servant" without the stain of sin (raising the human, not lowering the divine). This emptying out, through which the Invisible One presented himself in a visible way, represents a gesture of mercy rather than a deficiency in power.

3. Consequently, to recall us to eternal beatitude from our original chains and from worldly errors, he himself came down to us, he to whom we could not of ourselves rise up. Certainly there was a love of truth in many. Yet, among a plurality of uncertain opinions, they were being led astray through the cleverness of lying demons. "By what is falsely called knowledge,"[70] human ignorance was being dragged into differing and contradictory ideas.

To stop the overweening devil from toying with our minds

---

70. Cf. 1 Tm 6.20.

and thereby having them serve him in captivity, teaching from the law was not sufficient. Nor could our nature be restored through prophetic exhortations alone. But the actual reality of Redemption had to be added to moral precepts. Our origin, corrupted right after its start, needed to be reborn with new beginnings. A victim had to be offered for reconciliation, a victim that was at one and the same time both related to our race and foreign to our defilement. In this way alone could the plan of God—wherein it pleased him that the sin of the world should be wiped away through the Birth and Passion of Jesus Christ—in this way alone could the plan of God be of any avail for the times of every generation. Nor would the mysteries—as they pass through various developments in time—disturb us. Instead, they would reassure us, since the faith by which we live would not have differed at any stage.[71]

4. Let them stop complaining, those who speak up against the divine arrangements with a disloyal murmuring and object to the lateness of our Lord's Nativity—as if that which was done in the last age of the world was not applied to previous eras as well. For the Incarnation of the Word accomplished by being about to take place the very same thing that it did by having taken place—as the mystery of human salvation never ceased to be active in any earlier age. What the apostles preached, the prophets had also announced. Nor was it too late in being fulfilled, since it has always been believed.

But the wisdom and "kindness of God"[72]—by this delay in his salvific work—has made us better disposed to accept his calling. That way, what had been foretold through so many ages by numerous signs, numerous words, and numerous mysteries would not be open to doubt in these days of the Gospel. That way, the Birth of the Savior—which was to exceed all wonders and the whole measure of human intelligence—would engender in us a faith all the more steadfast, the more often and the earlier it had been proclaimed beforehand.

No, indeed, it is not that God has just recently come up with

---

71. Cf. Rom 1.17, Gal 3.11, Heb 10.38, and Hb 2.4.
72. Cf. Ti 3.4.

a plan for attending to human affairs, nor that it has taken him this long to show compassion. Rather, he laid down from the very "foundation of the world"[73] one and the same "cause of salvation"[74] for all. For, the grace of God—by which the entire assembly of saints has always been justified—was not initiated at the time when Christ was born, but augmented. This "mystery of great compassion,"[75] with which the whole world has now been filled, was so powerful even in its prefigurations that those who believed it when promised attained to it no less than those who received it when actually given.

5. It is, therefore, with an unmistakable tenderness that so great a wealth of divine goodness has been poured out on us, dearly beloved. Not only has the usefulness of foregoing examples served for calling us to eternity, but the Truth himself has even "appeared"[76] in a visible body. We ought, then, to celebrate this day of the Lord's Birth with no listless and no worldly joy. Each one of us would do it worthily and with a proper understanding, if all remember whose body it is of which they constitute members and whose head it is to which they have been fitted—to prevent any incongruous appendage from being attached to the sacred "edifice."[77]

Consider, dearly beloved, and pay careful attention by the light of the Holy Spirit as to who it is who has taken us to himself and whom we have received in ourselves. As the Lord Jesus was made our flesh by being born, so we are made his body by being reborn. Consequently, "we are members of Christ and a temple of the Spirit"[78] of God. It is for this reason that the blessed Apostle says, "Glorify God and bear him in your body."[79]

He it is who suggests to us the image of his own "meekness and humility,"[80] who fills us with that very power whereby he redeemed us—as the Lord himself promises: "Come to me, all you who labor and are burdened, and I will refresh you. Take my yoke upon you and learn from me, for I am meek and hum-

73. Cf. Eph 1.4.
74. Cf. Heb 5.9.
75. Cf. 1 Tm 3.16.
76. Cf. Ti 2.11 and 3.4.
77. Cf. 1 Cor 3.9.
78. Cf. 1 Cor. 6.15 and 19.
79. 1 Cor 6.20.
80. Cf. Eph 4.2.

ble of heart, and you will find rest for your souls."[81] Let us therefore take up this yoke of the Truth—neither "heavy"[82] nor rough—and allow him to rule over us. Let us be like him in humility, since we want to be patterned after him in glory—with him aiding us and leading us to his promises. In his mercy, he has the power even to wipe away our sins and to perfect his gifts in us, Christ our Lord, who lives and reigns forever and ever. Amen.

Sermon 24

25 December 443

Certainly, dearly beloved, the goodness of God has always looked after the human race—in various "ways" and to "many" degrees.[83] God has imparted very many gifts of his providence to ages past. But, "in these last days,"[84] he has surpassed all the abundance of his usual generosity. At this time, mercy itself came down in Christ for sinners, "truth" itself for the straying, and "life" itself for the dead.[85] As a result, the Word (the one that is co-eternal with and equal to the Father) takes up our lowly nature into the unity of his divinity. God born of God becomes a human being born of a human being.

(2) This indeed had been promised "from the foundation of the world,"[86] and had been continually heralded with many signs of deeds and words. But how great a portion of humanity would those figures and shrouded mysteries save if Christ by his coming were not fulfilling those distant and hidden promises, if what at that time profited only a few believers (as something yet to be done) were not now (fully accomplished) bringing real advantages to innumerable faithful?

In these times, therefore, we are not led to faith through signs and images. Reassured by the Gospel account, we believe and we worship what has been accomplished. Added to this—for our enlightenment—are the helps of prophecy, so that we

81. Mt 11.28–29.
82. Cf. 1 Jn 5.3.
83. Cf. Heb 1.1.
84. Cf. 1 Pt 1.20.
85. Cf. Jn 14.6.
86. Cf. Eph 1.4 and Gn 3.15.

might in no way consider doubtful what we know to have been foretold in such predictions.

(3) This is why the Lord says to Abraham, "In your seed will all peoples be blessed."[87] This is why David sings the promise of God in a spirit of prophecy, saying: "The Lord swore to David (and will not deceive him): 'I shall set upon my throne someone from the fruit of your loins.' "[88] This is why the Lord says through Isaiah, "Behold, a virgin will conceive in her womb and will bear a son, and they will call his name Emmanuel, which means 'God with us.' "[89] And also through Isaiah, the Lord says: "There will come forth a branch from the root of Jesse, and from this root a flower will rise up."[90] Certainly, in this branch the Blessed Virgin Mary was foretold, who sprung from the stock of Jesse and David, made fruitful by the Holy Spirit, bringing forth a new flower of human flesh, from a mother's womb indeed, but through a virgin birth.

2. As a result, let the hearts of believers exult in praise of God. "Let the children of human beings acknowledge his wonders,"[91] since it is in this work of God especially that our lowliness realizes how great a value its Creator has placed upon it. Although he had given much to our human origin (in making us to his own image), the Lord put far more into our restoration (when he accommodated himself to the "form of a servant."[92]) Though whatever the Creator expends on the creature comes from one and the same concern, nevertheless it would be less amazing that a human being should advance to divine things than that God should descend to human ones.

Unless Almighty God were willing to do this, no superficial justice, no sketchy wisdom could rescue anyone from the devil's captivity and the abyss of eternal death. Condemnation, passing with the sin "from one onto all,"[93] would remain. Debilitated with a lethal wound, nature could find no remedy, since it would not be able to alter its condition by its own powers.

(2) For, the first man received the substance of his flesh from

---

87. Gn 22.18.
88. Ps 131(132).11.
89. Mt 1.23 and Is 7.14.
90. Is 11.1.
91. Ps 106(107).8.
92. Cf. Phil 2.7.
93. Cf. Rom 5.12 and 18.

the earth and was animated with a rational spirit by his Creator breathing into him. This way, living "according to the image and likeness"[94] of his Maker, he might preserve the form of God's goodness and justice with the brilliance of imitation, as if in the reflection of a mirror. Had he but cultivated with perseverance this magnificent dignity of his nature through the observance of the law that had been issued, his uncorrupted mind would have led that very quality of his earthly body to heavenly glory.

But he rashly and unhappily believed the invidious deceiver and, giving in to the advice of pride, he preferred to seize the increase of honor set aside for him rather than earn it. Yet it was not only he, but the sum of his posterity in him as well that heard: "Earth you are, and into earth shall you go."[95] Therefore, "as with this man from the earth, so we too, human beings from the earth."[96] No one is immortal, since no one is of heaven.

3. And so, to undo the chain of this sin and death, the almighty Son of God, filling all things, containing all things, equal in all things to the Father, and co-eternal in one essence (from him and with him), took on himself our human nature. He, Creator and Lord of all things, saw fit to become one of the mortals, from a mother whom he had both chosen for himself and made. She, without harm to her virginal integrity, was the provider of his bodily substance only, so that, with the contagion of human seed brought to an end, purity and truth inhered within the new man.

In Christ, born from the womb of a virgin, though his birth was miraculous, his nature is not on that account different from ours. He who is true God is also true man; there is nothing false in either substance. "The Word became flesh,"[97] by an elevation of the flesh, not by a falling away from divinity. His divinity conducted his power and goodness in such a way that he raised what was ours by taking it up and did not lose what was his own by sharing it. In this Birth of Christ, according to the

---

94. Cf. Gn 1.26.
96. 1 Cor 15.48.
95. Gn 3.19.
97. Jn 1.14.

prophecy of David, "truth has risen up from the earth and justice has looked down from heaven."⁹⁸

Also in this Birth of Christ, the words of Isaiah were fulfilled where he says: "Let the earth produce and blossom forth a Savior, and let justice spring up as well."⁹⁹ For, the earth of human flesh—which had been cursed in the first one to go astray—issued forth (but only in this Birth from the Holy Virgin) a blessed sprout, one foreign to the vice of its stock. We arrive at a spiritual beginning in rebirth. To every human being who is "reborn,"¹⁰⁰ the water of Baptism is an image of the Virgin's womb—as the same Holy Spirit fills the font who also filled the Virgin, so that the mystical washing cancels in our case the sin which the holy Conception lacked entirely in theirs.

4. Far removed from this mystery, dearly beloved, is that deranged error of the Manichaeans. Nor have those any share in the regeneration by Christ who deny that he was physically born of the Virgin Mary. Because they do not believe his true Nativity, they do not accept his true Passion. As they do not confess that he was truly buried, they refuse to acknowledge that he is truly risen.

Having entered upon this precipitous road of execrable doctrine—where there is nothing that is not dark, nothing that is not slippery—they come crashing down headlong from the cliff of falsehood into the abyss of death. They find nothing solid to lean on. Beyond all the other disgraceful activities of diabolical invention, during that most prominent festival which they observe (as has been recently made clear by their own admission), they rejoice in the defilement of their bodies no less than in that of their hearts. Since they do not preserve the integrity either of the faith or of decency, they are found to be both blasphemous in their doctrines and obscene in their rituals.

5. With other heresies, dearly beloved—though all of them deserve to be condemned in their contradiction among themselves—each heresy, taken in isolation, has something that

---

98. Ps 84(85).12.
100. Cf. Jn 3.3 and 5.
99. Is 45.8.

might be true with respect to some part of it. Arius brought himself to ruin with great impiety, declaring that the Son of God is less than the Father and is a creature, and thinking that the Holy Spirit was created by the Son along with all other things. But he did not deny the eternal and immutable divinity in the essence of the Father, the divinity which he did not see in the unity of the Trinity.

Macedonius, estranged from the light of truth, did not accept the divinity of the Holy Spirit, but acknowledged that there is one power and the same nature in the Father and the Son. Sabellius was confused with an inexplicable error. Realizing that the unity of substance in the Father and the Son and the Holy Spirit are inseparable, he attributed to singularity what he should have attributed to equality. Since he was not able to understand a real Trinity, he believed it to be one and the same person under a triple name.

Photinus, deceived in the blindness of his mind, confessed the man in Christ to be true and of our substance, but he did not believe the same to be God from God, begotten before all ages. Apollinaris, bereft of stability in faith, believed that the Son of God took on the true nature of human flesh in such a way as to say that the soul was not in that flesh because the divinity itself occupied its place.

If all the errors which the Catholic Faith condemns would be reviewed in this way, something is found in one or the other that can be separated from the what is to be condemned. In that most depraved teaching of the Manichaeans, however, there is absolutely nothing at all that can in any way be considered tolerable.

6. But, as for you, dearly beloved, I cannot find any words with which to address you more fittingly than those of the apostle Peter himself: "a chosen race, a royal priesthood, a holy nation, a people set apart,"[101] built on Christ the impregnable rock, grafted into our Lord and Savior himself through his true assumption of our flesh. "Remain steady then in that faith"[102]

101. 1 Pt 2.9.
102. Cf. Col 1.23.

which you have "confessed before many witnesses,"[103] in which, reborn "through water and the Holy Spirit,"[104] you have received the "anointing of salvation" and the "seal of eternal life."[105]

"If anyone" should proclaim "to you" anything else "besides what" you have learned, "let them be accursed."[106] Do not prefer godless fables to the manifest truth. Whatever you might happen to read or hear contrary to the rule of the Catholic and Apostolic Creed, consider it to be deadly and diabolical.

Let not their pretended fasts, contrived by their lying skills, lead you astray; these profit not unto the purification of souls but unto their perdition. Manichaeans put on the appearance indeed of devotion and chastity, but with this ruse they draw a veil over the shamefulness of their actions. From the depths of their profane hearts, they spew forth "darts"[107] by which simple souls are wounded, so that, as the prophet says, "they might shoot under cover the upright of heart."[108]

(2) There is great safety in a complete faith, in a true faith. In it nothing can be increased or diminished by anyone, because, unless it is one, it is not faith, as the apostle says: "One Lord, one faith, one baptism, one God and Father of all, who is above everyone and throughout all things and in us all."[109] Cling to this unity, dearly beloved, with unshaken minds. "Pursue" all "holiness" in it.[110] Serve devotedly in it the commandments of the Lord, since, "without faith, it is impossible to please God,"[111] and without it nothing is holy, nothing pure, nothing alive.

"For the just live by faith,"[112] and those who lose their faith through the devil's deception are "dead while they live."[113] As justification is gained through faith, so also eternal life is gained through true faith, as the Lord our Savior says: "This is life

---

103. Cf. 1 Tm 6.12.
104. Cf. Jn 3.5.
105. Cf. Gelasianum 450 and 452
106. Cf. Gal 1.9.
107. Cf. Ps 54(55).22.
108. Ps 10(11).3.
109. Eph 4.5–6.
110. Cf. Heb 12.14 and 1 Cor. 14.1.
111. Heb 11.6.
112. Cf. Heb 10.38, Rom 1.17, Gal 3.11, and Hb 2.4.
113. Cf. 1 Tm 5.6.

eternal, to know you, the only true God, and Jesus Christ, whom you have sent."[114] May he have you make progress and bring you to "persevere up until the end,"[115] he who lives and reigns for ever and ever. Amen.

Sermon 25

25 December 444

However ineffable the Nativity of Our Lord Jesus Christ might be, dearly beloved, in which he clothed himself with the flesh of our nature, I take heart, nevertheless, not presuming upon my own ability but trusting in his inspiration. I take heart that, on the day chosen for this mystery of human restoration, something might be drawn out of me which would be able to edify those listening. Even though the Church of God, for the greater part, understands what it believes, it is not on that account unnecessary to say even things that have already been said. We owe the service of our mouth to many who have just come to the faith. It would be preferable to burden the instructed with things already known than to defraud the ignorant of what needs to be learned.

(2) God's Son, who has a single essence in common with the Father and the Holy Spirit, not a single person, willed to become a partaker of our lowliness, to become one of those capable of suffering, one of those capable of dying. So sacred and so marvelous is this that the rationale for God's plan could not be accessible to the wise ones of this world unless true light would have dispelled the darkness of human ignorance.

Not only on works of virtue, not only on observance of the commandments lies that "narrow and difficult way leading to life,"[116] but—along with these—on the path of faith. It involves great labor and great peril to walk, without stumbling, down the one path of sound doctrine among the dubious opinions of the unlearned and falsehoods which have the appearance

---

114. Cf. Jn 17.3.
115. Cf. Mt 10.22 and 24.13. Cf. 1 Cor 1.8.
116. Mt 7.14.

of truth. It involves great labor and great peril to avoid every risk of deception, when from all around snares of error set themselves in the way.

"Who would be fit for this,"[117] unless it be one who receives instruction and guidance from the Spirit of God? "We," as the Apostle says, "have not received the spirit of this world, but the Spirit who is from God, so that we might know what things have been given to us by God."[118] "Blessed is the one," David also sings, "whom you have instructed, o Lord, the one whom you have taught about your law."[119]

2. Since we, dearly beloved, have the safeguard of truth amid dangers of error, since we have been instructed, not "in the words of human wisdom,"[120] but in the teaching of the Holy Spirit, we believe what we have learned, and we proclaim what we believe: that the Son of God, begotten by the Father before the ages and co-eternal with the Father in an eternal and consubstantial equality, has come into this world through the womb of the Virgin who had been chosen for this "mystery of compassion."[121] In her and from her, "Wisdom has built itself a house,"[122] and the immutable divinity of the Word has fitted to himself the "form of a servant, unto the likeness of sinful flesh."[123]

Yet his glory, the one which he shares with the Father and the Holy Spirit, in no way decreases, for his nature cannot admit of diminution or change with respect to the supreme and eternal essence. On account of our infirmity, however, he made himself smaller for [human beings] (who did not have the capacity to receive him) and covered the splendor of his majesty (which human sight could not bear) with the veil of his body. Thus is he said "to have emptied himself."[124] He voided himself, so to speak, of his own power. In this lowliness through which he attended to our needs, he became inferior not only to the Father but even to himself.

Nothing was lacking to him in this condescension, to him

---

117. Cf. 2 Cor 2.16.
118. 1 Cor 2.12.
119. Ps 93(94).12.
120. Cf. 1 Cor 2.4.
121. Cf. 1 Tm 3.16.
122. Prv 9.1.
123. Cf. Rom 8.3.
124. Cf. Phil 2.7.

who has an "essence"[125] in common with the Father and the Holy Spirit. We understand it to be an aspect of omnipotence that he who becomes less with respect to our characteristics does not become less with respect to his own. Light became concerned with the blind, strength with the weak, mercy with the miserable. Consequently, it has come about through his great power that the Son of God took up human substance along with its need—to rebuild the nature which he created and to abolish the "death which he did not make."[126]

3. Once they have repudiated and cast far away every last notion held by the godless (for whom Christ is either "foolishness" or "scandal"[127]), let the faith of orthodox minds exult. Let it recognize the true and only Son of God, not just according to the divinity in which he was begotten by the Father, but also according to the humanity in which he was born of his Virgin Mother. There is only one [Person] in our lowliness and in divine majesty, true man and true God, eternal in his own state, temporal in ours, one with the Father in a substance which has never been less than the Father, one with his Mother in the body which he created.

In taking on our nature, he became for us a step whereby we might rise up to him through him. That essence—which exists everywhere (all the time and in its entirety)—did not require a descent with respect to place. It was every bit as compatible with this essence to be grafted whole into a human being as it was for it not to be separated even in part from the Father. As a result, it continues to be what "in the beginning was the Word,"[128] and it could not in any way have the property of ceasing to be what it once was.

(2) For the Son is eternally the Son, and the Father eternally the Father. So when the Son himself says, "Who sees me, sees

---

125. I have translated Leo's expression *hoc quod est esse* as "essence". He may have employed this circumlocution ("to be that which he is") to bring across the fact that God does not, properly speaking, have an essence, but only a pure existence. Thus, I have enclosed the word "essence" in quotation marks to suggest an improper usage.
126. Wis 1.13.   127. Cf. 1 Cor 1.23.
128. Jn 1.1.

the Father also,"[129] your godlessness, o heretic, has very much blinded you. Not seeing the majesty of the Son, you do not see the glory of the Father either. By saying that he was begotten who [at one point] did not exist, you assert that the Son is temporal, and, as long as you assert that the Son is temporal, you believe the Father to be changeable. For, the term "changeable" applies not only to that which has diminished but also to whatever has increased.

If, therefore, the Begotten is unequal to the Father (since begetting, as you define the term, brought forth someone who had not been), then the essence of the Begetter was also imperfect, in so far as it made progress (through begetting) in the acquisition of something which it did not have before. Yet the Catholic Faith curses and condemns this godless perversity of yours. It recognizes nothing temporal in the true divinity, but acknowledges both the Father and the Son to have the same eternity.

For the beam that emanates from light does not come after the light. True light never lacks a beam, having it as part of its substance to shine, just as it always has it as part of its substance to exist. But the manifestation of this beam has been called a "sending"—by which Christ appeared to the world. Although he filled all things with his invisible majesty, he came, nevertheless, to those who had not known him, as if from a very remote and deep seclusion. At that time, he took away the blindness of ignorance, as it has been written: "For those sitting in darkness and in the shadow of death, a light has risen."[130]

4. Of course the light of truth has been sent out in prior ages to enlighten the holy fathers and prophets, as when David said, "Send out your light and your truth."[131] Of course the divinity of the Son has made clear the works of his presence "in various ways and by many signs."[132] Yet all these prefigurations and all these miracles bore testimony about that "sending" of which the Apostle speaks: "When the fullness of time came, God sent his Son, made from a woman, made under the Law."[133]

129. Jn 14.9.
131. Ps 42(43).3.
133. Gal 4.4.
130. Is 9.2 and Mt 4.16.
132. Cf. Heb 1.1.

What could this be except that the Word becomes flesh, that the Creator of the world is born through the womb of a virgin, that the Lord of majesty adapts himself to essential human nature?[134] Although the contagiousness of earthly seed has not infected this spiritual Conception, what could this be except that the Lord—in order to take on, nevertheless, the essence of true flesh—assumes only the nature itself from his mother.

(2) With respect to this mission (wherein God has been united to man), the Son is unequal to the Father, not in that which comes from the Father, but in that which has been made from a human being. His humanity has not destroyed the equality which remains inviolable in the divinity, and the descent of the Creator to the creature is really the elevation of believers to eternal life. "Because in the wisdom of God," as the Apostle says, "the world did not know God through its own wisdom, it pleased God to make believers saved through the foolishness of preaching."[135]

To the world, that is, to the clever ones of this world, their wisdom has become blindness. Nor could they know God by it, for no one can come to knowledge of him except in his wisdom. Because the world was taking pride in the emptiness of its doctrines, the Lord grounded the faith of those who are to be saved in this, that—although it might seem both unworthy and foolish[136]—with all presumptions of opinion falling away, the grace of God alone might reveal what human intelligence would not be capable of understanding.

5. Let the Catholic Faith, therefore, recognize its own glory in the Lord's humility. Let the Church (which is the body of Christ) rejoice in the mysteries of its salvation, because unless "the Word" of God "had become flesh and lived among us,"[137] unless the Creator himself had descended to a communion with the creature and by his Birth recalled human oldness to a

---

134. Leo literally says "adapts himself to human origins." This expression clearly refers to the argument he has often made, to the effect that Christ took on unfallen human nature, i.e., the essence of that nature without the defect or stain of concupiscence.
135. 1 Cor 1.21.   136. Cf. 1 Cor 1.23.
137. Jn 1.14.

new beginning, "death would reign from Adam up to"[138] the end. Over all human beings would remain an unremediable condemnation, since, from nothing more than the condition of being born, all would have a single cause for perishing.

Consequently, the Lord Jesus—alone among the sons of human beings to have been born innocent, since he alone had been conceived without the defilement brought by concupiscence of the flesh—was made a man of our race, so that we might be able to become "partakers of the divine nature."[139] He placed in the font of Baptism that very origin which he had assumed in the Virgin's womb. He gave to the water what he had given to his Mother. For, the same "power of the Most High" and "overshadowing" of the Holy Spirit[140] that caused Mary to bear the Savior makes the water regenerate the believer.

What was more suitable for healing the sick, for opening the eyes of the blind, for raising the dead, than that the wounds of pride should be attended to with the remedies of humility? Adam, disregarding the instructions of God, brought in the "domination"[141] of sin; Jesus, "made under the Law,"[142] restored the liberty of justice. Adam, listening to the devil all the way to his going astray, merited that "all should die in him;"[143] Jesus, obeying his Father "all the way to the cross,"[144] brought it about that "all should be brought to life in him."[145] Adam, coveting the honor of angels, lost the dignity of his own nature; Jesus, taking on the condition of our infirmity, placed among the inhabitants of heaven those for whom he descended into hell. Finally, to Adam (fallen on account of his self-exaltation) was said: "Earth you are, and into earth shall you go;"[146] but to Jesus (exalted on account of his humility) was said: "Sit at my right hand until I put your enemies down as a footstool for your feet."[147]

6. These works of our Lord, dearly beloved, are useful to us,

---

138. Cf. Rom 5.14.
139. Cf. 2 Pt 1.4.
140. Lk 1.35.
141. Cf. Rom 6.14.
142. Cf. Gal 4.4.
143. Cf. 1 Cor 15.22.
144. Cf. Phil 2.8.
145. Cf. 1 Cor 15.22.
146. Cf. Gn 3.19.
147. Ps 109(110).1.

not only for their communication of grace, but as an example for our imitation also—if only these remedies would be turned into instruction, and what has been bestowed by the mysteries would benefit the way people live. Let us remember that we must live in the "humility and meekness"[148] of our Redeemer, since—as the Apostle says—"if we suffer with him, we shall also reign with him."[149] In vain are we called Christians if we do not "imitate Christ."[150] For this reason did he refer to himself as "the Way,"[151] that the teacher's manner of life might be the exemplar for his disciples, and that the servant might choose the humility which had been practiced by the Master, who lives and reigns forever and ever. Amen.

Sermon 26

25 December 450

When the faithful meditate about divine things, dearly beloved, the Birth of our Lord and Savior from his Mother comes to mind every day and all the time. For, a mind that is poised to acknowledge its Maker—whether occupied in the sighs of entreaty, or the exultation of praise, or the offering of sacrifice—such a mind touches upon nothing more frequently in its spiritual insights, touches upon nothing more confidently, than the fact that God the Son of God, begotten by his co-eternal Father, was also born through a human birth.

But no day suggests to us more than today that this Nativity should be worshipped in heaven and on earth. With a new light radiating even in the atoms themselves,[152] no day more than today impresses the entire splendor of this amazing mystery upon our senses. We recall not only to mind, but even—in a way—to sight, the conversation of Gabriel with the astonished Mary, the Conception by the Holy Spirit (as marvelous in being promised as it was in being actually granted), the Maker of the

---

148. Cf. Eph 4.2.   149. Cf. Rom 8.17 and 2 Tm 2.12.
150. Cf. 1 Cor 11.1.   151. Jn 14.6.
152. Leo used the term *elementa*, meaning the first principles or most elementary building blocks (here, of matter—as becomes obvious from what follows). I have rendered this with the equivalent modern notion of "atoms."

world brought forth from a virginal womb, and the one who established all natures made the Son of her whom he had created.

On this day, the Word of God appeared clothed in flesh, and, what could not even have been seen by human eyes before, "could" now "be touched with the hands."[153] On this day, the shepherds learned from angelic voices that a Savior had been born in the substance of our body and soul.[154] On this day, a new archetype for proclaiming the Gospel was deposited with those who preside over the Lord's flock, so that we too might say with the celestial host: "Glory to God in the highest, and on earth peace to people of good will."[155]

2. That infancy, which the majesty of God's Son did not scorn, was eventually brought to perfect manhood with the increase of age. When the triumph of his Passion and Resurrection had been brought to completion, all the activities of the lowliness he had undertaken for our sake passed away. Today's feast, nevertheless, renews for us the sacred beginnings of Jesus' Birth from the Virgin Mary. As we worship the Birth of our Savior, we find ourselves celebrating our own origin as well. For the Conception of Christ is the origin of the Christian people, and the birthday of the Head is the birthday of the body.

All of the elect have their own special place, and the Church's children are set off from one another by the passage of time. Yet all of us, the whole sum of believers who have sprung from the baptismal font, just as we have been crucified with Christ in his Passion, been raised with him in his Resurrection, and been set at the right hand of the Father in his Ascension, so too have we been born along with him in his Nativity.

Whenever believers in any part of the world undergo regeneration in Christ, they become transformed into "new human beings"[156] through a rebirth—once the path of their original "former selves" has been cut off. They are no longer considered to be in the lineage of their carnal father, but are counted

153. Cf. 1 Jn 1.1.
155. Lk 2.14.
154. Lk 2.11.
156. Cf. Col 3.10.

among the descendants of their Savior. It was precisely so that we might be able to become children of God that he was made the child of a human being. Had he not come down to us in this humility, none could come to him by any merits of their own.

(2) May earthly wisdom not bring murkiness here into hearts of the elect. May this dust, possessed of earthly thoughts and destined to go back soon into the depths, not raise itself up against the sublimity of God's grace. Now, "at the end of ages,"[157] what had been arranged "before time began"[158] has been accomplished. Now that the symbolism of figures has given way to the actual presence of reality, the law and prophecy have been turned into truth.

Abraham has indeed become "the father of all nations,"[159] and "the promised blessing" has been given to the world "in his seed."[160] No, it is not only those whom flesh and blood has begotten that are Israelites. Rather, the whole adopted group have entered into that inheritance prepared for the children of faith. Let the deceitful insolence of foolish questions not cause an uproar. Let human reasoning not dilute the effects of God's work. We "with Abraham put our faith in God, nor do we hesitate in reservation."[161] "Instead, we know full well that God has the power to bring about what he has promised."[162]

3. Our Savior, dearly beloved, was born not from the seed of flesh, but from the Holy Spirit. As a result, the condemnation of that first transgression did not have a hold on him. Hence, the very magnitude of the gift that was bestowed demands of us a reverence worthy of its splendor. As the blessed Apostle teaches, therefore, "we have not received the spirit of this world, but the Spirit who is from God, so that we might know what things have been given to us by God."[163] He cannot be duly worshipped except by offering back to him what he himself has given.

What can we find in the treasure of the Lord's generosity so

---

157. Cf. 1 Cor 10.11.
158. Cf. Ti 1.2.
159. Cf. Gn 17.4.
160. Cf. Gn 22.18.
161. Cf. Rom 4.3.
162. Rom 4.20–21.
163. 1 Cor 2.12.

appropriate to the honor of this celebration as peace? Peace was the first thing proclaimed by the angelic choir at the Lord's Nativity. It is peace which gives birth to "children of God."[164] Peace nurses love, engenders "unity,"[165] gives "repose" to the blessed,[166] and provides a home to eternity. It has for its own particular work and special benefit the joining to God of those whom it separates from the world. Wherefore, the Apostle urges us to this good when he says, "Justified then by faith, we are at peace with God."[167] In this brief sentence is contained the force of almost all the commandments. Where the truth of peace has been, no virtue can be lacking.

Indeed, what is it, dearly beloved, to be at peace with God except to will what he bids and to refuse what he forbids? If like minds and similar wills seek one another out in human friendships, and differences in lifestyle can never attain to a stable concord, how will someone have a share in peace with God if that someone takes pleasure in things that displease God and purposely takes delight in things by which he knows God to be offended?

Children of God do not take that kind of attitude. No, adopted nobility does not admit of such wisdom. Let the "chosen and royal race"[168] respond to the dignity of its regeneration, let it love what its Father loves, and let it not rebel from its Creator in anything—so that the Lord might not say once again: "I have given birth to children and raised them, but they have repudiated me. Oxen recognize their owner, while an ass knows its master's stall; but Israel does not realize who I am, and my people have not understood me."[169]

4. This favor involves a great mystery, dearly beloved, and this gift surpasses all gifts—that God should call a human being his child and that human beings should refer to God as their Father. From these titles, we perceive and we learn who it is that can rise up to so great a height of affection. If, in human offspring and earthly lineage, the vices of an evil life draw a

164. Cf. Mt 5.9.
166. Cf. Ps 4.9.
168. Cf. 1 Pt 2.9.
165. Cf. Eph 4.3.
167. Rom 5.1.
169. Is 1.2–3.

cloud over the children of illustrious parents, if unworthy descendants are put to shame by the very reputation of their ancestors, how badly will they finish up who for love of this world are not afraid to be disowned from the lineage of Christ. But, if it wins praise among men for the honor of fathers to be reflected in their progeny, how much more glorious is it for those born of God to mirror brightly the image of their Creator and to show in themselves the one who created them? As the Lord said, "So must your light shine before human beings, that upon seeing your good works they may extol your Father who is in heaven."[170]

(2) We know too well that, as the Apostle John says, "the whole world rests under the sway of the evil one."[171] Laying down traps, the devil and his angels strive through innumerable temptations either to scare off human beings (with obstacles) from their struggle toward the things above or to corrupt them (with success). But "greater is the one with us than the one" against us.[172] No battles can overpower us, no conflicts harm us if "we are at peace with God"[173] and continually say to the Father with all our heart, "Thy will be done."[174] When we accuse ourselves by our own confession and deny a consent of the heart to carnal appetites, we of course rile up against us the enmity of the one who gave rise to sin, but we build up an invincible peace with God. In rendering service to the grace of God, we are not only made subject to our King through obedience, but are even joined to him through the will. If we are of one mind with him (willing what he wills, disapproving of what he disapproves), he himself will bring us victory in all our battles. He who has given the "will"[175] will bestow also the ability. In this way can we "cooperate"[176] with his works, speaking that prophetic utterance in the exultation of faith: "The Lord is my light and my salvation. Whom shall I fear? The Lord is the defender of my life. Of whom shall I be afraid?"[177]

5. Let those then "who were born not from blood, nor from

---

170. Mt 5.16.
171. 1 Jn 5.19.
172. Cf. 1 Jn 4.4.
173. Cf Rom 5.1.
174. Mt 6.10.
175. Cf. Phil 2.13.
176. Cf. 1 Cor 3.9.
177. Ps 26(27).1.

SERMON 26

the will of flesh, but from God"[178] offer concord to God as peace-loving children. Let all the adopted members join together into that "firstborn" of new "creation"[179] who came "not to do his own will, but that of the one who sent him."[180] For the Father's grace has not adopted as heirs those who disagree or differ, but, rather, those who "think the same thing"[181] and love the same thing. Those who have been "re-fashioned" according to one and the same image ought all to have the same kind of heart.

(2) The birthday of the Lord is the birthday of peace, for, as the Apostle says, "He is our peace who made both things one."[182] Whether Jew or Gentile, "we have access to the Father through him, in a single Spirit."[183] On the day before his Passion (a day chosen beforehand according to a voluntary arrangement), it was this doctrine especially in which he instructed his disciples, so as to say: "My peace I give you, my peace I leave you."[184] So that the particular characteristics of his peace would not lie hidden beneath a generic word, he added [the following qualification]: "Not as the world gives do I give to you."[185] He was saying that the world has its own kinds of friendship, joining many hearts together with a distorted love. There are even some who are like-minded in vices, and the similarity of their desire engenders an equivalence in their affection. If perhaps some should be found who take no pleasure in perverse and dishonorable things, who exclude unlawful concords from the bond of their mutual affection, they do so—if they be Jews or heretics or infidels—not out of a friendship with God, but from the peace of this world.

When it comes to those who belong to the Spirit and who have kept the universal faith, peace comes down from above and leads right back up. It does not wish to mingle in communion with lovers of this world, but, rather, to resist all obstacles and to fly away from destructive pleasures to true joys—as the

---

178. Jn 1.13.
179. Cf. Col 1.15, Rom 8.29, Gal 6.15, and 2 Cor 5.17.
180. Jn 6.38.   181. Cf. Phil 2.2.
182. Eph 2.14.   183. Eph 2.18.
184. Jn 14.27.   185. Jn 14.27.

Lord says, "Where your treasure has been, there also will be your heart,"[186] that is to say, if the things which you have affection for are down below, you will go down to the depths; if the things which you love "are up above,"[187] you will go up to the heights.[188] May the Spirit of peace guide us and lead us there, with us willing the same thing and "thinking the same thing,"[189] with our hearts joined in faith, hope, and love. For, "whoever are guided by the Spirit of God, they are children of God,"[190] who lives and reigns with the Son and with the Holy Spirit for ever and ever. Amen.

Sermon 27

25 December 451

Only they have genuine reverence for today's feast, dearly beloved, only they worship devoutly who do not have any false ideas about the Lord's Incarnation, who do not have any that are unbecoming to his divinity. For it would be equally dangerous to deny either the reality of our nature in him or his equality with the Father in glory. When we attempt to understand the mystery of Christ's Birth, how he sprang from a virgin mother, let all the mist of earthly reasoning be driven far off, let the smoke of worldly wisdom be cleared away from the "eyes of enlightened"[191] faith. For the authority in which we believe comes from God; the teaching that we follow comes from God.

(2) Whether we lend our inner ear to that testimony given by the law, or to the pronouncements made by prophets, or to the Gospel's trumpet, how true it is what blessed John thundered forth while filled with the Holy Spirit: "In the beginning was the Word, and the Word was with God, and the Word was God. He was with God in the beginning. All things were made

---

186. Mt 6.21.   187. Cf. Col 3.1 and 2.
188. Leo uses two different words for "love" in this sentence: 1) *amare* for lower things, a lesser kind of love (I have rendered it "to have affection for")—probably corresponding to the Greek *philia*; and 2) *diligere* for higher things, a more sublime kind of love (I have rendered it with the English "to love")—probably corresponding to the Greek *agapē*.
189. Cf. Phil 2.2.   190. Rom 8.14.
191. Cf. Eph 1.18.

through him, and without him was made nothing."[192] Likewise true is that which the very same preacher added later on: "The Word became flesh and dwelt among us, and we have seen his glory, the glory as of an Only-Begotten Son coming from the Father."[193]

(3) In each nature it is the same Son of God who both assumes our characteristics and does not lose his own, who both renews human nature in human beings and remains unchangeable in himself. For, the divinity which he shares with the Father did not suffer any damage to its omnipotence, nor did the "form of a servant" harm the "form of God."[194] That supreme and eternal essence which condescended to save the human race has drawn us into its own glory, without ceasing to be what it was. When, therefore, the Only-Begotten Son of God professes himself to be less than the Father—with whom he also claims to be an equal—he demonstrates the reality of each form in himself.[195] Inequality points to the human form, while equality brings to light the divine one.

2. Corporeal birth did not take anything away from the majesty of God's Son, nor add anything to it, for the unchangeable substance can neither be diminished nor increased. "The Word became flesh"[196] does not mean that the nature of God was changed into flesh, but that flesh was taken up by the Word into the unity of his Person. Within the identity of this Person, complete human nature has been received, a nature with which the Son of God was inseparably united inside the womb of the Virgin, a womb made fruitful by the Holy Spirit and never to lack virginity. He was inseparably united with this human nature in such a way that the one who had been begotten from the Father's essence (before time) was born from the Virgin's womb (in time). We could not be released from the chains of eternal death had he not become lowly in our condition while remaining at the same time omnipotent in his own.

(2) In being born as a true man while never ceasing to be true

---

192. Jn 1.1–3.
194. Cf. Phil 2.6–7.
196. Jn 1.14.

193. Jn 1.14.
195. Cf. Jn 14.28 and 10.30.

God, our Lord Jesus Christ made in himself the beginning of a "new creature."[197] In the manner of his coming forth, he gave to the human race a spiritual beginning. In order to wipe out the contagiousness of carnal generation, those to be regenerated would have an origin without the seed of crime. About these has it been said: "Who were born not from blood, nor from the will of a human being, nor from the will of flesh, but from God."[198]

What mind can understand this mystery, what tongue has the capability of explaining this grace? Iniquity turns back into innocence, oldness into newness. Strangers come into adoption, and foreigners enter upon an inheritance. Godless people have started to be just, the covetous to be beneficent, the incontinent to be chaste, the "earthly" to be "heavenly."[199] What has effected "this change" but the "right hand of the Most High"?[200] For "the Son of God came to undo the devil's works."[201] He grafted himself into us and us into himself in such a way that God's descent to human affairs became the elevation of human beings to those divine.

3. We cannot fathom, dearly beloved, how great a mercy God has toward us. Yet Christians must take great care not to be ensnared again by the devil's traps and not to "become entangled once more in the very errors"[202] which they have renounced. For the ancient enemy, "transforming himself into an angel of light,"[203] does not stop laying down everywhere the snares of deception, does not stop trying to do whatever it takes to corrupt the faith of believers. He knows to which one he should apply the flames of desire, to which one he should suggest the enticements of gluttony, to which one he should offer the allurements of sensuality, into which one he should pour the slime of envy. He knows which one to disturb with sadness, which one to deceive with joy, which one to oppress with fear, which one to seduce with flattery. He dissects the character of each one, exposes their cares, and pries into their inclinations.

---

197. Cf. 2 Cor 5.17.
199. Cf. 2 Cor 15.49.
201. Cf. 1 Jn 3.8.
203. Cf. 2 Cor 11.14.

198. Jn 1.13.
200. Ps 76(77).11.
202. Cf. 2 Pt 2.20.

Whenever he has observed an individual to be excessively taken with something, it is there that he looks for ways to do harm.

Of those whom he has bound more tightly, there are many well suited to his wiles. He makes use of both their abilities and their words to deceive others. Through them are promised remedies for illnesses, indications of future events, the appeasement of demons, and the dispelling of shades. To these are joined those who falsely claim that the entire condition of human life depends upon the effects of stars, and those who say that the things which pertain either to God's will or to ours are under the power of inexorable fates. To compound the harm that is done, they assert that these fates can be changed—if only supplication be made to those stars which are unfavorable. Whereupon this godless contrivance falls apart through internal contradiction. If the aforementioned fates do change, then they need not be feared. If they do not, then the stars should not be venerated.

4. From such customs as this has the following godlessness been engendered, where the sun—as it rises at daybreak—would be worshipped from the higher elevations by certain sillier people. Even some Christians think that they behave devoutly when, before arriving at the basilica of the blessed Apostle Peter (which has been dedicated to the one living and true God), they climb the steps which go up to the platform on the upper level, turn themselves around towards the rising sun, and bow down to honor its shining disk.

This thing, done partly through the fault of ignorance and partly in a spirit of paganism, eats away at me and grieves me very much. Even if some of these perhaps revere the Creator of this beautiful light rather than the light itself, still we must refrain from even the appearance of this homage. When someone who has left behind the worship of the gods finds this among us, will they not bring this aspect of their former persuasion along with them, thinking it credible—upon having seen it to be something that both Christians and unbelievers hold in common?

5. Let this damnable perversion be cast aside from the usage

of the faithful. Let the honor due to God alone not be mingled with the ceremonies of those who render service to creatures. Holy Scripture says: "You shall do homage to the Lord your God, and him alone shall you serve."[204] Blessed Job—"a man without complaint," as the Lord says, "refraining from every evil"[205]—asked "have I ever looked upon the sun as it shined, or the moon as it waxed bright, and rejoiced secretly in my heart as I kissed my hand? This is the greatest iniquity and a denial against the Most High God."[206]

What is the sun and what is the moon except the sources of visible creatures and of physical light? One has a greater shine, the other a lesser light. Just as there is day time and night time, so the Creator has given the luminaries a different quality—although, even before these were made, days went ahead without the function of the sun and nights without the service of the moon.

(2) These lights were set up for the use of the human beings that were going to be made. That way, this rational animal would not lack the means to distinguish months, to count years, and to divide up seasons. It is through the varying durations of different measures of time and through the clear signs of distinct revolutions that the sun measures years and the moon cycles through months. On the fourth day, as we read, God said: "Let there be luminaries in the vault of heaven. Let them shine upon the earth and divide day from night. Let them mark the seasons, the days, and the years. Let them be in the vault of heaven, that they may shine upon the earth."[207]

6. Wake up then, o friend, and acknowledge the dignity of your nature. Recall that you have been made "according to the image of God."[208] This nature, although it had been corrupted in Adam, has nevertheless been re-fashioned in Christ. Use visible creatures in whatever way they should be used—just as you use the earth, the sea, the sky, the air, the springs, and the rivers. Whatever in them is beautiful and wonderful, refer it to

---

204. Mt 4.10.
206. Jb 31.25–28.
208. Cf. Gn 1.26.

205. Jb 1.8.
207. Gn 1.14–15.

the praise and glory of their Maker. Do not have devotion toward that light in which birds and serpents, wild beasts and domesticated animals, flies and worms take pleasure.

Touch the physical light with your physical senses, but embrace with the whole inclination of your mind that true light "which enlightens everyone coming into this world,"[209] that light about which the Prophet says: "Approach him and be made bright. Your faces will not blush."[210] If we are "the temple of God and the Spirit of God dwells in us,"[211] what each believer has in their heart exceeds the marvels of heaven.

(2) Yet we do not thereby suggest, dearly beloved, we do not urge, that you despise the works of God or think anything contrary to your faith about those things the good God has made "good."[212] Only use every kind of created thing and the "whole array"[213] of this world with reason and moderation. "Visible things," as the Apostle says, "last only for a time, but invisible things are eternal."[214]

Wherefore, since we have been born for the present but reborn for the future, let us not be given over to temporal goods but inclined toward the eternal. That we might be able to look toward our hope from up close, let us think about what divine grace—in this very mystery of Christ's Birth—has conferred upon our nature. Let us hear the Apostle when he says: "You have died, and your life is hidden with Christ in God. When Christ your life appears, then you also will appear in glory with him,"[215] who lives and reigns with the Father and the Holy Spirit for ever and ever. Amen.

Sermon 28

25 December 452

Though all the divine pronouncements encourage us to rejoice always in the Lord, dearly beloved, today we are doubtless roused to spiritual gladness in a much greater degree, as this

---

209. Jn 1.9.
210. Ps 33(34).6.
211. Cf. 1 Cor 3.16.
212. Cf. Gn 1.18.
213. Cf. Gn 2.1.
214. 2 Cor 4.18.
215. Col 3.3–4.

mystery of the Lord's Birth shines before us more brightly. Turning our attention to that ineffable condescension by which the Creator of human beings deigned to become himself a human being, may we be found in the nature of the one whom we adore in our own.

God the Son of God—only begotten of the eternal and unbegotten Father, remaining eternally in the "form of God,"[216] having unchangeably and beyond time no other being than that which the Father has—received the "form of a servant."[217] This happened without any damage to his majesty, so that he might lift us up to his state rather than that he should decline into ours.

As a result, so strong a bond of unity has been made between the two natures that, though each retains its own proper characteristics, whatever belongs to God cannot be separated from the man, while whatever belongs to the man cannot be disjoined from the divinity.

2. As we celebrate the birthday of our Lord and Savior, dearly beloved, let us consider in detail the child-bearing of the Blessed Virgin, so we might believe that at no moment in time was the power of the Word lacking to the body and soul once conceived. No, it was not that the "temple of Christ's body"[218] had been fashioned and animated beforehand, and only then did he claim it for his own, coming down into it in the manner of an inhabitant. Instead, the new man took its beginning through him and in him.

In the one Son of God and of a human being, the divinity had no mother, the humanity no father. Virginity, made fertile through the Holy Spirit, brought forth without any trace of corruption, at one and the same time, both a descendant of its own race and the Maker of its stock. Wherefore, this same Lord—as the Evangelist tells us—asked the Jews whose son the Christ would be, in so far as they had learned this from the authority of the Scriptures. When they replied that it had been revealed that he would come from the seed of David, he asks:

216. Cf. Phil 2.6.   217. Cf. Phil 2.7.
218. Cf. Jn 2.21.

"How then does David call him his Lord when he says in the Spirit, 'The Lord said to my Lord: "Sit at my right hand until I put your enemies down as a footstool for your feet." '?"[219] No, the Jews could not answer the question that had been put to them, for they did not understand that in the one Christ both an offspring of David and a divine nature had been foretold.

3. But the majesty of the Son (equal to that of the Father), clothing itself in the humility of a servant, had no fear of being diminished, nor was there any room for it to be increased. Through the power of the divinity, this majesty alone was able to accomplish the effect of its mercy (which it was expending on the restoration of humanity), namely, to rescue from servitude under a cruel oppressor that creature which had been made "according to the image of God."[220]

Yet, since the devil had not dealt with the first human beings so violently as to bring them over to his side without the consent of free will, that voluntary sin, along with the enemy's plan, needed to be destroyed in such a way that the standards of justice would not be violated by the gift of grace. In the general downfall of the entire human race, there was only one remedy in the secrets of the divine plan that could help those who had been laid low, namely, if a son of Adam, with no part in and innocent of the original betrayal, would be born to profit others with both his example and his merits.

Natural generation did not allow this, however, and a branch could not come from a diseased root through seed. Scripture says about this: "Who can make clean what has been conceived from an unclean seed? Is it not you, who alone are?"[221] As a result, David's Lord was made the son of David. From the "fruit" of the promised "stock,"[222] a shoot without defect sprang up, the two natures coming together into one Person. In one and the same Conception, one and the same Birth, our Lord Jesus Christ was brought forth. In him were both true divinity (for working miracles) and true humanity (for enduring sufferings).

219. Mt 22.43–44.
221. Jb 14.4.
220. Cf. Gn 1.27.
222. Cf. Is 4.2 and Jer 23.5.

4. As a result, dearly beloved, the Catholic Faith scorns the errors of barking heretics. Deceived by the emptiness of worldly wisdom, these have withdrawn from the Gospel of truth. Not capable of understanding the Incarnation of the Word, they have turned a source of enlightenment into an occasion of blindness for themselves. In tracing the opinions of almost all those who believe falsehoods—even those which lead to a denial of the Holy Spirit—we realize that practically no one has gone astray who did not disbelieve the reality of two natures in Christ while at the same time acknowledging a single Person.

Some have ascribed to the Lord only his humanity, others only his divinity. Some have said that his divinity was real enough, but that his flesh was only an appearance. Others have declared that he took on real flesh but did not have the nature of God the Father. These, attributing to his divinity what belongs properly to the human substance, have fabricated for themselves a greater and a lesser god, though there can be no degrees in the true divinity, for whatever is less than God is not God.

Some realized that Father and Son are not separable on a natural level. Yet, because they could not understand the unity of divine nature without a unity of Person, they insisted that the Father and Son are one and the same. As a logical consequence, to be born and to be nourished, to suffer and to die, to be buried and to rise again, all this would be predicated of the same one who, through everything, occupies both the person of a human being and the person of the Word.

There are those who thought that the Lord Jesus Christ did not have a body made of our substance but one taken from higher and finer elements. Others felt that there was no human soul in the body of Christ, but that the very divinity of the Word took the place of his soul. Their nonsense has even gone so far as to say that, though there was a soul in the Lord, it lacked a mind, because the divinity sufficed for the man to carry out all the functions of reason. Finally, these same people have presumed to assert that some part of the Word was turned into flesh. Thus, in the many-faceted variations of a single doctrine, not only the nature of flesh and of the soul, but even the very essence of the Word has been wiped out.

5. There are many other prodigious falsehoods. I ought not burden your kind attention by listing them. Yet, after these various types of godlessness (which are interconnected by the fact that they are all blasphemies of one form or another), I warn you—please give close heed—to resist especially the following errors. One of them, founded by Nestorius some time ago, tried to build up momentum—and not without considerable peril. As fully execrable, the other broke out just recently with Eutyches as its proponent.

Nestorius had the temerity to preach that the Blessed Virgin Mary was mother only to the man. This led to the belief that, in his Conception and Birth, no union occurred between the Word and the flesh, for the Son of God would not himself have become the son of a human being, but would merely have associated himself to a created human being by his good pleasure alone. Catholic ears could never tolerate this, ears so imbued with the Gospel of truth that they know with the greatest firmness that there could be no hope of salvation for the human race were he not himself both the Son of the Virgin and the Creator of his Mother.

(2) Eutyches, impious proponent of the more recent sacrilege, admitted the union of two natures in Christ. Yet he asserted that—as a result of this union—only one of the two natures remained while there was nothing at all left from the other's substance. This could only be accomplished either by absorption or separation. These things are so inimical to a sound faith that they cannot be accepted without destroying the very name of Christian.

If the Incarnation of the Word is the union of the divine and human natures in such a way that—through this very combination—what had been double became single, then the divinity alone would have been born from the Virgin's womb. It alone—in a counterfeit appearance—would have undergone nourishment and bodily growth. To leave aside all else that is subject to change in the human condition, the divinity alone was crucified, the divinity alone died, the divinity alone was buried.

Accordingly, there would be no reason for hope in resurrection, nor would Christ be the "first born from the dead,"[223] for no one should have been raised if there was no one who could be killed.

6. Far from your hearts be those poisonous lies inspired by the devil, dearly beloved. You know that the eternal divinity of the Son did not grow with any accretion in the presence of the Father. Take careful note of how to the nature which in Adam was told, "You are earth, and into the earth will you go,"[224] the same nature in Christ is told, "Sit at my right hand."[225]

According to that nature in which Christ is equal to the Father, the Only-Begotten was never inferior to the Begetter in sublimity, nor is his glory with the Father only temporal, for he is the very right hand of the Father. Concerning him is it said in Exodus, "Your right hand, o Lord, has been glorified in power,"[226] and in Isaiah, "Lord, who has believed what we have heard? To whom has the arm of the Lord been revealed?"[227]

(2) Man, taken up into the Son of God, was so received into the unity of Christ's Person from its very bodily origins, that he was not conceived without the divinity, nor born without the divinity, nor nourished without the divinity. He was the same Person in miracles as he was in dishonor. Through human weakness, he was crucified, died, and was buried. Through divine power, he rose again on the third day, ascended into heaven, and sat at the right hand of the Father. In the nature of man, he received from the Father what, in the nature of his divinity, he himself gave.

7. Meditating upon these things with a reverent heart, dearly beloved, bear always in mind that precept of the Apostle, for it gives warning to us all: "See to it that no one deceive you through philosophy and empty deceit, according to human tradition and not according to Christ. For, in him dwells all the fullness of divinity according to the flesh, and you have been filled in him."[228] He did not say "according to the spirit," but "according to the flesh," so that we may understand the true

---

223. Cf. Col 1.18.
225. Ps 109(110).1.
227. Is 53.1.
224. Gn 3.19.
226. Ex 15.6.
228. Col 2.8–10.

substance of flesh to be where there is the bodily dwelling of the fullness of divinity. With it is the whole Church thereby filled. Clinging to the head, the Church is the body of Christ, who lives and reigns with the Father and the Holy Spirit for ever and ever. Amen.

Sermon 29

25 December 453

Indeed, dearly beloved, the greatness of God's work surpasses and completely transcends the powers of human eloquence. What makes it so difficult to speak, however, also forbids us to remain silent. In Jesus Christ the Son of God, that which has been said through a prophet (i.e., "Who will recount his generation?"[229]) pertains not only to the divine essence, but to the human one as well. Speech cannot explain how the two substances came together into a single Person. Faith simply believes it. As a result, subject matter for praise never runs out, since the talent of a praiser can never exhaust it.

Let us rejoice, therefore, in the fact that we cannot measure up to expounding a mystery that involves such great mercy. Since we are incapable of expressing the profoundness of our salvation, let us think it good for us to be overwhelmed. No one draws closer to an understanding of the truth than the one who realizes that, when it comes to divine things, even if much progress has been made, there always remains something to be sought after. Whoever presumes to have arrived at the goal has not lighted upon what was being sought. Instead, that person has given out in the searching.

(2) Let us not, however, be disturbed by the constraints of our weakness. Words from the Gospels and the prophetic writings lend us a hand. By them, we are inflamed and instructed. We do not feel that we are so much reflecting back upon the Nativity of our Lord (when "the Word was made flesh"[230]) in the past as we are viewing it in the present.

What the angel of the Lord announced to the shepherds as

---

229. Is 53.8.
230. Jn 1.14.

they stayed up to keep watch over their flocks has also filled our ears. As a result, we have charge over the Lord's sheep because we heed the words spoken by God in the ears of our heart. It is as if it were being said during today's feast as well, "I proclaim to you the Gospel of great joy which all peoples will have. On this day, a Savior has been born for you, who is Christ the Lord, in the city of David."[231]

Angels without number join their exultation to this sublime announcement, uttering their praise in unison for the honor of God: "Glory to God in the highest, and on earth peace to people of good will."[232] Singing in concert, this multitude of the heavenly host provided a more distinguished testimony to what had taken place.

God receives glory from the infancy of Christ, who had been born from a virgin mother. Restoration of the human race would by all rights be referred to the glory of its Maker. Why, the angel Gabriel, sent by God, had said to Blessed Mary herself: "The Holy Spirit will come down upon you, and the power of the Most High will overshadow you. Wherefore, the holy offspring to be born from you will be called the Son of God."[233]

On earth, however, that peace has been established which makes human beings to be of good will. By the same Spirit through whom Christ was born from the body of an undefiled mother, Christians are reborn from the womb of the Holy Church. True peace for a Christian means not being separated from the will of God and taking delight only in those things which God loves.

2. We celebrate the Birthday of our Lord, dearly beloved, a day chosen from all those that have gone by. Of course the physical activities that had been preordained according to the eternal plan have been carried out. Of course the entire lowliness of the Redeemer has been carried up into the glory of his Father's majesty, "so that every knee would bend at the name of Jesus (of those in heaven, on earth, and under the earth), and every tongue would confess that Jesus is in the glory of God the Father."[234]

---

231. Lk 2.10.
233. Lk 1.35.
232. Cf. Lk 2.14.
234. Phil 2.10–11.

(2) We nevertheless adore without end this child-bearing of the salvific Virgin. We accept that indissoluble union of the Word and flesh no less as he lies in the manger than when he sits on the heights of his Father's throne. Certainly the immutable divinity contains its glory and its power within itself. Simply because it did not lie open to human view, however, does not mean that it had not been engrafted in the one being born.

These unusual beginnings of a true man indicate that he had been born, the one who was to have been both the "Son" and the "Lord" of King David.[235] David himself sings in a spirit of prophecy: "The Lord said to my Lord. Sit at my right hand."[236] Through this testimony, as the Gospel relates, the godlessness of the Jews was refuted. When Jesus had asked the Jews whose son the Christ would be, they answered, "David's." At once, the Lord points out their blindness, saying: "How, then, does David call him Lord, saying in the Spirit, 'The Lord said to my Lord.' "Sit at my right hand." '?"[237]

You have blocked off the path of understanding, o Jews. While you see only the nature of flesh, you have deprived yourselves of all the light of truth. According to the false inventions of your mindset, you look for the son of David to come from a merely physical stock. While building up your hope in a mere man, you have repudiated God the Son of God. Consequently, what is glorious for us to profess cannot benefit you at all.

We too, when asked whose son the Christ is, confess in the Apostle's words: "He was made from the seed of David according to the flesh."[238] From the very beginning of the Gospel's preaching, we receive instruction [to this effect] when we read: "Book of the generation of Jesus Christ, Son of David."[239] Yet we are distinguished from your godlessness by virtue of the fact that we believe the one whom we know to have been born as man from the lineage of David to be God as well, coeternal with God the Father, according to [the formula], "The Word was made flesh."[240]

Wherefore, if you keep to the dignity of your name, o Israel,

---

235. Cf. Mt 22.45.
237. Mt 22.43–44.
239. Mt 1.1.
236. Ps 109(110).1.
238. Rom 1.3.
240. Jn 1.14.

and you review without a blinded heart the announcements made by prophets, then Isaiah would open up for you the Gospel truth. You would hear him without being deaf when he says: "Behold a virgin will conceive in her womb and will bear a son, and they will call his name Emmanuel, which means 'God with us.' "[241]

Even if you did not recognize him to be God by virtue of his having this sacred name, you should at least have learned this from the words of David. You would then have been prevented from denying—contrary to the testimony of both the New and Old Testaments—that Jesus Christ is the son of David, in spite of the fact that you do not acknowledge him to be David's Lord.

3. Wherefore, dearly beloved, through the ineffable grace of God, the Church of believing Gentiles has obtained that which the synagogue of Jews has not deserved. As David said, "the Lord has made his salvation known and has revealed his justice in the sight of the nations."[242] Isaiah likewise announces: "People who were sitting in darkness have seen a great light. A light has arisen for those who were living in the realm of death's shadow."[243] Elsewhere, Isaiah says: "Nations that have not known you will call upon you, and people who do not recognize you will take refuge in you."[244]

Therefore, let us rejoice in the day of our salvation, dearly beloved. We have been taken up through the New Covenant into a participation with him, who was told by the Father through a prophet: "You are my Son, this day I have begotten you. Ask it of me, and I will give you the nations for your inheritance and the ends of the earth for your possession."[245] Let us glory, therefore, in the mercy of the one adopting us. As the Apostle says, "You did not receive a spirit of slavery again in fear, but you have received the spirit of adoption as children, in which we cry out 'Abba, Father.' "[246] It would be fitting and appropriate that the will of a father's testament be carried out by adopted sons. As the Apostle says, "If we suffer with him,

241. Mt 1.23 and Is 7.14.
243. Mt 4.16 and Is 9.2.
245. Ps 2.7–8.
242. Ps 97(98).2.
244. Is 55.5.
246. Rom 8.15.

we shall also be glorified with him."²⁴⁷ Let those who are going to be co-heirs with Christ in glory participate in his lowliness as well.

(2) Let the Lord be honored in his infancy. His birth and bodily growth should not be regarded as compromising the divinity. Our nature has not added anything to his immutable nature nor taken anything away from it. He who condescended to be conformed to human beings "unto the likeness of sinful flesh"²⁴⁸ remains all the while equal to the Father in the unity of the divinity. With the Father and with the Holy Spirit he lives and reigns for ever and ever. Amen.

Sermon 30

25 December 454

As you are aware, dearly beloved, we have often carried out our duty to you of giving a salutary talk concerning the excellence of today's feast. We do not doubt but that the power of divine goodness has shined so brightly in your hearts that what has found root in you by faith has also been grasped by your intelligence. The Birth of Our Lord and Savior, whether that of his divinity from the Father or that of his flesh from his Mother, surpasses the power of human eloquence. As a result, the saying ("Who will recount his generation?"²⁴⁹) may rightly be referred to either.

In that very matter which cannot be properly explained, a reason for holding forth always abounds—not because there is freedom to think any number of things, but because no tongue can measure up to the dignity of this subject matter. Consequently, this great "mystery,"²⁵⁰ planned "from all eternity"²⁵¹ for the salvation of the human race and reserved "for the end of the ages,"²⁵² does not allow anything to be taken from its completeness nor anything to be added to it. As it does not lose anything of its own, so it accepts nothing from the outside.

---

247. Rom 8.17.
248. Cf. Rom 8.3.
249. Is 53.8.
250. Cf. 1 Tm 3.16.
251. Cf. Ti 1.2.
252. Cf. 1 Cor 10.11.

Many, however, clinging to their own opinions and more ready to teach than to learn what they have not yet understood, have, as the Apostle says, "suffered a shipwreck of their faith."[253] I will touch upon their twisted and contradictory opinions in summary. When the darkness of these errors has been distinguished from the light of truth, divine benefits may thus be honored with devotion and worldly lies avoided with knowledge.

2. Evidence about the Birth of our Lord Jesus Christ served to demonstrate that he was the real son of a human being. Certain ones, drawing conclusions from this, have believed him to be nothing more than a mere man. They do not feel that divinity should be attributed to him since his earliest infancy, his bodily growth, and then his ability to suffer in general (right up to his Crucifixion and Death), had allegedly proven him to be not unlike other human beings.

Others, however, moved by an admiration for his powers have understood that the uniqueness of his origin and the power of his words and deeds pertain to a divine nature. Yet, they felt that he did not have any part of our substance and that the whole entity which was responsible for his physical activities and physical form either issued forth from a more refined type of material or had only the appearance of flesh (so that the sense perceptions of those who saw him and touched him were deceived by an illusory likeness).

Some of those going astray have even come to the conclusion that something from the substance of the Word had been turned into flesh, that Jesus (born of the Virgin Mary) possessed nothing of his Mother's substance. According to them, both that which was God and that which was man pertained to what the Word is. As a consequence of this, the humanity in Christ would have been false by virtue of the fact that it did not have its own substance, and the divinity would have been untrue by virtue of the fact that it was defective through mutability.

3. These and other forms of godlessness, dearly beloved, conceived through diabolical inspiration and poured out

253. 1 Tm 1.19.

through vessels of destruction for the harm of many, the Catholic Faith, for which God serves as both Teacher and Helper, has crushed once and for all. Meanwhile, the Holy Spirit encourages and teaches us through the witness of the law, through the predictions made by prophets, through the Gospel's trumpet, and through the teaching of the Apostles. He encourages and teaches us to believe with perseverance and understanding that, as blessed John says, "The Word became flesh and dwelt among us."[254]

"Among us" [he dwelt], indeed, us whom the divinity of the Word fitted to himself. We are his flesh, the flesh that had been taken up from the Virgin's womb. If this flesh had not been from ours, that is, had it not been truly human, the Word made flesh would not have dwelt among us. "He did" in fact "dwell among us,"[255] however, for he made the nature of our body his own. "Wisdom built itself a house,"[256] not from just any material, but from the substance that is properly ours. The fact that he had taken it on has been made clear from when it was said, "The Word became flesh and dwelt among us."[257]

(2) With this most holy pronouncement, the teaching of blessed Paul the apostle also agrees: "See to it that no one deceive you through philosophy and empty deceit, according to human tradition, according to the elements of this world, and not according to Christ. For in him dwells all the fullness of divinity according to the flesh, and you have been filled in him."[258] The entire divinity fills the entire body.

As nothing of his majesty remains that does not dwell in the dwelling filled by it, so nothing of the body remains unfilled by his indwelling. In that phrase, "and you have been filled in him,"[259] certainly it was our nature being referred to. That "filling" would not pertain to us had not the Word of God united both a body and a soul of our kind to himself.

4. We must surely acknowledge, dearly beloved, and confess with all our heart that this Generation surpasses every origin

---

254. Jn 1.14.
256. Prv 9.1.
258. Col 2.8–10.
255. Jn 1.14.
257. Jn 1.14.
259. Cf. Col 2.10.

of human creation. By it both the Word and the flesh, that is, God and man, are made into a single Son of God and a single Christ. "Adam's being molded from the clay of the earth,"[260] the fashioning of Eve "from the flesh of the man,"[261] and the making of other human beings from a mingling of the two sexes, none of these can compare with the appearance of Jesus Christ.

Abraham, when an old man, begot the heir of God's promise, while Sarah, though sterile and past the age of fruitfulness, conceived.[262] Jacob, was "loved by God"[263] before he was born. As grace directed his willful actions, he was set apart by the hairy roughness of his twin brother.[264] Jeremiah was told, "Before I formed you in the womb, I knew you; before you came out from the womb, I made you holy."[265] Anna, long a stranger to fruitfulness, brought forth in labor the prophet Samuel, whom she offered to God.[266] So she became renowned both for the birth and for her vow. Zachariah the priest received a holy progeny from the sterile Elizabeth.[267] John, to be the precursor of Christ, had received the prophetic spirit within the body of his mother.[268] As a child not yet born, he had pointed out the Lord's Mother by the sign of joy within his enclosure.[269]

These are all great matters and replete with miracles worked by God. Yet the more numerous they are, the less are they to be marveled at. But the Birth of our Lord Jesus Christ exceeds all understanding and goes beyond any precedent. No, what is entirely unique cannot be compared with anything else. To the chosen Virgin—it had already been promised by the words of prophets and by mystical signs that she would come from the seed of Abraham and the root of Jesse—to the chosen Virgin, the archangel announces a blessed fruitfulness, one without any harm to her honor, one which would not do any damage to her holy virginity either in conception or in child-bearing. Indeed, when "the Holy Spirit came down upon her and the

---

260. Cf. Gn 2.7.
261. Cf. Gn 2.21–22.
262. Cf. Gn 21.2.
263. Mal 1.2 and Rom 9.13.
264. Cf. Gen 25.25 and Hos 12.3.
265. Jer 1.5.
266. Cf 1 Sm 1.11–20.
267. Cf. Lk 1.24.
268. Cf. Lk 1.15.
269. Cf. Lk 1.41.

power of the Most High overshadowed her,"[270] the immutable Word of God took upon himself from her untouched body the clothing of human flesh. It did not carry any pollution from concupiscence, yet it lacked nothing of those things which pertain to the nature of soul and body.

5. Let the monstrosities of heretical ideas and the blasphemies of wild falsehoods go far away and recede into their own shadows. As for us, a "great throng of the heavenly host"[271] exulting in praise of God, and shepherds informed by the angels, they have taught us to adore both the Word in Christ the man and Christ the man in the Word, since we have come to know the evidence for both natures. If, as the Apostle says, "the one who inheres in the Lord constitutes a single spirit with him,"[272] how much more does the Word made flesh constitute a single Christ, where nothing belongs to either nature that does not belong to both!

(2) Let us not be weakened, then, in the plan of God's mercy. It restores us to innocence and to life. Since we recognize in our Savior the clear signs of the dual nature, let us not in the glory of God have doubts about the reality of his flesh, nor in the lowliness of man have doubts about the majesty of the divinity. He who took on the "form of a servant" also has the "form of God."[273] He who took up a body also remains incorporeal. He who can suffer in our weakness cannot be harmed in his strength. He who was crucified by the godless on a piece of wood has not been separated from his Father's throne. He who ascended over the heights of heaven as a victor over death will not abandon the universal Church "up to the consummation of the world."[274] Finally, he who submitted to judgment at the hands of the godless will sit in judgment over the actions of every mortal, coming with the same flesh as that in which he ascended.

Wherefore, let us not linger over very many proofs for this. It would be enough to adduce a single one from the Gospel of

---

270. Lk 1.35.
272. 1 Cor 6.17.
274. Cf. Mt 28.20.

271. Cf. Lk 2.13.
273. Cf. Phil 2.6–7.

Blessed John. In it, our Lord himself said as follows: "Amen, amen, I say to you, that the hour is coming, and now is at hand, when the dead will hear the voice of God's Son, and those who hear will live. For, as the Father has life in himself, so has he given it to the Son also to have life in himself. He has given to him as well the power to render judgment because he is the son of a human being."[275] Through a single statement, he shows that the Son of God is also the son of a human being. Hence, we see how we ought to believe in Christ the Lord as having a unity of Person. He is both the Son of God through whom we were made and the son of a human being by his taking on flesh ("so that he might die," as the Apostle says, "for our sins and rise for our justification."[276])

6. This profession of faith, dearly beloved, fears no contradictions, yields to no errors. We acknowledge the mercy of God, promised from the beginning and prepared before the ages. Through it alone could those chains of human captivity be loosened, the chains by which the ill-advising originator of evil had bound the first human being and all his posterity, the chains by which he was claiming for himself the offspring that had been surrendered in advance by the original sentence.

This was primarily responsible for justifying human beings, that the Only-Begotten of God saw fit to become the son of a human being as well. He, one in being with the Father, became true man, consubstantial as well with his Mother according to the flesh. We rejoice, therefore, in both, since we are not saved except with both. We cannot in any way divide the visible from the invisible, the corporeal from the incorporeal, the passible from the impassible, the tangible from the intangible, the "form of a servant" from the "form of God."[277]

Although one remains from eternity and the other began in time, both have nevertheless come together into a unity. They can neither be separated nor come to an end. Exalting and exalted, glorifying and glorified, the two have inhered in one another so that, whether in omnipotence or in disgrace, neither

---

275. Jn 5.25–27.   276. Rom 4.25.
277. Cf. Phil 2.6–7.

the divine in Christ goes without the human, nor the human without the divine.

7. If we believe this, dearly beloved, we are true Christians, "true Israelites,"[278] and have been truly adopted into the fellowship of God's children. Even all the saints who came before the time of our Savior have also been justified through this faith and made the body of Christ through this mystery. They awaited the universal redemption of believers in the seed of Abraham, about which the Apostle says: "Promises were made to Abraham and to his seed. Scripture does not say 'and to his seeds' as if in the plural, but as if in the singular: . . . and to your seed which is Christ."[279]

That is why the evangelist Matthew, to prove that the promise made to Abraham was fulfilled in Christ, started off with the order of generations, showing that the blessing for all nations had led up to him.[280] Luke also delineated the progression of this line, backwards from the Birth of the Lord himself, reversing the order so that he could explain that even those ages that preceded the deluge had been connected to this mystery and that all the steps of succession, from the beginning, were directed to him, in whom alone lay the salvation of all.[281]

(2) It must not then be doubted that "there is no other name under heaven given to human beings by which they can be saved"[282] besides that of Christ who, equal in the Trinity with the Father and the Holy Spirit, lives and reigns for ever and ever. Amen.

278. Cf. Jn 1.47.
280. Cf. Mt 1.1–16.
282. Acts 4.12.

279. Gal 3.16.
281. Cf. Lk 3.23–28.

EPIPHANY

These eight sermons, delivered on the feast of the Epiphany, cover numerous aspects of that event. Leo bewails the blindness of Jews in the person of Herod (whom he addresses several times, e.g., *Serms.* 31.2 and 34.2). Yet he points out that, in consequence of this, Gentiles owe thanks to God for giving his light to them (*Serm.* 32.2). Jews were "unwilling to recognize with their eyes the one whom they had pointed to from their sacred books" (cf. *Serms.* 32.2 and 33.3).

In the image of three wise men following the light of a star, Leo finds many opportunities for encouraging believers to follow the light of Christ, a light exemplified especially in love—". . . When an inclination to good will abounds in us all, the poison of hate might not be found in any one" (*Serm.* 37.4.2); in forgiveness—"To inflict and to pay back injury belongs to the wisdom of this world, but 'to repay evil for evil to no one' represents the childhood of Christian self-possession" (*Serm.* 37.4); and in humility—". . . the entire victory of the Savior, the one that overcame the devil and the world, began in humility and ended in humility" (*Serm.* 37.2).

Sermon 31

6 January 441

WE HAVE JUST celebrated the day when undefiled virginity brought forth a Savior for the human race. Now, dearly beloved, this revered feast of the Epiphany prolongs our joy. Since the mysteries of these kindred solemnities are closely related, the intensity of our joy and the ardor of our faith are not allowed to grow cold. It concerns the salvation of all humanity that the Infancy of the "Mediator between God and human beings"[1] was now being made known to the whole world, even while it was still confined to this meager little village. He had chosen the nation of Israel and—from that nation—one family in particular as the one from which to take

---

1. Cf. 1 Tm 2.5.

up the nature of all humanity. Still, he did not want the beginnings of his appearance to remain hidden within the dwelling of his Mother. Instead, he wanted to be acknowledged right away by all, since he had seen fit to be born for all.

(2) Consequently, a star with new brilliance appeared to three wise men in the East. Since it was brighter and more beautiful than others, it easily attracted to itself the eyes and hearts of those looking on. Immediately they realized that what seemed so unusual could not be without meaning. He who furnished the sign also gave understanding to those who saw it. What he granted to be understood, he also granted to be sought. At last, he who was sought offered himself to be found.

2. Three men follow the lead of this heavenly light. While trailing the signal of its gleam ahead of them with their attention focused upon it, they are led by the splendor of grace to knowledge of the truth. According to their human feeling, they surmised that the appearance of the king that had been signified to them was to be sought in the royal city. But he, who had taken up the "form of a servant"[2] and "had come not to judge"[3] but to be judged, chose Bethlehem for his Birth, Jerusalem for his Death.

(2) Herod, on the other hand, hearing that a leader of the Jews had been born, grew afraid at the thought of a possible successor. Plotting death for the Author of Salvation, he pledged a false compliance. How happy he would have been had he but imitated the faith of these wise men, had he but turned into an act of religion that which he was arranging for deception! O blind godlessness of foolish jealousy, thinking that the divine plan can be upset by your raging! The Lord of the world does not seek a temporal kingdom but gives an eternal one. Why are you trying to throw off the unchangeable plan of the things that have been arranged? Why are you trying to outdo the crimes of others?

Christ's Death does not belong to your time. First the Gospel must be established, the kingdom of God preached, illnesses

2. Cf. Phil 2.7.
3. Cf. Jn 12.47.

cured, miracles performed. Why, when the work is to be done by another, do you wish it to be your crime? Since you will not attain to the desired end of your misdeed, why do your hurl yourself alone into the guilt of having willed it? You accomplish nothing by your plotting, you bring nothing to completion. He who was born by his own wish will die "by the power"[4] of his own discretion.

As a result, the wise men fulfill their desire, coming to the child, the Lord Jesus Christ, as the same star leads them. They adore the Word in flesh, Wisdom in infancy, Strength in weakness, and the Lord of Majesty in the reality of a man. To reveal the mystery of their faith and understanding, they confirm with gifts what they believe in their hearts. They offer incense to God, myrrh to the man, and gold to the king. Knowingly do they venerate the divine and human nature in their unity. What was a proper characteristic of one or the other substance did not remain separated [from the other] in power.

3. When the wise men had returned to their land and Jesus had been taken to Egypt in accordance with the divine warning, a desperate insanity rages in the thoughts of Herod. He orders all the young boys in Bethlehem to be killed. Since he does not know the child he fears, he directs his cruelty against the entire age-group under suspicion. But those whom this godless king removes from the world, Christ establishes in heaven. Those whom [Christ] has not yet redeemed with his blood are granted the honor of martyrdom.

(2) Raise your faithful hearts, dearly beloved, to the shining beauty of eternal light. As you revere the mysteries devoted to human salvation, put your energy into all those things that have been done on your behalf. Love the purity of a chaste life, since Christ is the Son of a Virgin. "Abstain from carnal desires, since they wage war against the soul,"[5] as the apostle here present encouraged us in his own words (which we have just read). "Be little children with respect to wickedness,"[6] because the Lord of glory conformed himself to the infancy of mortals. Earnestly

4. Cf. Jn 10.17–18. 5. 1 Pt 2.11.
6. 1 Cor 14.20.

pursue "humility,"⁷ which the Son of God saw fit to teach his disciples. "Clothe" yourselves in the virtue of "patience,"⁸ "in which" you can possess "your souls,"⁹ since he who is the "Redemption"¹⁰ of all is also the "Fortitude"¹¹ of all. "Relish the things which are on high, not those things upon the earth."¹² Walk steadily along the path of truth and of life. Do not let the things of earth hinder you, you for whom the things of heaven have been prepared, through Jesus Christ our Lord.

Sermon 32

6 January 442

"Rejoice in the Lord," dearly beloved, "again I say, rejoice."¹³ In the short space of time after the solemnity of Christ's Birth, the feast of his Manifestation has dawned. On this day, the world recognizes the one whom the Virgin bore on that day. In such a way did the Word made flesh arrange the beginnings of his taking on our nature, that Jesus, born for and manifested to believers, would be hidden from his persecutors. On both occasions, therefore, "the heavens have proclaimed the glory of God,"¹⁴ and "the sound" of truth "went out through all the earth"¹⁵—when the host of angels appeared to the shepherds as heralds of the new-born Savior, and when the star, going on ahead, led the wise men to him for worship. "From the rising of the sun to its setting,"¹⁶ the Birth of the true King shone forth, when the kingdoms of the East learned the truth through the wise men, and it did not remain hidden from the Roman empire.

Even the ferocity of Herod, who wanted to snuff out the suspected king at the very beginning, unwittingly played right into the hands of this arrangement. Obsessed with his brutal crime, he goes after a boy unknown to him with the indiscriminate slaughter of infants. As he does so, a more widely known report

---

7. Cf. Lk 14.11 and Mt 23.12.
8. Cf. Col 3.12.
9. Cf. Lk 21.19.
10. Cf. 1 Cor 1.30.
11. Cf. Ps 27(28).8.
12. Col 3.2.
13. Cf. Phil 4.4.
14. Ps 18(19).2.
15. Ps 18(19).5.
16. Cf. Ps 49(50).1.

spreads everywhere, declaring this appearance of the Lord which had been proclaimed in the heavens. Both the novelty of that heavenly sign and the godlessness of this blood-drenched persecutor caused the report to be passed on more eagerly and more carefully. Then, the Savior was taken down even to Egypt, so that a nation given over to error from ancient times should now be marked out, through a secret grace, as being near to salvation. That nation which had not yet cast superstition from its heart would receive Truth as its guest.

2. Fittingly, therefore, this day—consecrated by the Lord's Manifestation—has obtained throughout the world a special dignity. This dignity ought to shine forth clearly in our hearts with a worthy splendor. It ought to shine forth clearly, so that we might revere the manner of these events not merely by believing, but by understanding as well. Blindness on the part of the Jews demonstrates what great thanks we owe to the Lord for his enlightenment of the Gentiles. What could be so blind, what so unacquainted with light, as those priests and scribes of the Israelites? When Herod asked the wise men "where," according to the testimony of Scripture, "the Christ was born,"[17] they made an investigation and gave reply from the prophet's words that it was where the star from heaven indicated.

Certainly, this star, with its signal light, could have led the wise men, upon leaving Jerusalem, right to the child's cradle—as later it did. To confound the obduracy of the Jews, however, the Savior's Birth became known not only by the star's lead, but by their acknowledgment as well. Now, the words of the prophet were moving on to instruct the nations, and the hearts of foreigners were learning about the Christ who had been foretold by ancient prophecies. Meanwhile, the infidelity of Jews uttered truth with the lips but kept falsehood in their hearts. They were unwilling to recognize with their eyes the one whom they had pointed to from their sacred books. As a result, the one whom they did not worship when humbled in the weakness of infancy, they would go on to crucify when resplendent at the height of his powers.

17. Mt 2.4.

3. What, Jews, is that unknowing knowledge which you have, that unlearned learning? When you were asked "where the Christ was born,"[18] you say truly and accurately, according to what you have read: "In Bethlehem of Judah. For thus was it written through the prophet, 'And you, Bethlehem of Judah, are not the least among the princes of Judah. For out of you will come the leader to rule my people Israel.'"[19] Angels announced this leader at his Birth to the shepherds and the shepherds to you.[20] Distant nations of Eastern peoples learned about this leader at his Birth from the unusual brilliance of a new star. To remove all doubt about the place from which the King would come forth, your learning produced what the star did not teach.

Why do you block off for yourselves the path that you open up for others? Why does any doubt remain in your unbelief, a doubt which was dispelled by your own reply? You demonstrate the place of his Birth from the witness of Scripture. You ascertain from the witness of signs in heaven and on earth that the time has come. Yet, when the heart of Herod burned to persecute him, your feelings became hardened for unbelief. As a result, those infants whom the persecutor murdered were better off in their ignorance than you in your knowledge—which has turned against you in accusation. You were unwilling to accept his kingdom, though you could point out his town. They were able to die for him, though they were not yet able to confess him.

So Christ, that he might not go for any length of time without a miracle, displayed the Word's power in silence, before he had the use of his tongue, as if to say: "Let the small children come to me, for the kingdom of heaven is made up of such as these."[21] New glory crowned the infants, and this glory consecrated their earliest years from the very start—this to teach that no human being is unsuitable for receiving a divine mystery, since even that time of life was compatible with the glory of martyrdom.

4. Let us recognize, dearly beloved, the first-fruits of our call-

---

18. Mt 2.4.
19. Mt 2.5–6 and cf. Mi 5.2.
20. Cf. Lk 2.10 and 18.
21. Mt 19.14 and Lk 18.16.

ing and of our faith in the wise men who worshipped Christ. Let us celebrate with joyful hearts the beginnings of blessed hope. It is from this point that we began to enter into our eternal inheritance. It is from this point that the secrets of Scripture began to speak and to reveal Christ to us. It is from this point that the truth, which the blindness of Jews did not accept, began to carry its own light to all the nations. Wherefore, let us honor this most sacred day, the day on which the author of our salvation appeared. Whom the wise men revered as an infant in his crib, let us worship as all-powerful in heaven.

Just as they offered to the Lord mystical kinds of gifts from their treasures, so let us bring forth from our hearts things that are worthy of God. Although he himself bestows all good things, he nevertheless asks for the fruit of our effort. For the kingdom of heaven comes not to those who sleep, but to those who work and "watch"[22] according to the Lord's command. If we do not render his gifts ineffective, we may deserve to receive what he promised through the very things which he has given.

(2) We encourage you to "abstain," in love, "from every wicked deed"[23] and to pursue chastity and justice. Children of light ought "to cast off the works of darkness."[24] So turn aside hatred, deflect lies, dispel pride with humility, wipe out avarice through generosity. It becomes the members [of a body] to be compatible with their head, so that we may deserve to share in the blessedness he has promised, through our Lord.

Sermon 33

6 January 443 (Recension A)[25]

I know, dearly beloved, that the occasion for today's feast does not escape you in your holiness. As usual, the Gospel read-

---

22. Cf. 1 Thes 5.6.   23. Cf. 1 Thes 5.22 and 2 Tm 4.18.
24. Cf. Rom 13.12.
25. This sermon comes down to us in two recensions. Recension A had been composed in 443. Recension B appears to represent a revision made by Leo himself at some later date. Material found in both recensions will appear in normal text. Material found only in Recension A will appear in **bold**. Material found only in Recension B will appear in *italics*. Some material found in both recensions but in a different order will be reproduced in both bold and italics in their proper order. Some material that does not coincide between the two

ing has made this known to you. So that I may not fail at all in my duty *toward you*, I will venture to say about it whatever the Lord will inspire. I do so with the hope that the more this feast is understood, the more devoted will be the reverence of all in our shared joy.

(2) God, in his providential mercy, planned to help the dying world "in these last days."[26] He determined beforehand the salvation of all nations in Christ. Since godless error had for some time turned all nations away from worship of the true God, and, since even Israel, the special people of God, had almost completely fallen away from the established laws—in short, "since all had been confined under the dominion of sin,—he had mercy on all."[27]

(3) Justice was lacking everywhere, and the whole world had fallen into worthless and evil things. Had divine power not put off passing judgment, all of mankind would have received the sentence of condemnation. But wrath was converted into mercy. In order to make the magnitude of the grace that was to be bestowed more evident, it then pleased him that the mystery of forgiveness should be applied to the sins of men that were to be wiped out—when none could boast about their own merits.

2. This ineffable mercy, dearly beloved, was manifested when Herod held royal power among the Jews. With legitimate succession broken down and the authority of priests undermined, a foreigner obtained the leadership. In this way, the rise of a true King was proven through the words of that prophecy which stated: "There will not be lacking a prince from Judah, nor a leader from his loins, until the one for whom it has been reserved should come, and he it is whom the nations await."[28]

At one time, the most blessed patriarch Abraham had been promised countless descendants from these nations. These were to be generated not from the seed of flesh, but from the fecundity of faith. These were compared to the stars in num-

---

versions of the Latin text but does not affect the English translation (such as word order or certain syntactical variants) will not be indicated.
26. Cf. 1 Pt 1.20.   27. Cf. Gal 3.22 and Rom 11.32.
28. Cf. Gn 49.10.

ber, so that the father of all nations would hope for a heavenly offspring and not an earthly one. In order to create this promised posterity, the heirs (symbolically represented in the stars) are quickened by the birth of a new star, so that this new honor given by heaven might serve the one for whom the witness of heaven had been summoned.

A star brighter than the rest stirs the wise men, inhabitants of the distant East. From the brilliance of that marvelous light, these men—not unpracticed at realizing such things—understand the greatness of its meaning. No doubt divine inspiration effected this in their hearts, so that the mystery of so great a spectacle would not escape them and that the extraordinary thing put before their eyes would not be obscure to their minds. At last, they carry out their roles with devotion, outfitting themselves with these gifts. This served to show that, though they were going to worship one, they believed at the same time in three—honoring his royalty with gold, his humanity with myrrh, and his divinity with incense.

3. So they enter the principal city of the Jewish kingdom. In the royal city, they ask to be shown *the boy*, the one who, as they had ascertained, was born *for them* to be king. Herod is disturbed. He fears for his safety. He becomes concerned about his power. He makes an inquiry of **the priests and** doctors of the law as to what Scripture foretold concerning the appearance of Christ. As what was prophesied comes to light, truth enlightens the wise men while infidelity blinds the teachers. Israel of the flesh does not understand what it reads, does not see what it reveals, makes use of writings whose contents it does not believe.

Jew, "where is your self-respect?"[29] Where is the nobility derived from father Abraham? "*Has not your circumcision become prepuce?*"[30] Behold, "you who are greater serve the lesser."[31] While foreigners enter upon the right to your inheritance, you wait upon them by reciting that Testament which you hold to only in a literal sense. "Let the multitude of nations come in,

29. Rom 3.27. 30. Rom 2.25.
31. Gn 25.23.

let them come into"³² the household of your patriarchs. Let "children of the promise" receive that blessing in the seed of Abraham which the "children of flesh" relinquish.³³ Let all peoples, in the three wise men, worship the Maker of the universe. Let "God be known," not only "in Judea," but in the whole world, so that "his name might be great in the Israel"³⁴ of everywhere. Just as faithlessness shows that dignity of the chosen race to have degenerated in his descendants, so faith makes it available to all.

4. When they had worshipped the Lord and completed all their devotion, the wise men—in accordance with the warning given in a dream—do not go back the same way they had come. It was appropriate for them, now that they believed in Christ, not to walk along the paths of their former way of life, but to take a new path and refrain from the straying that had been left behind. Also, they foiled in this way the plots of Herod, who was making arrangements for a godless plot against the **Lord** *child* Jesus under the guise of reverence.

Because the hope he entertained for that machination had been dashed, the king's ire rages even more. Taking into account the period of time which the wise men had mentioned, he pours out the ravages of his cruelty on all the little boys at Bethlehem. In a wide-scale slaughter, **he rages against the blessed infants of that city** *he massacres the infants of that entire city, infants who would pass over into eternal glory.* He reckons that, by killing every little boy there, he would kill Christ as well.

(2) But he, who put off to another time the shedding of his blood for the world's redemption, had betaken himself to Egypt, carried by the service of his parents. He was going back, of course, to the ancient cradle of the Hebrew nation. By the power of a greater providence, he made arrangements for the reign of the true Joseph. Coming "from heaven as the Bread"³⁵ of Life and food of reason, he dispelled that famine—more dreadful than any other kind of hunger—by which the minds of Egyptians were suffering through a deficiency of truth.

32. Cf. Rom 11.25.
34. Ps 75(76).2
33. Cf. Rom 9.8.
35. Cf. Jn 6.51.

Without that land, the preparations would not have been made for the mystery of this unique Victim, since it is there, in the slaying of a lamb, that the saving sign of the Cross and the Passover of the Lord had first been prefigured.

5. Now that we have been instructed in these mysteries of divine grace, dearly beloved, let us celebrate with an informed joy the day of our first-fruits and the beginnings of that call to the nations. Let us give thanks to the merciful God who, **as the blessed Apostle said,** "made us worthy of a share in the lot of the saints in light, who has snatched us from *darkness and* the power of darkness, and relocated us in the kingdom of his beloved Son."[36] For, as Isaiah prophesied, "the people who were sitting in darkness have seen a great light. A light has arisen for those who were living in the realm of death's shadow."[37] Concerning these, the same prophet also said to the Lord: "Nations that have not known you will call upon you, and people who do not recognize you will take refuge in you."[38] Abraham "saw" this day "and rejoiced."[39] He rejoiced when he realized that the children of his faith would be blessed "in his seed, which is Christ."[40] By believing, he foresaw that he would become "the father of" all "nations,"[41] "giving glory to God and knowing full well that what God promised he is capable of doing also."[42]

(2) David used to sing about this day in the Psalms, as when he said: "All the nations which you have made will come and make adoration before you, Lord, and they will bring honor upon your name."[43] At another point, he said: "The Lord has made known his salvation, and revealed his justice in the sight of the nations."[44] We know that this took place, of course, when a star led three wise men, roused from their distant land, to the knowledge and the worship of the King of heaven and earth.

This star's subservient function incites us to imitate its submission, so that we may render service to this grace which invites all to Christ, in as much as we can. Whoever lives in

36. Col 1.12–13.
37. Cf. Is 9.2 and Mt. 4.16.
38. Cf. Is 55.5.
39. Jn 8.56.
40. Cf. Gal 3.16.
41. Cf. Rom 4.18.
42. Rom 4.20–21.
43. Ps 85(86).9.
44. Ps 97(98).2.

the Church with devotion and chastity, who "relishes the things which are above, not the things upon the earth,"[45] resembles in a way the celestial light. Preserving the glow of a holy life, that person, just as the star, points out for many the way to the Lord. In this zeal, dearly beloved, you ought all to benefit each other, so that, in the kingdom of God to which we come by a correct faith and good works, you may shine as "children of light"[46] through Christ our Lord.

It does not cease appearing to those who look upon it rightly. If it could make Christ known, hidden in his Infancy, how much more can it manifest him reigning in majesty with the Father and the Holy Spirit forever and ever. Amen.

Sermon 34

6 January 444 (Recension A)[47]

Justice and reason demand a service of genuine reverence, dearly beloved, in these days which make known the works of divine mercy. We must rejoice with all our hearts and celebrate with honor the things that have been done for our salvation. Even the law of recurring seasons calls us to this devotion, which, after the day on which the Son of God (co-eternal with the Father) was born of the Virgin, in a short time introduced to us the feast of the Epiphany, consecrated by the Lord's appearance.

On this day, divine providence established a great protection for our faith. While we reflect with solemn reverence upon the Savior's Infancy (adored in its very beginnings), it is demonstrated through these earliest proofs that the nature of true man has appeared in him. This it is that "justifies the wicked,"[48]

---

45. Cf. Col 3.2. 46. Cf. Eph 5.8–9 and 1 Thes 5.5.
47. This sermon comes down to us in two recensions. Recension A had been composed in 444. Recension B appears to represent a revision made by Leo himself at some later date. Material found in both recensions will appear in normal text. Material found only in Recension A will appear in **bold**. Material found only in Recension B will appear in *italics*. Some material found in both recensions but in a different order will be reproduced in both bold and italics in their proper order. Some material that does not coincide between the two versions of the Latin text but does not affect the English translation (such as word order or certain syntactical variants) will not be indicated.
48. Cf. Rom 4.5.

this it is that makes saints from sinners, our belief that both true divinity and true humanity are in one and the same Lord Jesus Christ. It is by the divinity that, before all ages in the "form of God,"[49] he is equal to the Father. It is by the humanity that, during these "last days,"[50] he has been united to man in the "form of a servant."[51]

(2) Consequently, to strengthen this faith which was being fortified against all errors, it came about by the great goodness of the divine plan that a nation living in the distant regions of the East (*a nation which possessed the skill of reading stars*) should receive a sign that the child who was to rule **in** *over all* Israel had been born. The unusual clarity of a brighter star appeared to the wise men and filled the hearts of those looking on with an admiration for its splendor. As a result, they felt that they must by no means neglect what had been shown through so great a portent.

As the nature of the event had shown, it was the grace of God that governed this miracle. Although, up to this point, not even all of Bethlehem had learned about Christ's Nativity, [this sign] brought knowledge of [his Birth] to nations that were going to believe. What could not yet be described with human eloquence was made known by the proclamation of heaven.

2. Although it was a gift of divine favor that the Birth of the Savior should become recognizable to the nations, nevertheless, to understand the wonder of the sign, the wise men were also able to be reminded through the ancient pronouncements of Balaam, for they knew that it had at one time been spread abroad in a famous and memorable prediction: "A star will appear out of Jacob, and a man will rise up from Israel. He will rule over the nations."[52] So the three men, stirred by God through the shining of this unusual star, follow the course of its gleaming light ahead of them, thinking that they would find the indicated child in the royal city of Jerusalem.

When this conjecture had failed them, however, they learned from scribes and teachers of the Jews what the Sacred

49. Cf. Phil 2.6.
51. Cf. Phil 2.7.
50. Cf. 1 Pt 1.20.
52. Cf. Nm 24.17.

Scriptures had told about the Birth of Christ. Encouraged by the double evidence, they sought him out with an even more ardent faith, the one to whom both the brightness of the star and the authority of prophets pointed.

(2) When the divine oracle was put forth in the responses made by priests, the word of the Spirit was made clear, the one which said: "And you, Bethlehem of Judah, are not least among the princes of Judah, for out of you will come the leader who will rule my people Israel."[53] How easy and how logical it would have been for the Hebrew leaders to believe what they taught. Evidently, however, they understood it in a carnal manner (just as Herod did) and reckoned that Christ's kingdom would be like the powers in this world. They hoped for a temporal leader while Herod feared an earthly rival.

You are disturbed by a useless fear, Herod. In vain do you attempt to rage against the Child you suspect. Your realm does not encompass Christ, nor does the Lord of the world care about the meager limits within which you wield *the rod of* your power. He whom you do not wish to see reign in Judea reigns everywhere. You yourself would reign more happily if you would submit to his rule. Why not turn into honest service that which you resolve to do in falsehood and guile? Go with the wise men and worship the true King in humble adoration. More inclined as you are toward the Jewish blindness, you do not imitate the faith of these Gentiles. You turn your perverse heart to cruel wiles. Yet you are not going to kill the one you fear, nor will you harm those whom you eliminate.

3. Then, dearly beloved, when the wise men had been led into Bethlehem by following the star's guidance, "they rejoiced with a very great joy," as the Evangelist has related, "and, entering the abode, they saw the Child with Mary his Mother. Prostrating themselves, they adored him. Upon opening their treasure chests, they offered him gifts of gold, frankincense, and myrrh."[54] *O wonderful faith of perfect knowledge, which earthly wisdom did not teach, but the Holy Spirit instilled!*[55]

---

53. Mt 2.6 and cf. Mi 5.2.   54. Mt 2.10–11.
55. Cf. 1 Cor 2.4–5.

How did these men, when they were setting out from their own country, having not yet seen Jesus nor noticed anything at the sight of him which they would venerate in such a fitting way, how did they make this selection of gifts to offer him? It could only have been because a brighter ray of truth—over and above the sight of the star which excited their gaze—taught their hearts. Even before they began to undertake the journey, they understood that the one who had been indicated to them would require royal honor with gold, divine worship with frankincense, and the confession of mortality with myrrh.

(2) These things, certainly, in being believed and understood (to the extent that they pertained to the enlightenment of faith) were able to suffice for them. They did not search out with physical vision that which they had seen in the fullest sight of mind. Yet their diligence in this service to wisdom persevered until they saw the child, and this diligence thereby benefited the people of a future age and those of our own time. Just as it benefited us for Thomas *the apostle* to feel with his hand the marks left by wounds on the Lord's body after his Resurrection, so also it profits us that the wise men gave proof of his Infancy in beholding him. So the wise men saw and worshipped this Child from the tribe of Judah, "from the seed of David according to the flesh,"[56] "made from a woman, born under the law,"[57] the law which "he had come not to destroy, but to fulfill."[58]

(3) They saw and adored the Child, small when it came to size, dependent on others for help, unable to speak, and in no way different from the general condition of human infancy. Certainly, the proofs which attributed to him the majesty of an invisible divinity were reliable. Likewise, it ought to have great probative value that the Word made flesh and that the eternal essence of God's Son took up true human nature, preventing the miracles of ineffable works that would follow or the punishments of sufferings he would undertake from disturbing the mystery of faith through contradictory elements. No one could in any way be justified unless they come to believe that the Lord Jesus is both true God and true man.

---

56. Rom 1.3.   57. Gal 4.4.
58. Mt 5.17.

4. It is to this unique faith, dearly beloved, and to the truth preached through all ages that the diabolical godlessness of Manichaeans gives resistance. They have woven for themselves a web of cursed doctrine from sacrilegious and made-up lies, in order to kill the souls of those who had been deceived. Through the disasters of these insane opinions, they rushed forth headlong—to the point of contriving for themselves a Christ with a false body, who in himself presented nothing solid and nothing real to the eyes and actions of men, but showed off an empty image of pretended flesh. They would have it seem unfitting that God the Son of God should be believed to have inserted himself into the womb of a woman and to have subjected his majesty to this disgrace. They would have it seem unfitting that God the Son of God, intertwined with the nature of flesh, would have been born in a real body of human substance.

In point of fact, however, this whole work does not constitute an insult to him, but a manifestation of his power. It should not be thought of as defilement, but as glorious condescension. If visible light does not become damaged by any of the dirt with which it may be surrounded, and if dirty and murky places do not infect the glow of the sun's rays (which no one doubts to be a physical creation), then what thing could by any quality of its own defile the essence of that eternal and incorporeal light? This essence offered purification to the creature (which it had made according to its own image) by becoming associated with it. It did not thereby contract any stain, but healed the wounds of infirmity in such a way as not to allow any compromise of its power.

(2) This "great" and indescribable "mystery of" divine "compassion"[59] was announced by all the testimonies of Holy Scripture. Still, those of whom we speak—enemies of truth—have scorned the "law given through Moses"[60] along with the divinely inspired oracles of prophets. They have adulterated the pages of the Gospels themselves and those of the apostolic writ-

---

59. Cf. 1 Tm 3.16.
60. Cf. Jn 1.17.

ings by deleting certain things and adding others. They invent many books of falsehoods for themselves under the names of the apostles and even put words in the mouth of the Savior himself—all this in order to reinforce the fabrications of their error and to pour a deadly poison into the minds of those they want to deceive.

They saw how everything was opposed to them, all things were contradicting them, and how the madness of their sacrilegious impiety was refuted not only by the New Testament but even by the Old. Persisting nevertheless in their furious lies, they do not cease to disturb the Church of God by their deceits, and they persuade those pitiable people whom they could ensnare to deny that the Lord Jesus Christ took on true human nature, to deny that he was truly crucified for the salvation of the world, to deny that the blood of Redemption and the water of Baptism flowed from his side after it had been wounded by the lance, to deny that he was buried and raised on the third day, to deny that, as the disciples looked on, he was raised above all the heights of heaven to sit at the right hand of the Father. When the whole truth of the Apostolic Creed has been taken away, there is no fear to frighten wicked men, no hope to arouse the holy, and so they deny that Christ will judge the living and the dead. They teach those, from whom they have taken away the power of such great mysteries, to worship Christ in the sun and the moon, and, under the name of the Holy Spirit, to adore Manes himself, the very teacher of such godlessness.

5. Let today's festival then, dearly beloved, benefit all "for strengthening **our** *your* hearts in" fidelity and "truth."[61] Let the Catholic Faith be reinforced by the fact of that visible Infancy of our Savior, and let the godlessness of those who deny the flesh of our nature in Christ be accursed. Blessed John the apostle warned us of this in no uncertain terms when he said: "Every spirit who acknowledges that Christ Jesus has come in the flesh is of God. Every spirit who [refuses to acknowledge this of] Jesus is not from God and is antichrist."[62]

61. Cf. Jas 5.8 and 2 Pt 1.12.
62. 1 Jn 4.2–3.

No Christian, therefore, has anything in common with people of this kind, and there should be no alliance and no fellowship with such. May it be of benefit to the whole Church that many of them by the Lord's **discovery** *mercy* have been found out, and that the sacrileges in which they were living have been revealed by their own confession. May they deceive no one by their abstinence from foods, by the dirt on their clothes, by the pallor of their faces. Those fasts are not pure which come not for the sake of self-control, but for the art of pretense. Thus far they have harmed only the unwatchful; thus far they have deluded only the uninformed. After this, however, no one's lapse will be excusable, nor can anyone be considered simple-minded. Wicked indeed and perverse is the one who will then be discovered to have been bound up in this abominable error.

(2) We not only do not hold back, but even encourage, compassion, wisely and divinely set up by the Church, that even for such people you should pray to the Lord with us. We also, with tears of sorrow, have pity upon the downfall of misled souls. Following the example of the Apostle's compassion, "we are made weak with the weak,"[63] and "we weep with those who weep."[64] We hope that the mercy of God may be gained with many tears and requisite satisfaction on the part of those who have lapsed. While we live in this body, no one's rehabilitation is to be despaired of. We should desire the amendment of all, with the Lord helping us, who "raises up those who have been broken down, sets captives free, gives sight to the blind,"[65] to whom is honor and glory *with the Father and with the Holy Spirit* forever and ever. Amen.

Sermon 35

6 January 445

Today's feast, dearly beloved, has been made illustrious as you know by the appearance of our Lord and Savior. This is

63. Cf. 2 Cor 11.29.
64. Cf. Rom 12.15.
65. Cf. Ps 145(146).7–8.

the day on which a guiding star led three wise men to recognize and worship the Son of God. It has been determined that the memory of this event should be celebrated with annual ceremonies, so that, while the Gospel story is repeated over and over, the mystery of salvation may always, by its wonderful power, work itself into the hearts of those who understand.

(2) Many proofs that declared by clear signs the bodily Birth of the Lord had preceded it: when the Blessed Virgin Mary heard and believed that she would be made fruitful by the Holy Spirit and would bear a son; when, at her greeting, John (in the womb of Elizabeth and not yet born) was stirred with prophetic exultation—as if even from within the body of his Mother he were already crying out, "Behold the Lamb of God, behold the one who takes away the sins of the world"[66]; or when the angel announced the Lord's arrival and the shepherds were surrounded by the light of the heavenly host, so that they could have no doubts about the majesty of the Boy whom they were to see in the manger, nor could they think he had been brought forth only in the nature of a man, since the multitude of the heavenly host were at his service.

But these and other things of this kind seem to have come to the notice of only a few persons at that point, to those who were related to the Blessed Virgin Mary or belonged to the family of Saint Joseph. This sign, however—which effectively moved the wise men who lived far away and drew them irresistibly to the Lord Jesus—was undoubtedly a mystery of that grace and the beginning of that call by which the Gospel of Christ was to be preached not in Judea only, but also in the whole world. Through that star, brilliant to the sight of these wise men but not reflected in the eyes of Israelites, through that star was signified both the enlightenment of Gentiles and the blindness of Jews.

2. As is clearly evident, the pattern of these mystical events remains, dearly beloved, and what was begun by way of a symbol has been filled out with the reality. When the star shines from heaven by grace, three wise men in every nation, sum-

---

66. Jn 1.29.

moned by the brilliance of the Gospel's light, hurry on a daily basis to worship the power of the supreme King.

Personifying the devil, Herod too rages and groans over seeing the kingdom of his wickedness taken from him in those who pass over to Christ. Wherefore, if he kills the children, he thinks that he is putting Jesus to death. He does indeed strive to do this incessantly, trying to tear the Holy Spirit away from those who have been just recently born again, and trying to snuff out what appears to be the infancy of a tender faith.

As for the Jews who wanted to be outside the kingdom of Christ, they are still in a way under the rule of Herod. While the enemy of the Savior has dominion over them, they serve a foreign power as if they did not know the prophecy of Jacob: "There will not be lacking a prince from Judah, nor a leader from his loins, until the one for whom it has been reserved should come, and he it is whom the nations await."[67] Still, they do not yet understand what they nevertheless cannot deny, and their minds do not grasp what they know by the word of Scripture.

Truth proves a stumbling block to impaired teachers, and light becomes darkness to blind instructors. So, when asked, they reply that it is in Bethlehem that Christ is born. Yet they do not follow their own knowledge, a knowledge in which they instruct others. They have thus lost the royal succession, the worth of their sacrifices, the very place of prayer, and the priestly order. Since all things are closed to them and they find all things at an end for themselves, they do not see that these things have been transferred over into Christ.

(2) What these three men (representing all nations) obtained when they worshipped the Lord, the whole world acquires in its peoples through the faith that "justifies the godless."[68] Adopted children receive the Lord's inheritance, prepared from all eternity, while those who seemed to be the lawful heirs lose it. Come to your senses, Jew, come to your senses at last. Abandon your infidelity and convert to the Redeemer who re-

---

67. Gn 49.10.
68. Cf. Rom 4.5.

deemed you as well. Do not fear the enormity of your crime, for "he calls not the virtuous but sinners,"[69] nor will he who prayed for you when he was crucified[70] reject you because of your [past] godlessness. Cancel the harsh sentence of your cruel ancestors. Do not allow yourselves to be bound by the curse of those who shouted concerning Christ, "His blood be upon us and upon our children,"[71] and in so doing poured over onto you the guilt for their crime. Return to the Merciful One. Avail yourselves of the clemency of the Forgiving One. The cruelty of your wickedness has been changed into the cause of your salvation. He lives, the one you wanted to kill. Acknowledge the one who was denied, worship the one who was sold, so that you might benefit from the goodness of the one whom your ill will could not harm.

3. We ought then, dearly beloved, to desire and to work for what belongs to true love, which we owe even "to our enemies" (according to the Lord's words),[72] so that this same people who fell away from that spiritual nobility of their fathers might be "engrafted"[73] back into the branches of their tree. This sort of good will recommends us very much to God. Their failure has made room for mercy on our part, so that our faith might recall "them" to that "desire" to receive salvation.[74] It is becoming that the life of holy ones should benefit not only themselves but others as well. What cannot be accomplished in them with words can often be brought about through example.

When we consider, dearly beloved, the ineffable generosity of God in his gifts to us, we should be "cooperators"[75] with the grace of God "working in us."[76] Not into the possession of those who sleep does the kingdom of heaven come, nor is the beatitude of eternity bestowed upon those who are sluggish with idleness and laziness. Instead, as the Apostle says, "if we suffer with him, we will also be glorified with him."[77] We must run

69. Mt 9.13.
70. Cf. Lk 23.34.
71. Mt 27.25.
72. Cf. Mt 5.44.
73. Cf. Rom 11.23.
74. Cf. Rom 11.11.
75. Cf. 1 Cor 3.9.
76. Cf. 1 Cor 12.6, Eph 3.20, and Phil 2.13.
77. Rom 8.17.

along the "Way" which the Lord has told us he himself is.[78] He saw to our interests both with the objective mystery and with the example he provided, without any merits recommending us—in order to bring those who have been called into adoption to salvation through the former, and, through the latter, to encourage their labors.

These labors, dearly beloved, are not only far from harsh and burdensome to loyal sons and good servants, but are even pleasant and light, as the Lord said: "Come to me, all you who labor and are burdened, and I will refresh you. Take my yoke upon you and learn from me, for I am meek and humble of heart, and you will find rest for your souls. For my yoke is pleasant and my burden light."[79] Nothing, then, poses any difficulty for the humble, dearly beloved, or any harshness for the gentle. All commandments are easy to carry out when grace provides help and obedience softens authority.

Day after day the words of God sound in our ears, and every one is made to know what pleases divine justice. Because that judgment by which "each one will receive, in accordance with how they have behaved, either good or bad,"[80] because that judgment has been postponed by the "patience and goodness"[81] of the one that is to judge, the hearts of unbelievers bank on receiving impunity for their wickedness. They think that the quality of human actions has no relationship to the disapproval of divine providence—as if evil deeds were not routinely struck down with the most obvious punishments, or as if the fear of heavenly threats had not made itself known. By these has faith been encouraged and faithlessness rebuked.

4. In spite of all these things, God remains well disposed toward everyone. To no one does he deny his mercy. Why, he even bestows many good things indiscriminately upon all. He prefers to invite with acts of kindness those whom he could rightly subdue with punishments. Delay in retribution makes room for repentance. It cannot be said, however, that there is no vengeance where conversion does not take place. For, a

78. Cf. Jn 14.6.
80. 2 Cor 5.10.
79. Mt 11.28–30.
81. Cf. Rom 2.4.

hard and ungrateful mind becomes already its own punishment. It suffers in its conscience whatever has been deferred by the goodness of God.

Not for that reason, however, should offenders enjoy their sins, lest the end of this life find them in their actions. In hell there is no amendment. No means of satisfaction can be given where no act of the will remains any longer, as David says in prophecy: "Since in death there is no one who remembers you. Who will give you thanks in hell?"[82] Let us flee harmful pleasures, dangerous joys, and desires which perish right away. What fruit is there, what use is there, in wanting these things incessantly, things that we must abandon even if they do not abandon us? Let the love of ephemeral things be transferred to incorruptible ones. Let hearts called to lofty things find their enjoyment in heavenly delights.

Strengthen your friendships with the holy angels. Enter into the "city" of God[83] promised us as a home. Join yourselves with patriarchs, prophets, apostles, and martyrs. Take your joy from the same source as they. Desire their riches. Canvass for their prayers by imitating them closely. We shall have a common dignity with those to whom we have been united in fellowship. While time has been conceded to us for accomplishing the commands of God, "Glorify God in your body,"[84] and "Shine," dearly beloved, "like bright stars in this world."[85] May the lamps of your minds be always "burning."[86] May nothing "shadowy" remain in your hearts.[87]

As the Apostle says, "You were darkness once, but now you are light in the Lord."[88] Let that which has gone before in the figure of the three wise men be filled out in you. "Let your light shine before human beings in such a way that they, upon seeing your good works, might glorify your Father who is in heaven."[89] As it is a great sin when, on account of bad Christians, "the name of the Lord is blasphemed among the infi-

---

82. Ps 6.6.
83. Cf. Heb 11.16.
84. 1 Cor 6.20.
85. Phil 2.15.
86. Cf. Lk 12.35.
87. Cf. Mt 6.23 and Lk 11.34–35.
88. Eph 5.8.
89. Mt 5.16.

dels,"⁹⁰ so there is great merit in love when that name is blessed on account of the holy lives led by his servants. To him is honor and glory forever and ever. Amen.

Sermon 36

6 January 451

We must, dearly beloved, honor with special devotion the day on which Christ, the Savior of the world, first appeared to the nations. We must take into our own hearts today those same joys which were in the hearts of the three wise men. Roused by the signal of a new star that led them, they worshipped before their eyes the King of heaven and earth—in whom they had believed when he was but promised. This day was not so limited that the power of its work (revealed back then) would have passed away and nothing would have come to us but the report of its occurrence—which faith would accept and memory celebrate. Rather—with God multiplying his gifts—even our own times experience from day to day whatever those first days held.

Of course the narrative of the Gospel passage chiefly records those days when three men, whom neither prophetic preaching had taught nor the authority of law instructed, came from the most remote parts of the East to meet God. Still, it is this same thing that we see happening more clearly now—and more frequently—in the enlightening of all those who have been called. Isaiah's prophecy has been fulfilled, the one that said: "The Lord has revealed his holy arm in the sight of all the nations, and all the nations of the earth will see the salvation which is from our God."⁹¹ At another point, he says: "Those who were not told about him will see, and those who did not hear, will understand."⁹²

Consequently, when we see people given over to worldly wisdom and far removed from the confession of Jesus Christ, when we see them being led out from the depths of error and

90. Cf. Rom 2.24 and Is 52.5.   91. Is 52.10.
92. Is 52.15 and Rom 15.21.

called to a knowledge of the true light, the splendor of divine grace is undoubtedly at work. Whatever new light appears in clouded hearts shines with the rays of this same star, so that souls touched with its brightness are both moved with wonder on account of it and drawn by its lead to adoration of the Lord.

(2) But if we are willing to look carefully with the mind into how that threefold splendor of gifts would be offered by all who come to Christ with the steps of faith, would not the same offering be celebrated in the hearts of those who have a correct faith? Whoever acknowledges Christ as King of the universe pulls gold from the heart's coffer. Whoever believes that the Only-Begotten of God has united the true nature of humanity to himself gives an offering of myrrh. Whoever confesses that in nothing is [the Son] unequal to his Father's majesty worships him with a kind of incense.

2. When we look at these comparisons in detail, dearly beloved, we find that the role of Herod is not absent either. As the devil goaded him on in secret back then, so now he imitates him without tiring. He suffers torment from the enlightenment of all nations, torture from the daily erosion of his power—grieving that he has been deserted on all sides, while the true King receives worship throughout the world. He prepares deceit, devises plots, and erupts into slaughter. So as to make use of those whom he had up to then deceived, he burns with jealousy against the Jews, lies in wait with pretense for heretics, becomes inflamed with rage against pagans. He sees that the power of the eternal King cannot be overcome, the King whose Death has extinguished the power of death itself. As a result, the devil has marshaled all his skill for doing harm against those who truly serve the King. He hardens some through the "puffing up of knowledge"[93] about the law, perverts some through his invention of false religions, and incites still others to the rage of persecution.

Yet the one who has crowned the little boys with the glory of martyrdom also overcomes and destroys this madness of the

---

93. Cf. 1 Cor 8.1.

other Herod. He has imparted such unconquerable love to his believers that they dare to say in the Apostle's words: "What will separate us from the love of Christ? Tribulation? Distress? Persecution? Hunger? Nakedness? Danger? The sword? As it has been written, 'For your sake we are being put to death all day long. We are looked upon as sheep to be slaughtered. Yet, in all this, we overcome on account of the one who has loved us.' "[94]

3. We believe, dearly beloved, that this fortitude was necessary not only in those times when kings of the world and all rulers of the earth were raging against the people of God in impious bloodshed. These rulers considered it to be for their greater glory if they could remove the name of Christian from the earth. Yet they were unaware of the fact that the Church of God was being enlarged by the madness of their cruelty. Through the torture and death of blessed martyrs (who were thought to be thereby diminished in number), they were, rather, being increased as a result their example. Finally, the assaults made by these persecutors contributed so much to our faith that nothing adorns royal leadership more than the fact that lords of the world are members of Christ. They do not glory so much in having been born for sovereignty as they rejoice in their rebirth through Baptism.

(2) Storms of earlier disturbances have quieted down, and a certain calm appears to smile upon battles that have ended just a short time ago. Yet we must be vigilant to avoid those dangers which arise from the relaxation of peace itself. Ineffective in open persecutions, the adversary vents his fury through the wile of stealthy harm. Those whom he has not destroyed by the onslaught of affliction he lays low by a downfall through pleasure. Upon seeing that the faith of princes stands in his way and that the undivided Trinity of the one divinity is worshipped no less actively in palaces than in churches, he grieves that the shedding of Christian blood has been forbidden him, and he attacks the morals of those whose death he cannot bring about.

---

94. Rom 8.35–37.

He exchanges the terror of proscriptions for the fire of avarice, ruining with greed those whom he could not break with losses. Accustomed to his own wickedness as a result of long practice, he has not in his malice set aside hate. He has merely turned his abilities toward subjecting to himself the minds of believers through enticement. Those whom he cannot disturb with torture he inflames with lust. He sows discord, ignites hatred, and stirs up tongues. To prevent more cautious hearts from withdrawing out of his unlawful snares, he suggests the means for carrying through with crimes. This for him constitutes the fruit of all his falsehood, that he who is not worshipped by the sacrifice of animals and the burning of incense might be served by any sort of crime whatsoever.

4. Our peace also has its dangers, dearly beloved. In vain do people feel secure as a result of freedom for their faith if they do not resist the desires of vice. By the quality of works is the human heart made known, and outward actions disclose the beauty of souls. There are some, as the Apostle says, who "profess to know God, but deny him through their deeds."[95] Truly the guilt of denial is incurred when the ears have heard what is good, but the conscience does not hold on to it. The frailty of the human condition easily slides into sin. Because there is no sin without taking pleasure in it, human frailty readily gives in to the deceptive enjoyment.

Let us retreat quickly from carnal desires to the spiritual shelter. Let the soul that has knowledge of its God turn itself away from the suggestions of the ill-advising enemy. Let the patience of God be its defense. Let it not relish obstinacy in sin merely because vengeance has been put off. Let sinners not feel complacent about impunity. If they lose the time for repentance, they will find that there is no longer any room for mercy, since the prophet says: "Because in death there is no one who remembers you. Who will give you thanks in hell?"[96]

(2) Whoever finds the healing of correction to be difficult should flee to the mercy of God for help and beg that the chains

---

95. Ti 1.16.
96. Ps 6.6.

of evil habit be broken away from them, for "the Lord lifts up all who collapse, and raises up all who have been broken down."[97] No, the prayer of a believer will not be empty, since our merciful God "will accomplish the intentions of those who fear him."[98] He will give what has been asked for, since he provided the inspiration to ask it. Through our Lord Jesus Christ, living and reigning with the Father and the Holy Spirit for ever and ever. Amen.

Sermon 37

6 January 452

Recalling the deeds performed by the Savior of the human race brings us great profit, dearly beloved—if what we venerate as something believed we also take on to be imitated. In the arrangement of Christ's mysteries, there are both effects of grace and influences from doctrine, for we follow in the example of his works the one whom we acknowledge in the spirit of faith. Those very first things which the Son of God experienced in being born of his Virgin Mother set us on the road to progress in holiness.

There appear to those of an upright heart in one and the same Person both human lowliness and divine majesty. Whom the cradle shows to be an Infant, heaven and heavenly things call their Maker. That Boy with a small body is Lord and Ruler of the world. He who is encompassed by no limits is held in the arms of his Mother. But it is in these things that the healing of our wounds and the raising up of our abasement rest, for, unless such diversity had come together as one, human nature could not be reconciled to God.

2. Our remedies, then, have established for us a rule of living, and a pattern has been given for our conduct, a pattern from which medicine can be applied to the dead. Not inappropriately, when the brightness of a new star had led three wise men to worship Jesus, they did not see him ruling over demons, not

---

97. Ps 144(145).14.
98. Cf. Ps 144(145).19.

raising the dead, not restoring sight to the blind or mobility to the lame or speech to the dumb, nor in any action of divine power. They saw him, rather, as a Child—silent, at rest, placed in the care of his Mother—in a situation where there appeared no indication of power.

From this lowliness, however, a great miracle was presented. Consequently, the mere sight of that Sacred Infancy to which God the Son of God had adapted himself was bringing to their eyes a preaching that would be imparted to their ears. What the sound of his voice was not yet presenting, the activity of sight was teaching them. For the entire victory of the Savior, the one that overcame the devil and the world, began in humility and ended in humility. Its appointed time began under persecution and ended under persecution. Neither the endurance of suffering was lacking to the child, nor the gentleness of a child to the one who would suffer. For, the Only-Begotten Son of God undertook by a single inclination of his majesty both the will to be born as a human being and the ability to be killed by human beings.

3. Almighty God, therefore, made our extremely bad situation good[99] through his unique lowliness and "destroyed death" along with the author "of death."[100] He did not refuse anything that his persecutors brought down on him. In obedience to the Father, he bore the cruelties of violent men with the meekest docility. How humble we ought to be, then, how patient, we who, when we meet with any distress, never undergo anything we do not deserve! "Who will boast that they have a pure heart or that they are clean from sin?"[101] Blessed John says, "If we say we have no sin, we are deceiving ourselves and the truth is not in us."[102]

Who will be found so free from guilt that they have not in themselves anything for justice to condemn or mercy to forgive? Consequently, dearly beloved, the whole learning of Christian wisdom consists not in abundance of words, not in cleverness at disputing, not in desire for praise and glory, but

99. Cf. 1 Tm 1.10.
101. Prv 20.9.
100. Cf. Heb 2.14.
102. 1 Jn 1.8.

in a true and willing humility. This is what the Lord Jesus Christ chose and taught from within the womb of his Mother right up to his torment on the cross—by enduring everything with fortitude.

(2) When the disciples, as the Evangelist says, arguing among themselves as to "which one of them would be greater in the kingdom of heaven, [Jesus] called a little child and stood him in their midst and said: 'Amen, I say to you, unless you change yourselves and become like little children, you will not enter the kingdom of heaven. Whoever, therefore, humble themselves like this child will be the greater in the kingdom of heaven.' "[103]

Christ loves the Childhood that he first took up in both soul and body. Christ loves childhood, the teacher of humility, the rule of innocence, the image of gentleness. Christ loves childhood, to which he directs the characters of older people, to which he brings back old age. Those whom he would raise up to an eternal kingdom he disposes to follow his own example.

4. So that we may be able to recognize clearly how this wonderful change might be accomplished and by what alteration we might return to the level of childhood, let blessed Paul teach us and say, "Do not be made into children with respect to your senses, but become very little with respect to wickedness."[104] It is not to the amusements of childhood and to our imperfect beginnings that we must return, but we must extract from childhood something fitting for later years. May disturbances pass speedily and peace return quickly. May there be no memory of offenses, no desire for importance, but only a love for sharing things together and a natural equality. It is a great good not to know how to harm and not to have a taste for malice. To inflict and to pay back injury belongs to the wisdom of this world, but "to repay evil for evil to no one"[105] represents the childhood of Christian self-possession.

(2) It is to this likeness of little children, dearly beloved, that the mystery of today's feast invites you. Our Savior, the child

103. Mt 18.1–4.
105. Cf. Rom 12.17.
104. 1 Cor 14.20.

worshipped by those wise men, suggests this pattern of humility to you. In order to show what glory he has prepared for those who imitate him, he has consecrated with martyrdom those who came forth at the time of his appearance. Begotten at Bethlehem, where Christ was born, they became participants in his Passion by sharing his age.

Let humility be loved. Let every exaltation be avoided by the faithful. Let all prefer others to themselves. "Let none seek their own thing, but that of another."[106] That way, when an inclination to good will abounds in us all, the poison of hate might not be found in any one: "For, those who exalt themselves will be humbled, and those who humble themselves will be exalted."[107]

Sermon 38

6 January 453

Both the Gospel narrative and the regularity of this observance, dearly beloved, have disclosed to you the source of and reason for today's solemnity. It is not necessary now to repeat what happened with regard to the human beginnings of our Savior, that is, to speak about the brightness of a new star, about the wise men and their gifts, about the fury of Herod and the slaughter of the innocents. You know that the shining star prefigured God's grace, those three men the calling of Gentiles, that godless king the cruelty of pagans, and the murder of those children the prototype for all martyrs.

I must, nevertheless, meet your expectations by fulfilling the priestly duty of giving a talk on this most sacred day. I will try—as much as I can with the help of God's Spirit—to go along the paths of understanding, until we arrive at a realization of the fact that the mystery of this feast pertains to the times of all believers and until that which had been adored of old in the planned arrangement should not in any way be considered something remote.

---

106. Cf. 1 Cor 10.24.
107. Lk 14.11.

2. No Christian soul ought to think anything unworthy about the majesty of God's Son. Each one is bound to progress toward higher levels when the rudiments of a growing faith have been passed by. Yet the infirmity of the human mind, as it comes to accept the true humanity of Christ, cannot help but tremble on account of this participation with our nature. It cannot help but arrive only with great difficulty (through his bodily origins and growth) at an acknowledgment of a single divinity with the Father. Where the ray of heavenly light has been reflected in murky thoughts, the splendor of truth breaks off any resistance to faith. Then, a free heart (set loose from visible things) may follow the light of understanding as it would a star that was leading.

As the Apostle says, "the Lord Jesus Christ is in the glory of God the Father."[108] Along these lines, the one whom he venerated lying humbly in the cradle, he also confidently adores reigning with the Father. This manifestation, dearly beloved, dispels the clouds of hesitant souls and makes the Son of God known in such a way that these souls feel no obstacle in the fact that the same one is also the Son of a human being. It pertains to the dignity of this present feast when carnal senses are carried across from human to divine things. In this way, the signs of his power raise up those whom the experiences of infirmity weigh down. Thus, the real Infancy of our Savior serves to reveal his divinity. Our nature and our condition stood in need of such help, for humility could not restore the human race without majesty, nor majesty without humility.

3. Now, however, a keeping of God's commandments shines forth in the progress of individual believers and that saying becomes fulfilled where it was stated, "Let your light shine before human beings in such a way that they might see your good works and give praise to your Father in heaven."[109] If that is the case, who would not understand the divinity to be present where they behold a manifestation of true power? Indeed, without God there is no true power. Power does not hold any

108. Phil 2.11.
109. Mt 5.16.

characteristic of divinity unless it grows with the spirit of his Maker. Since the Lord said to his disciples, "Without me you can do nothing,"[110] there is no doubt that a human being who does good has from God both the effect of his work as well as the beginnings of the intention to do it.

So the Apostle, that most prolific adviser to the faithful, states: "With fear and trembling, work out your salvation, for it is God who (out of his good will) works in you both the will to do something and the ability to accomplish it."[111] It causes trembling and fear for the saints to think that, by becoming complacent with the works of compassion, they might lose the assistance of grace and be left to the weakness of their nature.

If any wish to find out whether God dwells in them (God, about whom it is said, "God is wonderful in his saints"[112]) let them investigate with a sincere examination the depths of their own hearts. Let them wisely ask how they can resist pride with humility, how they can struggle against ill will with benevolence, how they might not be taken in by the tongues of flatterers, and how they might take pleasure in the successes of others. Let them ask whether they do not want to "return evil for evil,"[113] and whether they prefer to forget injuries and let them go unavenged rather than to lose the image and likeness of their Creator. With gifts for everyone, God arouses all "to a knowledge of him"[114] and "rains on just and unjust, making his sun rise over the good and the bad."[115]

4. If in many people, however, the examination of a diligent search causes difficulty, let them seek out love, that mother of all virtues, in the secret places of their mind. If, with their hearts focused, they find that love of God and neighbor which causes them even to want for their enemies what they desire for themselves, whoever happen to be of this sort should not doubt that God rules over them and dwells in them. They receive God so much the more honorably if "they glory" not in themselves but "in the Lord."[116] Those who are told, "The king-

---

110. Jn 15.5.
111. Phil 2.12–13.
112. Ps 67(68).36.
113. Cf. Rom 12.17.
114. Cf. 1 Tm 2.4.
115. Cf. Mt 5.45.
116. Cf. 1 Cor 1.31 and 2 Cor 10.17.

dom of God is within you,"[117] "are led" to do nothing except "by the Spirit"[118] of the one by whose command they are ruled.

Since we know then, dearly beloved, that "God is love,"[119] "who works all things in everyone,"[120] pursue love in such a way that the hearts of all believers everywhere might flow together into a single desire for chaste love. May passing and empty things not take hold of us. Let us strive with a constant desire toward those things that will always remain. For the mystery of the present feast ought to be with us perpetually. It will undoubtedly be celebrated without end, if in all our actions the Lord Jesus Christ becomes manifest, who with the Father and the Holy Spirit lives and reigns forever and ever. Amen.

117. Lk 17.21.
118. Cf. Rom 8.14.
119. 1 Jn 4.16.
120. 1 Cor 12.6.

DAYS OF FAST IN LENT

These sermons cover the years 441–445, 451–455, and perhaps also 457–458. As he had with the *Collection* sermons, Leo reminds his audience that the "fasts have been ordained by the holy apostles through the Holy Spirit" (*Serms.* 47.1 and 50.2), and that ". . . there are none who do not need renewal" (*Serm.* 43.1). Preparation for the coming Feast of the Resurrection includes the many ways in which people can repair their souls for celebrating the great miracle. "There are none so perfect and so holy that they cannot be more perfect and more holy" (*Serm.* 40.1). Thorough examination of the heart's recesses (*Serm.* 41.1) will not only reveal the trickeries to which we are susceptible, but will reveal also the goodness and the works of mercy that will overcome them (*Serms.* 39.5, 40.5, 42.2, 43.5, 49.1, and 50.2).

In sermon 42.2, Leo inveighs against the Manichaeans who refuse to eat and drink certain things, believing them to be evil. Leo says: ". . . the good Creator has made all things good, it is our motive which brings evil" (*Serm.* 42.4). He thereby clearly delineates the meaning of Christian fasting.

Sermon 39

9 February 441 (Recension A)[1]

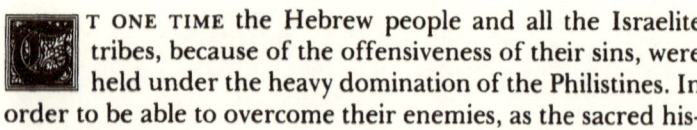T ONE TIME the Hebrew people and all the Israelite tribes, because of the offensiveness of their sins, were held under the heavy domination of the Philistines. In order to be able to overcome their enemies, as the sacred history shows, they restored strength of soul and body with a self-

---

1. This sermon comes down to us in two recensions. Recension A had been composed in 441. Recension B appears to represent a revision made by Leo himself at some later date. Material found in both recensions will appear in normal text. Material found only in Recension A will appear in **bold**. Material found only in Recension B will appear in *italics*. Some material found in both recensions but in a different order will be reproduced in both bold and italics in their proper order. Some material that does not coincide between the two versions of the Latin text but does not affect the English translation (such as word order or certain syntactical variants) will not be indicated.

imposed fast. They had judged rightly that they deserved that hard and wretched subjection because of neglect of God's commandments and the corruption of their lives, and that in vain did they fight with weapons unless they had first made war on their sins. By abstaining, therefore, from food and drink they imposed the penalty of severe punishment on themselves, and to conquer their enemies, they first conquered the enticement of gluttony in themselves. In this way it happened that the fierce adversaries and harsh masters yielded to them fasting whom they had overcome when full.[2]

(2) We too, dearly beloved, situated as we are among many struggles and battles, **if we wish to overcome our enemies in the same way, we may be healed by the same practice. Indeed, our situation is the same as theirs, seeing that they were attacked by bodily adversaries, we by spiritual enemies.** *if we wish to use the same remedies, we will be healed by the same practice. Our situation is nearly the same as theirs, seeing that, as they were attacked by bodily adversaries, so we are greatly attacked by spiritual enemies.* If our spiritual enemies may be overcome by the correction of our lives bestowed on us through the grace of God, even the force of our bodily enemies will also give way to us. They will be weakened by our correction, since, not their merits, but our own sins, made them onerous to us.

2. Wherefore, dearly beloved, in order that we may be able to overcome *all* our enemies, let us seek divine help by observing the commands of heaven, knowing that in no other way can we *hope to* prevail over our foes except by prevailing over ourselves as well. We have many struggles within ourselves; "the flesh lusts [after one thing] against the spirit, and the spirit [after another thing] against the flesh."[3] If in this opposition the desires of the body are stronger, the soul will shamefully lose dignity proper to it, and it will be calamitous for it to be a slave to what it ought to govern. But if the mind, submissive to its Ruler and to heavenly gifts, tramples on the lures of earthly indulgence and does not allow "sin to reign

2. Cf. 1 Sm 7.6–11.
3. Cf. Gal 5.17.

in its own body,"⁴ reason will hold a well-ordered leadership, and no deceit of "spiritual evil"⁵ will weaken its defenses. There is true peace for a human being and true liberty when the flesh is ruled by the soul, and the soul is governed by God as Director.

(2) Although this exercise, dearly beloved, may be undertaken profitably at any time in order to overcome with constant zeal the ever-watchful enemy, nevertheless, we ought to pursue it more carefully and more eagerly now when those very cunning adversaries are lying in wait with shrewder craftiness. For they know that the holy days of Lent are pressing on us in the observance of which all past sloth is chastened and all negligence repaired. They concentrate the whole power of their ill will on this, that **we** *those* who are going to celebrate the holy Passover of the Lord may be found unworthy in some way, and the clemency **we** *they* had obtained may thus be changed to an offense.

3. As we come then, dearly beloved, to the beginning of Lent, that is, to more diligent service of the Lord, *because we are entering as if into some struggle in the holy work*, let us prepare our souls for the fight against temptation. Let us be clear that, as we are more zealous for our own salvation, so much the more violently will the adversaries attack us. But the one "who is with us" is stronger "than the one" against us,⁶ and we have power through him in whose strength we trust, because it was for this that the Lord allowed himself to be tempted by the tempter, that he might teach us by his example, as he strengthens us by his help. He conquered the adversary, as you just heard, dearly beloved, by the witness of the law,⁷ not by forceful power, so that by this very fact he might honor mankind more and punish the adversary more, since the enemy of the human race was to be overcome not as if by God, but rather as if by man.

He fought the battle then so that we too might fight it afterwards; he has conquered so that we too might conquer in the same way. There are

---

4. Cf. Rom 6.12.
6. Cf. 1 Jn 4.4.
5. Cf. Eph 6.12.
7. Cf. Mt 4.1–11.

no works of virtue, dearly beloved, without the trial of temptations, no "faith without testing,"[8] *no struggle without an enemy, no victory without a confrontation. This life of ours is in the midst of pitfalls, in the midst of battles. If we do not wish to be ensnared, we must watch; if we wish to overcome, we must fight. Thus said Solomon, "Son, when coming to the service of God, prepare your soul for temptation."*[9] *People filled with God's wisdom know that the pursuit of religion brings on the suffering of strife. When they foresee the danger of a battle, they give warning ahead of time that they are going to fight, lest, if the tempter approach them when unsuspecting, he would the more quickly wound them unprepared.*

4. *Dearly beloved, we who, established in divine learning, consciously approach the crisis of the present struggle should hear the Apostle saying, "Our struggle is not against flesh and blood, but against principalities and powers, against the rulers of this world of darkness, against spiritual evils in the heavens."*[10] *Let us not be unaware that these our enemies know that everything is done against them when we make attempts to act for our salvation, and in the very things that we want for our own good we provoke the adversary. So, by the spark of the devil's jealousy, this is the chronic disagreement between us and them, that because they have fallen from these good things to which we are born by God's help, they are tormented by our justifications. If we are raised, they fall; if we are healed, they are weakened. Our remedy is their injury, for by the curing of our wounds they are wounded.*

"So stand firm," dearly beloved, as the Apostle says, "in the truth of your mind as a belt around your waist, your feet shod in the preparation of the Gospel of peace, in all things carrying the shield of faith, by which you may be able to put out all the fiery darts of the evil one, and put on the helmet of salvation and the sword of the Spirit which is the word of God."[11] See then, dearly beloved, with what powerful weapons, with what unconquerable defenses *our leader, marked out by many triumphs and* the invincible captain of the Christian hosts has armed us. He has bound our loins with the bond of chastity, he has shod our feet with the cords of peace, for

---

8. Cf. Jas 1.3 and 1 Pt 1.7.
9. Sir 2.1.
10. Eph 6.12.
11. Eph 6.14–17.

a soldier ungirded is overcome quickly by the instigator of lewdness, and one unshod is easily bitten by the serpent. *He gave us the shield of faith as a protection for the whole body, he placed the helmet of salvation on our head, he equipped our right hand with the sword, that is, the "word of truth,"*[12] *so that the spiritual contenders may not only be safe from a wound but may also be able to wound their attacker.*

5. Relying on these weapons, dearly beloved, let us *promptly and* fearlessly enter the "struggle facing us,"[13] so that *in that exercise of fasting* we may not be content with this limit only, to think that we should cultivate abstinence from food alone. It is too little if the substance of flesh is made thin but the strength of the soul is not nourished. After the outer human being has been afflicted a little, let the inner one be refreshed; after satisfaction has been withdrawn from the body, let the mind be strengthened with spiritual delights. Let every Christian soul examine itself and, with a close scrutiny of its own heart, look closely at its depths. Let it take care that no discord cling there, no avarice inhabit it.

In short, "let every plant which the heavenly Father has not planted be pulled up by its roots."[14] **Let chastity drive out incontinence, let the light of truth dispel the darkness of falsehood, let pride be set aside, let humility be taken on and the tongue of detraction be reined in, because the "mouth which lies kills the soul of the liar."**[15] **Let vengeance cease and injuries be assigned to oblivion.** *Let chastity drive incontinence far away, and the light of truth dispel the shadows of deceit. Let pride sink down, let wrath subside, let harmful darts be weakened and the lashes of the tongue be restrained. Let acts of vengeance cease and injuries be assigned to oblivion. Finally "let every plant which the heavenly Father has not planted be pulled up by its roots."*[16] *The seeds of virtue will then be well nourished in us when every alien sprout has been torn out from the field of our heart.*

(2) If people are so inflamed with a desire of vengeance

12. Cf. Eph 1.13 and Col 1.5.
13. Cf. Heb 12.1.
14. Mt 15.13.
15. Cf. Wis 1.11.
16. Mt 15.13.

against someone that they either throw the latter in prison or bind him up in chains, let them hasten the forgiveness, not only of the one who is innocent, but even of the one who seems worthy of punishment, in order that they might confidently use the rule of the Lord's prayer which says, "Forgive us our debts, as we forgive those who are in debt to us."[17] The Lord has bound this part of the petition with a special bond, in such a way that the effect of the whole prayer rests on this condition. *The Lord has commended this part of the petition to us with special emphasis, in such a way as if the effect of the entire prayer rests on this condition. He says, "For, if you forgive people their failings, your Father who is in heaven will forgive you. If, however, you do not forgive others, your Father will not forgive you your sins."*[18]

6. Therefore, dearly beloved, mindful of our own weakness, by which we easily fall into any and every fault, let us by no means neglect this most powerful remedy and that *most efficacious* cure of our wounds. Let us forgive, that we might be forgiven;[19] let us grant the pardon which we ask, and let us not be anxious to be avenged since we ourselves **pray** *wish* to be forgiven. Let us not pass over the groans of the poor with a deaf ear, but let us offer mercy to the needy with unhesitating kindness, that we may deserve to find mercy at the judgment. Those who direct their energy to this perfection with the help of God's grace will go through the holy fast faithfully; strangers to the "yeast of old malice,"[20] they will come to the blessed Passover *"with the unleavened bread of sincerity and truth."*[21] **In newness of life,**[22] **with the gift of God's goodness, they will merit the fellowship of eternal glory, through Christ our Lord.** *In newness of life they will worthily rejoice in the mystery of the regeneration of humanity, through Christ our Lord who with the Father and with the Holy Spirit lives and reigns forever and ever. Amen.*

17. Mt 6.12.
18. Mt 6.14–15.
19. Cf. Lk 6.37.
20. Cf. 1 Cor 5.8.
21. Cf. 1 Cor 5.8.
22. Cf. Rom 6.4.

Sermon 40
1 March 442 (Recension A)[23]

Although the recurrence of the appointed time itself, dearly beloved, reminds us of the Lenten fast, with its approaching Paschal Feast, still we must add the exhortation of our sermon, which, with the help of God, will be neither useless to the slothful nor burdensome to the devout. When the reason for these days requires that all our observance be increased, there is no one of you, I believe, who will not be glad to be encouraged to good works.

Our nature, even if it may rise to every possible height in the pursuit of virtue, as long as we are mortal, is changeable; nevertheless, just as it always has the possibility of slipping, so it has the possibility of growing. This is the real justification of the perfect, that they never presume they are perfect, lest, relaxing from the effort of a journey not yet completed, they may fall into the danger of failure when they have lost the desire of perfection.

(2) Since none of us, dearly beloved, are so perfect and so holy that they cannot be more perfect and more holy, let us all hasten together in earnest desire, with no difference of rank, no distinction of merit, away from what we have been toward that which we have not yet achieved; and to the measure of our usual acts, let us add something with needed increases. People are shown to be not particularly spiritual at other times if they do not prove themselves to be more spiritual in these days.

2. The reading, then, of the Apostle's preaching sounds timely in our ears when it says, "Behold, now is the acceptable time, now is the day of salvation."[24] What time could be more

---

23. This sermon comes down to us in two recensions. Recension A had been composed in 442. Recension B appears to represent a revision made by Leo himself at some later date. Material found in both recensions will appear in normal text. Material found only in Recension A will appear in **bold**. Material found only in Recension B will appear in *italics*. Some material found in both recensions but in a different order will be reproduced in both bold and italics in their proper order. Some material that does not coincide between the two versions of the Latin text but does not affect the English translation (such as word order or certain syntactical variants) will not be indicated.

24. 2 Cor 6.2.

acceptable than this time, what days more hopeful for salvation than these, in which war is declared on vices and the progress of all virtues is increased? You, o Christian soul, always have to be alert against the adversary of your salvation lest any place lie open to the wiles of the tempter, but you must practice a greater caution and more careful prudence when this same enemy rages against you with keener "ill will."[25] Now throughout the world the power of his ancient domination is "taken from" him, and his innumerable "vessels" of captivity are seized.[26]

Renunciation of barbarous pillage has come from people of all nations and all tongues, and there is now no race of humanity which does not struggle against tyrannical laws; while to the ends of the earth thousands upon thousands are being prepared for rebirth in Christ. With the appearance of a "new creature,"[27] "spiritual infamy"[28] is pushed out from those whom it possessed.

The wicked fury of the plundered enemy rages and seeks a new advantage, for he has lost his ancient rights. Unwearied and ever watchful, if he should find any sheep carelessly wandering from the sacred flock, he would take them captive and lead them by the steep slopes of pleasure and the by-paths of luxury into the lodgings of death. He therefore inflames wrath, nourishes hate, sharpens greed, laughs at continence, and incites gluttony.

3. Whom will he not dare to tempt, he who did not withhold his efforts at guile from even our Lord Jesus Christ himself? As the history of the Gospel shows,[29] when our Savior *who was true God, to show himself also as true man, and to cut off the wicked suggestions of every error,* after a fast of forty days and forty nights, felt the hunger of our weakness in himself, the devil, rejoicing to have discovered the sign in him that he suffered and was of mortal nature, in order to test the power which he feared, said: "If you are the Son of God, tell these stones to become bread."[30]

25. Cf. Wis 2.24.
26. Cf. Mt 12.29, Mk 3.27, and Lk 11.22.
27. Cf. Gal 6.15 and 2 Cor 5.17.   28. Cf. Eph 6.12.
29. Cf. Mt 4.1–11.   30. Mt 4.3.

The omnipotent could certainly do it, and it would be easy for a creature of any kind, at the command of the Creator, to pass into what form it might be ordered, as when he changed water into wine at the marriage feast when he so wished.[31] But here it was more in keeping with his plans for salvation, that the guile of the **very evil** *very proud* enemy should be overcome *by the Lord* not with the power of his divinity, but by the mystery of his lowliness.

Finally, when the devil had been put to flight, and all the arts of the cunning tempter had been shattered, *and the tempter with all his arts had been frustrated,* "angels came to the Lord and ministered to him,"[32] *so that of the true man and of the true God, both the humanity would be inviolate among the scheming questions and the divinity would be manifested among the holy obediences.*

May both the children and the disciples of the devil be confounded, those who, filled with the venom of serpents, deceive any simple-minded person by denying that in Christ each nature is true, whether they strip the divinity of its humanity or the humanity of its divinity. With the double witness, at a single time, each falsehood is destroyed, for the perfection of his humanity is clearly shown by the discomfort of his body, and the perfection of his divinity by the ministering of the angels.

4. So then, dearly beloved, as we have been taught by the authority of our Redeemer that "not on bread alone does a human being live, but on every word of God"[33]—*it is right that a Christian people, engaged in whatever fast, should rather desire to be filled with the word of God than with bodily food*—let us then take up this solemn fast with unhesitating devotion and a living faith, not in a meaningless abstinence which often both the helplessness of the body and the disease of avarice require, but let it be celebrated in large generosity, so that indeed we may be of those about whom the Truth himself said, "Blessed are those who hunger and thirst for justice, for they shall be satisfied."[34]

Let works of mercy be our delight, and let us be filled with

31. Cf. Jn 2.1–10.
33. Lk 4.4.
32. Cf. Mt 4.11.
34. Mt 5.6.

those foods which nourish us even to eternity. Let us rejoice in refreshing the poor, whom our gifts have made content. Let us be happy in clothing those whose nakedness we have covered with the needed garments. Let our human kindness touch the sick in their confinement, the feeble in their weakness, exiles in their suffering, orphans in their destitution, and widows in the sorrow of their loneliness. In aiding them, there is no one who can fail to receive some portion of this kindness. No wealth is small if love is great, nor is the measure of mercy or devotion dependent on property. *The riches of goodwill are rightly never lacking even with property which is insignificant.* Donations of the rich are greater and of the less endowed smaller;[35] but the fruit of their work is no different where there is the same goodwill in the workers.

5. In this very opportunity of exercising virtue, dearly beloved, there are occasions for other rewards which we receive with no expenditure from the barns, no lessening of our money, if only license is withstood, if the love of drink is renounced, and carnal lust is controlled by the laws of chastity, if hate passes into love, if hostility turns into peace, if serenity puts out wrath, if mildness cancels injury, if finally the relations of masters and servants are so ordered that the power of the former is gentler and the service of the latter is more dedicated. With this observation, dearly beloved, we will obtain God's mercy, and, when the guilt of sinners has been abolished, we will devoutly celebrate a worthy Passover.

(2) Even the most dutiful emperors of the Roman world observe this by a sacred custom of old, and in honor of the Passion *and Resurrection* of Christ, they alter their own lofty power, and with the severity of their own regulations softened, direct that those guilty *of many crimes* be released, in order that in the days on which the world is saved by the divine pity, their clemency may be praised as the imitator of heavenly goodness. Let the Christian people imitate their leaders, and, by the royal examples, be aroused to forbearance at home. It is not right for private laws to be more rigorous than the public ones. Let faults

---

35. Cf. Tb 4.9.

be forgiven, "chains loosened," offenses wiped out, revenge cut off. Let the sacred feast keep us all joyful, all free from harm, by divine and human favor, through our Lord Jesus Christ *who lives and reigns with the Father and with the Holy Spirit for ever and ever. Amen.*

Sermon 41

21 February 443

It is indeed fitting for us at all times, dearly beloved, to live wisely and purely, and to direct our wills and actions to what we know is pleasing to divine justice. But, when those days approach which the mysteries of our salvation have made brighter for us, our hearts must be made clean with more zealous care, and the discipline of virtue must be exercised more earnestly. As these mysteries are greater than any one part of them, so our observance also should surpass in some way our usual custom, and those who celebrate the feast with more solemnity should also find themselves so much the more elevated by it.

If it seems reasonable and in some way devotional to appear in more elaborate clothes on a festival, and to show a joyful spirit by the clothing of the body, and if we decorate the house of prayer at that time as far as we can with more attentive care and greater ritual, then is it not right that a Christian soul, which is the true and living temple of God, should prepare its appearance carefully, and when it is going to celebrate the mystery of its redemption, take every precaution that no spot of sin cloud it, nor any wrinkle of doublemindedness mar it?[36] For what benefit is an exterior reverence presenting an appearance of virtue if the interior of the person is sordid with the defilement of some vices? Everything that clouds the purity of the soul and the mirror of the mind must be wiped away vigorously and be rendered brighter by a certain filing away.

Let all examine their own consciences and place themselves in front of themselves for the scrutiny of their own judgment.

---

36. Cf. Eph 5.27.

Let them see if in the secret of their own heart they find that peace which Christ gives,[37] if no lust of the flesh assails the desire of the spirit,[38] if they do not scorn the lowly and seek the heights,[39] if they do not delight in unjust gain, if they do not take pleasure in the inordinate growth of their own possessions, if finally they are not burned up at another's happiness or rejoice in the misery of an enemy.

When perhaps they find nothing of all this disturbance in themselves, let them seek out with close scrutiny the kind of thoughts that go on there, or whether they succumb to vain images, and how quickly they pull their souls away from those which entice them to harm. To be moved by no allurements, to be excited by no greed is not characteristic of this life, which is all temptation.[40] They are already conquered by temptation if they do not fear to be conquered by it. It is pride to presume on the ease of not sinning, since the presumption itself is sin, as blessed John the Apostle says: "If we say we have no sin in us, we are deceiving ourselves and the truth is not in us."[41]

2. Let none beguile themselves, dearly beloved, none deceive themselves, and let none so trust in the purity of their own hearts that they think that they are ever not subject to the danger of temptation, for that watchful tempter may strike with more crafty devices those especially whom he sees refraining from sin. From whom will he withhold his wiles, if he dared to tempt the Lord of majesty himself with the deceit of his craftiness? He had seen his own pride trampled in the humility of the Lord Jesus' baptism; he understood that by the forty days' fast all the desire of the flesh was cut off, but still his spiritual wickedness did not despair of the arts of his malice. He so well convinced himself of the inconstancy of our nature that the one whom he saw as true man he presumed could be made a sinner.

If then the devil did not hold back the trickery of his deceits from the Lord himself, our Savior, how much more will he dare to attack our weakness! He has pursued us with fiercer hatred

37. Cf. Jn 14.27.
38. Cf. Gal 5.17.
39. Cf. Rom 12.16.
40. Cf. Jb 7.1.
41. 1 Jn 1.8.

and more savage jealousy from the moment we renounced him in Baptism and passed by divine regeneration, from that beginning which he dominated, into a new creature.[42] Because we are clothed in mortal flesh, the ancient enemy does not cease to put forward the snares of sin for us everywhere, and at that time especially to rage against the members of Christ[43] when they are going to celebrate the sacred mysteries, and when the teaching of the Holy Spirit has so rightly imbued the Christian people with this instruction that it prepares them for the Paschal Feast by the discipline of the forty days. The order of this purification now invites us to the observance of its healing, and points out the diligence of correction asked of us. As all of us are seen to have used these days in holiness, so they will be shown to have honored the Passover of the Lord with new devotion.

3. In these days then of the holy fast, let us pursue even more fruitfully the works of compassion which must always be the aim of our zeal. "We must do good to all, and especially to those of the household of the faith,"[44] so that in the very distribution of alms also, we may imitate the goodness of the heavenly Father "who causes his sun to rise on good people as well as evil, and his rain to fall on the just and unjust alike."[45] Although the poverty of the faithful ought especially to be helped, still those who have not yet received the Gospel must receive mercy in their troubles. We must love the mutual participation in human nature of all people, and it ought to make us benevolent to those also who are subject to us in whatever condition, especially if they are now reborn in the same grace,[46] and redeemed at the same price of the blood of Christ.[47]

We have this together with them, that we are created in the image of God,[48] and they are not separate from us in bodily origin or in spiritual birth. We are sanctified by the same Spirit, we live by the same faith, we come together to the same myster-

---

42. Cf. Gal 6.15 and 2 Cor 5.17.
44. Lk 6.36 and Gal 6.10.
46. Cf. Jn 3.5.
48. Cf. Gn 1.27.

43. Cf. 1 Cor 6.15.
45. Mt 5.45.
47. Cf. 1 Cor 6.20.

ies.⁴⁹ Let this unity not be despised, and let not such a deep communion be cheap to us, but let this very fact make us gentler in everything, that we share their subjection and with them are subjected to the one Lord in the same service. If any of these have hurt their masters by serious offenses, let them now receive leniency in the days of reconciliation. Let pity take away harshness, and let favor destroy vengeance. Let confinement hold no one, let prisons shut no one in, for our God has promised his own mercy on this condition, that people should know that their own sins will be remitted to them only if they remit those of others.⁵⁰ Destroy the material of dissension, dearly beloved, and the sting of enmity. Let hatred cease, let envy give way, let all the members of Christ⁵¹ come together in the union of love. "Happy the peacemakers; they shall be called children of God,"⁵² not only children but even heirs, "co-heirs with Christ,"⁵³ who lives and reigns forever and ever. Amen.

Sermon 42

*12 March 444 (Recension A)*⁵⁴

Since I am going to speak to you, dearly beloved, about the sacred and great fast, what more apt introduction should I use than that I begin with the words of the Apostle, in which Christ was speaking, and I say what was read: "Behold, now is the acceptable time; now is the day of salvation?"⁵⁵ Although there is no time which is not filled with divine gifts, and although access to the mercy of God is always provided for us through

---

49. Cf. Eph 4.4–5.
50. Cf. Mt 6.14.
51. Cf. 1 Cor 6.15.
52. Mt 5.9.
53. Cf. Rom. 8.17.
54. This sermon comes down to us in two recensions. Recension A had been composed in 444. Recension B appears to represent a revision made by Leo himself at some later date. Material found in both recensions will appear in normal text. Material found only in Recension A will appear in **bold**. Material found only in Recension B will appear in *italics*. Some material found in both recensions but in a different order will be reproduced in both bold and italics in their proper order. Some material that does not coincide between the two versions of the Latin text but does not affect the English translation (such as word order or certain syntactical variants) will not be indicated.
55. 2 Cor 6.2.

his grace, now, however, the souls of all ought to be moved with greater earnestness to spiritual progress and be animated with greater faith.

The recurrence of that day on which we were redeemed invites us to all the duties of mercy, so that we might celebrate the mystery of the Lord's Passion, supreme above all others, with bodies and souls purified. Unceasing devotion and continued reverence were owed to the great mysteries in such a way that we would always remain in the sight of God as it is proper that we be found on the Paschal Feast itself. But, because this strength is found only in the few, and as long as more rigorous observance is relaxed because of weak flesh, and as long as the care of this life is spread out through various actions, even religious hearts are bound to become soiled with earthly dust. It was foreseen by the great healing of the divine instruction that the discipline of forty days would be good for us for restoring the purity of our souls, so that our devout acts might redeem the faults of other times and our pure fasts might melt them down.

2. As we are about to go into the holy days, dearly beloved, days consecrated for purifying our souls and bodies in a more devoted way, let us be diligent in obeying the Apostle's precept, "cleansing ourselves from every defilement of flesh and spirit."[56] When the struggle that exists between the two elements is subdued,[57] let the soul, which properly is constituted as ruler of the body under the direction of God, retain the dignity of its mastery. For the chief point of our fast is not in mere abstinence from food, nor is nourishment profitably kept from the body, unless the mind is recalled from iniquity and the tongue restrained from slander.

2. *As we are about to go into the holy days, dearly beloved, days made holy by the healing fasts, let us be diligent in obeying the Apostle's precepts, that, "giving no offense to anyone," we might not be subject to the "blame" of harsh critics.*[58] *For we may be reviled by the infidels with a just condemnation, and by our fault wicked tongues will arm*

---

56. 2 Cor 7.1.   57. Cf. Gal 5.17.
58. Cf. 2 Cor 6.3.

themselves to injure religion, if the characters of those fasting does not match with the purity of perfect self-control. For the chief point of our fast is not in mere abstinence from food, nor is nourishment profitably kept from the body, unless the soul is recalled from evil.

(2) Consequently, we must moderate our freedom in eating, so that our other desires may be reined in by the same control. This is the time of gentleness and patience, of peace and tranquillity. When the defilement of all faults is cleared away, our business is to learn eternal virtues. Now let the courage of devout souls accustom itself to give up blame, to overlook insults, and to forget injuries. **Now let the faithful soul train itself "with the weapons of justice on the right hand and on the left,"[59] so that,** "through honor and dishonor, through blame or praise,"[60] flattery might not puff up nor reproaches weary a secure conscience *and constant uprightness. The modesty of religious people is not gloomy but holy, nor should the murmurs of any complaints be found in those for whom the solace of holy joys is never lacking.* Let not a lessening of earthly riches be feared among the works of mercy. Christian poverty is always wealth, *because what one has is more than what one does not have.*

(3) Poor people do not fear to suffer in this world, for it has been given them to "possess all things" in the Lord of all things.[61] Those who carry out good works must not at all fear that this power may fail them, since both in the two coins the devotion of that Gospel "widow" was praised,[62] and also, the generous liberality of a "cup of cold water" has a reward.[63] From the compassion of good people, the measure of kindness is judged, and the effects of mercy will never be lacking to those in whom mercy itself is not lacking. The widow of Sarepta experienced this[64] when, in the time of famine, she placed before the blessed Elijah the food for one day, which was all she had, and putting the hunger of the prophet before her own necessity, she expended on him without hesitation her scant grain and bit of oil. What she asked in faith did not fail her, and,

---

59. 2 Cor 6.7.
61. Cf. 2 Cor 6.10.
63. Cf. Mt 10.42.
60. 2 Cor 6.8.
62. Cf. Mk 12.41–44 and Lk 21.2–4.
64. Cf. 1 Kgs 17.9–16.

when the vessels were emptied by her dutiful outpouring, a spring of new richness arose, so that by her holy use the fullness of her substance did not diminish, nor was there fear of its failure.

3. You have no doubt, dearly beloved, that the devil, who is the enemy of all virtues, hates these pursuits to which we entrust you prepared with good will, and that he arms the force of his malignity for this purpose, that he may lay snares for the devout person from the devotion itself and may try to overcome through ambition those whom he could not throw down by their want of confidence. *The evil of pride is near to upright actions, and from this, self-exaltation always creeps in on virtues.* It is difficult for one living a praiseworthy life not to be taken in by human praise, unless, as it is written, "Those who glory, let them glory in the Lord."[65]

Whose purposes would not that wicked enemy dare to attack? Whose fast would he not attempt to break, when he did not restrain his craftiness even from the Savior of the world himself, as the Gospel reading shows?[66] For, terrified in him at the fast of forty days and forty nights, the devil wanted to determine with cunning whether Christ had this self-denial as a gift or as his own, so that he would not fear that the works of his deception would be weakened if Christ belonged to the same creation which his human body belonged to.

So first he examined through cunning whether he himself was the Creator of substances who could change the nature of corporeal substance into whatever he wished and, secondly, whether under the appearance of human flesh his hidden divinity was covered, for whom it would be easy to make the air a passageway for himself, and to balance his earthly limbs in the vacuum.

Since, however, the Lord preferred to exhibit the goodness of a true man to him rather than to display the power of his divinity, the devil turned the skill of a third scheme to this, that he should test, with desire for domination, the one in whom the signs of divine power had ceased, and should lead him to

65. 1 Cor 1.31 and 2 Cor 10.17.
66. Cf. Mt 4.1–11.

the worship of himself by promising the kingdoms of the world. But the wisdom of God "made foolish" the devil's "prudence,"⁶⁷ **so that the proud enemy, seeing man whom he had overcome at one time, did not fear to persecute the man who must be killed for all.** *so that the proud enemy would be bound by that which he had formerly bound, nor did he fear to persecute the man who must die for the world,*

4. Let us then be on our guard against the wiles of the adversary, not only in the pleasures of appetite, but even in our resolution of abstinence. For he who knew how to bring death to the human race through food,⁶⁸ knew also how to harm it through the fast itself; and, for the purpose of deceit in a contrary way, *by using the Manichaeans as his lackeys* just as through the serpent he urges human beings to take forbidden things, so through the fast he urges them to avoid permitted things.

Discipline is useful which accustoms us to frugal food and represses the appetite for luxuries, but woe to the teaching of those among whom even fasting is sinful! For they condemn the nature of creatures to the injury of the Creator, and they assert that when eating they are defiled by those things whose Creator they say is not God but the devil.

*Certainly there is no evil substance, nor is there any nature evil in itself. For the good Creator has made all things good,*⁶⁹ *and the Creator of all things is one, "who made heaven and earth, the sea, and all the things that are in them."*⁷⁰ *Whatever of these is granted to human beings for food and drink is holy and clean in the quality of its own kind. If it is taken in hasty greed, it is the excess which disgraces eaters and drinkers, and the nature of the food and drink does not defile them,* as the Apostle says: "To the pure, all things are pure; but to those who have been corrupted and lack faith, nothing is pure, but their minds and consciences are corrupted."⁷¹

5. You, however, dearly beloved, the holy offspring of the Catholic Mother, whom the Spirit of God has instructed in the school of truth, control your liberty with reasonable judgment, knowing that it is good to abstain even from lawful things, and,

---

67. Cf. 1 Cor 1.19–20.
68. Cf. Gn 3.3–4 and 19.
69. Cf. 1 Tm 4.4.
70. Ps 145(146).6 and Acts 14.15.
71. Ti 1.15.

when it is necessary to live more sparingly, to distinguish foods in such a way that enjoyment of it may be set aside but its nature not condemned. And so, may no wickedness of this infection sully you. These are polluted especially by their own observance, "serving the creature rather than the Creator,"[72] vowing foolish abstinence to the stars of the sky, whom no one doubts are Manichaeans, who have been observed to fast in honor of the sun and moon on Sunday and Monday. They are twice wicked by this one act of their perversity, twice profane, who have set up their fast both to the worship of the stars and to the contempt for the Resurrection of Christ.

They take themselves away from the mystery of human salvation, and, as they deny that he was born in the reality of our flesh, so they do not believe that Christ our Lord truly died and rose. On account of this, they condemn with the gloom of their fast the day of our joy. And when to hide their infidelity they dare to take part in our mysteries, they adapt themselves in the communion of the Sacraments in such a way that sometimes, in order to conceal themselves more safely, they receive the Body of Christ with an unworthy mouth, but they absolutely refuse to drink the blood of our redemption. We wish you to know this in your goodness, so that people of this kind might also be recognized by these signs, and those whose sacrilegious pretense shall have been understood, then noted and published, might be driven from the society of holy people *by priestly authority*.

(2) Blessed Paul the apostle prudently warns the Church of God about such people when he says, "We implore you, brethren, be on your guard against those who cause dissension and put hindrances in the way of the doctrine you have learned, and avoid them. People of this kind do not serve Christ the Lord but [their own appetite]. They seduce the hearts of the innocent by pious talk and persuasive blessings."[73]

6. With these admonitions of ours, dearly beloved, which we frequently pour into your ears against the detestable **sect** *error*, take up the holy days of Lent, and, fully instructed, prepare

---

72. Rom 1.25.
73. Rom 16.17–18.

yourselves to deserve the mercy of God by your works of mercy. Quench your anger, put aside hate, love harmony, and "anticipate one other" in sincere kindnesses.[74] Rule your servants and subordinates with justice, let no one of them be tortured behind bars or in chains. Let acts of vengeance cease, let offenses be forgiven, let severity be changed to mildness, contempt to gentleness, discord to peace. **Since, however, we are "joined" by no agreement**[75] **to the "enemies of the Cross of Christ,"**[76] **let not the sanctity of the faithful be polluted with the fellowship of the wicked. Let "light" be separated from "darkness,"**[77] **and let the children of truth flee from the children of the devil.**

Into the "temple of God"[78] **which is the Church of Christ, nothing contaminated ought to be brought, nothing profane ought to be admitted, so that, when all impurity has been shut out from the depths of the heart, our fast may be sanctified, and we may be the eternal "dwelling place of the Holy Spirit,"**[79] **who deigns to possess us washed from the stains of our sins, and to rule us forever.**

Let us fast, therefore, on Monday and Wednesday and Friday. On Saturday, however, let us celebrate the vigil with the blessed apostle Peter who, not ceasing to have care for the flock entrusted to him, will obtain protection for us by his prayers.

Let all find us modest, peaceful, kindly, so that our fast may be accepted by God. To him finally we offer our sacrifice of true abstinence and true devotion, if we keep ourselves from all malice, with him helping us through all things, to whom, with the Son and with the Holy Spirit is one divinity, one majesty, forever and ever. Amen.

Sermon 43

25 February 445

The Apostle's teaching advises us, dearly beloved, that, "putting aside the old self with its deeds,"[80] "we should be renewed

---

74. Cf. Rom 12.10.
76. Cf. Phil 3.18.
78. Cf. 2 Cor 6.16 and 1 Cor 3.16.
80. Col 3.8–9.
75. Cf. 2 Cor 6.14.
77. Cf. 2 Cor 6.14.
79. Cf. 1 Cor 3.16 and Rom 8.9.

day by day with a holy way of life."[81] If indeed we are the "temple of God" and the "Holy Spirit lives" in our hearts[82]—for, as the Apostle says, "You are the temple of the living God"[83]—we must work with much vigilance to make the chamber of our heart not unworthy of so great a guest. Just as in houses made by human beings we provide with praiseworthy care that if there is any leakage of rain or drafts of storms or decay from its very age, we take great pains to repair it at once, so we ought to watch with constant solicitude to see that no disorder and nothing unclean be found in our souls. Although our building does not stand without the support of its builder, nor can our foundation remain unharmed unless it has the protection of its founder, still, since we are rational "stones" and "living" material,[84] the hand of our Creator has so made us that those who are renewed build along with their Master Builder.

May human obedience never withdraw itself from the grace of God nor may it fall from that good without which it cannot be good. If it feels anything impossible for itself or arduous in the performance of the commandments, let it not abide in itself but return to the one who commanded it, for he gives an order to excite desire and afford help, as the prophet says: "Cast your care on the Lord and he himself will support you."[85] Are there any so immoderately proud that they assume themselves to be so perfectly untouched and unstained that they need no renewal? Such an opinion is thoroughly mistaken, and they grow old in excessive vanity if, among the temptations of this life, they believe themselves immune from every wound. Everything is full of danger, everything full of pitfalls. Desires drive us, enticements lure us, money attracts us, loss hinders us, and the tongues of slanderers are bitter. The mouths of those who praise us are not always trustworthy; here hate rages, there a lying service deceives, so that it is easier to avoid discord than to escape falsehood.

2. In achieving these virtues, the way is so dubious and choice

---

81. Cf. 2 Cor 4.16.
83. 2 Cor 6.16.
85. Ps 54(55).23.

82. Cf. 1 Cor 3.16.
84. Cf. 1 Pt 2.5.

is so uncertain that, between the boundaries of good and evil, if anyone could preserve the measures of highly subtle distinctions, it would be difficult for the goodness not to be harmed, that goodness well known to itself, with the tongue of detractors, and, for one who is a friend of holiness, to evade the reproaches of the wicked. When the thoughts of human beings turn to this diversity of temporal matters, how many shadows oppose them, how many errors of distorted ideas rise up against them, so that from the opposition of disagreements comes the material of quarrels.

Although the hearts of all the faithful do not doubt that divine providence is never absent in any part of the world or at any time, or that success in temporal affairs does not rest on the power of the stars (which is no power), but it acknowledges that all things are disposed according to the most just and most kind decision of the King on High, as it is written: "All the paths of the Lord are mercy and truth."[86] Still, since some things happen not according to our desires, and since the cause of the wicked is often favored over that of the righteous in the mistakes of human justice, it is a fact very near to us and well known that these things trouble even great souls and drive them to some complaint of an unlawful matter. Even David, most renowned of prophets, confessed himself distressed by these diversities to the point of danger, and said: "My feet were almost stumbling, my steps were all but slipping, because I was envious of the arrogant, seeing the prosperity of the sinners."[87]

Because to few people belongs such firm endurance that they are shaken with no resentment of injustice, and because it is not so much adversity as success which destroys many of the faithful, we are bound to apply a strong remedy to heal the bruises with which human weakness is wounded. For this reason I have briefly gone over certain aspects of the dangers of which the world is full, so that all may recognize that clemency for sin and the medicine of reparation is necessary, since Scrip-

---

86. Ps 24(25).10.
87. Ps 72(73).2–3.

ture says: "Who will boast that they have pure hearts, or that they are cleansed from sin?"[88]

3. When should we run more appropriately, dearly beloved, to the divine remedies than when these very mysteries of our redemption are presented to us by the law of the seasons? To celebrate them more worthily, let us prepare ourselves most profitably by the fast of forty days. Not only must those who are coming into the new life through the mystery of the Death and Resurrection of Christ by the regeneration of Baptism take up the practical and necessary defense of this sanctification, but also all the people of the reborn, the former to receive what they do not yet have, and the latter to guard what they have received. As the Apostle says, "Let those who are standing upright watch out lest they fall,"[89] for none are supported by such strength that they can be sure of their own stability.

Consequently, dearly beloved, let us use the revered institutions of this health-giving time and cleanse the mirror of our heart with greater care. However purely and soberly we lead this mortal life, it is nevertheless stained with some dust of our earthly condition, and the brightness of our minds, created "in the image of God,"[90] is not so far from the smoke of every vanity that it cannot be clouded by some filth and is not always in need of polishing. If this is necessary even to the most careful souls, how much more must those seek it who have passed the space of almost a whole year too confidently or perhaps too carelessly? We warn them in dutiful charity lest they flatter themselves that the consciences of individuals cannot be open to us, for no hiding places and no walled enclosures keep out the eyes of God who sees all things at the same time.

Not only are deeds and thoughts known to him, but also things about to be done and thought. This is the knowledge of the Judge on High, this is the inspection to be dreaded, for whom every solid is pierced, every secret is open, to whom the dark is clear, the dumb respond, silence speaks out, and the voiceless spirit talks.[91] Let none "scorn" the "patience of the

---

88. Prv 20.9. 89. 1 Cor 10.12.
90. Cf. Gn 1.27.
91. Cf. Sir 23.27–29 and 42.20. Cf. Heb 4.13.

goodness" of God in the matter of unpunished sins,[92] nor let them think God is not hurt since they have not yet felt his wrath. The reprieves of mortal life are not long, nor does the license of foolish wills last, passing into the sorrow of eternal punishment, if, while the sentence of judgment is suspended, we do not seek the medicine of penitence.

4. As a result, let us flee to the mercy of God, everywhere present, so that the holy Passover of the Lord may be celebrated with a worthy observance. Let the hearts of all the faithful sanctify themselves. Let harshness be softened, let wrath be calmed, let all forgive faults one to another, and let those who seek forgiveness not exact vengeance. When we say, "Forgive us our debts as we forgive those in debt to us,"[93] we bind ourselves with the most unyielding chains unless we fulfill what we profess. If the sacred pact of this prayer is not yet observed in its totality, now at least all know their own consciences. By forgiving others' faults, people can obtain the forgiveness for their own sins. For the Lord says, "If you forgive others their failings, your Father who is in heaven will forgive you yours."[94] What he demands from all does not lie far from them, since the sentence of the Judge depends on the kindness of the suppliants themselves. He who is merciful and just in hearing the prayers of humanity has ordained his justice according to our kindness, so that the law of severity would not hold for us, whom he had found not greedy for vengeance.

Generosity also is proper to merciful and gentle souls. There is nothing more worthy of human beings than to be the imitators of their Creator, and, according to the measure of their own faculties, to be executors of divine work. When the hungry are fed, the naked clothed, the sick cared for, does not the help of God fill full the hands of the minister, and is not the kindness of the servant a gift of the Lord? Although he has no need of help in applying his mercy, he so regulates his power that he supports the sufferings of human beings through human beings. We properly thank the grace of God in the services of

---

92. Cf. Rom 2.4. 93. Mt 6.12.
94. Mt 6.14.

mercy when his works are seen in his servants. Because of this, the Lord himself says to his disciples: "So let your light shine before human beings, that, seeing your good works, they might give the praise to your Father who is in heaven."[95]

Sermon 44

25 February 451

Always indeed, dearly beloved, "the earth is full of the Lord's kindness,"[96] and the nature of things itself is the teacher to each one of the faithful in the worship of God, while "heaven and earth, the sea and all things which are in them,"[97] proclaim the goodness and power of their Creator, and the wonderful beauty of the elements that serve him demands a due thanksgiving from the understanding creature.[98]

But when we come around to those days which more especially mark the mysteries of human Restoration and precede in close order the Paschal Feast, a still more careful preparation of devout purification is called for. Although in any time there are many who lead an innocent life, and very many commend themselves to God by their habitual performance of good deeds, we should not however trust in the integrity of our conscience to such a point that we think that human weakness, living among scandals and temptations, can meet nothing that will harm it. The chief of prophets says, "Who will boast that they have pure hearts, or that they are cleansed from sin?"[99] On another occasion, he says: "From my hidden faults cleanse me, o Lord, and from dangerous ones spare your servant."[100]

If, on the other hand, as has been proven by experience, such is the state of those who resist sinful desires, who repress the motions of wrath, and chastise their secret thoughts, that they are never able in their own hearts not to discover something to correct and even often are deceived by hidden faults or weighed down by those of others, what vices in others, what

---

95. Mt 5.16.
96. Ps 32(33).5.
97. Cf. Pss 68(69).35 and 145(146).6. Cf. Acts 14.15.
98. Cf. Rom 1.20–21.
99. Prv 20.9.
100. Ps 18(19).13–14.

weaknesses, how many wounds there may be for which a more rigorous remedy must be used, so that they might not be found strangers to that mystery through which the "works of the devil are destroyed!"[101]

This is in keeping with the Paschal Feast, that the whole Church should rejoice at the remission of sins, which happens not in those only who are reborn in holy Baptism but also in those who have long been numbered among the adopted. Although the washing of regeneration chiefly makes "people new,"[102] nevertheless, because there is still for all of us a daily renewal against the rust of mortality, and in the path of progress there is no one who ought not always to be better, in general we still have to struggle so that in the Day of Redemption no one may be found in sins of long standing.

2. What therefore, dearly beloved, any Christian ought at all times to do should now be pursued more carefully and more devotedly, to fulfill the apostolic institution of forty days of fast, not only by scant food, but especially by fasting from sins. When for this reason that correction is undertaken to remove the kindling of bodily desires, no kind of restraint is to be followed more than that we never be intoxicated by an unjust will and are always fasting from dishonorable acts. This devotion does not disregard the sick, nor does it separate invalids, for even in a feeble and useless body there can be found an integrity of soul, if, where there was a disposition of irregularity, there also the foundations of virtue may be strengthened. Consequently, the sickness of weak flesh is enough, and often exceeds the measure of voluntary suffering, so that the intention only fulfills the parts of its duty, and what does not enjoy a bodily feast does not nourish itself with wickedness.

(2) To these reasonable and holy fasts nothing is joined more carefully than the works of almsgiving, which in the one name of mercy include many praiseworthy acts of devotion, so that the spirits of all the faithful can be equal, even with unequal means. The love which is owed at the same time to God and to

---
101. Cf. 1 Jn 3.8.
102. Cf. Eph 4.24 and Col 3.10.

human beings is never so hindered with obstacles as not to be free to wish them well. Though the angels said: "Glory to God in the highest, and on earth peace to people of good will,"[103] not only are human beings made happy by the virtue of good will but also by the good of peace, whenever they suffer in charity with others who are laboring under whatever misery.

The works of mercy are very broad, and by their variety they confront true Christians with this, that in the distribution of alms not only the rich and well-provided have their own portions, but also the less wealthy and the poor. Those who are unequal in the power of liberality still are alike in the affection of the spirit. Although in the eyes of the Lord many contributed "much" from their wealth to the treasury,[104] a certain widow put in two coins and merited to be crowned by such an excellent testimony of Jesus Christ that in such a small size of gift hers was worthy to be preferred to the offerings of all the rest. Among the large gifts of those to whom much still remained, that gift of hers, though small, was "complete."

If any are constrained by the difficulties of such great poverty that they have not even enough to offer two coins to a poor person, they have nevertheless in the commandments of the Lord enough to fulfill the duty of good will. Those who serve a "cup of cold water" to a thirsty poor person will receive a "fee" for their work.[105] Such advantages the Lord prepares for his servants in reaching his kingdom that even the offer of water, whose use is free and common, does not lack its reward. Lest any difficulty should intervene, the example of cold water is the image of mercy for those who lack the price of wood for heating the drink, so they will not fear to lose their reward. As to this cup, the Lord warns us, and not without purpose, that it be offered in his name, for faith makes these things precious which are of themselves common, and what is given by unbelievers, though they be of great cost, are empty of all justification.

3. Now that you are about to celebrate the Passover of the

---

103. Lk 2.14.
105. Cf. Mt 10.42.
104. Cf. Mk 12.41–44.

Lord, dearly beloved, practice the holy fasts so that you might come to the sacred feast free of all distraction. The spirit of pride, from which all sins arise, must be driven out by the love of humility, and those who swell with self-praise must be softened with gentleness. If any offense irritates other souls, let them be reconciled to each other and make an effort to return to the unity of concord. "Giving back to no one evil for evil, and forgiving each other as Christ has forgiven you,"[106] wipe out enmity between human beings with peace, and, if your subordinates deserve to be either imprisoned or in chains, let them be released in mercy, so that we who need the remedy of daily forbearance might pass over the faults of others without difficulty. When we say to the Lord our Father, "Forgive us our debts, as we have forgiven those who are in debt to us,"[107] it is certain that, when we show mercy to others' faults, we are preparing divine mercy for ourselves. Through our Lord Jesus Christ who with the Father and with the Holy Spirit lives and reigns forever and ever. Amen.

Sermon 45

10 February 452

The strength and the wisdom of the Christian faith, dearly beloved, is the love of God and the love of neighbor, and those who are eager to worship God and to help their fellow servant lack nothing of the performance of devotion. We must exercise the double union of these affections all the time, and steadily increase it, but at this time we must amplify it more and more so that the forty days' fast, the prelude to the Paschal Feast, might move the inner ear of our heart as did the voice of John the Baptist quoting the prophet Isaiah, "Prepare a way for the Lord, make his paths straight."[108]

Whether we are thinking of that part of the people having long since entered the contest of the evangelical struggle, which ceaselessly reaches for the palm of victory through the

---

106. Rom 12.17 and Col 3.13.   107. Mt 6.12.
108. Lk 3.4. Cf. Is 40.3.

course of the spiritual race; or that part, conscious of deadly sins, which hastens to forgiveness through the process of reconciliation; or that part, about to be reborn in the Baptism of the Holy Spirit, which wishes to be divested of the old Adam and to be clothed in the newness of Christ; in every case the words are spoken fittingly and usefully, "Prepare a way for the Lord, make his paths straight."[109]

What these ways of the Lord are, what these paths are, we can learn from the exhortation of the preacher, who in promising the works and gifts of divine grace opened up the effects of the future changes, adding the word of the prophet's speech, saying, "Every valley will be filled in, every mountain and hill will be laid low, the crooked ways will be made straight and the rough ways into smooth paths."[110] The valley means the gentleness of the humble, the mountain and hill the exaltation of the proud. Since, as the Truth says, "All who humble themselves will be exalted, and those who exalt themselves will be humbled,"[111] rightly is the filling for the valleys foretold and the leveling for the mountains, so that the valley might have no stumbling block and the plain no crookedness. Although "it is a narrow and hard road that leads to life,"[112] those whom truth and devotion strengthen walk it without difficulty, nor do they lack delight in the journey if their road becomes the solid rock of virtue and not the sand of shifting vices.

2. So that we may know more fully through what sort of roads we may reach the promises of God, let us listen to the prophet David when he teaches us, "All the ways of the Lord are mercy and truth."[113] The form of the life of the faithful comes from the example of divine works, and justly does God demand from them the "imitation of himself,"[114] for he has made them "in his image and likeness."[115] Let us then take possession of the dignity of his glory in the measure in which mercy and truth are found in us. With these the Savior came to save us, and with these, the ones saved must hasten to the One who saves them,

---

109. Lk 3.4. Cf. Is 40.3.
111. Lk 14.11.
113. Ps 24(25).10.
115. Cf. Gn 1.26.

110. Lk 3.5. Cf. Is 40.4.
112. Mt 7.14.
114. Cf Eph 5.1.

that the mercy of God might make us merciful and his truth may makes us truthful.

Consequently, as the just soul walks along the way of truth, so the gentle soul walks along the way of mercy. Yet these roads are never divided, as if parts of these virtues were sought by different paths, as if it were one thing to grow in mercy and another to progress in truth. People are not merciful if they are strangers to truth, nor are they capable of justice who are beyond the reach of compassion. Those who are not endowed with both virtues enjoy neither. Love is the power of faith; faith is the strength of love. Only then is the name true and the fruit true of both when the union remains intact.

When they are not together they fail together, for they are help and light to each other until the rewarding vision fulfills the desire of belief and is seen and loved in permanence, because there is no loving without faith and there is no believing without love. Since, as the Apostle says, "In Christ Jesus neither circumcision nor prepuce counts for anything, but faith which expresses itself through love,"[116] let us be eager for charity and faith at one and the same time. This is indeed a most powerful flight of two wings by which a pure spirit is raised to be worthy to see God so that the weight of human cares may not "hold it down."[117] He who said, "Without faith it is impossible to please God,"[118] also said, "If I have faith in all its fullness so that I might move mountains, but I do not have love, I am nothing."[119]

So that the divine liturgy of the Paschal Mysteries might be performed with worthy solemnity, the two things in which the teaching of all the commandments concurs must be more earnestly sought, in which each separate believer is made both the sacrifice to God and his temple. Let faith continue "to hope" for what it believes,[120] let charity continue to render favorable what it loves; each is a part of loving, each is a part of believing. Let us be joined to him by imitation of his goodness, to whom

116. Gal 5.6.
118. Heb 11.6.
120. Cf. Heb 11.1.
117. Wis 9.15.
119. 1 Cor 13.2.

we are subject by the yielding of our minds. The voice of God is, "Be holy, because I am holy,"[121] and the voice of the Lord is, "Be compassionate, as your Father is compassionate."[122]

3. Lest we doubt that what we spend on the poor is given to God, let us hear what trade the distributors of alms enter into when the Lord tells what the kind of judgment will be, when he says to those placed on his right: "Come, you blessed of my Father, possess the kingdom prepared for you from the creation of the world. For I was hungry and you gave me food. I was thirsty and you gave me drink. I was a stranger and you welcomed me, naked and you covered me. I was sick and you visited me. I was in prison and you came to me."[123] When the virtuous ask when and how they could have given all this, the King will answer them and say, "I assure you, in as much as you did these things for one of my least brethren, you did them to me."[124]

What is more fruitful than this work? What is more blessed than this kindness? It should therefore not be deprived of its praise if, because of this very community of nature, it is an excellent thing for human beings to be helped by human beings. But, since what does not come out of the font of faith does not reach the eternal reward, the value of heavenly works is one thing, that of earthly works another. The kindness of the world has a limit among those whom it helps. Christian devotion moves toward its Author, and we are called kind in the one whom we confess "to be working in us,"[125] as the Lord says: "So let your light shine before men, that, seeing your good works, they might give praise to your Father who is in heaven."[126]

4. Be glad, then, faithful spirits, and recognizing your glory "in the glory" of the one who works in you,[127] be fervent in celebrating this Paschal Feast. It is your duty to be prepared to suffer with the one who suffered for all, since the holy life of the saints is never far from the Cross of Christ. The key of re-

---

121. Lv 11.44 and 19.2.
122. Lk 6.36.
123. Mt 25.34–36.
124. Mt 25.40.
125. Cf. 1 Cor 12.6, Eph 3.20, and Phil 2.13.
126. Mt 5.16.
127. Cf. 1 Cor 1.31 and 2 Cor 10.17.

straint "holds" the desires of flesh[128] and kills off the bodily passions by virtue of the Spirit dwelling in them.

That any would not have within themselves something which they should destroy is a difficult thing. Wrath must be quenched, pride must be humbled, luxury must be abolished, the "root" of avarice must be sought ever deeper, so that the seed "of all evils" can be cut off if their first growth can be torn out.[129] Because the soul must be ceaselessly cultivated with this care, and we must so use the body that the lower nature furnishes the necessary obedience to its ruler, now especially must the flesh be controlled by the reins of discipline, and whatever hinders the highest desires must be cut off. When both parts of us are prepared with suitable purification to celebrate the Passion of the Lord, the habit is being engendered for all time to come.

Let severe commands toward our subjects be reduced, let vengeance for a fault cease, and let those guilty of crimes rejoice that they have come to those days in which the harshness of public penance is removed under holy and devout rulers. Let hate be abolished, rivalry fall away, the acts of peace and goodwill be multiplied, and, if any have allowed themselves to be defiled by malice, let them work earnestly to be cleansed by kindness. The judgment of God is as harsh to the pitiless as it is kind to the merciful, and, when those on the left have been thrown out into the fire of hell for their inhumanity, the eternal blessedness of the heavenly kingdom will receive those on the right, praised for the generosity of their alms. Through our Lord Jesus Christ, who with the Father and with the Holy Spirit lives and reigns forever and ever. Amen.

Sermon 46

1 March 453

We know, dearly beloved, that the fervor of your devotion is such that in this fast which leads to the Passover of the Lord,

---

128. Cf. Ps 118(119).120.
129. Cf. 1 Tm 6.10.

many of you outrun our admonitions. But because the use of self-restraint is necessary not only for disciplining the flesh but also for purifying the soul, we want your observance to be so perfect that, as you cut away sensuality from the desires of the body, so you may shut out errors from the senses of the mind. For the Paschal Feast, in which all the mysteries of our worship converge, that one only is prepared with a true and reasonable purification whose heart is not defiled by unfaithfulness. As the Apostle says, "Every act done in bad faith is a sin,"[130] and the fasts of those whom the "father of lies"[131] deceives with his illusions and of those whom the true flesh of Christ does not nourish will be empty and fruitless.

We must keep the divine commandments and sound doctrine with our whole heart, to hold ourselves free from evil sensations with all prudence. The soul will keep a holy and spiritual fast when it casts out the food of wrong and the poison of falsehood, for the wily and skillful enemy introduces these now all the more, when the whole Church in its entirety is reminded by the recurrence of the solemn feast to learn the mysteries of its salvation.

Those who are not disillusioned by the Death of Christ and not deceived about his Human Birth are the true witnesses and worshippers of his Resurrection. Those who are "ashamed of the Gospel" of the Cross of Christ,[132] so as foolishly to "empty" of its meaning the suffering undertaken for the redemption of the world,[133] have denied the very nature of the Lord's true flesh. They do not understand that the unchangeable divinity of the Word of God, subject to no suffering, so humbled itself for the salvation of humanity that in power it did not lose its own nature but in mercy it took up ours. So there is one Person of the twofold "nature" in Christ, and the Son of God, also the son of a human being, is one Lord, in the wisdom of his mercy taking on the "form of a servant."[134] He was not submitting to the law of necessity, for by his power he became humble, by his

---

130. Rom 14.23.
131. Cf. Jn 8.44.
132. Cf. Rom 1.16.
133. Cf. 1 Cor 1.17.
134. Cf. Phil 2.6–7.

power he suffered, by his power he was mortal, that in order to destroy the dominion of sin and death, both the substance of his weakness might be capable of punishment, and the nature of his power might lose nothing of its glory.

2. Thus, dearly beloved, if in reading or hearing the Gospel you recognize certain things in our Lord Jesus Christ that are subject to injury, and certain things illumined by miracles, as if he at one time appeared human and at another time shone as divine, do not consider anything of this as false—as if in Christ there was humanity alone or divinity alone—but in faith believe both, in humility worship both. In the unity of the Word and flesh there is no division, nor do Jesus' bodily proofs seem false because divine signs were manifest in him. The testimony for each nature is true and abundant in him, coming together from the height of divine wisdom to teach that the divinity in the flesh and the flesh in the divinity take part in every way in the inviolable Word, unseparated from the suffering of the flesh.

(2) Thus, Christian soul, disciple of truth, you have fled deceit; now use the Gospel story with faith, and note carefully, here with a spiritual mind and there with bodily sight, what things were visibly done by the Lord, as if you yourself were there together with the apostles. Give to the man what as a child he took from a woman; give to God the fact that his Mother's virginity was in no way harmed by his Conception nor by his Birth. Recognize the "form of a servant,"[135] "wrapped in swaddling clothes" and lying "in a manger;"[136] but in the one announced "by angels,"[137] declared by the heavens,[138] worshipped by "wise men,"[139] confess the "form of the Lord."[140]

See him as human when he did not decline the "wedding" feast,[141] admit him to be divine when he turned the "water" into "wine."[142] Let our own affections find their echo when he shed tears at the death of a "friend,"[143] and feel the divine power when that same person, now a "fetid" body after the "four

---

135. Cf. Phil 2.7.
136. Cf. Lk 2.7.
137. Cf. Lk 2.8–15.
138. Cf. Mt 2.2, 7, 9, and 11.
139. Cf. Mt 2.11.
140. Cf. Phil 2.6.
141. Cf. Jn 2.2.
142. Cf. Jn 2.9.
143. Cf. Jn 11.35–36.

days' " burial, was raised alive by the power of his word alone.[144] To make "mud of his spittle" and the dust was the work of his body; but to open the blind man's "eyes besmeared" with this[145] was certainly a work of that faculty which he had not given to the elements of nature because he had reserved it for the revelation of his glory. It is characteristic of true man to relieve the tired body in quiet sleep;[146] but of true God to restrain the force of raging "storms" by the "rebuke" of his command.[147] It is the work of human kindness and a responsible spirit to "provide" food for the hungry;[148] but to satisfy "five thousand men, as well as their wives and children, with five loaves and two fish,"[149] who would dare to deny that this is the work of the divinity which, these functions of true flesh cooperating with divinity, showed itself to be in man and man in itself? In no other way could the ancient wounds of original sin be healed in human nature but by the Word of God assuming flesh from the womb of the Virgin and, in one and the same Person together, both being born as flesh and being the Word.

3. Keeping in a firm heart this faith of the Lord's Incarnation, dearly beloved, by which the "whole Church is the Body of Christ,"[150] fast from all the deceits of the heretics, and trust that the works of mercy will benefit you as the purity of restraint is fruitfully guarded, if only your souls are not defiled with any taint of wicked thoughts. Cast out those questions of worldly wisdom, hateful to the Lord, for by it, no one can come to the knowledge of truth. Rather, hold fixed in your mind what you have learned in the Creed.

Believe the Son of God, "through whom all things were made, without whom nothing was made,"[151] to be co-eternal with the Father, and also born "according to the flesh" at the end of time.[152] Believe that he was crucified bodily, died, and rose again, and was "set above" the heights of the heavenly "realms," at the right hand of the Father,[153] and is to come in

---

144. Cf. Jn 11.39 and 43–44.
145. Cf. Jn 9.6.
146. Cf. Mt 8.24, Mk 4.38, and Lk 8.23.
147. Cf. Lk 8.24.
148. Cf. Mk 8.6–7.
149. Mt 14.17 and 20–21.
150. Cf. Eph 1.22–23.
151. Jn 1.3.
152. Cf. Rom 1.3.
153. Cf. Eph 1.20–21.

the same flesh in which he ascended, "to judge the living and the dead."[154]

The Apostle urges this on all the faithful when he says, "If you have risen with Christ, seek the things which are above, where Christ is sitting at the right hand of God; be intent on the things which are above, not those on earth. For you have died, and your life is hidden with Christ in God. And, when Christ your life appears, then you also will appear with him in glory."[155]

4. "Having confidence" in such a great "promise,"[156] dearly beloved, be "citizens of heaven" not only "in hope" but also "in your daily life."[157] Although we must at all times be earnest in the sanctification of mind and body, now during this fast of forty days purify yourselves with more careful works of mercy, not only "in giving alms," which have a great effect of "amendment,"[158] but also in pardoning offenses and in releasing sinners from their guilt.

The condition that God has put between himself and human beings does not show opposition to sinners. For, when we say, according to the teaching of the Lord, "Forgive us our debts as we forgive those who are in debt to us,"[159] we ought to fulfill with our whole heart what we say. Then what we ask in the following words will be entirely fulfilled, that "we be not put to the test," and that "we be freed from all evils,"[160] through Christ our Lord, who reigns with the Father and with the Holy Spirit forever and ever. Amen.

Sermon 47

21 February 454

Among all the Christian festivals, dearly beloved, we well know that the Paschal Mystery is the chief, and the calendar of the whole year disposes us to enter into it properly and worthily. But the present days especially demand our devotion, for

---

154. Cf. 1 Pt 4.5.
156. Cf. Heb 10.19 and 23.
158. Cf. Lk 11.41.
160. Mt 6.13.
155. Col 3.1–4.
157. Cf. Phil 3.20.
159. Mt 6.12.

we know them to be near to that most holy mystery of the divine mercy. Among them the major fasts have been ordained by the holy apostles through the direction of the Holy Spirit, so that we too, in the common veneration of the Cross of Christ, should take some part in what he did for us, as the Apostle says: "If we suffer with him, we shall also be glorified with him."[161] The expectation of the promise of blessedness is certain and sure where there is a sharing of the suffering of the Lord.

There is no one, dearly beloved, to whom the association of this glory is denied because of the condition of our times, even though the calm of peace gives no opportunity for valor. The Apostle teaches us this when he says, "All those who wish to live devoutly in Christ will suffer persecution,"[162] for the pressure of persecution is never lacking if the practice of religion is not lacking. The Lord himself in his discourses said, "Those who do not take up their cross and follow me are not worthy of me."[163] We ought not to doubt that this word belongs not only to Christ's disciples but to all the faithful and the whole Church which everywhere heard his salvation in the persons of those who were present.

As we must live righteously all the time, so we must bear the cross all the time, for to all of us have been assigned our own crosses, and all of us carry them in our own way and in our own measure. There is one word for persecution, but not only one cause of struggle, and there is infinitely more danger in hidden traps than in an obvious enemy. Blessed Job, well-versed in the alternating good and evil of this world, spoke well and truly when he said, "Is not the life of human beings on earth a trial?"[164]

Faithful souls are attacked not only by sorrows and trials of the body but also, even if the bodily members are unharmed, they are oppressed by grave illness if they have been softened by indulgence of the flesh. But, since "the flesh lusts against the spirit and the spirit against the flesh,"[165] the rational mind is

---

161. Rom 8.17.
163. Mt 10.38.
165. Cf. Gal 5.17.

162. 2 Tm 3.12.
164. Jb 7.1.

protected by the safeguard of the Cross of Christ, and it does not consent when enticed by harmful desires, because it is "held fast" by the "nails" of continence and "by the fear of God."[166]

In those who have been well situated, at the devil's instigation, there is no lack of enmities toward those unlike themselves, and they easily burst out into hatred, and then their wicked lives become even more detestable in comparison with the just. "Iniquity" makes no peace with "justice,"[167] drunkenness hates temperance, and there is no agreement between falsehood and truth; pride does not like gentleness, wantonness modesty, or greed generosity. These differences breed such obstinate conflicts that even if the exterior is at rest, they do not cease to disquiet the inner hearts of the devout. It is true that "those who wish to live a godly life in Christ will suffer persecution,"[168] and it is true "that all this life is a trial."[169] Let all of the faithful who have learned this from their own experience be armed with the Cross of Christ so that they might be worthy of Christ.

2. The devil's craft lies in wait, dearly beloved, for those especially who are struggling through this trial to reach eternal rewards, and he undermines the faith of those whose honor he cannot upset. Whoever are led astray from the confession of truth are turned onto another road, and their whole life is a withdrawal. The farther they are from the light of the Catholic Faith, the nearer they are to death.

In our own days, some have taken up again their old madness in the spirit of an already disapproved and condemned error, and they suffer from their indifference. They dare to deny the twofold nature in Christ, either because they do not accept the reality of the flesh or that divinity was made flesh. According to the Manichaeans, there is no resurrection when there is no death, or according to Apollinaris, the very divinity of the Word is changeable and was itself made capable of suffering. But to think this, to put this into the ears of the Christian people, what else is it but to overturn the very foundations of our

166. Cf. Ps 118(119).120.
168. 2 Tm 3.12.
167. Cf. 2 Cor 6.14.
169. Jb 7.1.

religion and to deny that the true Son of God is the true son of a human being?

In him alone the restoration of the human race is evidenced in the law, promised through the prophets, and announced by all the signs of the Old Testament, and therefore this "great mystery" of divine mercy,[170] of profit to all the ages, often and for a long time prefigured, is most surely fulfilled in the appointed time. Since "the Word became flesh,"[171] in Christ there is the one Person of God and man, and no division of either nature happens in any of his acts, and thus the truth of the Gospel shows him whom it asserts to be the Son of God to often be called the son of a human being.

Of those things that are told of him, some are of his humanity and some of his divinity, but both are reported under the name of the son of a human being. A faith that believes the Lord Jesus Christ to have been born of the Virgin Mary, and to be at the same time God and man, must not hesitate to acknowledge the humanity in God or the divinity in the man, and, as in the Word there is true lowliness of the manhood taken up, so in the flesh is the true majesty of God who took it up.

3. Since you remember that you have been instructed from here many times, it is enough to have touched on these things concerning the Incarnation of the Word, dearly beloved, on the occasion of the Paschal Feast for which we ought to prepare the purity of our hearts. Now I ask your devout attention for what the season demands, so that you might carry out a holy and healthy fast in works of mercy. Since we must work especially hard for the pardon of sins, you assure yourselves of divine mercy without any doubt if you also give over to pardon every offense in respect to your subjects. It is fitting for the people of God to assemble in peace and concord for such a great feast, and the severity of vengeance which is now relaxed even in public courts should be much more mitigated in the hearts of Christians, for the care of the holy people ought rather to be intent on this, that no one be cold, no one be hun-

---

170. Cf. 1 Tm 3.16.
171. Jn 1.14.

gry, no one lack necessities, no one pine in sorrow, that no chains hold anyone bound, that no prison shut anyone in.

Whatever causes of offense there are, still they are from person to person, and the greatness of the fault is not so much to be considered as the fact of the common nature. From the "judgment by which we judge another,"[172] we shall obtain the mercy of God's judgment. "Blessed are the merciful, for God will be merciful to them,"[173] God who lives and reigns forever and ever. Amen.

Sermon 48

13 March 455

Among all the days, dearly beloved, which Christian devotion holds honorable in many ways, there is none more excellent than the Paschal Feast, through which the dignity of all the solemnities in the Church of God is consecrated. Indeed, even the Birth of the Lord from his Mother is credited to this mystery, for there was no other reason for the Son of God to be born than that he could be fixed to a cross. Our mortal flesh was taken up in the womb of the Virgin, the ordering of his Passion was completed in our mortal flesh. It was brought about in the ineffable wisdom of the mercy of God that he should be for us the sacrifice of redemption, the destruction of sin, and the beginning of the resurrection to eternal life.

Remembering what the whole world obtained through the Cross, we realize that we are duly prepared for celebrating the Day of the Passover by a fast of forty days, so that we can be worthy to enter on the divine mysteries. It is not only the highest bishops or the priests of the second order, nor the ministers of the Eucharist alone, but the whole body of the Church, the total number of the faithful, who ought to be cleansed from all contamination, so that the temple of God, whose foundation is the Founder himself, might be beautified in every stone and be full of light in all its parts.

---

172. Cf. Mt 7.2.
173. Mt 5.7.

If the houses of kings and the courts of high officials are with reason honored with every adornment to make more noble residences for those whose services are greater, with how much labor should the "home of divinity itself be built," and with how much honor it should be decorated![174] Although it could not be begun and completed without its Author, still its Builder has granted that we may seek its increase by our own labor. Living and rational material is used for the construction of this temple, and he encourages us through the Spirit of grace to fit it together of our own will into a single whole.

For this reason, this material is loved, for this reason it has been sought, so that, from one not seeking, it itself is seeking, and from one not loving, it is now loving, as the blessed John the apostle says: "Let us love, then, because God has first loved us."[175] When all the faithful together and separately are one and the same "temple of God,"[176] as it must be perfect in its whole, so it must be perfect in its parts, for though its beauty is not the same in all its members, nor can there be equality of merit in so great a variety of parts, the union of charity produces a fellowship of splendor. Sharers in holy love, even though they do not use the same benefits of grace, they yet rejoice with one other in their blessings, and what they love cannot be outside of them, for they become rich in their own increase when they rejoice in another's progress.

2. In this union of the saints, dearly beloved, where they love the same things, and delight in the same things, and think the same things, there is no place for the proud or for the envious or for the greedy. Whatever there is in which vanity glories or anger rages or sensuality indulges, it is considered not in the company of Christ but on the side of the devil, and is shut far away from the home of devotion. The adversary of innocence and the enemy of peace frets, and because "he himself has not stood fast in truth"[177] and has lost all the glory of his nature by being proud, he grieves that human beings are restored by the mercy of God and are brought into that good which he himself

---

174. Cf. Eph 2.22. 175. 1 Jn 4.19.
176. Cf. 1 Cor 3.16 and 2 Cor 6.16. 177. Jn 8.44.

lost. No wonder the author of sin is tortured by the honesty of those who act rightly, and anguished by the steadfastness of those he cannot cast down, since indeed even among human beings some are found to imitate the works of his malice.

Many, to our grief, burn with envy at others who are righteous, and, because they know that vices are displeased with virtues, they are armed for hatred of those whose example they do not follow.[178] But servants of God and disciples of truth love even those who are unlike them, and they declare war on vices rather than on people, "to no one returning evil for evil,"[179] but wishing always for the correction of sinners. It is beautiful indeed and comparable to the divine goodness when all are mindful of themselves in others, and love their own nature even in the enemy.

We know that many have gone into good lives from bad, have become sober from being drunken, merciful from cruel, generous from avaricious, chaste from promiscuous, peaceful from fierce. As the Lord said, however, "I came not to call the virtuous, but sinners,"[180] and to no Christian is it permitted to hate anyone, for no one is saved except by the remission of sins. We do not know how priceless the grace of the spirit is going to make those whom worldly wisdom has debased.

3. May the people of God be holy, may they be kind; holy, to refuse forbidden things; kind, to do what is commanded. Although it is a great thing to have a right faith and sound doctrine, and worthy of much praise to be circumcised in appetite, to have gentle meekness and pure chastity, nevertheless, all virtues are naked without charity, nor can any excellence of life be called fruitful which love has not brought to birth. In the Gospel of John, the Lord says: "In this all people will know that you are my disciples, if you have love for one another,"[181] and in the letter of that same apostle is written, "Beloved, let us love one another, because love is of God, and every one who loves is begotten of God and knows God; the one who does not love does not know God, because God is love."[182]

---

178. Cf. Prv 29.27.
180. Mt 9.13.
182. 1 Jn 4.7–8.

179. Cf. Rom 12.17.
181. Jn 13.35.

Let the souls of the faithful examine themselves and judge the innermost affections of their hearts with true discernment, and, if they find anything planted in their consciences from the fruits of charity, they need not doubt that God is within them, and, as they are more and more receptive of such a Guest, let them become more and more generous in the works of enduring mercy. If "God is love,"[183] charity should have no end, for divinity can be closed off by no boundary.

4. Therefore, dearly beloved, although every time is suitable to practice the good of charity, nevertheless, the present days are urged on us especially, so that those who want to undertake the Passover of the Lord with sanctification of soul and body should try to acquire this grace above all, in which the summit of all virtues is contained and by which a "multitude of sins is covered."[184] Consequently, since we are about to celebrate that grandest mystery of all, by which the blood of Jesus Christ has destroyed our sins, we should first prepare "sacrifices" of mercy,[185] that what the goodness of God has brought us, we too should provide for those who have sinned against us.

Let injuries be dropped into oblivion, let faults know no punishment, and let all the offenses of our subjects be released from the fear of retribution. Let the prison walls hold no one, and let no sad groans of culprits continue in dark cells. If any are holding such, being guilty of some dereliction, let them know that they themselves are sinners, and that, to receive mercy for themselves, they should be glad that they have found someone to whom they can be merciful. When we say, according to the Lord's teaching, "Forgive us our debts, as we have forgiven those who are in debt to us,"[186] we do not doubt that because of this form of our prayer we will obtain divine forgiveness.

5. Toward the poor also and those handicapped by various disabilities, let a kinder generosity be held out, that gratitude might be rendered to the "grace of God" by the voices "of many,"[187] and that the needy might obtain refreshment by our

183. Cf. 1 Jn 4.16.
185. Cf. Heb 13.16.
187. Cf. 2 Cor 9.11–12.

184. Cf. 1 Pt 4.8 and Prv 10.12.
186. Mt 6.12.

fasts. God is pleased by no devotion of the faithful more than by what is spent on the poor, and, where he finds "merciful" care, there he recognizes the likeness of his own holiness.[188]

Have no fear for the failure of your means in these expenses, for kindness itself is a great possession, and the substance of generosity cannot lack where Christ both feeds and is fed. In all this work, that hand supports it which increased the bread by "breaking" it and multiplied it by distributing it.[189]

May givers of alms be secure and "cheerful,"[190] because they will have a very great reward when they have kept back for themselves only very little, as the blessed apostle Paul says: "The one who provides seed for the sower and bread for eating will provide in abundance; he will multiply your seed, and will increase the yield of the fruits of your goodness,"[191] in Christ Jesus our Lord, who lives and reigns with the Father and with the Holy Spirit forever and ever. Amen.

Sermon 49

(17 February 457)?

At all times and every day, dearly beloved, certain signs of the divine goodness are set up before us, and no part of the year is estranged from the holy mysteries, so that, while protections for our salvation meet us everywhere, we may always look more eagerly for the welcoming mercy of God. But whatever it is that is given in different works of grace, and in gifts for the restoration of human souls, all of it is now more clearly and more fully presented to us when things are not to be done one by one, but all are to be celebrated together.

When the Paschal Feast is nearing, we are in the great and holy fast, which announces its observance to the faithful without exception. None are so holy that they cannot be holier, none so devout that they ought not to be more so. Who is there, living in the uncertainty of this life, who is either immune to

188. Cf. Lk 6.36.
189. Cf. Mt 14.15–21 and 15.36. Cf. Mk 6.41 and Lk 9.16.
190. Cf. 2 Cor 9.7.   191. 2 Cor 9.10.

temptation or free from blame? Who is there who wishes to add no virtue or to remove no fault? Adversity harms us and prosperity corrupts us, and it is no less dangerous to lack what is desired than to be full of what is granted. There are snares in the abundance of wealth, there are snares in the distress of poverty; the former raises us to pride, the latter goads us into complaint. Health is a trial, infirmity is a trial, for the first is a reason of negligence, the second a cause of sadness. There is a trap in security, and a trap in fear, and it makes no difference whether the mind held by affections for earth is occupied by joys or cares, since the sickness is the same whether one is weakening under empty luxuries or suffering under anxious care.

2. The word of Truth is fulfilled in everything by which we learn that "it is a narrow and difficult road that leads to life"[192] and though the wide road leading to death is crowded with great throngs, only here and there are the footsteps of the few entering the path of salvation. Why is the road on the left more populous than the right, unless the mass of people are given over to joys of the world and the good of the body? Although what they want is transitory and uncertain, they will undertake labor more willingly for the desire of pleasure than for the love of virtue. And, although unnumbered are those who long for things they can see, scarcely can any be found who put eternal things before temporal. The blessed apostle Paul says: "The things which are seen are transitory, but those not seen are eternal,"[193] and the way of virtue lies in some ways hid and concealed, since "in hope we are saved,"[194] and true faith loves that above all which it reaches with no interference of the flesh.

It is a great labor and accomplishment to keep the unstable heart from all sin, and not to relax the vigor of the soul for any defilement though endless allurements of pleasure entice it from all sides. "Whoever touch pitch, will they not also be defiled by it?"[195] Who is not weak in the flesh? Who is not soiled in dust? Who indeed are of such great purity that they are not defiled by those very things in which life consists? The divine

---

192. Mt 7.14.
193. 2 Cor 4.18.
194. Cf. Rom 8.24.
195. Sir 13.1.

teaching commands us through the Apostle: "Those who have wives should live as though not having [them], and those who weep as though not weeping, those who rejoice as though not rejoicing, those who buy as though possessing nothing, and those who use this world as though they are not using it, for the figure of this world is passing away."[196] Blessed is the soul which runs the course of its journey in simple moderation and does not linger in those things through which it must walk, so that it is a steward, rather than an owner, of the things of the earth. Such a soul will not lack human affection but will rely on the divine promises.

3. This courage, dearly beloved, is demanded of and instilled in us by nothing so much as these present days in which, while we go through their special observance, we acquire the habits in which we are to persevere. It is well known to you that this is the time when throughout the world the Christian battle-line must combat the raging devil. If sloth holds any lukewarm or cares hold them occupied, now is the time to be equipped in spiritual arms and, aroused by the heavenly trumpet, to enter the battle, for that one "by whose envy death entered the world"[197] burns especially at this time with jealousy and is at this time tortured by very great grief.

For he sees a new people from all the human race being brought into adoption as children of God, and, through the virginal fertility of the Church, the births to regeneration being increased. He sees that he is deprived of the power of his domination, expelled from the hearts of those he once possessed; that thousands of the old of both sexes are snatched from him, thousands of the young, thousands of children; and that neither one's own sin nor Original Sin stand in the way of anyone, when justification is not granted by merits but is given by the generosity of grace alone. He sees that the lapsed also and those deceived by the falsehood of his snares are washed in the tears of penitence and admitted to the healing of reconciliation, when the key of the apostles has opened the gates of mercy.

196. 1 Cor 7.29–31.
197. Wis 2.24.

He knows too that the day of the Lord's Passion is coming soon, and that he will be ground down by the power of that Cross which in Christ, who is a stranger to everything owed to death, was the redemption of the world, not the penalty of sin.

4. And so, that the malice of the raging enemy might have no consequence because of his envy, we must cultivate a still more earnest devotion in following the Lord's commands. Let us use the time, in which all mysteries of divine mercy converge, with a preparation of soul and body, begging the guidance and the help of God, "without whom we can do nothing,"[198] but with whom we are able to accomplish all things. For that reason is the command given, that we should seek the aid of the one who gave it. None should excuse themselves on the grounds of infirmity, when he who incites the "will" also gives the power,[199] as the blessed apostle James says: "If any of you are without wisdom, let them ask it of God, who gives generously to all and does not reproach, and it will be given to them."[200]

What believer does not know what virtues ought to be worked for and what vices fought against? Who are so lenient, or so unskilled at judging their own consciences, that they do not know what they should choose to be removed from themselves or what increased in themselves? None indeed are so beyond reason that they do not know the quality of their lives or recognize the secrets of their own hearts. Let them not be satisfied with themselves in everything, nor judge their pleasure according to the flesh. Instead, let them put their lives in the scales of the divine commands, for where some things must be done by order and others are forbidden to be done, they will weigh themselves with a just scrutiny and judge the habits of their lives by comparison with both weights.

The mercy of God is the architect which, in its commands, built the shining mirror in which human beings might examine the faces of their souls and know how they conform to the "image of God,"[201] or how they are unlike, especially so that when the cares of the body and its disturbing employments are little

---

198. Cf. Jn 15.5.
200. Jas. 1.5.

199. Cf. Phil 2.13.
201. Cf. Gn 1.27.

by little cast out, at least in these days of our redemption and reparation, we might turn ourselves from earthly to heavenly things.

5. Indeed, as it has been written, "We all offend in many things,"[202] so the first feeling should be of mercy, and the faults of others toward us should be forgotten, so that no love of revenge can make us violate that holy contract by which we have bound ourselves in the Lord's prayer, saying, "Forgive us our debts as we have forgiven those who are in debt to us."[203] Let us not then be surly in forgiveness, for either the desire of vengeance or the kindness of mercy will come back on us. People must rather wish, since they are always exposed to the danger of temptation, that their own faults may be unpunished rather than that they should strike a blow at the faults of others. What would be more in harmony with the Christian faith than that there be forgiveness to sinners not only in the Church but also in every home?

Let threats be put aside and chains be loosened, for those who have not loosened them will bind themselves with them far more destructively. What any impose upon others they have decreed for themselves by their own ruling. "Blessed are the merciful, for God will have mercy on them."[204] God is just and benign in his judgments, allowing some to be under the power of others for this reason, that the use of discipline and the mildness of clemency might be preserved in equal moderation, and that none should dare to deny that pardon to another's sin which they want to receive for their own.

6. Because the Lord said, "Blessed are the peacemakers, for they will be called children of God,"[205] all strife of discord and hate should be put aside, and none should think they are going to have fellowship in the Paschal Feast if they neglect to rebuild fraternal peace. With the Father on high, those who have not been in charity with their brethren will not be held in the number of the children.

In the distribution of alms and in the care of the poor, the

---

202. Cf. Jas 3.2.
203. Mt 6.12.
204. Mt 5.7.
205. Mt 5.9.

Christian fasts should grow fat, and what any take from their own pleasure they should spend on the sick and the poor. Let care be given that all might bless God with one voice. Those who give some portion of their own substance should know that they are ministers of God's mercy, God who has placed the lot of the poor in the hands of the generous, so that the sins which are washed in the Baptismal Water or the tears of repentance might also be taken away by almsgiving, for Scripture says: "Water quenches a blazing fire; almsgiving atones for sins,"[206] through our Lord Jesus Christ, who with the Father and with the Holy Spirit lives and reigns forever and ever. Amen.

Sermon 50

(9 March 458)?

As the Paschal Solemnity is nearing, dearly beloved, the custom of the preceding fast is upon us, which trains us for forty days in the sanctification of body and soul. As we are about to enter on this greatest of all festivals, we ought to prepare ourselves by this observance so that we might be found dying with him in his Passion if we are to rise with him in his Resurrection. As blessed Paul the apostle says, " For you have died, and your life is hidden with Christ in God. But, when Christ your life appears, then you also will appear with him in glory."[207]

What is the participation with Christ for us except that we cease to be what we were? Or what is the "likeness to the Resurrection" except the putting off of the "old self?"[208] Consequently, those who understand the mystery of their restoration ought to divest themselves of the faults of the flesh and cast away all the filth of sin, so that when they go into the "marriage" feast they will shine in the "garment" of virtue.[209]

Although the kindness of the bridegroom invites everyone to share the royal banquet, all who are called must be eager to prove themselves worthy of the honor of the sacred meal. Certain ones abuse the patience of God, and, though they are

---

206. Sir 3.33.
208. Cf. Rom 6.5–6.
207. Col 3.3–4.
209. Cf. Mt 22.11–12 and 9.

not undisturbed in conscience, they become secure because of the long impunity; although the punishment is delayed for this reason, that correction might be able to have its time.[210] Let none, thinking they have not received what they deserve, delay to embrace the mercy of our God "by which he does not wish the death of sinners but only that they be converted and live."[211] What is delayed is not then taken away, nor do they escape condemnation by not seeking mercy.

There is not one reason only that all people ought to ask for it, since sin differs from sin and crime from crime in many ways and to many degrees. Because all believers ought to strive for perfect innocence and full purity, in order to deserve to be enrolled in the fellowship of those about whom it is said, "Blessed are the pure in heart, for they will see God,"[212] with all urgency and with all our strength we must struggle to see that whatever stains the secret conscience, whatever obscures the keenness of the soul, is wiped away with the most thorough purging. It has been written, "Who will boast that they have pure hearts or are clean from sin?"[213] Yet we must not despair of achieving purity and this, while it is always being sought, is always received, nor does there remain to be condemned by judgment anything which has been purged by confession.

2. This it is, dearly beloved, that all the children of the Church, praying in one and the same manner from the teaching of the Lord, say: "Forgive us our debts, as we have forgiven those who are in debt to us."[214] None are so holy, none so upright that, in this time "in this life, which is wholly a trial,"[215] they should not need remission of some sin. The dangers of innumerable offenses surround us on all sides and we go from allowed enjoyments to extreme excess, while the delight of pleasure creeps in under the guise of concern for health, and what would be enough for nature does not satisfy appetite. Hence arises the love for possessions, never satisfied; hence the desire for prominence, which falls back either on its ancestry or its offspring to boast now of its descendants, now of its parents.

210. Cf. Rom 2.4.
212. Mt 5.8.
214. Mt 6.12.
211. Ez 33.11.
213. Prv 20.9.
215. Jb 7.1.

To these and other temptations, whose combination is complex and infinite, what virtue is opposed more surely than abstinence, which, by nourishing and preserving the good of soul and body, both furnishes growth and strengthens it? Thus, in the heavenly discipline of the Church, the divinely instituted fasts bring much of use to subdue the bodily appetite by the laws of abstinence, and to temper internal movements, and, as the body fasts from food, so does the mind from wickedness. For the Lord says, "Blessed are they who hunger and thirst for holiness, for they will be satisfied."[216]

God's people have spiritual feasts and pure delicacies which it is healthy for them to look for and laudable for them to desire, for the prophet says in praise of them, "Taste and see that the Lord is sweet."[217] Whoever have touched with the taste of their hearts the sweetness of the justice and mercy of God, by which all his ordinances are carried out, and have drunk from the experiences of supernal joys never to be diminished by any pride, they will despise the corruptible and temporal good in their admiration of the eternal, and they will glow in that fire which the love of God kindles.[218] As when cold is changed to warmth, and night is changed to daylight, the Holy Spirit by one stroke in the hearts of the faithful takes away darkness and destroys sin.

3. While self-restraint, the mother of virtues, brings to birth such fruits and leads those who are fasting from sin to ineffable delights, let us, dearly beloved, carry out the heavenly commands with even more earnest effort, and, because the whole Paschal Mystery was established for the remission of sins, let us imitate what we want to celebrate. For our "merciful and just Lord"[219] has so promised his pardon that he reveals it even to those whom he spares. Explaining by what rule he wanted us to pray to God the Father, he said: "If you forgive others their failings, your Father who is in heaven will forgive you. If, however, you do not forgive others, your Father will not forgive you your sins."[220] This represents a just and kindly condition,

---

216. Mt 5.6.
217. Ps 33(34).9.
218. Cf. Lk 12.49.
219. Cf. Ps 114(116).5.
220. Mt 6.14–15.

by which human beings are made partakers of divine power, that they might activate the word of God by his own will and bind the Lord to themselves by that judgment with which they themselves have judged their fellow servants.

Whether it is in respect to equals or to servants, the nature identical in all must be loved, and, since there is no one who has not sinned, there is no one who should not pardon. Let us offer with no difficulty what we receive with gratitude, so that, by our generosity in alms or our clemency to sinners, the more merciful we are, the more perfectly innocent we shall be, through our Lord Jesus Christ who lives and reigns with the Father and with the Holy Spirit forever and ever. Amen.

LENTEN SERMON ON THE TRANSFIGURATION

Sermon 51

445

EADING FROM the Holy Gospel according to Matthew. "At that time, Jesus took Peter, James, and John his brother, and led them up onto a high mountain," etc.[1]

This Gospel reading, dearly beloved, which has struck the interior hearing of our souls through the ears of the body, calls us to the knowledge of a great mystery, and we shall seek for it all the more easily with the breath of God's grace if we turn our thoughts to those things which were told a little while ago. Christ, the Savior of the human race, God, when he established this faith which calls the "wicked to justice"[2] and the "dead to life,"[3] so filled his disciples with the admonitions of doctrine and his miraculous works that the same Christ was believed to be both Only-Begotten Son of God and also son of a human being. For one of these without the other does not benefit us for salvation. It would be equally dangerous to believe the Lord Jesus Christ either to be God alone without man, or man alone without God, since we must confess both equally. As true humanity was in God, so true divinity was in the man.

To strengthen the vigor of this faith, the Lord asked his disciples what they themselves, among the diverse opinions of others, believed or what they felt about him; and the apostle Peter, through the revelation of the Father on High, surpassing bodily senses and transcending things human, saw with the eyes of his soul the Son of the Living God, and he confessed

---

1. Cf. Mt 17.1–9.
2. Cf. Rom 4.5.
3. Cf. Rom 4.17.

the glory of the divinity, for he did not look only for the substance of flesh and blood. In this sublimity of faith, he was so pleasing that, gifted with the joy of blessedness, he received the sacred strength of the impregnable rock, founded on which the Church was to prevail against the gates of hell and the laws of death, nor in loosing and binding the cases of anyone at all was any other thing to be ratified than what it had confirmed by the judgment of Peter.

2. But this height of excellent understanding, dearly beloved, had to be built up concerning the mystery of the inferior substance, lest the faith of the Apostle should be so carried away in respect to the glory of confessing the divinity in Christ that he might think the taking on of our weakness would be unworthy of and unsuitable to the God who cannot suffer, and so now he might believe the human nature to be glorified in him in such a way that he could not be affected by suffering or be dissolved in death.

As a result, when the Lord said that, "it was necessary that he go to Jerusalem and suffer many things from the elders and scribes and chief priests, and to be put to death and rise again on the third day,"[4] blessed Peter, who was filled with heavenly light and fervent in his ardent acknowledgment of the Son of God, rejected the shame of ridicule and the disgrace of a very cruel death, from, as he thought, his devout and spontaneous aversion. But a kindly reproach from Jesus took hold of him and stirred in him a desire to share in his Passion.[5] The following exhortation of the Savior inspired him and taught him this, that as far as they are concerned, "those wishing to follow him must deny themselves" and consider as trifling the loss of temporal things in the hope of things eternal, for those who did not fear to "lose" their lives for Christ "would save them" in the end.[6]

(2) So that the apostles might accept this strong and happy perseverance with their whole hearts, and that the harshness of the acceptance of the Cross might in no way agitate them,

4. Mt 16.21.   5. Cf. Mt 16.22–23.
6. Cf. Mt 16.24–25.

and that they should never be ashamed of the suffering of Christ or believe this patience, which was about to support the cruelty of his Passion, ought to be scandalous for him, in order that he might not lose the glory of his power, "Jesus took Peter and James and his brother John,"[7] and, when he had gone up on a high mountain with them, he showed them the splendor of his glory.

Although they had learned that the majesty of God was in him, still they knew nothing of the power of that body of his where divinity was concealed. Then he had promised clearly and explicitly that "certain of the disciples there present would not taste death before they saw the son of a human being coming in his kingdom,"[8] that is, in royal splendor, which, in a special manner pertaining to the nature of the manhood he had taken up, he wished to be visible to these three men. For, encompassed up to now in mortal flesh, in no way were they able to look at and see that ineffable and inaccessible vision of the divinity itself, which is saved for the clean of heart in eternal life.[9]

3. The Lord disclosed his glory before chosen witnesses and illumined that form, common to other bodies, with such splendor that "his face" was like the glory of the "sun," and his clothing was like glistening "snow."[10] He used this Transfiguration chiefly that the scandal of the Cross would be lifted from the hearts of the disciples, and that the humility of his voluntary suffering would not upset the faith of those to whom the perfection of his hidden dignity had been revealed. But, with no less foresight the hope of the holy Church was made firm, so that it might know with what sort of exchange the whole body of Christ was to be given, and that the members might promise to themselves a sharing in the honor of the one who had shone as their Head.

The Lord himself had said, when speaking about the majesty of his coming, "Then the just will shine like the sun in the kingdom of their Father."[11] Blessed Paul the apostle assures us of

---

7. Mt 17.1.
8. Mt 16.28.
9. Cf. Mt 5.8.
10. Cf. Mt 17.2.
11. Mt 13.43.

the same thing when he says, "For I think that the sufferings of this time are not to be compared to the future glory which will be revealed in us."[12] On another occasion, the same Apostle said, "For you have died, and your life is hidden with Christ in God. And, when Christ your life appears, then you also will appear with him in glory."[13]

4. To strengthen the apostles and to advance them in all knowledge, yet another lesson came in this miracle. Moses and Elijah, meaning the law and the prophets, appeared speaking with the Lord, so that, very truly in the presence of these five men, what was written might be fulfilled: "Among two or three witnesses every word will stand."[14] What is more stable, what is more firm, than this saying in whose message the trumpet of the Old and of the New Testaments sound, and with whose Gospel teaching the records of the ancient pronouncements concur? The pages of both Testaments agree with one other, and the splendor of his present glory shows, manifest and clear, the one whom the preceding signs had promised under a veil of mystery. As blessed John says, "The law was given through Moses, grace and truth have come through Jesus Christ,"[15] in whom both the promise of the prophetic figures and the reason of the commands of the law have been fulfilled, whilst he both teaches that the prophecy is true through his presence, and makes the commandments possible through his grace.

5. The apostle Peter, stirred by these revelations of the mysteries and rejecting things of the world just as he scorned earthly matters, in his desire of eternal things, was seized by some sort of ecstasy, and was filled with the joy of the whole vision, and wanted to live with Jesus there where his manifested glory brought delight. He therefore said, "Lord, it is good for us to be here; if you wish, let us make here three tents, one for you, one for Moses, and one for Elijah."[16] But the Lord did not respond to this suggestion, indicating that what Peter wanted was not only base but disordered, for the world could not be

---

12. Rom 8.18.
13. Col 3.3–4.
14. Dt 19.15 and 2 Cor 13.1. Cf. Mt 18.16.
15. Jn 1.17.
16. Mt 17.4.

saved except by the Death of Christ. By the Lord's example, the faith of believers is called to this, that although it behooves us not to doubt the promise of beatitude, we should understand that, in the vicissitudes of this life, perseverance must be requested before glory, because the happiness of reigning cannot come before the times of suffering.

6. And so, while he was still speaking, a bright cloud overshadowed him and a voice from the cloud said, "This is my beloved Son, in whom I am well pleased. Listen to him."[17] The Father was certainly present in the Son, and in that clarity of the Lord which he had tempered for the disciples' sight, the essence of the Father was not separated from his Only-Begotten, but in order to distinguish the quality of both Persons, the splendor of the body showed the Son to their sight, as the voice from the cloud made the Father known to their hearing.

When the voice was heard, the disciples fell on their faces and they were much afraid, but they trembled not only because of the majesty of the Father, but also because of the majesty of the Son, for by a higher sense they understood the one divinity in both. Because there was no hesitation in their faith, they made no distinction in their fear. This witness was broad and multiple, and it was heard rather in the force of the words than in the sound of the voice.

When the Father said, "This is my beloved Son, in whom I am well pleased. Listen to him," was it not clearly understood as "This is my Son" to whom it belongs to be eternally from me and with me? Neither is the Father prior to the Son, nor is the Son after the Father. "This is my Son" whom divinity does not separate, nor power divide, nor eternity distinguish from me. "This is my Son," not adopted but my own, not created by another but begotten from me, and not made comparable to me from any other nature but equal proceeding from my essence. "This is my Son," "through whom all things were made, and without whom nothing was made."[18] All the things I do, "he does likewise,"[19] and whatever "I cause, he causes" inseparably with me and no differently.[20]

17. Mt 17.5.
19. Cf. Jn 5.19.
18. Mt 17.5 and Jn 1.3.
20. Cf. Jn 5.17.

The "Son is in the Father and the Father in the Son," and our unity is never divided.[21] Although I am the one who begot, and he is another whom I have begotten, nevertheless, it is not right for you to think anything other concerning him than it is possible to think about me. "This is my Son," who has "not" sought by "robbery the equality" he has with me,[22] nor seized it by usurpation; but, existing in the form of my glory, in order to execute our common plan to restore the human race, he bent down the unchangeable divinity to the "form of a servant."[23]

7. Listen without delay, therefore, to the one in whom I am well pleased in all things, by whose preaching I am made known, by whose humility I am glorified, because he is "Truth and Life,"[24] he himself is "my Power and Wisdom."[25] "Listen to him," whom the mysteries of the law foretold, whom the mouths of the prophets announced. "Listen to him" who "redeemed" the world "with his blood,"[26] who "binds" the devil and "seizes his vessels,"[27] who has canceled the "decree" of sin"[28] and destroyed the pact of deceit. "Listen to him" who opens the way to heaven and, through the penalty of the Cross, prepares for you the steps of ascension to his kingdom. Why do you fear to be redeemed? Why, when bound, are you afraid to be freed? Let what Christ wills be done, with me willing it as well. Cast out human fear and arm yourselves with faithful constancy, it is unbecoming to fear in the suffering of the Savior what by his help you do not fear in your own end.

8. These things were said, dearly beloved, not only for the good of those who heard them with their own ears, but, in these three apostles, the whole Church has learned what their eyes have seen and their ears have heard. Let the faith of all then be strengthened by the teaching of the Holy Gospel, and let no one be ashamed of the Cross of Christ by which the world was redeemed. Subsequently, let no one "fear to suffer for justice,"[29] or be anxious about the repayment of the promises, because we pass through labor to rest, and through death to life.

---

21. Cf. Jn 10.38.
22. Cf. Phil 2.6.
23. Cf. Phil 2.7.
24. Cf. Jn 14.6.
25. Cf. 1 Cor 1.24.
26. Cf. Rv 5.9.
27. Cf. Mt 12.29.
28. Cf. Col 2.14.
29. Cf. 1 Pt 3.14.

Since he has taken on himself all the weakness of our lowliness, if we "remain" in him in faith and in "love,"[30] we conquer what he conquered and we receive what he promised. Whether in carrying out his commands or in bearing adversities, the prophetic voice of the Father ought always to sound in our ears: "This is my beloved Son, in whom I am well pleased. Listen to him,"[31] who lives and reigns with the Father and with the Holy Spirit for ever and ever. Amen.

30. Cf. Jn 15.9.
31. Mt 17.5.

PASSION OF THE LORD

Leo delivered a sermon on the Lord's Passion during Holy Week, breaking it up into parts over a couple of days, as he himself explained: "These things that I have put into your devout ears are enough today, dearly beloved, lest the weariness caused by too many words distress you. What still needs to be added we promise to give you on Wednesday, God willing, since he who has given what we have said, will give, we believe, what to say then, through Jesus Christ our Lord" (*Serm.* 52.5). Upon resuming that particular sermon, Leo states: "Fidelity demands, dearly beloved, that we should return to that part of the sermon which we promised concerning the Lord's Passion, he himself helping us, and I do not doubt that you are helping us in this with your prayers as well" (*Serm.* 53.1).

Within this series of sermons, Leo touches on many aspects of the Passion—from the Last Supper all the way through the Resurrection. Some of his deepest reflections on the mystery of Redemption come from this collection, a fact that brings us to regret very much the loss of sermons from 446 to 451 and from 455 to 461. Leo explains to the congregation—simply, clearly, but sublimely—his personal insights into the real meaning of every person, place, and thing involved in the Passion—from the foreshadowings of the Old Testament to the realities of the New. He urges them continually to meditate upon the Passion because "never can enough be said [about it]" (*Serm.* 62.1).

While the specific incidents upon which he chooses to focus vary throughout these sermons, Leo always manages to reiterate the truth about the Incarnation—generally with a view to refuting current heresies. "We should not let either of these groups make it seem that what has been done for us, not only humbly but sublimely as well, would be either impossible (with respect to human beings) or unworthy (with respect to God). But both should be accepted, both believed. No human being can be saved except through both" (*Serm.* 56.1).

Leo often remarks that the Passion continues to be real for all believers, as real as it was to those who were actually present during it. Leo's eloquence waxes as he becomes personally involved in the events, directly addressing the participants and thereby increasing the pathos. "Return[, o Judas,] to your former state. Abandon your fury. Come to your senses. Kindness invites you. Your salvation demands it. Life calls you back to life" (*Serm.* 58.3). "From what fountain of error, o

Jews, from what lake of ill will have you drunk the poison of such blasphemies? What teacher instructed you, what doctrine persuaded you, that you ought to believe someone to be King of Israel, someone to be the Son of God, if he would not allow himself to be crucified or would shake his body free from the grip of nails? No mysteries of the law, no rites of the Paschal observance, no words of the prophets proclaimed this to you" (*Serm.* 55.2).

Sermon 52

16 March 441—Palm Sunday

TODAY'S PASSAGE from the Gospel has unfolded for us, dearly beloved, the mystery of our Lord's Passion. Our Lord Jesus the Son of God undertook it for the salvation of the human race. According to his promise, "he has drawn all things to himself in being lifted up."[1] So plainly and clearly has the Gospel unfolded this mystery that, to devout and holy hearts, hearing it read is the same as seeing the actual events. Since the sacred narrative holds undoubted authority, we are obliged to try, with the Lord's help, to have our intellect grasp what history has made known.

After that first and universal fall of human transgression—from which "through one man sin entered into this world, and through sin death, and death has thereby spread to all people, in that all have sinned"[2]—no one could escape the terrible dominion of the devil nor the chains of harsh captivity. Reconciliation to pardon would lie open for no one, nor a return to life—had God the Son (co-eternal with and co-equal to God the Father) not condescended to become the son of a human being, coming "to seek out and to save what had been lost."[3]

As "death" came "through Adam," so "through" our Lord Jesus Christ came "resurrection of the dead."[4] According to the impenetrable design of God's wisdom, simply because "the Word became flesh"[5] "in these last days,"[6] this does not mean that the Savior's Birth from the Virgin profited the generations

---

1. Cf. Jn 12.32.
2. Rom 5.12.
3. Lk 19.10.
4. Cf. 1 Cor 15.21.
5. Jn 1.14.
6. Cf. 1 Pt 1.20.

of these last days only and did not pour itself out also for ages past.

Certainly all the ancients who worshipped the true God, the entire multitude of saints in former ages, lived in this faith and pleased God. There was no salvation or justification for patriarchs, or for prophets, or for anyone of the saints at all, except in the Redemption of the Lord Jesus Christ. Just as the promise was foretold by many words and signs of the prophets, so it is now itself made present by the same grace and action.

2. Thus it is, dearly beloved, that in the whole course of the Lord's Passion, we should not make so much of human infirmity that we think divine power to have been lacking there. Nor should we look at this "form"[7] of the Only-Begotten (co-eternal with and equal to the Father) in such a way that we should not believe true the things that seem unworthy of God. Certainly, in both natures and in the one Christ, neither the Word is cut off from the man, nor the man separated from the Word. Humility was not despised because majesty had not been diminished. Nothing which had to be inflicted on the suffering nature has harmed the inviolable one.

This whole mystery (which both humanity and divinity have completed together) was a dispensation of mercy and an act of love. With such chains are we held bound that only by this grace can we be released. Condescension by the divinity therefore becomes our advancement. "By so great a price" are we redeemed,[8] at such great cost are we healed. What return would there be from wickedness to justice, from misery to blessedness, unless the just leaned down to the wicked and the blessed bent himself down to the miserable?

3. We must not, then, be ashamed of the Cross, dearly beloved, for it comes from the strength of divine wisdom, not from a state of sin. Our Lord Jesus truly suffered with our weakness and truly died. Yet he did not so deprive himself of his own glory that, in the midst of the insults of his Passion, he exercised nothing of his divine operations.[9]

---

7. Cf. Phil 2.6.   8. Cf. 1 Cor 6.20 and 7.23.
9. Cf. (for the following section) St. Augustine, *Tractatus in Iohannem* 112.2–3.

Wicked Judas—no longer covered in sheep's clothing but flushed out into the open as a ravenous wolf[10]—embarked upon the violence of crime through the appearances of peace, offering as the sign of his treason a kiss more deadly than any weapon. That raging crowd which had converged to apprehend the Lord with a cohort of armed soldiers, blinded by their own shadows, could not discern the true light amid torches and lanterns. At this point, the Lord (who had chosen to wait for the crowd rather than withdraw—as John the Evangelist shows), when he had not yet been recognized, asked whom they sought. When they said that they were looking for Jesus, he answered, "I am he."[11]

This response, like a blast of thunder, so struck and scattered that band (made up of the wildest men) that all of them—cruel, menacing, and fierce as they were—retreated and fell down. Where was the conspiracy of violence? Where was the fire of wrath? Where were the arms that had been drawn? When the Lord said, "I am he,"[12] the mob of wicked men was flung down at the utterance. What, then, will his majesty not be able to do when he sits in judgment, he whose lowliness could not be judged?

4. Indeed, however, the Lord (knowing what belonged more to the mystery he had chosen to undergo) did not insist upon using his power. He allowed his persecutors to return to their plan for the crime that had been arranged beforehand. For if he were unwilling to be taken, he certainly would not have been. But what human being could be saved if that human being had not allowed himself to be apprehended?

Blessed Peter—who lived with the Lord in the staunchest loyalty and burned with the fire of holy love against the attacks of violent men—used his sword on the servant of the high priest and cut off the ear of that fiercely threatening man. But the Lord did not allow this zealous initiative of the eager apostle to proceed further. He ordered him to sheathe his sword and did not allow himself to be defended against the attackers with hand or steel.[13]

---

10. Cf. Mt 7.15.
12. Cf. Jn 18.4–5
11. Cf. Jn 18.4–5.
13. Cf. Mt 26.51–52.

It was contrary to the mystery of our Redemption that he who came to die for all should be unwilling to be apprehended. If the triumph of the glorious Cross would have been delayed, the domination of the devil would have continued longer and the captivity of humanity been drawn out. He therefore gives his attackers freedom to rage against himself, for divinity does not want to manifest itself to such as these. Christ's hand restores the servant's ear (already dead as a result of the cut and severed from the frame of the living body), returning it to its place on the injured head.[14] He forms again what he himself had formed in the first place, and the flesh at once follows the command of the one who made it.

5. These works now have divine force. Because the Lord conceals the power of his majesty and gives access to the force of his persecutor against him, it is from this very will that "he loved us and handed himself over for us."[15] Cooperating in this, the Father "did not spare his own Son, but handed him over for us all."[16] There is one will of the Father and the Son, just as there is one divinity. For the result of this action we owe no thanks to you, Jews, nor to you, Judas. Your wickedness served the purposes of our salvation indeed, though without your willing it, and through you there happened "what the hand of God and the plan of God had decreed to happen."[17]

Consequently, the Death of Christ frees us but accuses you. According to justice, you alone do not possess what you wished to destroy for all. Still, so great is the goodness of our Redeemer that even you can receive pardon—if, by confessing Christ to be the Son of God, you put aside this murderous ill will. It was not in vain that the Lord prayed on the cross, "Father, forgive them, for they know not what they do."[18]

This healing would not have passed you by, Judas, if you had fled to that penitence which would recall you to Christ—and not to that which would urge you on to the noose. But, though saying, "I have sinned, handing over innocent blood,"[19] you persisted in the wickedness of your disloyalty. Even in the ulti-

14. Cf. Lk 22.51.
15. Eph 5.2.
16. Rom 8.32.
17. Cf. Acts 4.28.
18. Lk 23.34.
19. Mt 27.4.

mate danger of your own death, you believed Jesus to be not God the Son of God, but only a man of our own race. You would have drawn his mercy to you if you had not denied his omnipotence.

(2) These things that I have put into your devout ears are enough today, dearly beloved, lest the weariness caused by too many words distress you. What still needs to be added we promise to give you on Wednesday, God willing, since he who has given what we have said, will give, we believe, what to say then, through Jesus Christ our Lord.

Sermon 53

19 March 441—Wednesday of Holy Week

Fidelity demands, dearly beloved, that we should return to that part of the sermon which we promised concerning the Lord's Passion, he himself helping us, and I do not doubt that you are helping us in this with your prayers as well. It is to our common advantage if you can consider me beholden, for whatever has been attributed to my skill would be spent on your edification.

(2) After that wicked and detestable bribery of Judas—by which the Redeemer of the world was betrayed by him to the hostile Jews—and after those sacrilegious mockeries in which his meekness was led right up to the place of his punishment, two thieves were crucified with him, their crosses on either side.

One, up to now the equal in all things of his companion, a robber on the roads and always a danger to the safety of people, deserving the cross, suddenly becomes a confessor of Christ. Among those sharp tortures of body and soul—which at the same time both the pressure and the distress of death were increasing—he was changed by a wonderful conversion and said, "Remember me, Lord, when you enter into your kingdom."[20]

What discourse urged him to this faith? What doctrine infused it? What preacher aroused it? He had seen none of the miracles that had been performed earlier. By that time, cures

---

20. Lk 23.42.

of the sick had ceased, as had giving light to the eyes of the blind and giving life to the dead. On the other hand, those things which were soon to be done had not yet arrived. Nevertheless, he confessed him to be Lord and King, the one he sees as a companion in his own punishment.

Thence came this gift in which faith itself received a response, for Jesus said to him, "Amen, I say to you, today you will be with me in Paradise."[21] This promise surpasses the human condition, for it issued not so much from the wood of a cross as from a throne of power. From that height is reward given to faith. There the debt of human transgression is abolished,[22] because the "form of God" did not separate itself from the "form of a servant."[23] Even in the midst of this punishment, both the inviolable divinity and the suffering human nature preserved its own character and its own oneness.

2. For the reinforcement of our hope, the witness of all creation has been added. When Christ gave up his spirit, all the elements trembled, the brightness of the sun (obscured with thick shadows) turned the day into unnatural night, the earth (struck with deep shocks) could not keep its stability, and the firmness of rocks (their solidity broken) burst asunder. In addition, the veil of the temple (no longer to shadow the mysteries of the past) was torn, the bodies of many saints were stirred up, and—to strengthen faith in the coming resurrection—tombs were opened.[24]

Heaven and earth passed sentence against you, Jews—as the sun withdrew its service of giving daylight, and the laws of nature denied you their function. When the service of creation departs from its laws, it is your blindness and your confusion that have been signified. When you said, "His blood be upon us and upon our children,"[25] you received what was coming to you. That which the faithless part of your race has lost, the believing "fullness of the nations"[26] would attain.

3. As a result, dearly beloved, our Lord Jesus Christ crucified

---

21. Lk 23.43.
22. Cf. Col 2.14.
23. Cf. Phil 2.6–7.
24. Cf. Mt 27.50–53.
25. Mt 27.25.
26. Cf. Rom 11.25.

is not an "obstacle" nor "foolishness" to us, but "the power of God and the wisdom of God."[27] We, I say, are the spiritual offspring of Abraham, not born as children of slavery but reborn into the family of liberty.[28] For us "was Christ" the true and spotless Lamb "sacrificed,"[29] the one who had been led "with mighty hand and outstretched arm"[30] from the oppression of Egyptian rule.

Let us, then, embrace the wonderful mystery of the saving Passover, and be re-formed into the image of the one who conformed himself to our deformity. Let us be raised to the one who made the dust of our lowliness into the body of his glory. That we might deserve to be companions of his Resurrection, let us adapt ourselves to his humility and patience in all things. We are undertaking the service of a great name, the discipline of a great profession.

Followers of Christ may not stray from the king's highway. We are bound not to be preoccupied with temporal affairs as we head for the eternal. Because we have been redeemed by the precious blood of Christ, "let us glorify and carry God in our body,"[31] so that we may deserve to come to those things which have been prepared for the faithful through Jesus Christ our Lord, to whom is honor and glory forever and ever. Amen.

Sermon 54

5 April 442—Palm Sunday

Among all the works of God's mercy, dearly beloved, which from the beginning have been devoted to the salvation of mortals, none is more wonderful, none more sublime, than that Christ was crucified for the world. All the mysteries of former times serve this mystery. Whatever details had been laid down by sacred decree—in the assortment of victims, in the prophetic signs, and in legal regulations—all these predicted an outcome and promised a fulfillment. Now that images and

---

27. Cf. 1 Cor 1.23–24.
28. Cf. Gal 4.31.
29. Cf. 1 Cor 5.7.
30. Ps 135(136).12.
31. Cf. 1 Cor 6.20.

figures have ceased, we profit by believing what has already been done, just as they did by believing that it was going to be done.

(2) In everything that pertains to the Passion of our Lord Jesus Christ, dearly beloved, Catholic Faith has handed this down, has demanded this. We need to know that two natures have come together in our Redeemer, and that, while its own characteristics remain, so great a unity of the two substances came about that, from the time when—as the course of human nature demanded—"the Word was made flesh"[32] in the womb of the Blessed Virgin, we cannot think of him as God without that which is man, nor can we think of him as man without that which is God.

Each nature expresses its own truth in its own distinct actions, but neither separates itself from its connection with the other. Neither one lacks anything there, but the whole lowliness is in his majesty, while the whole majesty in his lowliness. Unity brings no confusion, nor does the distinctiveness ruin the unity. One is subject to suffering, the other inviolable.

Yet reproach belongs to the very one to whom glory belongs also. It is the same [Person] in weakness who is also in strength; the same [Person] is capable of death who is also victor over death. God took on the whole man and bound himself to man and man to himself by the plan of his mercy and power, in such a way that each nature is in the other and neither crosses over into the other from its own distinctiveness.

2. But because the dispensation of the mystery, planned for our restoration before eternal ages, was not to be completed without human weakness nor without divine strength, "each form"[33] does what is proper to it in communion with the other, that is, the Word doing what belongs to the Word, the flesh carrying out what belongs to the flesh. One of these shines forth in miracles, the other succumbs to injuries. The former does not withdraw from equality with the Father's glory, while the latter does not relinquish the nature of our race.

32. Jn 1.14.
33. Cf. Phil 2.6–7.

Nevertheless, even the acceptance of sufferings has not been exposed to the tendencies of our lowliness so much that it is drawn away from the power of divinity. Whatever mockery and disgrace, whatever harassment and punishment the rage of wicked people inflicted on the Lord, it was not tolerated through necessity but undertaken by free will. "The Son of Man has come to seek and to save what was lost."[34] Thus he used the malice of his persecutors for the redemption of all, so that even his murderers could be saved if only they would believe in the mystery of his Death and Resurrection.

3. You stand out, Judas, as more wicked than all the rest, and more unhappy, for penitence did not call you back to the Lord, but despair drew you to the noose. If only you had waited for the completion of your crime until the blood of Christ had been poured out for all sinners, you would have put off the gruesome death of hanging. When so many miracles of the Lord and so many of his gifts tortured your conscience, these mysteries at least would have called you back from your rash deed, the ones you had accepted when already at the Paschal meal you were detected in your treachery by the sign of divine knowledge.

Why do you distrust his goodness, who did not refuse you the communion of his body and blood, who did not deny the kiss of peace to you coming to arrest him with a crowd and a cohort of armed men? But, as you are an incorrigible man, "a breeze passing and not returning,"[35] you followed the madness of your own heart. "With the devil standing at your right hand,"[36] the wickedness that you had armed against the chief of all the saints you have now turned against your own head. Since your crime has surpassed all measure of punishment, your wickedness makes you the judge, and your punishment allows you to be your own executioner.

4. "God was in Christ, reconciling the world to himself,"[37] and the Creator himself was bearing the humanity that was about to be restored to the image of its Maker. Marvelous works

---

34. Lk 19.10.
36. Cf. Ps 108(109).6.
35. Ps 77(78).39.
37. 2 Cor 5.19.

of God had been accomplished, works that the prophetic spirit had foretold were one day to be done: "Then the eyes of the blind will be opened, the ears of the deaf will hear, then the lame will leap like stags, and the tongues of the dumb will be open."[38] Jesus knew that the time for the fulfillment of his glorious Passion was at hand and said, "My soul is sorrowful even unto death,"[39] and, on another occasion, "Father, if it is possible, let this cup pass away from me."[40] Since these words expressed a certain fear, he cured the emotion of our weakness by participating in it, and drove away the anxiety in the experience of suffering by undergoing it.

In us, therefore, the Lord trembled with our terror, that he might clothe himself by the putting on of our weakness, and wrap our inconstancy in the firmness of his strength. He had come into this world as the rich and merciful ambassador from heaven. He had entered the economy of salvation in a wonderful interchange, receiving our state and giving us his own, giving honors for insults, health for pain, life for death.[41] He, whom more than "twelve thousand of his angelic legions"[42] could serve by annihilating his persecutors, preferred to accept our fear rather than to exercise his own power.

5. Blessed Peter the apostle was the first to learn how much this humility bestowed upon all the faithful. When the violent storm of a cruel assault had overwhelmed him, he was turned by a sudden conversion to the restoration of his energy. He drew a remedy from the Lord's example, and the trembling member returned at once to the firmness of its Head. This servant could not be greater than his Lord, nor this disciple greater than his Teacher,[43] a Teacher who would not conquer the anxiety of human frailty without first experiencing fear—and conquering it.

Then "the Lord looked at Peter."[44] Standing amid the insults of priests, the lies of witnesses, the injuries of those who struck

---

38. Is 35.5–6.
39. Mt 26.38.
40. Mt 26.39 and Mk 14.36.
41. Cf. Augustine, *Enarratio in Ps. 30* (2.1.3).
42. Cf. Mt 26.53.
43. Cf. Jn 15.20.
44. Lk 22.61.

him and spat on him, he met the troubled disciple with his eyes, the same eyes with which he had foreseen that Peter would undergo a struggle. In so doing, the gaze of Truth entered into Peter, directed toward the place where the amendment of his heart was to be grounded. It was as if the Lord's voice were resounding within him and saying: What are you thinking, Peter? Why do you withdraw into yourself? Turn to me, trust in me, "follow me."[45] This is the time for my Passion; the hour of your suffering has not yet come. Why do you fear what you yourself will also overcome? Let not the weakness which I have accepted disturb you. I was anxious for you, but you should not worry about me.

(2) "When morning came, all the chief priests and the elders of the people met in council against Jesus, that they might hand him over to death."[46] O Jews, this morning it was not the rising of light that touched you, but its setting. No, the usual daylight did not benefit your eyes, but the night of dark blindness lay over your wicked souls. This morning destroyed for you the temple and the altars, removed the law and the prophets, abolished the kingdom and priesthood, and changed all the festivities into eternal sorrow. You embarked upon that wild and blood-drenched plan as "fat bulls, many calves," raging beasts, "mad dogs,"[47] so that you might hand over to death the "Author of Life"[48] and "Lord of Glory."[49]

As if the magnitude of your fury might be lessened in your dependence on the judgment of the one who presided over your province, you led Jesus bound to Pilate, so that when the tremulous judge had been overcome by the unjust clamors, you might select the assassin for pardon and might seek out the Savior of the world for punishment. After this condemnation of Christ, which the ignorance (rather than the power) of Pilate carried out, with hands washed and mouth polluted, he sent Jesus to the cross with the same lips with which he had pronounced him innocent. The abuse of the people, with the

---

45. Cf. Jn 21.22.
47. Cf. Ps 21(22).13 and 17.
49. Cf. 1 Cor 2.8.
46. Mt 27.1.
48. Cf. Acts 3.15.

priests as their spokesmen, forced on the Lord many mockeries, and the wild crowd raged against the meekness of the one who bore these things willingly.

(3) But, since there is a great deal to be said here, dearly beloved, let the remaining things be put off until Wednesday (assuming that the day's sermon should cover it all) when the reading of the Lord's Passion will be repeated. With your prayers, the Lord will be present, that we might carry out with his help what we have promised, through Christ our Lord. Amen.

Sermon 55
8 April 442—Wednesday of Holy Week

With the Lord's help, dearly beloved, I must repay the debt that you expect of me. Your prayers have earned that the one who gave you the inclination to ask for it should make me worthy to fulfill your expectation. Speaking in the last sermon about the Lord's Passion, we came to a point in the Gospel narrative where Pilate is said to have given way to the wicked clamor of Jews that Jesus should be crucified.

When everything that the divinity allowed to be done in the limiting veil of flesh had been carried out, Jesus the Son of God was nailed to a cross which he himself had carried—along with two thieves, one on his right, the other on his left, crucified in the same way.[50] Even in the very appearance of the gallows was shown that criterion which would be applied when he comes to judge all human beings. Faith on the part of the believing thief prefigured those who were to be saved, while wickedness on the part of the blasphemer foreshadowed those who were to be condemned.[51]

Christ's Passion, therefore, contains the mystery of our salvation. From the instrument which the iniquity of Jews devised as a punishment, the Redeemer's power has made for us a step up to glory. This is what the Lord Jesus undertook for the salvation of all when, as he was being held to the wood by nails, he

---

50. Cf. Mt 27.38 and Lk 23.33.
51. Cf. Lk 23.39–43.

implored his Father's mercy for his murderers, saying, "Father, forgive them, for they know not what they do."⁵²

2. Meanwhile, the chief priests for whom the Savior was asking forgiveness were intensifying the suffering of the cross with the sting of their ridicule. Against the one whom they were not able to injure further with their hands, they cast the weapons of their tongues, saying, "He saved others, himself he cannot save. If he is the King of Israel, let him come down from the cross, and we shall believe in him."⁵³

From what fountain of error, o Jews, from what lake of ill will have you drunk the poison of such blasphemies? What teacher instructed you, what doctrine persuaded you, that you ought to believe someone to be king of Israel, someone to be the Son of God, if he would not allow himself to be crucified or would shake his body free from the grip of nails? No mysteries of the law, no rites of the Paschal observance, no words of the prophets proclaimed this to you.

On the other hand, you have truly and in very many places read something which pertains to the detestable wickedness of your crime and to the voluntary suffering of the Lord. He himself speaks through Isaiah: "I gave my back to scourges, my cheeks to striking hands; my face I did not shield from the insult of spittle."⁵⁴ He says through David: "They put gall in my food, and in my thirst they gave me vinegar to drink."⁵⁵ On yet another occasion, he says through David: "Many dogs surround me, a pack of evildoers closes in upon me. They have pierced my hands and my feet, they have numbered all my bones. They watched me carefully and examined me. They divided my garments among them and cast lots for my clothes."⁵⁶ Lest only the kind of your crime might seem to be predicted and the power of the crucified one not foretold, you certainly did not read that the Lord descended from the cross. You did, however, read: "The Lord has reigned from the cross."⁵⁷

52. Lk. 23.34.
53. Mt 27.42.
54. Is 50.6.
55. Ps 68(69).22.
56. Ps 21(22).17–19.
57. Ps 95(96).10.

3. This Cross of Christ holds the mystery of its true and prophesied altar. There, through the Saving Victim, an oblation of human nature is celebrated. There, the blood of a Spotless Lamb effaced the pact of that ancient transgression. There, the whole perversity of the devil's mastery was abolished, while humility triumphed as conqueror over the vaunting of pride. So swift was the effect of faith that, of the two thieves crucified with Christ, the one who believed in the Son of God entered "Paradise" justified.[58]

Who could explain the mystery of such a great gift? Who could describe the power of such a marvelous transformation? In a brief moment of time, the guilt of a long-standing wickedness was abolished. In the midst of the harsh torments of a struggling soul, though fastened to the gallows, that thief passes over to Christ, and the grace of Christ gives a crown to him, someone who incurred punishment for his own wickedness.

4. When our Lord had tasted the "vinegar"[59] (having issued from a vineyard that had degenerated from its author's stock and been turned into the bitterness "of a spurious vine"),[60] the Lord said, "It is finished,"[61] that is to say, the Scriptures have been fulfilled. There remains nothing more for me to wait for from the madness of angry people. I have endured nothing less than I foretold I would suffer. Mysteries of weakness have been accomplished. Now let the evidence for power be produced. So, "bowing his head, he breathed forth his spirit,"[62] and, into the body that would be raised on the third day, he admitted the quiet of peaceful sleep.

When the Author of Life spent himself for this mystery and the structure of the whole world was shaken at so great an abasement of divine majesty, when all creation by its own disorder condemned the wicked crime, and the very elements gave out a clear judgment against the culprits—what then was your feeling, Jews, what was your conscience? When the judgment of all pressed upon you and your wickedness could not recall

---

58. Cf. Lk 23.43.
60. Cf. Jer 2.21.
62. Jn 19.30 and Mt 27.50.
59. Cf. Jn 19.30.
61. Jn 19.30.

itself from the completed crime, what confusion poured over you? What punishment seized your heart?

5. So great, dearly beloved, is the mercy of God that, even from such a people, he was willing to justify many through faith. Into the company of the patriarchs and into the family of the chosen race, he has adopted us, who were at one time perishing in the night of our long-standing ignorance. So then, let us run to the peak of our hope, not lazily and not listlessly, but recognizing prudently and faithfully from what captivity and from what wretched servitude, and with what "price," we have been "redeemed,"[63] and with what "arm" we have been "brought out."[64] Let us "glorify God in our bodies"[65] to show from the goodness of our lives that he lives in us.

Since there is nothing in the scale of virtues that has more worth than the holiness of mercy and the purity of chastity, let us equip ourselves more especially with these protections. That way, with the labor of love and the splendor of chastity, we might—as if raised up on a pair of wings—from "earthly" beings deserve to become "heavenly."[66] Whoever are filled with this desire (aided by the grace of God) and do not "boast" about their progress in themselves but "in the Lord,"[67] such people honor the Paschal Mystery properly. Into their house, the devastating angel does not come, since it bears the Lamb's blood and the sign of the Cross. They have no fear of the Egyptian plagues and leave their enemies annihilated in the same waters with which they themselves have been saved.

(2) And so, dearly beloved, let us embrace the wonderful mystery of our salvation with purified souls and bodies. Cleansed from all "leaven of the old evil,"[68] let us celebrate the Lord's Passover by a worthy observance. With the Holy Spirit ruling us, let us not "be separated from the love of Christ"[69] by any temptations, for he who has "made peace in all things by his own blood,"[70] has taken himself up to the height of his Father's

63. Cf. 1 Cor 6.20.
64. Cf. Ps 135(136).11–12 and Ex 15.16.
65. Cf. 1 Cor 6.20.   66. Cf. 1 Cor 15.48–49.
67. Cf. 2 Cor 10.17 and 1 Cor 1.31.
68. Cf. 1 Cor 5.7.   69. Cf. Rom 8.35.
70. Cf. Col 1.20.

glory and yet has not left the lowliness of those serving him. To him is honor and glory forever and ever. Amen.

Sermon 56

28 March 443—Palm Sunday

Christ, the Creator and Lord of all things—after he had been born miraculously from the Holy Virgin, after the wise men had worshipped him with homage at his cradle, and after teaching of the divine word had abounded and the healing of various maladies had been effected by the command of his powerful word[71]—after all this, Christ, the Creator and Lord of all things completes the dispensation of all mysteries and of all powers through his saving Passion.

Consequently, dearly beloved, the Cross of Christ represents the true reason for and the principal cause of Christian hope. Though it seems "to the Jews an obstacle, to the Gentiles foolishness," nevertheless, it constitutes for us "the power of God and the wisdom of God."[72] As a result, this highest and most powerful mystery of divine mercy must always be held in our hearts with all its dignity. Now, however, it demands a more lively disposition of soul and a purer apprehension of mind, when, not only by the return of this time of year but also by the text of the Gospel reading, the whole work of our salvation is presented to us.

Let thoughts of the wicked, then, have no place with us, and let neither Jewish outrages nor the derision of pagans disturb the integrity of a healthy discernment. We should not let either of these groups make it seem that what has been done for us, not only humbly but sublimely as well, would be either impossible (with respect to human beings) or unworthy (with respect to God). But both should be accepted, both believed. No human being can be saved except through both.

(2) God is just and merciful, but he did not use the rights of his will simply to exercise the power of his kindness for our

---

71. Cf. (for what precedes) Gaudentius, *Tr.* 12.5 (CSEL 68.110–11)
72. 1 Cor 1.23–24.

restoration. Because it followed as a natural consequence that "a human being, by sinning, should become the slave of sin,"[73] medicine was dispensed to the sick, reconciliation to the guilty, and redemption to captives—in such a way that the just sentence of condemnation might be rescinded by the just work of a liberator.

If divinity alone stood forth on behalf of sinners, the devil would have been conquered not so much by reason as by power. On the other hand, if mortal nature alone pleaded the cause of the fallen, it would not be divested of its condition nor free of its race. It was necessary that both the divine and the human substance come together into the one Lord Jesus Christ, so that, through the Word made flesh, both the birth of the new man and his suffering should come to the aid of our mortality.

2. Since, therefore, the blindness of Jews would not see the divine in Jesus Christ, and the wisdom of Gentiles despises the human, while the former are bringing false information against the glory of God and the latter are vaunting themselves against his lowliness, we worship the Son of God both in his strengths and in our weaknesses. We are not ashamed of the Cross of Christ, and, among the tongues of slanderers, we do not doubt his Death or Resurrection. What draws the proud to infidelity, this very thing directs us to faith, and what with them constitutes a matter for shame, with us gives cause for reverence.

(2) When the Lord had warned his disciples to fight against the strength of temptation by the constant prayer of watchfulness, he himself said in supplication to the Father, "My Father, if it is possible, let this cup pass away from me. Nevertheless, not as I will, but as you will."[74] The first is a petition of weakness, the second of strength; the former he asks from our condition, the other is a choice from his own.

The Son who is equal to the Father was not ignorant of the fact that all things are possible to God. He had not descended

---

73. Cf. Jn 8.34.
74. Mt 26.39.

into this world to take up the cross without a will of his own. That way, he would suffer the conflict between diverse feelings, with his judgment perturbed to some extent. That there should be a clear distinction between the nature taken up and the nature of the one who had taken it up, what was of man desired the divine power, what was of God had concern for the human cause. Subsequently, the lower will yielded to the higher.

It was soon shown what could be prayed for by one in fear, and what ought not to be granted by the healer. Because "we do not know how to pray as we ought"[75] and it is good for us very often not to have what we want, God (who is just and good) mercifully denies the harmful things asked for. The Lord then firmly strengthens the correction of our will with the threefold prayer. While the disciples are still heavy with grief, he says, "Sleep now and take your rest. The hour has come when the Son of Man will be betrayed into the hands of sinners. Get up. Let us go. My betrayer has already arrived."[76]

3. At these words of the Lord, those he had spoken of rushed in, and the crowd converged to apprehend Christ with swords and clubs, following the lead of Judas Iscariot, who had obtained pride of place in the crime by the privilege of his treachery. No honor was denied him, lest any offense should give him an excuse for crime. Instead, enkindled, he burned with the spirit of that one to whom he willingly offered himself as an accomplice. Such was the mind he had, such also was the leader he found. Deservedly, as the prophet said, "his prayer became sin,"[77] for when the deed was done, his conversion was so perverted that he sinned even in repentance.

(2) The Son of God then allowed wicked hands to be laid on himself, and what was set in motion by the rage of the aggressors is completed by the power of the sufferer. Here was that "mystery of great holiness"[78] which Christ consecrated by his injuries. If he had overthrown these men by straightforward power and manifest strength, he would only have been exercis-

75. Rom 8.26.
77. Cf. Ps 108(109).7.
76. Mt 26.45–46.
78. Cf. 1 Tm 3.16.

ing divinity, but not healing humanity. In all things that the madness of the people and priests insolently and shamelessly brought against him, however, it was our uncleanness that was washed away, our offenses that were expiated.[79] For the nature (which in us has always been guilty and captive) suffered in him, though innocent and free. To "take away the sin of the world," that "Lamb offered" himself "as a victim"[80] whom both his bodily substance joined to everyone else, and his spiritual origin distinguished from everyone else.

(2) This is enough to put in your ears today, dearly beloved. Let the other things be postponed until Wednesday, and, with God helping us by your prayers, he will deign to allow that we might fulfill our promise.

Sermon 57

31 March 443—Wednesday of Holy Week

Mindful of our promise, dearly beloved, we are rendering what we owe to your good faith. We hope that the grace of God will be with us, so that, from the very source that stimulated the promise, devotion might come forth for us. When the Lord Jesus Christ was taken by the crowds which the high priests and doctors of the law had armed, he curtailed his power in order to fulfill the plan that had been arranged, ordering the blessed apostle Peter (who had been aroused by human wrath against the attackers) to withhold his sword.[81] It would be incongruous that he who did not wish to be aided by the protection of angelic legions should want to be defended by the intervention of one disciple.

Although the ferocious crowd accomplished what it wanted and exulted at the result of its crime, nevertheless, there was greater strength in the captured than in those capturing. The blindness of Jews gained nothing, except that they lost themselves through their own wickedness, but the patience of Christ brought this about, that he saved everyone by his Passion.

79. Cf. Is 53.5–6 and 11–12.   80. Cf. Heb 10.12 and Jn 1.29.
81. Cf. Mt 26.52.

2. When Jesus was led to Caiaphas, the chief priest, where the scribes and all the priestly order had assembled, they searched for false testimonies against the Lord. Among the confused and dissonant voices, however, Jesus maintained a wonderful silence. When Caiaphas said, "I adjure you by the living God to tell us if you are the Christ, the Son of God,"[82] he replied with such true and far-seeing authority that with the same words he both struck at the consciences of unbelievers and strengthened the hearts of believers, answering all the interrogations with, "You have said it," and adding what follows: "Nevertheless, I say to you that, from this time onward, you will see the Son of Man being sitting at the right hand of power and coming on the clouds of heaven."[83]

Caiaphas, to exaggerate his ire at the words he had heard, "tore his clothes,"[84] and, not understanding what he had signified by this madness, deprived himself of the priestly honor. Where, Caiaphas, is your breastplate "of decision"? Where is your belt of continence? Where is the humeral of strength?[85] You have despoiled yourself on your own of the mystical and sacred robe. With your own hands did you rend the priestly garments, forgetful of that command which you had read concerning the chief priest, "He is not to remove the headdress from his head or rend his garments."[86] But you, by whom this dignity was now being removed, you yourself are the agent of your own disgrace, and, to show the end of the Old Covenant, the same destruction was taking away the priestly emblems which soon afterwards also tore asunder the veil of the temple.

3. From here, dearly beloved, when the night had passed in innumerable mockeries, they delivered Jesus bound to Pilate (who was presiding). The chief priests and the elders of the people were carrying out the affair with this plan, that they should seem removed from the action of their crime, withdrawing the work of their hands, and thrusting forth the weap-

82. Mt 26.63.   83. Mt 26.64.
84. Mt 26.65.
85. Cf. Ex 28 for a description of vestments worn by the high priest.
86. Lv 10.6 and 21.10.

ons of their tongues, themselves unwilling to kill, yet crying out, "Crucify him! Crucify him!"[87]

What is more unjust than this pretense of religion? What is more cruel than this caricature of mercy? By what law, Jews, are you permitted to will what you are not permitted to carry out? By what reasoning does that which defiles your body not violate your heart? You feared to be contaminated by the slaughter of the one whose blood you later demanded to be poured over you and your children. If your wickedness does not carry out the whole crime, allow the governor to judge as he thinks best. But you, severe and violent even against him, do not permit the governor to turn aside from the condemnation from which you yourselves hypocritically abstain.

(2) Pilate sinned in doing what he did not will, but into your conscience floods whatever your fury wrenched from him. Such also was your observance there, that you would not allow the price which the betrayer of Christ brought back to you to be put into the treasury, taking care lest blood money pollute the sacred chest. From what kind of heart comes this hypocrisy of yours? The conscience of the priests receives what the coffers of the temple do not. The price of this blood is rejected, but the pouring out of it is not feared. With however many shadows of falsehood you wrap yourselves around, the commerce entered into with the traitor remains. In it, just as it was not allowable to purchase just blood, so it was not allowable to shed it.

4. With Pilate yielding, therefore, to the seditious clamor of Jews, Christ is crucified in the place named Golgatha. He who fell because of a tree is raised up by the tree, and the food which occasioned sin is washed out by the taste of gall and vinegar. Before he was betrayed, the Lord had rightly said, "When I have been lifted up, I shall draw all to myself,"[88] that is, I will deal with the whole condition of humanity and will call back to integrity the nature lost long ago. In me will all weakness be abolished, in me will all wounds be healed.

---

87. Jn 19.6.
88. Jn 12.32.

It has been shown that Jesus, when lifted up, did draw all to himself, not only by suffering in our substance, but even by a disturbance of the whole world.[89] While the Creator was hanging on the gallows, all creation groaned, and all the elements at the same time felt the nails of the cross. Nothing was free from that punishment. By this he drew both earth and heaven into communion with himself, by this he broke the "rocks," opened the "tombs," unlocked hell,[90] and hid the sun's rays with the horror of thick "darkness."[91] The world owed this witness to its own Creator, so that in the fall of its Maker all things should want to come to an end. But the patience of God preserves his own order in matters and in times, and rather invites us to that love of him, that we may seek the salvation[92] of those at whose crime we shudder.

5. "Snatched from the powers of darkness"[93] at such a great "price,"[94] and by so great a "mystery,"[95] and loosed from the chains of the ancient captivity, make sure, dearly beloved, that the devil does not destroy the integrity of your souls with any stratagem. Whatever is forced on you contrary to the Christian faith, whatever is presented to you contrary to the commandments of God, it comes from the deceptions of the one who tries with many wiles to divert you from eternal life, and, by seizing certain occasions of human weakness, leads careless and negligent souls again into his snares of death.

(2) Let all those reborn through water and the Holy Spirit consider the one whom they have renounced. Let them consider by what profession they have shaken off from themselves the yoke of tyrannical domination, and let no one in prosperity or adversity run for the deadly aid of the devil. "He is a liar from the start,"[96] and he thrives only on the art of deceiving, to lead astray human ignorance by a show of false conscience, and to be now the wicked instigator of those for whom he will afterwards be the wicked accuser.

The years of our life and the qualities of our temporal actions

---

89. Cf. Mt 27.51.
90. Cf. Mt 27.51–52.
91. Cf. Mt 27.45.
92. Cf. Rom 10.1.
93. Cf. Col 1.13.
94. 1 Cor 6.20.
95. Cf. 1 Tm 3.16.
96. Jn 8.44.

stand not in the nature of the elements or in the movements of the stars, but in the power of the Most High and True God, whose help and mercy we ought to beg in all things that we rightly desire. Far be it from us that he should be offended, but if so, there is nothing beyond him which it would avail us to pray to; in the same way, if he is favorable, no adversity can harm us. "If God is for us, who can be against us? Since God did not spare his own Son but gave him up for us all, how has he not given to us all things with him?"[97] who lives and reigns forever. Amen.

Sermon 58

16 April 444—Palm Sunday (Recension A)[98]

I know indeed, dearly beloved, that the Paschal Feast represents so sublime a mystery that it exceeds not only the very slight comprehension of my lowliness but even the capacity of those with great talent. Yet the magnitude of God's work must not be contemplated in such a way that I should either distrust myself or be ashamed to carry out the service I owe, since it is not permitted to be silent about the mystery of human salvation, even if it cannot be explained.

With the help of your prayers, however, we can hope for the grace of God to moisten the sterility of our hearts with the dew of its inspiration. As a result, in things that are useful to their ears, the holy flock might profit by the service of the pastor's voice. The Lord speaks as the giver of all good things, saying, "Open your mouth and I shall fill it,"[99] and we have the courage to say in the same prophetic words, "Lord, you will open my lips, and my mouth will announce your praise."[100]

(2) As we begin, dearly beloved, to retrace the Gospel story of the Lord's Passion, we understand it to have been ordained by divine plan that the sacrilegious leaders of the Jews and the wicked priests (who had often sought occasions for raging against Christ) did not acquire the power to exercise their fury

---

97. Rom 8.31–32.
99. Ps. 80(81).11.
98. Cf. *Sermon* 24 Note 22.
100. Ps. 50(51).17.

except on the Paschal Solemnity. For it was fitting that those things which had long ago been promised by **prophetic** *prefigured* mystery should be fulfilled in clear actuality, that the True Lamb should replace the **prefigured** *symbolic* lamb, that by one sacrifice the variety of manifold victims should be brought to a close.

In fact, all of those things which had been **divinely** established through Moses concerning the immolation of the lamb had foretold Christ and had openly announced the killing of Christ. Consequently, that the shadow might yield to the body, and images cease in the presence of truth, the ancient ritual has been replaced by a new mystery, victims pass into the Victim, blood is removed by blood, and the feast held according to the law, in being transformed, was actually being fulfilled.

2. When the priests were convoking scribes and elders of the people to their wicked plan, and the task of fixing a crime on Jesus occupied the minds of all the priests, teachers of the law deprived themselves of the law, and, through a voluntary default, abandoned the ancestral rites. When the Paschal festival was beginning, in fact, those who should have adorned the temple, cleaned the vessels, provided the victims, and furnished a more consecrated diligence in the legal purifications, were seized by the rage of parricidal hatred. They were preoccupied with just one idea, that they conspire in one crime with the same cruelty.

As a result, did they attain anything by the punishment of Innocence **and the condemnation of Justice**, except a failure to understand *the new mysteries* **"our Pasch"**[101] and the destruction of *ancient ones* **their own festival**? When the leaders looked ahead, their concern was not for **devotion** *the festival* but for their own crime, lest a tumult should arise on the *holy feast* day.[102] And this concern did not serve their religion but their crime. Concerned high priests and anxious priests feared an uprising of the people on the principal feast, not because the people might sin, but because Christ might escape.

101. Cf. 1 Cor. 5.7.
102. Cf. Mt 26.5.

3. Jesus, however, sure of his resolution and fearless in the working out of his Father's plan, was putting an end to the Old Testament and establishing a new Passover. When the "disciples had reclined" with him "to eat" the mystical "supper,"[103] while in the atrium of Caiaphas the manner of killing Christ was being discussed,[104] he himself, establishing the Sacrament of his Body and Blood, taught them what kind of victim ought to be offered to God. Even the traitor was not kept away from this mystery, to make it quite evident that the Lord was not irritated by any injury, though he knew already of the willing treachery.

He, the traitor, was for himself the matter of his ruin and the cause of his perfidy, in following the devil's lead and being unwilling to have Christ's guidance. When the Lord said, "Amen I say to you, one of you is about to betray me," [105] he showed that the conscience of his betrayer was known to him. He did not distress the wicked man with harsh and open reproaches, but met him with a gentle and quiet warning, for penitence would correct more easily one whom no despondency had spoiled.

Why, wretched Judas, do you not make use of such great kindness? See how the Lord tolerates your escapades, and how Christ exposes you to no one except yourself. Neither your name nor your person was disclosed, but by the word of truth and mercy the secrets of your own heart alone are touched. Neither the honor of the apostolic order nor the communion of sacraments is denied you. Return to your former state. Abandon your fury. Come to your senses. Kindness invites you. Your salvation demands it. Life calls you back to life.

See how your spotless and innocent fellow disciples are greatly terrified at the disclosure of this crime. All fear for themselves, since the perpetrator of the crime had not been made known. They are "upset,"[106] not because of a guilty conscience but because of the uncertainty due to human changeableness, fearing lest what each knows about himself should be

---

103. Cf. Mt 26.20–21 and Jn 13.2.   104. Cf. Jn 11.47–53.
105. Mt. 26.21.   106. Cf. Mt 26.22 and Mk 14.19.

less true than what Truth itself had foreseen. But you, in the anxiety of these holy men, abuse the Lord's patience, and you believe yourself concealed by your boldness. You add presumption to your crime, nor are you frightened by a fully evident sign. When others held back from the food which the Lord had established for a sign, you did not withdraw your hand from the dish,[107] because you did not turn your mind from the crime.

4. Next, **dearly beloved**, as John the Evangelist says, when the Lord "handed over bread that had been dipped" to his betrayer as a clear sign, the devil seized on Judas completely. He now possessed, in the act of his wickedness, the one whom before he had shackled with evil thoughts.[108] While [Judas] reclined with the others at table only with respect to his body, in his mind he was arming the hatred of priests, the lies of witnesses, and the rage of ignorant people.

When the Lord saw what infamy Judas was intent upon, he said, "What you are doing, do quickly."[109] This was the word not of one commanding, but allowing; not of one in fear, but of one prepared. The Lord had power over all time but showed himself as allowing no delay for the traitor and as carrying out his Father's will for the redemption of the world, so that he neither forced nor feared the crime prepared by his persecutors.

(2) After Judas, won over by the devil, departed from Christ and cut himself off from the body of apostolic unity, the Lord, disturbed by no fear but concerned only about the salvation of those to be redeemed, spent all the time left before the assault of persecutors on mystic discourses and holy doctrine, as John the Evangelist says. He "raised his eyes to heaven"[110] and prayed to the Father for the whole Church, that all whom the Father had given—and would give—to the Son might become one[111] and forever remain undivided for the glory of the Redeemer.[112]

---

107. Cf. Mt 26.23.
109. Jn 13.27.
111. Cf. Jn 17.6, 11–12, and 21.
108. Cf. Jn 13.26–27.
110. Cf. Jn 17.1.
112. Cf. Jn 17.22–23.

Finally, he added that prayer in which he said: "Father, if it is possible, let this cup pass me by."[113] It is not to be supposed that the **Lord** Jesus wanted to withdraw from his Passion and Death, whose mysteries he passed on to the *his* disciples. Indeed, he himself had forbidden the blessed apostle Peter, who was burning with devout faith and love, to use his sword against the persecutors, saying, "The chalice which the Father has given me, do you not wish me to drink it?"[114]

What the Lord himself testifies to *What the Lord says according to the Gospel of John* cannot be doubted: "God so loved the world that he gave his Only-Begotten Son, in order that every one who believes in him might not perish, but might have eternal life."[115] Likewise certain is what the apostle Paul said about this same thing: "Christ loved us, and gave himself up in our place, an offering to God in the odor of sweetness."[116] In saving all by the Cross of Christ, the Father and the Son had one will and one plan, nor could that be upset by any consideration which had been mercifully established and unchangeably fixed before the eternal ages.

Consequently, therefore, he who has taken on the true and whole man, *dearly beloved*, has taken up also the true senses of the body and the true affections of the soul. Nor, because all within him was full of mysteries, full of miracles, does this mean therefore that he wept with false tears, or ate food with false hunger, or slept with pretended sleep. He was despised in our lowliness, saddened in our sorrow, and crucified in our pain. For this did his mercy undergo the sufferings of our mortality, that he might save it. For this did his strength accept [these sufferings], that he might overcome them. It is what Isaiah openly foretold, saying: "He bears our sins; he grieves for us, and we consider him in pain, in beatings, and in distress. He was wounded for our crimes, and weakened because of our sins, and by his wound are we healed."[117]

5. When, therefore, **dearly beloved**, the Son of God says, "Father, if it is possible, let this cup pass me by,"[118] he uses the

---

113. Mt 26.39 and Mk 14.35.
114. Jn 18.11.
115. Jn 3.16.
116. Eph 5.2.
117. Is 53.4–5.
118. Mt 26.39 and Mk 14.35.

voice of our nature, and he pleads the cause of our human frailty and disquiet—in order to strengthen patience and drive out fear in those things we shall have to bear. Finally, ceasing to ask even this, as if in some way excusing the fear in our weakness—in which it is hurtful for us to rest—he passes to another mood and says, "Nevertheless, not as I will, but as you will."[119] Later, the Lord states likewise, "If this cup cannot pass from me unless I drink it, your will be done."[120]

This saying of the Head is the salvation of the whole body. This saying has instructed all the faithful, inflamed all confessors, crowned all martyrs. Who can overcome the hatred of this world, the storms of temptation, the terrors of **persecutors** *persecutions*, unless Christ says to the Father in us all and for us all, "Your will be done"?[121] **Let all the children of the Church learn this saying: "(You) have been bought with a great price,[122] and have been justified by the free gift of his grace."[123] When the rush of any violent "temptation" falls on them, let them use the safeguard of this most powerful prayer,[124] that when the trembling of fear has been overcome, they might receive "patience in suffering."[125]**

(2) From here on out, dearly beloved, our sermon must be directed to drawing together the order of the Lord's suffering, which, lest we burden you with a surplus of words, we put off to **Wednesday** *Saturday*, to divide the labor *equally*. May the grace of God be added to your prayers, thus giving me the means of paying the debt. **Through Christ our Lord.** *Through our Lord Jesus Christ, living and reigning with the Father and with the Holy Spirit for ever and ever. Amen.*

Sermon 59

19 April 444—Wednesday of Holy Week (Recension A)[126]

In our last sermon, dearly beloved, we treated the things which preceded the Lord's arrest. It now remains—with the

---

119. Mt 26.39.
120. Mt 26.42.
121. Mt 26.42.
122. Cf. 1 Cor 6.20.
123. Cf. Rom 3.24.
124. Cf. Heb 2.18.
125. Cf. 2 Cor 1.6.
126. Cf. *Sermon* 24 Note 22.

help of God's grace—to talk about the sequence of events during the Passion itself, as we promised. Our Lord had declared in the words of his sacred prayer that *he had most truly and most fully* both the human and divine natures **were most truly in him**. He was showing whence it was that he would be unwilling to suffer and whence it was that he would be willing to do so. Putting aside human fearfulness and confirming the **divine** *strength of* power, he reverted to that purpose envisioned by the eternal plan.

Though the devil was raging through the works of Jews, [the Lord] held out before them the "form of a slave"[127]—without sin, so that the case of all people could be pleaded through someone in whom alone the nature of all remains without fault. As a result, the children of darkness rushed against the True Light. Though using torches and lanterns,[128] they did not avoid the night of their infidelity, because they did not recognize the Author of Light. They apprehended someone who was prepared to be held. They took away someone who was willing to be taken away. If he had wanted to oppose them, their wicked hands could bring no injury on him, but the Redemption of the world would be delayed. If unharmed, he would save no one, he who was to die for the salvation of all.

2. He allowed, then, to be brought on himself whatever the people's fury dared. With the encouragement of priests—*so he is led to Annas, father-in-law of Caiaphas,*[129] *and then to Caiaphas when Annas sent him on*[130]—then after wild accusations from calumniators in the house of Caiaphas, after the lying and falsehoods of witnesses, he is sent on by a delegation of priests[131] for interrogation by Pilate.[132] These neglected the divine right and claimed—as if they were really devoted to Roman laws—that they "have no king except Caesar,"[133] In reserving all judgment to the governor's power, they were looking for a prosecutor of savagery rather than the judge of a case.

They were bringing Jesus, bound with hard cords,[134] beaten

127. Cf. Phil 2.7.
128. Cf. Jn 18.3.
129. Cf. Jn 18.13.
130. Cf. Jn 18.24.
131. Cf. Mt 27.1–2.
132. Cf. Mt 26.57–62.
133. Jn 19.15.
134. Cf. Mt 27.2.

with many stripes and blows,[135] stained with spittle,[136] condemned already by the clamor—so much that in spite of all the preliminary judgments[137] Pilate did not dare to free him, since all wanted him to die. Afterwards, the investigation itself shows that Pilate found no guilt in the accused, but he did not remain constant in that verdict.[138] So the judge condemns someone whom he had found to be innocent, adding the "blood of a just man"[139] to that of wicked people, though he felt, both through his own realization and from the dream "of his wife," that he must abstain from his blood.[140]

[Pilate's] "washed hands" do not cleanse his stained soul.[141] No, what was to be committed at the instigation of his godless spirit would not be expiated by splashing his hands in water. Of course, the crime of those Jews exceeds the blame of Pilate, for the Jews drove him—terrified as he was at the name of Caesar and frightened by cries of hatred—to the execution of their crime. He himself, nevertheless, who had **given in to** *worked with* the rebels, did not escape guilt, having abandoned his own judgment and entered another's crime.

3. Pilate, overcome by the madness of implacable people, dearly beloved, allowed **the Lord** Jesus to be dishonored with much derision and harassed by innumerable troubles. Pilate displayed him to *his persecutors* **the scribes and priests** after he had been beaten with whips, crowned with thorns, and clothed in the garment of their mockery. He thought that the minds of his enemies would thereby undoubtedly be softened,[142] and that, when their envy and hatred had been satisfied, they would feel that he should be no further persecuted, having seen him afflicted in so many ways.

On the contrary, when their anger was inflamed into shouts that the special privilege should free Barabbas,[143] while the penalty of **hanging on** the cross should be applied to Christ,[144] and when the general cry from the crowd was, "His blood be

---

135. Cf. Mt 26.67 and Jn 19.3.
136. Cf. Mt 26.67 and 27.30.
137. Cf. Jn 19.6.
138. Cf. Jn 18.38 and 19.6.
139. Cf. Mt 27.24.
140. Cf. Mt 27.19.
141. Cf. Mt 27.24.
142. Cf. Jn 19.1–5.
143. Cf. Mt 27.21 and Jn 18.40.
144. Cf. Mt 27.22–23 and Jn 19.6.

upon us and upon our children,"[145] the unjust obtained for their own condemnation that which they steadily demanded.

"Their teeth," as the prophet bore witness, "are spears and arrows, their tongue a sharp sword."[146] In vain did they hold back **their own** *godless* hands from crucifying the Lord of Majesty when they **were hurling** *brandished* the deadly arrows of their voices against him and the poisoned weapons of their words. It is on you, on you, o false Jews, sacrilegious leaders of the people, that the whole weight of this evil deed falls. Though the cruelty of the crime bound both judge and soldiers, nevertheless, the whole accomplishment of the deed involves you. In the punishment of Christ, whatever fault there was either in Pilate's judgment or in the obedience of the cohort, it makes you more worthy of contempt from the human race, for it was by the influence of your fury that they could not be innocent, though they did not agree with your wickedness.

4. **And so, since the blindness of the unhappy Jews denied the Lord of the universe to be their king,**[147] when the Lord **Jesus** was handed over to the will of the mob, he was—in derision of his royal dignity—ordered to carry his own *punishment* **"cross."**[148] Indeed, he was worthy of this opprobrium, since his **"glory was turned into ignominy."**[149] *This was to fulfill what the prophet Isaiah had said: "Behold, a child is born for us, a son is given to us, whose dominion is on his shoulders."*[150] *When, therefore, the Lord carried the wood of the Cross which he converted into his scepter of power,* "he clearly became a great mockery in the eyes of the wicked" but a "great mystery" to the faithful.[151]

As renowned victor over the devil and most powerful conqueror of hostile *spirits* **powers**, in an admirable spectacle, he carried the trophy of his "victory." On the shoulders of his unconquered endurance, he bore the sign of salvation to be worshipped in every kingdom.[152] Even then he encouraged all his imitators by the sight of his labor, saying, "Any who do not take up their cross and follow me do not deserve me."[153]

145. Mt 27.25.
146. Ps 56(57).5.
147. Cf. Jn 19.15.
148. Cf. Jn 19.17.
149. Cf. Hos 4.7.
150. Is 9.6.
151. Cf. Augustine, *Tr. in Io.* 117.3.
152. Cf. Col 2.15.
153. Mt. 10.38.

5. *As the crowd went with Jesus to the place of punishment, Simon of Cyrene was found, and the wood of the cross was transferred from the Lord to him.*[154] *This served to prefigure the faith of nations to whom the Cross of Christ would not be confusion but glory. It was not then an accident but a figure and a mystery that, while the Jews were raging against Christ, a stranger met him to suffer with him, as the Apostle says:* "*If we suffer with him, we shall also reign with him.*"[155] *No Hebrew, no Israelite, but a foreigner became his stand-in during the most sacred humiliation of our Savior. Through this substitution, the propitiation of the spotless Lamb and the fullness of all mysteries passed from circumcision to prepuce, from carnal children to spiritual children.*

Indeed **Consequently**, "Christ our Passover has been sacrificed,"[156] **as the Apostle says**. Offering himself to the Father as a new and real sacrifice of reconciliation, he was crucified—not in the temple whose due worship is now completed, nor within the enclosure of the city which was to be destroyed because of its crime, but "outside and beyond the camp."[157] That way, as the mystery of the ancient sacrifices was ceasing, a new victim would be put on a new altar, and the Cross of Christ would be the altar not of the temple but of the world.

6. Then, dearly beloved, when Christ was lifted up by the cross, let the mind's eye not light upon only what was in the sight of the wicked, to whom it was said through Moses, "Your life will be put before your eyes, you will be afraid by day and by night, and you will not be secure about your life."[158] They could see nothing in the Crucified Lord beyond their crime, having not the fear by which true faith is justified, but the one by which their wicked consciences are tormented. Our minds, however, enlightened by the Spirit of Truth, should recognize with a pure and free heart the glory of the Cross shining in heaven and on earth. It should see with interior penetration what it is that the Lord said when he spoke about the imminence of his Passion: "The hour has come that the Son of man should be glorified."[159]

Further, he said: "*Now is my soul troubled, and what shall I say?*

---

154. Cf. Mt 27.32.
155. Rom 8.17 and 2 Tm 2.12.
156. 1 Cor 5.7.
157. Cf. Ex 29.14 and Heb 13.11–12.
158. Dt 28.66.
159. Jn 12.23.

Father, save me from this hour. But it was because of this that I have come to this hour."[160] "Father, glorify your Son."[161] When the voice of the Father had come from heaven, saying, "I have glorified and shall again glorify,"[162] Jesus responded to those standing around, saying: "It was not for me that this voice came, but for you. Now is the judgment of the world. Now the prince of this world will be sent down below. I, in being lifted up from the earth, shall draw all things to myself."[163]

7. O wonderful power of the Cross! O indescribable glory of the Passion! In this is the tribunal of the Lord, and the judgment of the world, and the power of the Crucified. You have drawn all things to yourself, Lord, and when "you had stretched out your hands all day for an unbelieving and rebellious people,"[164] all the world received the understanding to confess your majesty.

You have drawn all things to yourself, Lord, when all the elements expressed the same feeling in condemning that crime perpetrated by Jews. With the lights of heaven darkened and day turned to night, even the earth shook with unaccustomed motions, and all creation turned its back on the practices of the wicked.

You have drawn all things to yourself, Lord, when the veil of the temple was split apart and the Holy of Holies withdrew from unworthy priests, so that figure was turned into truth, prophecies into reality, and the law into the Gospel. You have drawn all things to yourself, Lord, so that what was done in the one temple of Judea with concealed meanings, the devotion of all nations everywhere celebrates in a clear and open mystery.

Now, when the variety of animal sacrifices has ceased, the one oblation of your body and blood fulfills all the many kinds of offering. You are the true "Lamb of God that takes away the sins of the world,"[165] and thus you perfect all mysteries in yourself. As one sacrifice is made on behalf of all victims, so there will be one kingdom for all nations.

160. Jn 12.27.
162. Jn 12.28.
164. Cf. Is 65.2.
161. Jn 12.28.
163. Jn 12.30–32.
165. Jn 1.29.

Now there is a higher order of Levites, a worthier order of elders, and a holier anointing of priests, since your Cross is the fountain of all benediction, the cause of all graces, through which there is given to believers strength from weakness, glory from reproach, and life from death.

8. Let us confess then, dearly beloved, what the *blessed* teacher of Gentiles, Paul **the apostle**, confessed in a glorious expression: "A trustworthy message and deserving to be accepted by all, that **Christ** Jesus came into this world to save sinners."[166] Hence, the mercy of God toward us is more wonderful, because it is not for the just nor for the holy, but "for the" wicked and "godless," that Christ "died."[167] Of course the divine nature could not receive the sharp point of death. In being born from among us, he undertook something which he could offer for us.[168]

At one time, the power of his Death threatened our death, saying through the mouth of Hosea the prophet, "I will be your death, o death, and I will be your sting, o infernal one."[169] By dying he submitted to the laws of death, but by rising he abolished them. So he put an end to the hold of death. From being eternal, he made it temporal. *For* **That way**, "just as in Adam all die, so in Christ all **would be** *will be* brought to life."[170]

(2) May it turn out, dearly beloved, as the apostle Paul says, "that those who live should live no longer for themselves, but for him who died and rose for all."[171] Since "the old things have passed away and all things have been made new,"[172] let no one remain in the old state of carnal life, but "let **us** all be renewed *by progress* from day to day"[173] through the increase of holiness. No matter how much one may be justified, there is still room— in **this life** *this body*—to become more honorable and better.

Whoever does not increase decreases. Whoever acquires nothing loses *not a little something*. As a result, we must run with the steps of faith, with the works of mercy, with the love of holiness, that we may celebrate the day of our Redemption **with**

---

166. 1 Tm 1.15.
167. Cf. Rom 5.6.
168. Cf. Augustine *En. in Ps.* 129.
169. Hos 13.14.
170. 1 Cor 15.22.
171. 2 Cor 5.15.
172. 2 Cor 5.17.
173. Cf. 2 Cor 4.16.

good works *in a spiritual way,* "not in the yeast of the old malice and wickedness, but in the unleavened bread of sincerity and truth."[174] Then might we deserve to participate in Christ's Resurrection, *who lives and reigns with the Father and with the Holy Spirit for ever and ever. Amen.*

Sermon 60

1 April 445—Palm Sunday

We no longer wait, dearly beloved, for the mystery of our Lord's Passion to be manifested, a mystery ordained "before the beginning of time"[175] for the salvation of the human race, a mystery announced to us by many signs through all ages past. Instead, we worship it now as fulfilled. Both the Old and the New Testaments agree for our instruction, and the Gospel story unfolds for us what the prophet's trumpet had sounded. As it has been written, "Abyss calls upon abyss in the sound of your waterfalls,"[176] since the depths of each Testament respond to the other with an echo in order to tell about the "glory of God's grace."[177]

What was hidden under the veil of figures becomes clear in the light of Revelation. Despite the miracles performed by our Savior for the people to see, few have felt the presence of Truth. Even the disciples—upset at the voluntary Passion of the Lord—did not escape that stumbling block arising from the Cross without temptation from fear. Whence, then, would our faith acquire its knowledge, whence would our constancy receive strength? Whence, indeed, except from reading predictions about the things we know to have been accomplished?

2. Now the Savior's triumph has been accomplished, dearly beloved, and the arrangements which all the words of the Old Testament announced have found their completion. Let carnal Jews mourn, therefore, while spiritual Christians rejoice. This feast—which has turned into night for the former—shines forth upon us with its light, because the same Cross of Christ

---

174. 1 Cor 5.8.
176. Ps 41(42).8.

175. Cf. 2 Tm 1.9 and Ti 1.2.
177. Cf. Eph 1.6.

brings glory to believers and punishment to unbelievers. Certainly, the fury of his persecutors worked nothing against the "Lord of Majesty"[178] except violent cruelty and bitter suffering. To those redeemed by the Lord's Passion, however, it has brought joy rather than sorrow—more genuinely and more appropriately.

It was understandable for the disciples to be afraid at that time, nor should grief exhibited by the apostles incur the charge of diffidence. For the proud ferment of "fat bulls" and the wanton insolence of "calves" raged.[179] Jews and leaders of the Jews were conspiring in a single crime. Before the eyes of sheep, the savagery of wild beasts hunted the blood of that Just Shepherd. Even he himself, who had come to suffer, said about his participation in our nature, "My soul is sorrowful even unto death."[180]

Now that his power and strength have been manifested through the acceptance of weakness, no sorrow on the part of believers must cloud over the Paschal Solemnity. We should not recollect the story of his sufferings with any sadness, because the Lord put the malice of Jews to such use that his will to show mercy has been fulfilled through their intention to do harm. If, "during the exodus of Israel from Egypt,"[181] a lamb's blood meant the restoration of freedom and the sacrifice of cattle made that feast holy by turning away the devastator's anger, then how much joy should the Chritian people take in the fact that the Almighty Father "did not spare his Only-Begotten Son, but handed him over for us all"?[182] Consequently, that Passover in the killing of Christ became the True and Only Sacrifice. Through it, not merely had one people been snatched from the domination of Pharoah, but the entire world has been snatched from the devil's captivity.

3. Such a mystery, dearly beloved, have all the figures waited upon from the very beginning. Now the blood of Abel the just proclaims this Death of the Chief Shepherd, while Cain, the

178. Cf. 1 Cor 2.8.
180. Mt 26.38.
182. Rom 8.32.
179. Cf. Ps 21(22).13.
181. Cf. Ps 113(114).1.

murderer of his brother, may be recognized in the parricide committed by Jews. Now the flood and the ark of Noah show what restoration takes place in Baptism and what salvation occurs on the wood of the Cross.[183] Now Abraham, the father of nations, obtains the promised heirs; not carnal offspring but the posterity of his faith have been blessed in his seed.[184] Now, during the feast predicted by all other feasts, a sacred month of new things has shone forth, so that Christian creation had its beginnings during the same month in which the world took its start.

(2) Clearly the furious Jews did whatever they wanted to against the Lord Jesus. God's power did not withdraw the reality of his assumed human nature from any of their audacious deeds. Yet the Lord in his patience carried out his service according to plan, while the persistence of their sacrilegious cruelty helped along the Savior's work, a work which neither scribes, nor Pharisees, nor high priests understood, "for if they had known, they never would have crucified the Lord of Majesty."[185]

Not even the devil realized that by raging against Christ he would destroy his own kingdom. He could not lose the prerogatives deriving from his ancient deception if only he would restrain himself from the blood of our Lord Jesus. Maliciously bent upon doing harm, however, he becomes destroyed by destroying and captured by capturing. Persecuting a mortal, he ends up cutting down the Savior.

For this endeavor, an undertaking characterized by reckless audacity, the devil found a fitting accomplice and a fitting companion. Wicked Judas preferred to become a servant of the devil rather than an apostle of Christ. He did not abandon Christ as a result of the disquiet caused by fear, but cast him aside in his greed for money.

4. See then, dearly beloved, and look carefully at what seeds and what fruits spring from this root of avarice, which the Apostle rightly called the "root of all evils."[186] No sin would be

---

183. Cf. 1 Pt 3.20–21.
185. 1 Cor 2.8.
184. Cf. Gal 3.7–9.
186. Cf. 1 Tm 6.10.

committed were it not for cupidity. Every illicit appetite comes as a sickness arising from this desire. No inclination toward the love of money has any worth, while the soul desirous of profit was not afraid to perish for even a little. No trace of justice can be found in a heart where avarice has made itself at home. Traitorous Judas, drunken with this poison, went to the noose while thirsting for profit. So stupid was his wickedness that he sold both a Lord and a Teacher for thirty pieces of silver.[187]

(2) When the Son of God offered himself to undertake the punishment for iniquity, blessed Peter the apostle—whose faith burned with such devotion that he would be "prepared" both to suffer for the Lord and to die for him[188]—frightened by the accusation of a priest's servant girl, runs into the weakness of denial. He had been allowed to waver, as it seems, in order that the remedy of penitence might be founded in the prince of the Church, and that no one would dare to trust in their own strength when not even blessed Peter could escape the danger of fickleness.

Yet the Lord Jesus—detained within that sanhedrin of priests in body only—looked with a divine gaze into the trepidation of that disciple who stood outside. As soon as he "looked over" at his fearful heart,[189] [the Lord] raised it up and stirred him to "tears" of repentance.[190] Blessed are your tears, holy apostle, tears which had the power of holy Baptism for washing away the guilt of denial. Beside you was the right hand of our Lord Jesus Christ. As you were slipping, it grabbed hold before you could fall away. You received strength to stand amid the very danger of falling. Our Lord saw in you not a faith overcome, not a love turned away, but a troubled stability. Tears flowed out since love had not given way, and the fountain of love washed away the words of fear. No, the remedy of washing away did not come slowly since there had not been a decision of the will. Quickly the rock returned to its firmness, becoming so strong that he did not fear afterward in his own suffering what had so terrified him in the Passion of Christ.

187. Cf. Mt 26.15–16.
189. Cf. Lk 22.61.
188. Cf. Lk 22.33.
190. Cf. Lk 22.62.

Sermon 61

4 April 445—Wednesday of Holy Week (Recension A)[191]

Jewish wickedness bent over backwards to fabricate any pretext whatsoever for perpetrating crime against the Lord Jesus, dearly beloved, and the lies which false witnesses had brought forth in the service of unjust priests were producing nothing worthy of death. They found it to be something of an insurmountable task to frame him, Lord of the world, with the stigma of having sought after a kingdom. Pilate wanted Jesus to be freed when he saw that their accusations were groundless. Whereupon they clamored falsely and menacingly in unison, "If you pardon him, you are not a friend of Caesar, for anyone who makes himself king goes against Caesar."[192]

O Pilate, you unwisely feared a ridiculous excuse. You would have had every reason to fear an arrogation of royalty and would have been bound to put down an attempted revolution to protect the empire of Caesar if the stirrings of tyranny had exposed a plan to take power, if provisions for equipment, amassing of finances, or encampments of soldiers had been uncovered. Why did you allow him to be encumbered with the charge of striving after power when his teaching dealt primarily with humility? He did not speak out against Roman laws. He submitted to "assessment" and paid the tax.[193] He did not hold back revenues, but laid down that "what belongs to God should be rendered unto God, and what belongs to Caesar rendered unto Caesar."[194] He chose poverty, encouraged obedience, and preached docility. Truly this does not constitute an attack upon Caesar but a help to him.

---

191. This sermon comes down to us in two recensions. Recension A had been composed in 445. Recension B appears to represent a revision made by Leo himself at some later date. Material found in both recensions will appear in normal text. Material found only in Recension A will appear in **bold**. Material found only in Recension B will appear in *italics*. Some material found in both recensions but in a different order will be reproduced in both bold and italics in their proper order. Some material that does not coincide between the two versions of the Latin text but does not affect the English translation (such as word order or certain syntactical variants) will not be indicated.

192. Jn 19.12.   193. Cf. Mt 17.24–25.
194. Cf. Mt 22.21.

2. So that the charges brought by these Jews might not seem completely vacuous, however, look carefully into what has been ascertained regarding the works of our Lord Jesus, o magistrate, see what has been discovered about his power. He bestowed sight upon the blind, hearing upon the deaf, walking upon the lame, and speech upon the mute. He drove away fevers, relieved sorrows, cast out demons, brought the dead back to life, and commanded both the sea and the winds to quiet down. Certainly these things point to a great King, one who has prominence, however, not through human authority but through divine strength. Let the Jews charge him with holding this power instead. Let them alter their case. Let them profess with their mouths what they really think in their hearts. Why do they fabricate charges about earthly matters when it is really heavenly things that they are prosecuting?

(2) Although Pilate felt it to be burdensome upon and hostile to himself when the Jews attacked him for reneging on friendship with Caesar, he nevertheless tried to placate their rage for a time. To that end, he either permitted or ordered that the Lord Jesus should be afflicted with various outrages, thinking that their wickedness would no longer rant once it had been satisfied. Yet their unrelenting malice continued to wax as it built up on itself. Although they had acquired the right to deride him at will, they began to insist upon that of killing him as well. Consequently, the chief priests and leaders of the Jews—as well as the whole multitude—kept shouting over and over again, "Crucify, crucify."[195] Pilate then handed Jesus over to the will of his persecutors, letting go the thief Barabbas. As a result, impunity was granted to a murderer—at the request of those who "were killing the Author of Life" on a feast day.[196]

3. So, dearly beloved, as the Lord was going to the place of his glorification and mercy was departing from the tents of the godless, what had been written realized its fulfillment, namely, "Salvation is far away from sinners."[197] Throngs "of people were following him, including women mourning and la-

---

195. Jn 19.6.
197. Ps 118(119).155.
196. Cf. Acts 3.15.

menting over him."[198] For the weaker sex are generally moved to tears even for those who are worthy of death, and they tend to pity the deaths of those who have been condemned in view of their shared human nature. Yet the Lord Jesus did not want their mourning to be directed towards him, since grief did not befit a triumph, nor lamentation a victory. Turning to them at last, he said, "daughters of Jerusalem, do not weep for me, but weep for yourselves and for your children. For the days will come when it will be said, 'Blessed are the infertile, the wombs which have not given birth, and the breasts which have not nursed.' "[199]

Where does the one to be crucified show any sorrow? Where does the one about to die exhibit any fear? No, the hour of punishment does not frighten his heart in anticipation of his suffering. Teaching that there is no reason to weep for him, he points the way to repentance by renouncing vengeance. There is no reason, he said, why you should weep over me, daughters of Jerusalem. Lament over yourselves and wail for your children. That grief of yours should be poured out on behalf of those whom your wombs have brought forth to be like these. Clearly you ought not to mourn for the Savior of believers, but for the wickedness of those who perish. I suffer the cross of my own free will. I am going to destroy that death which I allow to come upon me. Do not weep for someone dying in order to redeem the world. You will see him passing judgment [over it] in the Father's majesty.

4. Lifted up on the cross, therefore, Christ turned death back onto the one who gave rise to it and **put to scorn** *shattered* all "dominions"[200] and opposing powers by throwing in its way a flesh capable of suffering. *He allowed the boldness of the ancient enemy to come against him. That enemy, in raging against a nature subject to himself, had the audacity to exact a debt even where he could find no trace of sin.*

That universal "edict" of death which proclaimed our sale into bondage[201] has been made void, and the contractual rights

---

198. Cf. Lk 23.27.
200. Cf. Col 2.15.

199. Lk 23.28–29.
201. Cf. Col 2.14.

have been transferred to the Redeemer. Those nails which had pierced the hands and feet of our Lord have gouged out everlasting wounds in the devil, and the punishment of holy limbs meant the killing of hostile powers. Christ won so total a victory that all those who would believe in him triumphed in him and with him.

5. When the Lord, therefore, raised aloft in the lifting up of his crucified body, was carrying out the reconciliation of the world on a kind of fortress built up on torment, he invited the converted "thief" to the abode of "Paradise."[202] You, leaders of the Jews and teachers of the law, without any remorse for the wickedness of your conscience, not at all softened by the effect of your crime, you compounded the piercing of nails with the weapons of your tongues, saying, "He saved others, himself he cannot save. If he is the king of Israel, let him come down from the cross, and then we believe him."[203]

To these foolish and blasphemous words of yours, however, all the elements send back an answer. All together, the sky, the earth, the sun, and the stars bring a single judgment against you. Protesting that you are unworthy to benefit from their functioning, they show to the world that "darkness" of your unseeing[204] through terrifying "movement"[205] and unusual default. But if neither the phenomena in the heavens nor those down below suffice to convince you of your wrongdoing, if "rocks" and "tombs"[206] were better able to perceive the Cross of Christ than your hearts, pay attention at least to what happened in the temple. That veil which had been positioned in such a way as to close off the Holy of Holies was torn apart "from top to" bottom.[207] That holy and mystical sanctuary—which the high priest alone had been authorized to enter—was thrown open. There would be no sequestration for a place where no holiness resided any longer.

(2) Consequently, you ought to have acknowledged the fact of your repudiation, the fact that you had lost any right to exer-

---

202. Cf. Lk 23.43.
203. Mt 27.42.
204. Cf. Mt 27.45 and Lk 23.44–45.
205. Cf. Mt 27.51.
206. Cf. Mt 27.51–52.
207. Cf. Mt 27.51.

cise the priesthood, since what Truth had told you was true: "If you really believed Moses, you would believe me also."[208] Rightly do both Testaments condemn you, therefore, you who are both empty of grace and deprived of the law, you who resisted the new things precisely because you did not believe the old.

(3) We, on the other hand, dearly beloved, freed from the darkness of ignorance, have received the light of faith and have entered into the inheritance of the New Testament through the election of adoption. Let us rejoice, therefore, in the feast which carnal Israel lost, since "Christ our Pasch has been sacrificed."[209] Through his ineffable grace, we have been endowed with the blessing of all gifts. We have been transformed from oldness into newness in such a way that not only have we been restored to the abode of Paradise, but we are even now being made ready for the glory of the heavenly kingdom.

Sermon 62

16 March 452—Palm Sunday

At last the feast of our Lord's Passion has arrived, the feast that we have desired and the entire world has longed for, dearly beloved, and it does not allow us to remain silent amid the exultation of spiritual joys. It is difficult to speak often—in a worthy and fitting manner—about the same thing. Yet the bishop nevertheless does not have the liberty to withhold the duty of his sermon from the ears of believers when it comes to so great a mystery of divine mercy. Why, the subject matter itself—from the mere fact that it is indescribable—grants abundant material for speaking. What needs to be said cannot be left out. Never can enough be said about the Passion.

Let human weakness succumb to the glory of God. Let it always find itself no match for explaining the works of his mercy. May we struggle with our feelings, be at a loss with our talent, and fail in our speech. It is a good thing that we possess too little that we might even think rightly about the Lord's majesty.

---

208. Jn 5.46.
209. 1 Cor.5.7.

For the prophet says, "Seek the Lord and be strengthened. Seek his face always."[210] None must presume that they have found everything that they seek, lest someone who has stopped approaching fail to come near.

(2) What is there among all the works of God in which the attention of human admiration becomes so wearied, what so pleases and overwhelms the contemplation of our mind as the Passion of our Savior? As often as we are able to think about his omnipotence (which for him is of one equal essence with the Father), the humility in God becomes more to be wondered at than his power. His emptying himself of his divine majesty is more difficult to comprehend than his promoting to the highest place the "form of a servant."[211]

It does greatly help our understanding, however, that, although the Creator is one thing, the creature another; the inviolable divinity one thing, the suffering flesh another; nevertheless, the properties of each substance come together into one Person. Whether in instances of weakness or in those of strength, the degradation belongs to the same one whose is also the glory.

2. By this rule of faith, dearly beloved, which we have received in the very beginning of the Creed (established by apostolic authority), we confess "our Lord Jesus Christ," whom we call the "only Son" of God the Father Almighty, the same one who was "born of the Holy Spirit from the Virgin Mary." We do not disavow his majesty when we believe that he was "crucified, died, and raised on the third day."[212] Both the humanity and the divinity at the same time encompass all that belongs to God and all that belongs to man. Although the one above suffering is in the one suffering, the strength cannot be affected by the weakness, nor can the weakness be overcome by the strength.

Blessed Peter the apostle was rightly praised in his recognition of this unity. When the Lord inquired what the disciples thought about him, Peter quickly beat them all to saying, "You are the Christ, Son of the living God."[213] Certainly he saw this not with flesh and blood revealing it (by the use of which the

210. Ps 104(105).4.
212. Cf. the Apostles' Creed.
211. Cf. Phil.2.7.
213. Mt 16.16.

interior eyes can be hindered), but by the very Spirit of the Father, working in his believing heart. Prepared for the government of the whole Church, he might thereby first learn what he was to teach. For the confirming of that faith he was about to preach, he heard, "You are Peter and upon this rock I shall build my Church, and the gates of hell will not prevail against it."[214]

(2) The strength of the Christian faith, therefore, built on an impregnable rock, does not fear the gates of death, for it confesses one Lord Jesus Christ, both true God and true man. It believes him to be both Son of the Virgin and Creator of his Mother, both one born at a certain point in time and the very origin of time, both the "Lord of" all "strength"[215] and one from the stock of mortals, both "knowing no sin"[216] and yet sacrificed "in the likeness of sinful flesh" for sinners.[217]

3. That he might release humanity from the chains of baneful deceit, he hid the power of his majesty from the furious devil and also put forward the weakness of our lowliness. If, however, the cruel and proud enemy had been able to know the plan of God's mercy, he would rather have been eager to calm the spirits of Jews with gentleness than to fire them with unjust hatred—in order to keep from losing the servitude of all his captives by persecuting the liberty of someone who owes him nothing.

As a result, his malice failed. He inflicted punishment upon the Son of God, punishment that was to turn into healing for every child of human beings. He poured out that righteous blood which was the price and the cup for reconciling the world. Our Lord undertook what he chose according to the design of his will. He allowed the wicked hands of persecutors on himself. These, bent on their own crime, were serving the Redeemer's purpose.

So great was the movement of his love for his murderers, that from the cross he prayed the Father not to avenge him,

---

214. Mt 16.18.   215. Cf. Pss 23(24).10 and 45(46).8.
216. Cf. 2 Cor. 5.21, Jn 8.46, and Heb 4.15.
217. Cf. Rom 8.3.

but to pardon them, saying, "Father, forgive them, for they know not what they do."[218] Such was the power of his prayer that the preaching of Peter the apostle turned to repentance the hearts of many from among those who said: "His blood be upon us and upon our children."[219] On a single day, "almost three thousand" Jews "were baptized,"[220] and all were made "one in heart and soul,"[221] prepared now to die for him, the one for whom they had demanded crucifixion.

4. Judas, the traitor, could not come to this forgiveness. That "son of perdition,"[222] "at whose right hand stood the devil,"[223] sank into despair before Christ completed the mystery of Universal Redemption. When the Lord died for all the sinful, Judas could perhaps have been able to profit by this healing as well, had he not hastened to the noose. In his evil heart, however, now given over to the fraudulent thefts of a criminal, now busy with hired killers, there remained nothing at all from proofs of the Savior's mercy. He had heard with his wicked ears the words of the Lord when he said, "I did not come to call the just, but sinners,"[224] and "the Son of a Man has come to seek out and to save what had perished,"[225] but he had not understood the kindness of Christ.

Christ healed not only bodily illnesses but cared even for the wounds of feeble souls, saying to the paralytic, "Courage, my child, your sins are forgiven,"[226] and to the adulteress brought before him, "Neither will I condemn you; go and sin no more."[227] He showed through all his works that he had come as a Savior for the world, not as a judge. Yet this understanding was completely foreign to the wicked traitor, who rebelled against himself, not in the judgment of repentance but in the madness of destruction. He who would sell "the Author of Life to his murderers"[228] even sinned in dying and thereby increased his condemnation.

218. Lk 23.34.
219. Mt 27.25.
220. Cf. Acts 2.41.
221. Cf. Acts 4.32.
222. Cf. Jn 17.12.
223. Ps 108(109).6.
224. Mt 9.13.
225. Lk 19.10 and Mt 18.11.
226. Mt 9.2.
227. Jn 8.11.
228. Cf. Acts 3.15.

5. What the false witnesses, therefore, what the bloodstained elders, what the wicked priests did to the Lord Jesus Christ by making use of a cowardly judge and employing an unknowing cohort must be both detested and embraced by all ages. As cruel for the minds of Jews was the Lord's Cross as it was marvelous in the strength of the Crucified. People raged against one person, but Christ had mercy on all. Savagery that was done to him he accepted willingly, so that by allowing the crime he might complete the work of his eternal will.

6. The whole order of events that the Gospel narrative fully describes must be received by the faithful hearing it, so that, by a saving faith in the actions then completed during the time of our Lord's Passion, we should understand not only the forgiveness of sins to have been accomplished in Christ, but also the pattern of justice to have been set forth. So that this might be discussed in greater detail with the Lord's help, let this part of our sermon be saved for Wednesday of this week. The grace of God will be with us, as we hope, and this, with the help of your prayers, will enable us to fulfill our promises, through our Lord Jesus Christ who with the Father and the Holy Spirit reigns for ever and ever. Amen.

Sermon 63

19 March 452—Wednesday of Holy Week

Our Lord's Passion, dearly beloved, about which we promised to speak again today, has an especially wonderful glory due to the mystery of his humility. That humility both redeemed us all and taught us all, so that righteousness would spring from the same one who had paid the price.

God's Son, in his omnipotence (equal to the Father through the same essence), could in fact have rescued the human race from the devil's sway by nothing more than a command from his will. It was especially in conformity with his divine work, however, that the hostility of that enemy's wickedness should be overcome by what he had conquered, and that the liberty of one nature should be restored through the same nature by which the captivity of all had been brought into effect.

When, however, the Evangelist said, "The Word was made flesh and dwelt among us,"[229] and when the Apostle said, "God was in Christ reconciling the world to himself,"[230] it was shown that the Only-Begotten of the Father Most High entered into such fellowship with human lowliness that one and the same Son of God remained after he had taken on himself the substance of our body and soul, our substance (to enrich it) and not his own, because weakness had to be enriched and not strength. That way, when the creature was united to its Creator, nothing divine was lacking to what was assumed, nothing human to that assuming.

2. This design of God's holiness and mercy, though draped in past ages with some kind of veil, was not so hidden that it was denied to the understanding of holy people who, from the beginning up to the coming of Christ, stood out as praiseworthy. That salvation which was to come in Christ had in fact been promised both by the words of prophets and by the signs of all that happened. Not only did those who preached it attain to it, but all those who believed the preachers as well. One faith justifies the holy people of all times. Whatever we confess as having been done by Jesus Christ, the "Mediator between God and human beings,"[231] or whatever our fathers worshipped as still to come, all belongs to the same hope of the faithful.

There is no distinction "between Jews and Gentiles."[232] Indeed, as the Apostle says, "circumcision is nothing, prepuce is nothing; but the keeping of God's commands."[233] These commands, if they are maintained in the integrity of faith, make true "children of Abraham,"[234] that is to say, perfect Christians, as the same Apostle says: "All of you who have been baptized into Christ have clothed yourselves in Christ. There is neither Jew nor Greek, slave nor free, male nor female. All of you are one in Christ. But, if you belong to Christ, you are therefore the posterity of Abraham, heirs according to the promise."[235]

3. There can be no doubt, then, dearly beloved, that the hu-

229. Jn 1.14.
230. 2 Cor 5.19.
231. Cf. 1 Tm 2.5.
232. Cf. Rom 10.12.
233. 1 Cor 7.19.
234. Cf. Gal 3.7.
235. Gal 3.27–29.

man nature has been taken up into such a cohesion by the Son of God that he is one and the same Christ not only in that "firstborn of all creation,"[236] but in all his saints as well. Just as a head cannot be divided from its members, so the members cannot be divided from their head. It may not pertain to this life, but to eternal life, "that God is all in all."[237] Nevertheless, even now he is the Undivided Dweller in his own temple, which is the Church, as he himself promised, saying, "Behold, I am with you always, until the end of time."[238] Echoing this, the Apostle says: "He himself is the Head of the body, the Church, he who is the beginning, the first-born from the dead, so that he himself may be in all things, holding the primacy, because it pleased God that all fullness reside in him, and through him to reconcile all things in himself."[239]

4. By these and many other citations, what has been instilled in our hearts if not that we should be "renewed" through them all "into the image"[240] of that one who, remaining "in the form of God,"[241] condescended to become "the form of sinful flesh?"[242] He assumed all those weaknesses of ours which come as a result of sin, though "without" any part in "sin."[243] Consequently, he lacked none of the afflictions due to hunger and thirst, sleep and weariness, sadness and tears. He endured grievous sorrows even to the point of death. No one could be released from the fetters of mortality unless he, in whom alone the nature of all people was innocent, should allow himself to be killed by the hands of wicked men.

Our Savior, the Son of God, gave both a mystery and an example to all who believe in him, so that they might attain to the one by being reborn, and arrive at the other by imitation. Blessed Peter the apostle teaches this, saying: "Christ suffered for you, leaving you an example, that you should follow in his footsteps. He did no wrong, nor was deceit found in his mouth. When he was reviled, he did not revile in return. When he suffered, he did not counter with threats, but gave himself over

---

236. Cf. Col 1.15.
237. Cf. 1 Cor 15.28.
238. Mt 28.20.
239. Col 1.18–20.
240. Cf. Col 3.10.
241. Cf. Phil 2.6.
242. Cf. Rom 8.3 and Phil 2.7.
243. Cf. Heb 4.15.

to the one judging him unjustly. He himself bore our sins in his own body on the cross, so that, dead to sin, we might live for holiness."[244]

5. No believer, dearly beloved, is to be denied the gifts of grace. Likewise, no one has not become indebted to Christian discipline. Although the rigor of that figurative law has been revoked, the benefit of voluntary observance has increased nonetheless. As John the Evangelist said, "though the law was given through Moses, grace and truth have come through Jesus Christ."[245] All that has come according to the law—whether in the circumcision of flesh, or in the diversity of victims, or in the Sabbath observance—all bore witness to Christ and foretold the grace of Christ.

He himself "terminates the law,"[246] not by emptying out its figures but by fulfilling them, for he is the author of both old and new. He has changed the mysteries of the prefigured promises by completing these promises. He put an end to expectations when he came as the Expected One. Among the moral precepts, however, no decrees of the earlier Testament were repudiated. By the Gospel teaching, however, many have been broadened, so that those granting salvation would be more perfect and more clear than those promising a Savior.[247]

6. Consequently, all that the Son of God "did and taught" for reconciling the world, we have not so much learned from the account of past events as we have felt in the force of present works. He it is who, born from his Virgin Mother by the Holy Spirit, enriches his untainted Church with the same inspiration—until through the birth of Baptism an innumerable throng of God's children have been born. Concerning them it is said: "Who were born not from blood, nor from the will of human beings, nor from the will of flesh, but from God."[248]

He it is in whom the seed of Abraham was blessed with the adoption of the whole world. Consequently, that patriarch has been made father of the nations, since children of promise are

---

244. 1 Pt 2.21–24.
246. Cf. Rom 10.4.
248. Jn 1.13.

245. Jn 1.17.
247. Cf. Augustine, *Enar. in Ps* 72.3.

born not of flesh but in faith.[249] He does not make exceptions for any nation. From every nation under heaven,[250] he has made one flock of holy sheep, fulfilling on a daily basis what he had promised, saying: "I also have other sheep that are not of this fold, and I must lead them. They will hear my voice, and there will be one flock and one shepherd."[251]

It was primarily to blessed Peter that he said, "Feed my sheep."[252] All shepherds, however, are directed in this duty by the same Lord. So fruitful and so well-watered are the pastures in which he nourishes those who come to the rock,[253] that innumerable sheep, strengthened with the abundance of his love, do not hesitate to die for the name of their Shepherd, even as the Good Shepherd was willing to "lay down his life for the sheep."[254] With him, not only the glorious courage of martyrs but also the faith of all who have been reborn suffer together in that same rebirth.

Even while we renounce the devil and believe in God, while we pass into new things from old, while we put aside the "image" of this "earthly" human being and take on the form of that heavenly one,[255] a kind of "death" and a certain "likeness of resurrection" happens.[256] Taken up by Christ and taking on Christ, then, we are not the same after the purification of Baptism as we were before it. Instead, the bodies of those reborn turn into the flesh of the Crucified.

7. "This transformation," dearly beloved, belongs to the "right hand of the Most High."[257] He "accomplishes all in all,"[258] so that, from the quality of "good lives" led by every single believer, we might recognize the very Author of those "good works."[259] We give thanks to the mercy of God for adorning the whole body of the Church with innumerable gifts of grace. Through many rays of the one light, the same splendor appears everywhere, nor can Christians merit from anything

---

249. Cf. Rom 4.12–18.
250. Acts 2.5.
251. Jn 10.16.
252. Jn 21.17.
253. Cf. 1 Cor 10.4.
254. Cf. Jn 10.15.
255. Cf. 1 Cor 15.49.
256. Cf. Rom 6.5.
257. Cf. Ps 76(77).11.
258. 1 Cor 12.6.
259. Cf. 1 Pt 2.12.

besides the glory of Christ. This is that "true light" which justifies and "enlightens every human being."[260] This is what he has "rescued from the power of darkness, bringing it into the kingdom of "God's Son."[261] This is what raises up the soul's desire through a "newness of life"[262] while extinguishing lusts of the flesh. This is how the Lord's Passover is properly celebrated "with the unleavened bread of sincerity and truth."

When the "yeast of the old evil" has been thrown out,[263] the "new creature"[264] receives food and drink from the Lord himself. This partaking in the body and blood of Christ means nothing else than that we should pass over into what we have taken in. Since we have died with him and are buried with him and are risen with him, let us bear him through all things both in spirit and in flesh, as the Apostle says: "You have died, and your life is hidden with Christ in God. When Christ your life appears, however, you too will appear with him in glory,"[265] who lives and reigns with the Father and the Holy Spirit forever and ever. Amen.

Sermon 64

5 April 453—Palm Sunday

All times, indeed, dearly beloved, engage the souls of Christians in the mystery of our Lord's Passion and Resurrection. No observance in our religion fails to celebrate that reconciliation of the world and taking up of human nature in Christ. Now, however, the Universal Church ought to be instructed with greater understanding and inflamed with a more fervent hope—at a time when the dignity of these events finds direct expression in the recurrence of holy days and in the pages of Gospel truth, to such an extent that the Lord's Passover ought not so much to be remembered (to have happened in the past) as honored (like a present reality).

In none of these things which pertain to the Cross of Jesus

---

260. Cf. Jn 1.9.
261. Cf. Col 1.13.
262. Cf. Rom 6.4.
263. Cf. 1 Cor 5.8.
264. Cf. Gal 6.15 and 2 Cor 5.17.
265. Col 3.3–4.

Christ should the certainty of our faith waver. None of those things which have been unfolded in the Gospel story should be received apathetically by our ears. People have not been lacking—and are still not lacking—who assail the truth of the Lord's Incarnation: that the "Word was made flesh"[266] in the womb of his Virgin Mother, that the Infant who appeared made progress in bodily growth to the age of perfect manhood, and that (having been crucified, died, and been buried) he rose on the third day. They assert that these things took place in the appearance of our image, but not in the nature of our flesh.

We who by no means withdraw from the Gospel and apostolic witnesses are strengthened by the understanding of those whose indubitable experiences have taught us. We can say devoutly and continually that in these things we also have been instructed, we have seen what "they saw," we have learned what they learned, we have touched what "they handled."[267] Consequently, we are not confused by the Lord's Passion, since we have not been deceived about his Generation.

2. We indeed know, dearly beloved, and profess with our whole heart, that the Father, Son, and Holy Spirit have a single divinity, and that the consubstantial essence of the eternal Trinity does not in any way have division within itself or conflict, since the Trinity is equally eternal, equally unchangeable, and equally never ceasing to be what it is. In this ineffable unity of the Trinity (whose works and judgments act together in all things),[268] the Person of the Son by himself took on the restoration of the human race. It is he "through whom all things were made, and without whom nothing came to be."[269] It is he who animated by the breath of rational life a man molded from the mire of the earth. Consequently, he it was who restored our nature also, a nature fallen from the heights of eternity to its lost dignity. Because he made human nature, it was fitting that he should restore it as well. Guiding his plan to completion, he

---

266. Jn 1.14. 267. Cf. 1 Jn 1.1.
268. According to well-established theological principles, no real distinction can be made between the activities of individual Persons of the Holy Trinity *ad extra*.
269. Jn 1.3.

used the justice of reason rather than the power of force to destroy the domination of the devil.

Since the whole posterity of the first human being was felled simultaneously with that one wound and no merits of saints were able to overcome the well-deserved condition of death, one physician alone came from heaven—foretold often by many signs and long promised by the prophets' assurances. Remaining in the "form of God"[270] and losing nothing of his own majesty, he came forth in the nature of our body and soul without the contamination of that ancient falsehood. Only the Son[271] was born of the Blessed Virgin without stain—not a stranger to our race but foreign to sin, in whom were the perfect innocence and true nature of the one that had been created in the "image and likeness of God."[272] From the stock of Adam there emerged one in whom the devil had nothing he could call his own. While raging against someone he did not hold under the law of sin, the devil lost the right of his wicked rule.

3. Shedding innocent blood for the guilty[273] was so powerful for establishing freedom and so abundant for paying the ransom. If all of the captives believed in their Redeemer, the chains of the tyrant would hold no one. As the Apostle says, "Where sin abounded, grace has even more abounded."[274] Since those born under the prejudgment of sin have received "power" to be reborn in innocence,[275] the gift of liberty has been made more valuable than the debt of servitude.

What hope do they leave for themselves in the protection of this mystery, those who deny the reality of human substance in the body of our Savior? Let them tell us by what sacrifice they have been reconciled, by what blood they have been redeemed! Who is it "who has given himself for us as an oblation and sacrifice to God in the odor of sweetness"?[276] What sacrifice was ever more sacred than that which the true High Priest placed on the altar of the Cross by offering his own flesh?

270. Cf. Phil 2.6.
271. i.e., and not the Father nor the Holy Spirit.
272. Cf. Gn 1.26. 273. Cf. Lam 4.13.
274. Rom 5.20. 275. Cf. Jn 1.12.
276 Eph 5.2.

"In the sight of the Lord the death of" many "saints" has been "precious" indeed.[277] Yet the killing of no guiltless human being has been a propitiation for the world. Righteous people have received—not given—crowns. From the strength of believers have been born examples of long-suffering, not gifts of justice. Separate deaths indeed occur separately, nor can anyone pay the debt of another by his own end. Among the children of human beings, only one stands out, namely, our Lord Jesus Christ—in whom all have been crucified, all died, all been buried, and all even raised up. He himself said, "When I have been lifted up from the earth, I shall draw all things to myself."[278]

True faith, which "justifies the wicked"[279] and makes them "righteous,"[280] drawn to a participant of his nature, "obtains salvation" in that one in whom alone it finds itself innocent.[281] There is one "Mediator between God and human beings, Christ Jesus the human being."[282] By participation in his nature, human beings have come to the peace of that divinity,[283] being free to "glory" in his power.[284] He came to engage the proud enemy in the weakness of our flesh and gave his triumph to those in whose body he triumphed.

4. We acknowledge, therefore, the divine nature from the Father and the human substance from his Mother in our one Lord Jesus Christ, true Son of God and of a human being. Yet the Word of God and the flesh share a single Person. Each essence shares its activities with the other, but the distinctive qualities of their works must be recognized. We must observe by the contemplation of a sincere faith to what things the humility of weakness is drawn and to what things the height of strength is directed; what it is that flesh does not deal in without the Word and what it is that the Word does not effect without the flesh.

Without the power of the Word, in fact, the Virgin could not have conceived or given birth; without the reality of flesh, the

---

277. Cf. Ps 115(116).15.
279. Cf. Rom 4.5.
281. Cf. 1 Thes 5.9.
283. Cf. Eph 2.15–16.
278. Jn 12.32.
280. Cf. Rom 1.17.
282. 1 Tm 2.5.
284. Cf. Phil 3.3.

Infant could not have lain wrapped in its swaddling clothes.[285] Without the power of the Word, the wise men could not have worshipped the Child announced by that new star;[286] without the reality of flesh, the Boy could not have been taken to Egypt in accordance with an order from above when Herod wanted to kill him.[287] Without the power of the Word, the voice of the Father sent from heaven could not have said, "This is my beloved Son, in whom I am well pleased;"[288] without the reality of flesh, John could not have insisted, "Behold the Lamb of God, behold the one who takes away the sins of the world."[289]

Without the power of the Word, there could not have been any restoration of the infirm[290] and raising of the dead;[291] without the reality of flesh, food would not have been necessary for him after fasting[292] nor sleep for him when he was tired.[293] Without the power of the Word, finally, the Lord would not have proclaimed himself equal to the Father;[294] without the reality of flesh, he would not have said that the Father is greater than himself.[295] Catholic Faith takes up both and defends both, for it believes that—the distinctive natures of the divine and of the human substances notwithstanding—one and the same Son of God is both man and the Word.

There are many examples, dearly beloved, which we could take up from the whole body of Scripture for explaining this faith that we preach. Nothing has been commended more often by divine utterances than that the Son of God, according to his divinity (from the Father), is eternal and, according to the flesh (from his Mother), is temporal. So as not to tire out your kind attention, however, the length of today's sermon should be curtailed, so that on Wednesday we might deliver what needs to be added, with the help of the Lord Jesus Christ who, with the Father and the Holy Spirit, lives and reigns for ever and ever. Amen.

285. Cf. Lk 2.7.
286. Cf. Mt 2.11.
287. Cf. Mt 2.13.
288. Mt 3.17.
289. Jn 1.29.
290. Cf. Mt 15.30.
291. Cf. Lk 7.11–15 and Jn 11.
292. Cf. Mt 4.2.
293. Cf. Mt 8.24.
294. Cf. Jn 10.30.
295. Cf. Jn 14.28.

Sermon 65

8 April 453—Wednesday of Holy Week

I understand, dearly beloved, that I must meet your expectation by delivering my promised sermon concerning the glorious Passion of our Lord Jesus Christ—in such a way that this duty of preaching might both render service to the Paschal Feast and counteract the effrontery of wicked error. Those who deny that the Son of God took on the true nature of our flesh are "enemies" of the Christian faith[296] and question the Gospel teaching with exceedingly great presumption.

According to these people, the Cross of Christ was either the pretense of an imaginary being or a punishment endured by the divinity. This suggestion must be driven away far from the hearts of devout people, since Catholic integrity can have neither "taint" of perfidy nor "wrinkle" of falsehood.[297] It confesses one Christ, both God and man, in such a way that it cannot say either that the man was false or that God was capable of suffering.

From that very beginning (when the "Word was made flesh"[298] in the Virgin's womb), no division ever existed between the divine and the human substances. Throughout all the increases of bodily growth, his actions during that whole time belonged to one and the same Person. Yet we do not confuse those things which happened inseparably by mixing them up somehow. Instead, we realize the nature to which any given thing might pertain from its properties. Divine operations do not prejudice human ones, nor do human operations prejudice divine ones. Both join together without the deletion of any proper characteristic or a doubling of the Person.

2. Now that we have reviewed the events that preceded the Lord's Passion, let us deal with what proofs exist for the Paschal Mystery. While the wrath of Jews was burning to execute their crime—as "God in Christ was reconciling the world to himself"[299]—no force could have been brought against the "temple

---

296. Cf. Phil 3.18.
297. Cf. Eph 5.27.
298. Jn 1.14.
299. 2 Cor 5.19.

of his body"[300] unless he himself permitted it. Even when that terrible "cohort" of soldiers and that mob of people were "sent by the chief priests and the Pharisees with swords and clubs,"[301] they were driven back by one word from the Lord. When the people had said that they were looking for Jesus of Nazareth and he replied, "I am he,"[302] not one of them stood their ground. Intead, losing the use of their limbs, they all fell at once, driven "backward" and struck down.[303] This was an indication of divine power which frustrated the attempts of the wicked men, not by hostile arms or the help of any created power, but solely by the strength of his word.

It was another kind of work, however, that was appropriate for saving the human race, and the blood of Christ could not have become the price for [redeeming] believers had the Redeemer not allowed himself to be apprehended. So he permitted wicked hands to be laid on himself, and the power of divinity was held in check so that the glory of the Passion might be attained. Certainly a mere semblance would have been worthless, and the appearance of suffering would not have benefitted anyone, had true divinity not clothed itself with the true feelings of human flesh.

Son of God and of a human being, incapable of being violated by reason of the one state, capable of suffering by reason of the other, he renewed our mortal essence through his immortal one. He lacked neither sorrow nor fear so that he could strengthen us to overcome disturbances of this sort, not only by the mystery of having assumed our nature, but by his example of fortitude as well. His exhortation to endurance would seem unjust had he not participated in our weakness.

3. Isaiah the prophet foretold the real sufferings of the Lord, speaking in his place: "I presented my back for scourges, my cheeks to their blows. I did not turn away my face from the shame of their spittle."[304] What the flesh of the Word suffered was punishment not of the Word but of the flesh. Yet injuries

---

300. Cf. Jn 2.21.
302. Cf. Jn 18.4–5.
304. Cf. Is 50.6.

301. Cf. Jn 18.3 and Mt 26.47.
303. Cf. Jn 18.6.

and tortures redounded even onto the one who cannot suffer, so that the things which he permitted against his body are appropriately said to have been inflicted on him, as the Apostle says: "For if they had known, they would never have crucified the Lord of Majesty."[305] Jews, blinded in their malice, did not know into what crime they had precipitated themselves.

Wherefore, the merciful Lord Jesus—who wanted to save even his murderers by his Death—prayed from the height of the cross for the ignorance of those raging against him, saying, "Father, forgive them, for they know not what they do."[306] Not by the understanding of their heart, nor by the hearing of their ears, nor by the sight of their eyes[307] did they perceive who it was they had assailed with false witnesses, who it was they had forced to be hanged on the cross. They do not recognize in his human body the substance of divinity. They saw him to be lowly. They did not worship him as Maker of the universe. Disparaging the meekness of the one who had been judged, they did not understand the power of the one who would judge. One wickedness joined the persecution of true God and the rejection of true man. Jews see in Christ only the "form of a servant,"[308] while heretics claim it to be false.

4. Let these docetistic christians say what substance of the Savior was fastened to the wood, what lay in the sepulcher, what flesh rose on the third day when the stone of the tomb was rolled away, and what kind of body Jesus brought before the eyes of his disciples when he entered to them through closed doors, when he dispelled the hesitation of those who saw him when he asked them to behold with their eyes and to touch with their fingers the still-open holes caused by nails and the fresh wound in his pierced side.[309]

If heretical obstinacy does not abandon its darkness in so great a light of truth, let them demonstrate from where they assure themselves of a hope in eternal life, from where they believe themselves to be partakers in the Resurrection of

---

305. 1 Cor 2.8.
307. Cf. 1 Cor 2.9.
309. Cf. Jn 20.19–27.

306. Lk 23.34.
308. Cf. Phil 2.7.

Christ. They cannot say with the Apostle, "Christ has risen from the dead, the first fruits of those who are asleep,"[310] for he does not constitute the first fruits of humanity if he does not come from the stock of human nature. He who rose first of all represents the fullness of that portion which would follow. We devoutly believe that what had been initiated in the Head is to be completed also in the members, because "just as in Adam all die, so also in Christ will all be brought to life."[311]

5. Embracing then, dearly beloved, the sole pledge of the Christian hope, let us not be torn from our adhesion to the body of Christ, in whom, as the Apostle says, "dwells the fullness of divinity in bodily manner, and you have been filled out in him."[312] Since the substance of God is incorporeal, how does it dwell in bodily manner in Christ unless the flesh of our race has been made the flesh of the divinity? We filled out in that God in whom we have been crucified, in whom we have been buried, in whom we have even even been raised up. We can therefore say with the Apostle: "Our abode is in heaven. From heaven also we await the Savior, our Lord Jesus Christ, and he has transformed the body of our lowliness to be made like the body of his glory,"[313] living and reigning with the Father and with the Holy Spirit for ever and ever. Amen.

Sermon 66

10 April 453—Good Friday

Today's Gospel reading, dearly beloved, which has unfolded for us the sacred history of the Lord's Passion, has become so well known to the whole Church (from hearing it frequently in public) that each one of you recalls the order of events as if they were being held before your very eyes. Nor should we consider people to have made too little progress if they do not doubt what they have heard. Even if they are not strong enough to thoroughly appreciate any given mystery of the Scriptures, they firmly believe, nevertheless, that there is nothing false in

---

310. 1 Cor 15.20.
311. 1 Cor 15.22.
312. Col 2.9–10.
313. Phil 3.20–21.

the divine books. Because the "fullness of knowledge" was promised to a sincere "faith,"[314] therefore, let the vigor of enlightened souls rouse itself to deserve instruction from the Holy Spirit. Let it not be content to know the order of outward actions without examining also the reason for this mercy expended on it. That way, human nature might love the Creator more dearly by learning how deeply he loves it.

(2) God had no reason in fact to pity us—except his own goodness. That second creation of man is more wonderful than the first, because it is a greater thing for God to have restored ("in this last age")[315] what had perished, than (in the beginning) to have made what was not. No merits of the saints preceding us have in themselves regained the freedom of natural innocence. We lost this by the prevarication of our first parents, because the sentence levelled against sinners has fettered the whole offspring of its captive descendants. No one stands out as free from condemnation, because no one was free from the crime.

Yet the Savior's Redemption, in "destroying the devil's work"[316] and breaking the chains of sin, so arranged the "mystery of its great compassion"[317] that the predetermined number of generations should flow on right up to the end of the world. But the re-making of its beginnings through the justification of undivided faith belongs to all ages [including those] of times past. Indeed, the Incarnation of the Word as well as the Death and Resurrection of Christ have become the salvation of all the faithful. He gave the blood of a just man to those of us who believe it to have been poured out for the reconciliation of the world. He gave that same blood also to those of our ancestors who in like manner believed that it was going to be poured out.

2. Nothing in the Christian religion, therefore, dearly beloved, remains separated from the ancient prefigurations. No, salvation has never been hoped for by the just ones who have gone before us except in the Lord Jesus Christ. Circumstances were different, of course, according to the arrangements of God's will. It was for the very same purpose, however, that the

314. Cf. Col 2.2 and Heb 10.22.
315. Cf. 1 Pt 1.20.
316. Cf. 1 Jn 3.8.
317. Cf. 1 Tm 3.16.

clear testimonies given by the law existed, as well as the expectations of prophets and the offering of sacrifices. For, it was appropriate that those people should be taught in this way, that what they could not receive through revelation, they might accept in a shrouded manner.

Greater would be the authority of the Gospel by the fact that the pages of the Old Testament had served it with so many signs and so many mysteries. It was concerning these that the Lord declared publicly that "he had not come to destroy the law, but to fulfill it."[318] Jews should not think it to be of any benefit for them to stay on the outer surface of a word in an unspiritual way. They have clearly been shown to resist these Scriptures which among us retain their true dignity. We are both taught by the prophecies and enriched by their fulfillment.

Our Lord said: "When I am lifted up from the earth, I shall draw all things to myself."[319] Nothing remained of legal institutions, nothing of prophetic figures, nothing, that is, which has not passed entirely into the mysteries of Christ. We possess the sign "of circumcision,"[320] the sanctification of anointing, the consecration of priests. We possess the purity of sacrifice, the truth of Baptism, the honor of the temple. Rightly should messengers have ceased after the message had come to pass. Yet our reverence for these promises should not be diminished just because the fullness of grace has been shown.

As the Apostle says, "Blindness has come upon one part of Israel,"[321] and, "those who are children of the flesh are not children of the promise."[322] God's wonderful mercy has made an Israelite nation out of all the nations. Softening the stone-hard hearts of pagans, God's mercy raised up true "children of Abraham from the stones."[323] As a result, "when all were held bound by sin,"[324] those who were born of the flesh would be "reborn in the Spirit."[325] No, it does not matter of what father each would be born, since, by the undivided confession of a

---

318. Mt 5.17.
320. Cf. Phil 3.3.
322. Cf. Rom 9.8.
324. Gal 3.22 and cf. Rom 11.32.
319. Jn 12.32.
321. Rom 11.25.
323. Cf. Mt 3.9.
325. Cf. Jn 3.5.

single faith, the fountain of Baptism makes them innocent, while election through being adopted confirms them as "heirs."[326]

3. What else has the "Cross" of Christ done and what else does it do except "reconcile" the world "to God by destroying enmities"? What else except recall everything together into true "peace" through the true sacrifice of the immaculate Lamb?[327] Those who depart in professing the faith from what they had uttered at the time of rebirth cannot be in accord with God. Forgetful of that divine promise, they manifestly adhere to what they had renounced, demonstrating that they have fallen away from what had been believed.

Some do not believe that Jesus Christ "rose" with that same flesh in which he had been born, in which he suffered, in which he died, and in which he was buried. Some do not confess that the "first fruits" of our nature have been raised up again in him.[328] In vain do such as these arrogate unto themselves the name of Christian. Let them not think that they celebrate the Lord's Passover in any way.

(2) True worshipers of the Lord's Passion should look at the Crucified Jesus with the eyes of their heart in such a way as to recognize him as being of their own flesh. Let the earthly substance tremble in the punishment of its Redeemer. Let the rocks of unfaithful souls be broken. Let those on whom the tombs of mortality lie heavy break and leap over the shattered mass of obstacles. Let the proofs of the coming resurrection "appear" now "in the holy city"[329] as well, that is, in the Church of God. Let what must be done in the body come about in hearts.

To no one among the infirm has that victory of the Cross been denied. No one is there to whom the prayer of Christ will not be an aid. If it benefited many who were raging against him, how much more would it help those who turn to him? Ignorance is taken away, difficulties are smoothed over, and the sacred blood of Christ extinguished that fiery weapon by

---

326. Cf. Rom 8.17 and Gal 4.7.
328. Cf. 1 Cor 15.20 and 23.
327. Cf. Eph 2.15–17.
329. Cf. Mt 27.53.

which the boundaries of life had been confined.[330] Darkness of the ancient night has yielded to true light. Christian people are invited to the wealth of Paradise, and the way has been thrown open to all believers for returning to their lost homeland—provided they do not close off for themselves that way which could be opened to the faith of a thief.[331]

4. As we celebrate the wonderful mystery of this Paschal Feast, dearly beloved, let us announce—while the Spirit of God teaches us—whose glory we have been called to share in and into what hope we have entered. Let us not so anxiously or so proudly busy ourselves in the occupations of this present life as not to struggle—with the whole affection of our hearts—to be conformed with our Redeemer through his example. He did nothing and suffered nothing that was not for our salvation, in order that the strength which was in the Head might also be in the body.

(2) First of all, has that taking on of our substance in the divinity—by which "the Word became flesh and dwelt among us"—left any person outside his mercy except an infidel? Besides, who is there whose nature is not one with Christ if Christ has received him by taking our nature and if he has been "born again of" that "Spirit"[332] from which Christ was begotten?[333] Who then does not recognize the "stages of" his own "life" in him?[334] Who does not see that his taking of food,[335] his rest in "sleep,"[336] his anxiety in "sorrow,"[337] and his "tears" of compassion[338] made his "form" that "of a servant"?[339]

Since this form must be healed of its ancient wounds and purified from its off-scouring of sin, the Only-Begotten of God became also the son of a human being. That way, he would not lack either the whole reality of human nature or the fullness of divinity. Consequently, just as it was our nature (joined into one with the divinity) that the virginity of his Mother brought forth, so it was ours also that the Jewish wickedness crucified.

---

330. Cf. Gn 3.24.
331. Cf. Lk 23.43.
332. Cf. Jn 3.5.
333. Cf. Lk 1.35.
334. Cf. Lk 2.40 and 52.
335. Cf. Mt 11.19.
336. Cf. Mt 8.24.
337. Cf. Mt 26.37.
338. Cf. Jn 11.35–36.
339. Cf. Phil 2.7.

What lay lifeless was ours, and what rose on the third day was ours, as well as what ascended above the heights of heaven to the right hand of the Father's majesty. If we walk in the way of his commandments and if we are not ashamed to confess that which brings our salvation in the humility of the body, we too will be brought into the company of his glory. What has been foretold will be openly fulfilled: "Everyone who will confess me in the presence of human beings, I will also confess them in the presence of my Father who is in heaven."[340]

5. God's grace has been present in this exhortation of ours and has helped it, the grace which destroyed the enemies of Christ's Incarnation and Death and Resurrection[341] when the truth was revealed through all the churches. Believers of all the world—in agreement with the authority of apostolic faith—rejoice together with us in exultation, as the blessed apostle Paul says: "Or do you not know that whoever of us have been baptized in Christ have been baptized in his Death. For we were buried with him through Baptism in death so that, as Christ rose from the dead through the glory of the Father, so also shall we walk in the newness of life. For if we have been grafted into the likeness of his Death, so shall we be into that of his Resurrection. We know that our old human being has been crucified [with him] in order that the body of sin might be destroyed, so we might not be slaves to sin any longer. For whoever has died is justified from sin. If we have died with Christ, moreover, we believe that we shall also live together with him"[342] who reigns with the Father and with the Holy Spirit for ever and ever. Amen.

Sermon 67

28 March 454—Palm Sunday

Spirits of the faithful, dearly beloved, should indeed always be filled with admiration for the works of God. Rational souls should cling especially to those thoughts from which they gain

---

340. Mt 10.32.
342. Rom 6.3–8.
341. Cf. Phil 3.18.

an increase of faith. When the attention of a devout heart has been directed either to general benefits or to the special gifts of this particular grace, it drives away many frivolous thoughts and withdraws from bodily concerns into a kind of spiritual solitude. In this time of the Lord's Passion, however, we must be even more eager and more diligent that what has been reviewed in the sacred readings might be understood by the hearing of a sound intelligence, and that what has importance in the words themselves might appear even more important in their deeper meaning.

(2) Now the first reason "for lifting up our hearts"[343] is that those things which the Gospel truth has related to us have been foretold by the voices of prophets—not as something about to be done, but as already accomplished. What human ears did not yet know as about to be done, the Holy Spirit was announcing as accomplished. King David, whose offspring Christ is according to human lineage,[344] preceded the day of the Lord's crucifixion by more than eleven hundred years. He had suffered none of those tortures which he mentions as having been inflicted upon himself.[345] Because the Lord—who was going to take the suffering flesh from David's stock—spoke through his mouth, the history of the crucifixion has rightly been prefigured in the person of David. David bore in himself the bodily origin of the Savior. Truly David suffered in Christ, because Jesus was truly crucified in the flesh of David.

2. All the things, therefore, that the wickedness of Jews inflicted on the "Lord of Majesty"[346] had been fully predicted. Prophetic locution was interwoven not so much concerning future things as concerning those past. What else, then, did these things open up to us except the unchanging order of God's eternal plan? With God, things that are going to be discerned have already been decided, and future things have already been accomplished. Now, when divine knowledge foresees both the nature of our actions and the effects of all our wills, how much better known to God are his own works.

---

343. Cf. Preface of the Mass.
345. Cf. Ps 21(22).
344. Cf. Rom 1.3.
346. Cf. 1 Cor 2.8.

Surely it was pleasing to him that those things be considered as completed which were absolutely incapable of not being accomplished. Hence comes it that the apostles, full of God's Spirit, spoke with one voice[347] to God when they endured the threats and the cruelty of Christ's enemies: "In this very city, Herod and Pontius Pilate conspired with the pagan nations and the peoples of Israel to do against your holy servant Jesus (whom you anointed) what your hands and your plan decreed to be done."[348] Wickedness in persecuting Christ did not spring from the plan of God, did it? Likewise, the hand of his divine preparation did not arm that crime which is greater than any other crime, did it?

Clearly we must not think this about the Supreme Justice. What was foreknown about the malice of Jews and what was properly decreed regarding the Passion of Christ were very different and quite contrary. For the will to murder did not proceed from the same place as the will to die. Nor did their heinous crime and the Redeemer's patience arise from a single spirit. Our Lord did not himself cause the wicked hands of his attackers to be laid on him, but he permitted this. He did not force what was going to happen actually to happen simply by foreknowing it. Yet it was for this purpose that he had taken on flesh, so that it might happen.

3. Finally, so disparate were the motives of the Crucified and of those crucifying, that, while what was undertaken by Christ could not be abolished, what was committed by those others could indeed have been put to a halt. He who came "to save sinners"[349] did not deny his mercy even to his own murderers,[350] but turned the evil of godless people to the good of believers.[351] More wonderful was this grace of God in that it had been mercifully prepared—not according to human merit, but according to the "riches of God's wisdom and knowledge"[352]—when the water of Baptism received even those who poured out the Savior's blood.

347. Cf. Acts 4.24.
348. Acts 4.27–28.
349. Cf. 1 Tm 1.15.
350. Cf. Lk 23.34.
351. Cf. Rom 11.11–12.
352. Cf. Rom 11.33.

Scripture—which contains the *Acts of the Apostles*—tells us that, when the preaching of blessed Peter the apostle "goaded the hearts" of Jews,[353] and, when they had acknowledged the wickedness of their crime, they said, "What shall we do, brethren?" And the same apostle goes on: "Do penance. Every one of you should be baptized in the name of Jesus Christ for the remission of your sins, and you will receive the gift of the Holy Spirit. For the promise is to you, and to your children, and for all those who are far away, whom the Lord our God will call to himself."[354] Then the writer adds this: "Those who accepted his words were baptized, and that very day about three thousand souls were added to their number."[355]

(2) Although the Lord Jesus Christ wanted to suffer the anger of their complaints, in no way was he the author of their crime. He did not cause them to wish this, but he yielded—so that they could do it. He thus used the madness of these blinded people and, in the same way, the treachery of his betrayer. He was willing to call him back from the enormity of that crime through acts of kindness and through his words, by taking him in as a disciple, by elevating him to an apostle, by warning him with signs, by blessing him in the mysteries—so that, as no kindness was lacking to him for his correction, there was no occasion for sin.

4. You, however, most wicked man—"from the seed of Canaan and not of Judah"[356]—no longer a "vessel of election"[357] but the "son of perdition"[358] and of death, you believed that the devil's suggestions would be more profitable for you. Inflamed with the fire of avarice, you were burning for the acquisition of thirty silver pieces. You did not see what riches you lost. Even if you did not think that the promises should be believed, for what reason was so little a sum of money put ahead of what you had received? You were giving commands to demons, you were healing the sick, you were honored with the apostles, and, so that you might appease the hunger of your avarice, thefts from

---

353. Cf. Acts 2.37.
355. Acts 2.41.
357. Cf. Acts 9.15.
354. Acts 2.37–39.
356. Cf. Dn 13.56.
358. Cf. Jn 17.12.

the purse lay open to you. But the less lawful it was, the more it incited your soul (which had been warned about the prohibitions). No, the sum of the price did not please you so much as the magnitude of the sin. Hence, the crime of your commerce is not so much detestable because you assessed the Lord at too low a value, but because you sold even your Redeemer himself to prevent him from taking pity on you. It was right for you to incur that punishment of yours, since, in the punishment you inflicted, no one more cruel than you could be found.

5. When, therefore, at the predetermined time Jesus Christ was crucified, died, and was buried according to the plan of his own will, it was not a necessity brought upon him by his own condition but the redemption of our captivity. As a result, "the Word was made flesh"[359] so that our suffering nature could be taken from the Virgin's womb. What could not be carried out against the Son of God could be allowed against the son of a human being.

Although the mark of divinity shone on him even at his Birth and all the growth of bodily progress was full of divine miracles, he nevertheless took the reality of our weakness and excluded nothing of human infirmity from himself except participation in our sin. That way, he might bring his own nature to us and heal ours in himself. A double remedy has been prepared for us miserable people by the Almighty Physician, one of which is in the mystery, the other in his example. Through the one, divine grace is conferred; by virtue of the other, human response is required. As God is the author of justification, so human beings are debtors of devotion.

6. Consequently, this ineffable restoration of our salvation, dearly beloved, leaves no place for pride or idleness. "We" both "have" nothing beyond "what we have received"[360] and are continuously warned against holding on to the gifts of God's "grace without using them."[361] With all justice, then, the one who goes ahead of us with help also insists upon his conditions, and the one who leads us to glory urges us graciously to obedience. As

---

359. Jn 1.14.
361. Cf. 1 Tm 4.14.
360. Cf. 1 Cor 4.7.

a result, the Lord rightly became "the Way"³⁶² for us, since we cannot come to Christ except through Christ.

Whoever walks his path of patience and humility comes to Christ through Christ. On this journey, the heat of labor is clearly not wanting, nor the gloom of sorrow, nor the tempests of fear. On it are the treachery of wicked people, persecutions by the godless, threats from those in power, and insults from the proud. Yet the "Lord of Hosts" and "King of Glory"³⁶³ endured all things in the "form" of our weakness³⁶⁴ and "in the likeness of sinful flesh,"³⁶⁵ so that, among the dangers of this life, we should not so much wish to flee by running away as to overcome by enduring.

7. Hence it is that our Head, the Lord Jesus Christ, transforming all the members of his body into himself, cried out amid the punishment of the cross (assuming the persona of those redeemed), saying what on one occasion he had uttered in the psalm: "My God, my God, look at me. Why have you abandoned me?"³⁶⁶ This expression, dearly beloved, represents a teaching, not a complaint. Since in Christ there is but one Person for God and man, he cannot be abandoned by someone from whom he cannot not be separated. He asks on our behalf. We are frightened and feeble, wondering why the flesh, afraid of suffering, had not been heeded.

When his suffering pressed him to heal and correct that fear which comes from our frailty, he had said, "My Father, if it is possible, let this cup pass me by. Nevertheless, not as I will but as you will."³⁶⁷ Later, however, he said, "My Father, if this cup cannot pass me by unless I drink it, your will be done."³⁶⁸ When this fear residing in the flesh was cast out, when the flesh then made the transition over to his Father's will, and when the whole threat of death was trampled under foot, he was fulfilling the work of his design.

When, "exalted in" the very "triumph"³⁶⁹ of so great a vic-

362. Cf. Jn 14.6.
363. Cf. Ps 23(24).10.
364. Cf. Phil 2.7.
365. Cf. Rom 8.3.
366. Ps 21(22).2. Cf. Mt 27.46 and Mk 15.34.
367. Mt 26.39.
368. Mt 26.42.
369. Cf. Jn 12.32 and Col 2.15.

tory, he asked the cause and the reason why he should be abandoned, that is, not heard, was it not to show that this emotion which he accepted for the release of human fear was one thing, and that which he had chosen from the eternal will of the Father "for the reconciliation of the world"[370] another? That cry of not being heard provides the explanation for a great mystery, because the Redeemer's power would have brought nothing to humanity if our weakness had obtained what it sought.

Lest we burden you with too long a sermon, dearly beloved, let these words be enough for today. Let us put the remainder off until Wednesday. With your prayers, God will be present so that we might render to you what we promise to fulfill, with his generosity, who lives and reigns for ever and ever. Amen.

Sermon 68

31 March 454—Wednesday of Holy Week

My last sermon—which I want to finish for you as I promised, dearly beloved—had reached the point where we were talking about that cry of the Crucified Lord to the Father. Let no simple and careless hearer receive the words he spoke ("My God, my God, why have you abandoned me?"[371]) as though, when he was fixed to the wood of the cross, the power of God the Father had withdrawn from him. For the nature of God and man had joined into such a great union that they could not be divided by suffering or separated by death. Although each substance retained its own proper nature, God did not abandon his body during the Passion, nor did the flesh make God passible, because the divinity which was in the suffering man was not in the suffering itself.

Since there is a single Person for both the Word and the flesh, the one who was made (just like all other things) is the same one "through whom all things were made;"[372] the one who was taken by the hands of wicked men is the same one who is con-

---

370. Cf. 2 Cor 5.19.
371. Cf. Ps 21(22).2, Mt 27.46, and Mk 15.34.
372. Jn 1.3.

fined by no boundaries; the one who was pierced by nails is the same one who is hurt by no wounds; the one, finally, who underwent death is the same one who does not cease to be eternal. In each instance it is shown by undoubted signs that both the lowliness of Christ and his majesty are real.

Divine strength has so united itself to human weakness that, while God makes his powers to be what ours are, he has made ours to be what his are. Neither the Son was separate from the Father nor the Father from the Son. That unchanging divinity and indivisible Trinity could not have separated anything of itself from itself. Although the design of the Incarnation—in actually undertaking it—properly involves the Only-Begotten Son of God, yet the Father was not separate from the Son in so far as the flesh is not separate from the Word.

2. It was for this reason that "Jesus cried out in a loud voice, 'Why have you abandoned me?'"[373]—to make known to all that it was right that he should not be rescued or defended, but should be abandoned into the hands of violent men, that is, to become the Savior of the world and the Redeemer of all people. That cry did not come out of misery but out of mercy, not for lack of help but from his decision to die. What must we think of this cutting off of life when his soul was given up "by" his own "power" and recalled "by" his own "power?"[374] As the blessed Apostle said, "The Father did not spare his own Son but gave him up on behalf of us all."[375] On another occasion he said, "Because Christ loved the Church and gave himself over for her to make her holy."[376]

It was the will of his Father as well as his own will that the Lord should be given over to his Passion. That way, the Father not only abandoned him but—in a way—abandoned himself as well, not through a fearful departure but through a voluntary withdrawal. Now the power of the Crucified restrained itself from the wicked. So that he might employ a hidden design, he was unwilling to use his manifest strength. For how could he

---

373. Mt 27.46. Cf. Ps 21(22).2 and Mk 15.34.
374. Cf Jn 10.17–18.   375. Rom 8.32.
376. Eph 5.25–26.

make sinners whole if he who by his Passion had come to destroy death and the author of death would have resisted his persecutors?

(2) It was therefore, dearly beloved, the part of Jews to believe that Jesus—against whom they had been able to perpetrate such a crime—was abandoned by God. Not recognizing the mystery of his wonderful patience, they said with blasphemous mockery: "He saved others, himself he cannot save. If he is the king of Israel, let him come down from the cross now, and we shall believe him."[377]

Not at the whim of your blindness, foolish scribes and wicked priests, was the power of the Savior to be shown, nor ought the Redemption of the human race be given up in accordance with the demands of those blasphemous tongues. If you had been willing to recognize the divinity of God's Son, you would see his innumerable works, and this ought to strengthen you for that faith which you deceitfully profess. If, however—as you yourselves say—it is true that he saved others, why have so many and such great miracles, done in the sight of all, in no way softened the hardness of your hearts—unless it is because "you have always resisted the Holy Spirit,"[378] that you have turned all the benefits of God toward your own destruction? For, even if Christ would come down from the cross, you would nevertheless be fixed to your sin.

3. These taunts of empty scoffing have therefore been ignored. No affronts, no abuses, have moved the mercy of the Lord from the path of his design for restoring those lost and ruined. He was, then, offered to God as a unique Victim for the salvation of the world, and the killing of the true Lamb, foretold through many ages, has brought the children of promise into the liberty of faith. The New Testament was also confirmed, and these children were inscribed by the blood of Christ as heirs of the eternal kingdom. The Sovereign Pontiff entered "the Holy of Holies," and the "Unspotted" Priest[379] himself went "through the veil of his flesh"[380] in an appeal to God.

377. Mt 27.42.
379. Cf. Heb 9.14.
378. Cf. Acts 7.51.
380. Cf. Heb 10.20.

(2) Finally, then, the transition was made openly from the law to the Gospel, from the synagogue to the Church, from the many sacrifices "to the one Victim."[381] When the Lord "gave up his spirit,"[382] that mystical veil—which by its hanging there shut off the inner sanctuary of the temple and the holy chamber—"was torn from top to bottom" by sudden force,[383] for reality did away with figures, and announcements were unnecessary in the presence of the announced. There was, in addition, a tremendous commotion of all the elements[384] as the very functions of nature drew themselves away from those who had devised the crucifixion of Christ.

When the centurion, guard over the punishment, cried out in terror at what he saw, "In truth this man was the Son of God,"[385] no penitence was apparent to lessen the godlessness of Jews, a godlessness harder than all monuments and rocks. It seems that the Roman soldiers were more prepared to recognize the Son of God than were the Israelite priests.

4. Accordingly, the Jews, deprived of sanctification from all the mysteries, have turned their light into darkness for themselves and their festivals into sorrow. Let us, therefore, dearly beloved, worship with prostrate bodies and souls the grace of God poured out on all peoples. Let us beseech the merciful Father and the "wealthy" Redeemer[386] that day by day, aided by his help, we might flee all the dangers of this life. For the cunning tempter is everywhere present, leaving nothing empty of his snares. We must always resist him in faithful constancy, with the help of the God's mercy which is always extended to us in the midst of any adversity. As a result, though the evil one never ceases to attack, may he find no one to overcome.

Let the fasts, dearly beloved, carefully observed, benefit us all. Let the grace of temperance (which we know to be fitting for both soul and body) not be broken by any excesses. Things pertaining to sobriety and self-denial have been practiced more earnestly during these days. As a result, they have changed

---

381. Cf. Heb 10.12 and 14.
382. Cf. Mt 27.50.
383. Cf. Mt 27.51.
384. Cf. Mt 27.51.
385. Mt 27.54.
386. Cf. 2 Cor 8.9.

from a brief effort into a lifelong habit. Let the faithful not spend any time without deeds of mercy or efforts of self-denial. In the passing of days and the course of time, we ought to prepare the reward of our works, not the loss of merit. May the mercy of God be present in holy and devout souls, so that he will enable us to obtain what he has made us desire, who lives and reigns with our Lord Jesus Christ his Son and with the Holy Spirit forever and ever. Amen.

Sermon 69

4 April 454—Holy Saturday Vigil

Indeed, the greatness of this ineffable mystery, dearly beloved, exceeds the reach of human understanding and any possibility of being described. Likewise, the triumph of the Lord's Passion has a loftiness far above the most outstanding abilities and most eloquent tongues. Yet we should rejoice rather than be embarrassed about being overcome by the dignity of so great a subject matter. No one could think less adequately about it than someone who thought that what had been said would be sufficient.

Consequently, it would not be superfluous for us to preach something we have preached before. Nor should someone speaking about divine matters fear the peevishness of carnal ears—as if these things are to become contemptible simply because they are brought to mind by frequent repetition. On the contary, it pertains very much to the coherence of Christian faith—according to the teaching of the Apostle—that "we should all say the same thing and be perfect in the same understanding and in the same knowledge."[387]

Unfaithfulness, of course, which is the mother of all errors, gets broken apart into many opinions that it considers necessary to color in with the art of speaking. But the witness of truth never withdraws from its own light. It is the weakness of our vision—and not a variegation of the light—that causes it to shine less for some and more for others. Following the help of

---

387. 1 Cor 1.10.

enlightenment from above, my words must also render service to [this light]. Since you are "the cultivation of God, the building of God,"[388] may he grant that both distributor and receiver should measure up, for he knows how to collect a just interest for his outlays.[389]

2. Know, dearly beloved, that in going over this text of the Gospel reading—to which you paid close attention, the one dealing with the glory of Christ's Cross—all the mysteries of these divine utterances have been disclosed to you. Rejoice that whatever the shadows of the Old Testament used to veil beneath the testimonies of prophets has been brought out into the open through the mystery of the Lord's Passion. As a result, the various kinds of sacrifices and the different means of purification have come to a halt. As a result, the precept of circumcision, the distinction between foods, the Sabbath rest, and the killing of the paschal lamb have ceased—since "the law was given through Moses, but grace and truth have come about through Jesus Christ."[390]

Figures came first so that their fulfillment could follow. When the reality which had been announced finally arrived, there was no longer any need for the services of heralds. Reconciliation of the human race was conducted in such a way that the salvation which comes in Christ should have been available to all generations under the same justification. Delaying [this salvation] was a calculated move. It had the advantage of causing those things which were believed long before they actually took place to be honored without interruption. When the strength of faith has been established in those things that do not lie open to our vision,[391] heavenly doctrine treats us more leniently, us whom it has put off until these times. To help us understand more easily, we benefit from many more prophets and witnesses than former ages.

3. What the sacred Gospels, "written by the finger of God,"[392] tell us about the Passion of the Lord Jesus Christ, accept with-

---

388. 1 Cor 3.9.
389. Cf. Mt 25.27 and Lk 19.23.
390. Jn 1.17.
391. Cf. Heb 11.1.
392. Cf. Ex 31.18 and Dt 9.10.

out a shadow of hesitation. Consider this series of past events to be as clear as if you were in contact with them all through physical sight and touch. Let true divinity and true humanity be believed in Christ. He is flesh who is the Word. As he is of one substance with the Father, so he is of one nature with his Mother—not doubled in person, not confused in essence; in his power not subject to suffering; in his lowliness subject to death; but so using both that his strength could glorify weakness but weakness could not obscure strength.

He who contains the world allows himself to be apprehended by persecutors. He is killed by the hands of those in whose hearts he has not been received. Justice does not resist the unjust, and truth yields to false testimonies. Remaining "in the form of God," he fills out the "form of a servant."[393] He confirms the reality of his physical Birth by the severity of his physical Passion. Yet to undergo this was for the Only-Begotten and eternal Son of God not occasioned by necessity but motivated by mercy, so that "from the standpoint of sin he might condemn sin,"[394] and that "he might destroy the devil's work" as a result of the devil's work.[395]

(2) That enemy of the human race introduced a deadly wound into the whole world for the sake of destroying it in its very foundations, while the captive offspring of the seed surrendered to him could not parry his iron-clad rights. Consequently, in so many generations subjected to him by the law of death, when he saw one among the children of men whose power he marvelled at as exceeding that of all the saints who ever lived, this enemy thought himself secure about the continuance of his prerogative if no merits of justice would have been able to overcome the power of death.

By wildly arousing his servants and his mercenaries, he was raging toward his own destruction. Though he felt that a man whom he could kill was beholden to him somehow, in avenging the likeness of nature, he did not see the freedom of his unique innocence. He was not mistaken about his race, but he was de-

393. Cf. Phil. 2.6–7.   394. Rom 8.3.
395. Cf. 1 Jn 3.8.

ceived about his guilt. First Adam and Second Adam were one with respect to human flesh but not when it came to their respective work. In the former "all die." In the latter "all will be brought to life."³⁹⁶ The former, through his love of pride, made his way to misery. The latter, through the strength of his humility, paved the way to glory. For this reason had he said: "I am the Way, the Truth, and the Life"³⁹⁷—the Way, in the form of a righteous life; the Truth, in the anticipation of a sure thing; the Life, in the realization of eternal joy.

4. Jewish godlessness, dearly beloved, as well as the devil's pride, did not recognize this mystery of great compassion. "For if they had known, they never would have crucified the Lord of Majesty."³⁹⁸ But, since the design of God's mercy lay hidden from the enemy of the human race, "God in Christ reconciling the world to himself"³⁹⁹ was concealed behind the veil of flesh. So the devil continued to rage against someone in whom he could find nothing that belonged to him. It would rather have benefitted his malice if he would have been sparing and would have refrained from pouring out the blood of one through whom the captivity of all was to be released and their liberty restored. Yet "darkness did not overwhelm" the light,⁴⁰⁰ nor could lying blindness see the wisdom of truth.

So the Lord's gentleness maintained its constant patience. While the strength of the angelic legions that waited on him was held in check, he drank the cup of sorrow and death, thereby transforming the entire affliction into triumph. Deceptions were overcome, and the powers of evil were suppressed.⁴⁰¹ So the world received a new beginning in order that a condemned generation might not stand in the way of those whom regeneration was helping to be saved. "Old things have passed away, and all things have been made new."⁴⁰² For, through him and with him, a share both in the Passion and in the eternity of the Resurrection belong in a similar way to all those believing in Christ and reborn in the Holy Spirit. As the Apostle says, "You

---

396. Cf. 1 Cor 15.22.
397. Jn 14.6.
398. 1 Cor 2.8.
399. 2 Cor 5.19.
400. Cf. Jn 1.5.
401. Cf. 1 Pt 3.22.
402. 2 Cor 5.17.

have died, and your life has been hidden with Christ in God. When Christ your life will appear, however, you too will appear with him in glory."[403]

5. Grounded in this hope, then, dearly beloved, avoid all the craftiness of the devil. He lays traps not only through the lusts of flesh and carnal allurements. But, scattering the cockle of falsehood even among the seeds of faith themselves, he is eager to harm the cultivation of truth, to uproot with wicked errors those whom he could not corrupt with evil deeds. Flee the arguments of worldly doctrine and avoid the poisoned words of heretics. Let there be nothing in common between yourselves and those who are christians in name only because they oppose the Catholic Faith. They are not the "temple of" God's "Spirit" nor "members of Christ."[404] Instead, tangled up in false ideas, they have as many faces of the devil as they do idols of falsehood.

Freed from these evils through the Lord Jesus Christ, who is "the Way, the Truth, and the Life,"[405] let us bear all the temptations of that "life" and all the battles with the exultation of faith. "If we suffer with him, we shall also reign with him."[406] This reward has been prepared not only for those who have been killed for the Lord's name by the savagery of wicked people, since all of those serving God and living for God, as they are crucified in Christ, so are they to be crowned in Christ. This reward has been prepared indeed for those who, excelling in all glory, overcame fearful deaths and cruel torments by enduring them even to the point of giving up their lives. Yet it has also been prepared for those followers who have conquered the greed of avarice, the exaltation of pride, and the desires of sensuality by the mortification of their own flesh. Rightly does the Apostle say that "all those who wish to live in devotion to Christ suffer persecution."[407] Undoubtedly this applies to anyone who is not a stranger to holiness.

Those celebrate the Paschal Feast properly who work "not

---

403. Col 3.3–4.
405. Cf. Jn 14.6.
407. 2 Tm 3.12.

404. Cf. 1 Cor 6.19 and 15.
406. Rom 8.17 and 2 Tm 2.12.

in the yeast of the old malice, but in the unleavened bread of sincerity."⁴⁰⁸ They live no longer in the first Adam, but in the second Adam, having been made members of the body of Christ, Christ who, "though he was in the form of God," condescended to become the "form of a servant."⁴⁰⁹ "In the one Mediator between God and human beings, Jesus Christ the human being,"⁴¹⁰ there would be both the fullness of divine majesty and the reality of human nature. Had the divinity of the Word not received this nature into the unity of his own Person, there would be no regeneration in the water of Baptism nor Redemption in the blood of the Passion. Since, however, in the mystery of Christ's Incarnation we have received nothing false, nothing in figures, not in vain do we believe ourselves to have died with him dying, and to have been raised with him rising. He himself who "works all things in all"⁴¹¹ remains in us, he who lives and reigns with the Father and with the Holy Spirit forever and ever. Amen.

Sermon 70

2 April 443—Good Friday

I think, dearly beloved, that the sacred story of the Lord's Passion—which the Gospel narrative has told us as usual—remains so fixed in all of your hearts that the reading of it has become, as it were, a visual aid to each one of its hearers. True faith, indeed, has this power, that it does not quit the minds of those who could not be present in body. Whether the believer's heart returns to the past or reaches out to the future, the recognition of truth senses no lapse of time.

(2) There exists, then, in our minds the image of things done for our salvation. Whatever at that time captivated the disciples' hearts touches our affections too—not that we are either overcome with sorrow or frightened by the wrath of angry Jews, since the Resurrection and Ascension of the Lord brought to an invincible confidence even those whom the force

---

408. Cf. 1 Cor 5.8.
410. 1 Tm 2.5.
409. Cf. Phil 2.6–7.
411. Cf. 1 Cor 12.6.

of that tempest scared. When, however, we grasp in our minds the character of those people at Jerusalem and of the priests, we realize with trembling hearts the wickedness of their crime.

Although the Savior's Passion belongs to the salvation of the human race, and the chains of eternal death have been broken by the temporal death of the Lord, still the patience of the Crucified prompts one thing, and the madness of those crucifying him another. Nor do mercy and wrath come to the same conclusion. By the pouring out of the same blood, Christ freed the world from its captivity while Jews killed the Redeemer of all.

2. Its own malice hardened worldly Israel. In no way did it benefit from witness given by the law, from the figures of mysteries, or from the oracles of prophets—even though John showed that the Passover of the Lord, celebrated through so many ages, was being fulfilled in him when he said in a public speech, "Behold the Lamb of God, behold the one who takes away the sins of the world."[412] Wickedness fights against justice, blindness against light, falsehood against truth. But from the violence of those resisting him, from the wickedness of that cruel people, Jesus attained the result of his eternal plan.

He had such consideration for the human race in his own Death that he did not deny the mystery of salvation even to his persecutors. He who had come to forgive all the sins of every believer did not want to exclude even the crime of those Jews from the scope of his mercy. We would welcome faith for these very people whose faithlessness we detest—if only they be converted. Imitating the mercy of the Lord (who prayed for those by whom he had been crucified), we also join our prayers to those of blessed Paul the apostle. We hope that this people might "obtain mercy,"[413] the people through whose "offense" we have received the grace of reconciliation.[414] As the same teacher of the Gentiles said, "God has imprisoned all in their unbelief in order that he might have mercy on all."[415]

3. What, then, was it that both took away the understanding of Jews and disturbed the hearts of the "wise of this world"?[416]

---

412. Jn 1.29.
414. Cf. Rom 11.11.
416. Cf. 1 Cor 1.19–20.

413. Cf. Rom 11.31.
415. Rom 11.32.

What else besides the Cross of God's Son, which both made the prudence of philosophers vanish and caused the teaching of Israelites to become blurred? For the height of divine wisdom exceeded every sense of the human mind. "It pleased God to make believers saved through the foolishness of preaching,"[417] so that the constancy of faith might become more wonderful from the difficulty of believing.

It seemed illogical and irrational to take into one's mind [the belief] that an unspotted Virgin bore the Creator of all natures in the substance of real human nature, and that the Son of God, equal to the Father, who filled all things and contained the universe, should be seized by raging bands, condemned by the judgment of wicked people, and, after the disgrace of mockeries, should allow himself to be fastened on a cross. In all these things, however, there exist at the same time both the lowliness of human nature and the loftiness of the divine.

No, the method of [dispensing] mercy does not obscure the majesty of the one [dispensing it]. Through his ineffable power, it has come about that, while true man is in the inviolable God and true God is in the suffering flesh, glory is conferred upon human beings through shame, incorruption through punishment, life through death. If "the Word" had not "become flesh,"[418] and such a solid unity did not exist in both natures that even a short time of death could not separate the assumed nature from the one assuming it, never could mortality have returned to eternity. There was for us in Christ a special guard to prevent the condition of death from remaining in that suffering nature which the inviolable essence had taken up, so that what had died could be raised up through what could not die.

4. We must strive, dearly beloved, with great effort of soul and body, to join ourselves inseparably to this mystery. Just as it would be a very grave breach to neglect the Paschal feast, so it would be even more perilous to be united with congregations at church but have no association in the Lord's Passion. As the

417. 1 Cor 1.21.
418. Cf. Jn 1.14.

Lord said, "Any who do not take up their cross and follow me are not worthy of me."[419] As the Apostle said, "If we suffer with him, we shall also reign with him."[420] Who worship Christ suffering, dead, and risen except those who have suffered, died, and risen with him?

These things have been begun in all the Church's children by this very mystery of Regeneration, where the destruction of sin means life for the reborn and the triple immersion follows the pattern of our Lord's three-day Death. When the stone of the sepulcher has been removed, as it were, the water of Baptism brings forth new those souls that the fountain's bosom had received old. What has been celebrated in mystery, nonetheless, must be carried out in action. Whatever time remains in the world for children of the Holy Spirit should not be lived without taking up the cross.

While the "vessels" of that ancient theft "have been snatched"[421] from a cruel tyrant by the power of the Cross of Christ, and domination held by the "prince of this world" has been "cast out" out from bodies of the redeemed,[422] the same malice continues nevertheless to ensnare the just and attacks in many ways those whom it does not rule. If he finds any souls careless and imprudent, he fixes on them again with traps more ruthless still and brings them, snatched from the Church's paradise, into the company of his damnation. When any who belong to the Christian observance, then, know that they exceed the limits and that their desires tend toward something which makes them deviate from the right path, let such as these take refuge in the Cross of Christ and fasten the movements of their harmful will to the wood of life. In the prophet's words, let them cry out to the Lord and say, "Pierce my flesh with nails from fear of you, for I fear because of your judgments."[423]

5. What does it mean to have the flesh pierced by the nails of fear of God except to withhold bodily senses from the pleasures of unlawful desire under the fear of divine judgment?

---

419. Mt 10.38.
421. Cf. Mt 12.29.
423. Ps 118(119).120.

420. Rom 8.17 and 2 Tm 2.12.
422. Cf. Jn 12.31.

Those who resist sin and kill their strong desires—lest they do anything worthy of death—may dare to say with the Apostle: "Far be it from me to glory, except in the Cross of our Lord Jesus Christ, through whom the world has been crucified to me and I to the world."[424] Let Christians fasten themselves there where Christ has taken them with himself. Let them "direct" their every "path"[425] to where they know human nature to have been saved.

Our Lord's Passion has been drawn out to the end of the world. He himself is honored in his saints, he himself is loved, he is also fed in the poor, he is clothed. Likewise, in all those who bear adversities for the sake of justice, he himself suffers also—unless perhaps it should be thought that, with the faith spread over the entire world and the number of wicked people lessened, all persecutions and all struggles which raged against the blessed martyrs are ended, the necessity of taking up the cross, so to speak, having applied only to those on whom the most cruel punishments were inflicted in order to break down their love for Christ.

Yet the devotion of those serving God gives testimony to the contrary, as does the Apostle's preaching, where he said, "All who wish to live in devotion to Christ Jesus suffer persecution."[426] With these words, those who are struck by no persecution are shown to be exceedingly lukewarm and lazy. None can have peace in this world unless they love the world. There has never been any commerce between injustice and justice, no agreement between lying and truth, no harmony of "darkness" with "light."[427]

(2) Even when the devotion of good people wishes that the evil be corrected and obtains the conversion of many by the grace of our merciful God, the plots of evil spirits against the saints are not diminished. Whether by secret schemes or in open battle, they trouble the resolution of good will among all the faithful. Everything honorable, everything holy, they find repugnant. Although nothing would be allowed beyond what

---

424. Gal 6.14.
426. 2 Tm 3.12.
425. Cf. Ps 118(119).5.
427. Cf. 2 Cor 6.14.

divine justice permits, what serves the good of correcting God's people through discipline or the teaching of patience, these spirits treat with the crafty art of deceit, that they might seem to harm or to spare through their own free will.

Sad to say, they make such a mockery of many with the wickedness of pretense that some people both are afraid to deal with these spirits when enraged and want to keep them placated. Yet the benefits of demons are more harmful than all wounds, because it is safer for mankind to deserve the hatred of the devil than his peace. Wise souls, who have learned to fear only one, to love only one, and to hope in only one, when their desires have been regulated and their bodily senses crucified,[428] are not moved to any fear of or awe before the enemy.

They also prefer the will of God to their own, and the less they delight in themselves for love of God,[429] the more do they love themselves. When they hear the voice of God saying to them, "Do not go after your lusts. Restrain your desires,"[430] they divide their affections and distinguish between the law of the spirit and the law of the body. In a certain respect, they deny themselves for themselves, losing themselves in those things that they want bodily, and finding themselves in those that they desire spiritually.

6. In such members of Christ's body, dearly beloved, the Holy Passover would be celebrated properly. Those triumphs which the Passion of Christ has obtained lack nothing. In those who, after the Apostle's example, "train their own bodies" and bring them into "subjection,"[431] the same enemies are worn out by the same strength, and at this time the "world" continues to "be conquered" by Christ.[432]

(2) These things which pertain to our sharing in the Cross have been, I think, sufficiently brought to your attention today, so that the Paschal Mystery will also be celebrated duly in the members of Christ's body. It remains to speak of attaining to a share in the Resurrection. So that it will not be burdensome

---

428. Cf. Lk 10.42.
429. Cf. Jn 12.25.
430. Sir 18.30.
431. Cf. 1 Cor 9.27.
432. Cf. Jn 16.33.

for both you and myself that I should continue speaking, we shall put off the promised words till next Saturday.[433] May the grace of God be with us (as we believe to be the case), so that we might fulfill our duty with his help, who lives and reigns with the Father and with the Holy Spirit for ever and ever. Amen.

Sermon 71

3–4 April 443—Holy Saturday Vigil

In the last sermon, dearly beloved, we brought up our participation in the Cross of Christ—not inappropriately I think— so that the very lives of believers might incorporate the Paschal Mystery in themselves, and so that what has been honored by a feast might be celebrated through our conduct. You yourselves have demonstrated how appropriate this is. You have learned from your devotion how much benefit soul and body have derived from the longer fasts, the more constant prayers, and the more generous alms. Hardly any have not profited from this exercise and not confirmed in the recesses of their conscience something in which they can rightly rejoice. These gains must be preserved by constant watchfulness, however, lest, when the labor has been relaxed, the devil's ill will stealthily draw back into idleness what the grace of God has given.

(2) By the observance of these forty days, we have wanted to devote ourselves to this, namely, that we should know something about the Cross in this season of our Lord's Passion. Consequently, we must try very hard also to be found companions of Christ's Resurrection, moving from death to life while we are in this body. For any who have been changed from one thing to another by some conversion, there comes an end (in ceasing to be what they were), and there comes a beginning (in becoming what they were not). Yet it makes a difference for whom one dies or lives, since there is a death which brings life and a life which brings death.

Only during this passing age can each one be eagerly sought out. Differences in eternal compensation depend upon the na-

---

433. i.e., Holy Saturday.

ture of temporal activities. We must die, then, to the devil and live for God. We must die to sin in order to be raised to justice. Let the old things fall so that the new may rise. Since, as the Truth says, "no one can serve two masters,"[434] do not let the one who drives the upright into ruin become our master, but the one who has raised the fallen up to glory.

2. As the Apostle says, "The first human being (coming from the earth) is earthly, the Second (coming from heaven) heavenly. As was the earthly one, such also are the earthly. As is the Heavenly One, such also are the heavenly. Just as we have borne the likeness of the earthly human being, let us also bear the likeness of the one who comes from heaven."[435] We must rejoice a great deal over this transformation by which we are taken from earthly coarseness to heavenly dignity through that ineffable mercy of the one who descended to our state in order to lift us up to his.

He took on not only the substance but even the condition of sinful nature. Divine impassibility allowed those things to be brought upon him which human mortality suffers in its misery. Then, lest a lengthy sorrow should torture the troubled spirits of his disciples, he cut short the announced period of three days with such wonderful swiftness. While the last part of the first day and the first part of the third day met together in the second whole day, the span of time was shortened somewhat without the number of days being lessened.

Our Savior's Resurrection did not allow his soul to be kept for long in the nether regions or his flesh in the tomb. So quickly did his uncorrupted body become enlivened that death seemed more like sleep. Divinity, which did not withdraw from either the body or the soul of that human nature which he had assumed, joined by its power what it had divided by its power.

3. Many proofs followed. On these has the authority for preaching the faith throughout the whole world been founded. Certainly, the "rolled-away stone,"[436] the empty tomb, the "linen on one side,"[437] and angels proclaiming the whole event contributed abundantly to the truth of the Lord's Resurrection.

---

434. Mt 6.24.
436. Cf. Mt 28.2.
435. 1 Cor 15.47–49.
437. Cf. Jn 20.5–6 and Lk 24.12.

He nevertheless "appeared out in the open" before the women and often to the eyes of the apostles[438]—not only "speaking with" them but even dwelling and "eating with" them,[439] allowing himself to be touched with a loving and earnest touch by those who were being grazed by doubt.[440] He went through a "closed" door to the disciples.[441] "By his breath," he gave them the "Holy Spirit."[442]

When they had been given the light "of understanding," "he opened up" to them the hidden things "of the Holy Scriptures."[443] He showed them the wound "in his side," the "places of the nails,"[444] and all the signs of his recent suffering, so that the property of the divine and of the human natures might be understood as remaining inseparable in him. He wanted us to know that the Word was distinct from the flesh in its essence, but in such a way that we would confess one and the same Son of God to be both the Word and flesh.

4. Paul the apostle, teacher to the Gentiles, does not differ in this faith, dearly beloved, when he says, "Even if we knew Christ according to the flesh, yet at this time we no longer know him [that way]."[445] Our Lord's Resurrection did not put an end to his flesh, but changed it. No, the substance was not destroyed by an increase in power. Its state changed, but the nature did not give out. His body—which could be crucified—became impassible. His body—which could be killed—became immortal. What could be wounded became incorruptible.

Correctly was it said that the flesh of Christ became unknown in the state in which it had been known, for nothing remained in it that was capable of suffering, nothing infirm. Consequently, it both remains the same with respect to its essence and does not remain the same with respect to its glory.

What wonder, then, if he says this about the body of Christ when he says it of all Christian spirits as well: "From this, then, we do not regard anyone according to the flesh,"[446] that is to say: from this, the beginning of our resurrection was made in

---

438. Cf. Jn 21.1 and 14. 439. Cf. Acts 1.3–4.
440. Cf. Lk 24.39; Jn. 20.20 and 27.
441. Cf. Jn 20.19. 442. Cf. Jn 20.22.
443. Cf. Lk 24.27 and 45–46. 444. Cf. Jn 20.25–27.
445. 2 Cor 5.16. 446. 2 Cor 5.16.

Christ; from this, the pattern of all our hope went before us in the one who died for us all. We do not hesitate through lack of trust, nor do we become paralyzed before an uncertain future. Now that the beginning of the promise has been received, we see with the eyes of faith things that are to come. Rejoicing in the exaltation of our nature, we now hold fast to what we believe.

5. Let not the appearance of temporal affairs concern us. Let things of the earth not draw our thoughts from heavenly things back to themselves. Let the things which have not happened for the most part be considered as completed nevertheless. Let the mind, focused upon things that last, plant its desire where eternal things are presented to it. "Even though we have been saved [only] by hope"[447] while still wearing our corruptible and mortal bodies, we are nevertheless truly said "to be not in the body"[448] if bodily feelings do not dominate us. Rightly do we lay aside the name of a thing whose will we do not follow.

(2) When the Apostle says, "Do not satisfy the lusts of flesh,"[449] we understand that he does not forbid those things which are for our salvation and what human infirmity requires. Since, however, not every desire is to be indulged nor are we to give in to whatever pleases the body, we know that we are being warned to maintain a balance in self-restraint. With it, we would not grant superfluous things to the body (which has been placed under the spirit's control) nor deny it necessary things.

That same Apostle says in another place, "None ever hated their body, but nourished it and look after it."[450] Not for its faults, of course, nor for its comfort should the body be fed and nourished, but for the service that it owes. As a result, refreshed nature can keep its right order. Lower things will not prevail in shameful disorder over the higher, nor higher ones give way to the lower. When faults overcome the soul, servitude comes about where there ought to be mastery.

6. Let the people of God realize, then, that they are a "new creation in Christ."[451] Let them carefully perceive by whom this

---

447. Cf. Rom 8.24.
448. Cf. Rom 8.9.
449. Rom 13.14.
450. Eph 5.29.
451. Cf. 2 Cor 5.17.

creature has been taken up and what it has taken up. Whatever has been made new should not return to its old instability. Those who have "laid their hands to the plow" should not give up the work. Let them tend what they sow and not "look back on" what has been left behind.[452] Let none fall back into that from which they have risen. Even if—up until now—as a result of bodily weakness, they lie in some inertia, let them desire urgently to be healed and refreshed.

This represents the way of salvation and an imitation of the resurrection begun in Christ. Since in the vicissitudes of this life there must be some falls and slips, the footsteps of travelers should be moved from shifting soil to solid ground. As it has been written, "the steps of human beings will be directed by the Lord, who will approve their way. Though the just slip, they will not come crashing down because the Lord will hold out his hand beneath them."[453]

(2) This determination, dearly beloved, must be firmly kept up, not only during the Paschal feast but for sanctifying all of life. To this end must the present observance lead. Whatever of this brief practice has been a pleasant experience to faithful souls, it should turn into a habit and should remain without flaw. If any fault should creep in, however, it must be blotted out with speedy penitence. Since the healing of old sicknesses comes slowly and with difficulty, so much faster should the remedy be applied while the wounds are still fresh. That way, always rising from relapses to wholeness, we might deserve to arrive at that incorruptible resurrection of glorified flesh in Christ Jesus our Lord, who lives and reigns with the Father and with the Holy Spirit for ever and ever. Amen.

Sermon 72

21 April 444—Good Friday

Indeed, dearly beloved, the Gospel narrative has presented the entire Paschal Mystery to us. Through bodily ears, our

452. Cf. Lk 9.62.
453. Ps 36(37).23–24.

mental hearing has been so penetrated that we cannot fail to have formed an image of these events. So clearly does the text of this divinely inspired story show the wickedness with which the Lord Jesus Christ was betrayed, the judgment with which he was sentenced, the cruelty with which he was crucified, and the glory with which he was raised.

We must nevertheless add the duty of our sermon. As I know that you claim the debt of custom by your devout anticipation, so the bishop's exhortation should be added to the solemnity of this sacred reading. Since, then, there is no place for ignorance in the ears of the faithful, the seed of the Word (which comes through preaching the Gospel) ought to be increased in the soil of your heart. That way, when the suffocating thorns and weeds have been destroyed, the plants of holy thoughts and the shoots of upright desires might come up freely with their fruits.

(2) Now, indeed, the Cross of Christ (which represents the cost of saving mortals) contains both a mystery and an example. Divine power has been fulfilled through the mystery, human devotion aroused by the example. To those rescued from the yoke of captivity, redemption also offers the possibility of following it through imitation. For, if worldly wisdom so glories in its errors that it follows the opinions, customs, and all the principles of whatever leader it chooses, what will participation in the name of Christ mean for us? What else but an inseparable unity with the one who is, as he himself said, "the Way, the Truth, and the Life"?[454] Indeed, he is the Way of holy living, the Truth of divine teaching, and the Life of eternal blessedness.

2. Now, the entire human race has fallen in the fall of our first parents. Yet the merciful God wanted to help the creature "made in his own image"[455] through his only Son Jesus Christ—in such a way that the restoration of its nature should not be outside of that nature, and that the second creation should advance beyond the dignity of its original state. Happy the nature

---

454. Jn 14.6.
455. Cf. Gn 1.27.

which has not fallen away from what God made, but happier still the one which remains in what God has remade. It was a great thing to have received a form from Christ, but greater still to have its substance in Christ.

That nature took us up into its own particular nature, modulating itself into whatever measures of kindness it wanted. Yet it did not in any way incur an alteration due to instability. That nature which took us up neither lost its attributes in ours, nor consumed ours in its own. It joined in itself a single Person for both divinity and humanity. Yet, through the management of weakness and strength, the flesh could not be beyond suffering on account of the divinity, nor the divinity able to suffer by means of the flesh. That nature which took us up did not break off the shoot of our race from the common stock. Yet it separated from that shoot the contagion of the sin which passes over into all human beings.

Certainly that weakness and mortality (which were not sin but the punishment for sin) were accepted by the world's Redeemer as a penalty, in order that he might pay the price. As a result, that which used to be the transmission of condemnation onto all human beings becomes in Christ a "mystery of compassion."[456] He offered himself (though free of debt) to his cruel taskmaster, allowing the violence of Jews (as servants of the devil) to crucify his sinless flesh. He wanted this flesh to be subject to death until his speedy Resurrection. That way, persecution might not be insuperable for those who believe in him, nor death frightening. As we must not doubt our participation in his glory, so we must not doubt his participation in our nature.

3. If, dearly beloved, "we believe" unhesitatingly "in our hearts what we profess with our lips,"[457] we too are crucified in Christ, we too die, we too are buried, we too are raised with him on the third day. As the Apostle says, "If you have risen with Christ, seek the things that are above, where Christ is, sitting at the right hand of God. Savor the things which are above, not those that are on the earth. For you have died, and your

---

456. Cf. 1 Tm 3.16.
457. Cf. Rom 10.9 and 10.

life is hidden with Christ in God. But when Christ your life appears, then you also will appear with him in glory."[458]

So the hearts of believers might realize that they have the means to be raised up to heavenly wisdom (after having spurned the desires of flesh), the Lord promises his own presence to us by saying, "Know that I am with you all days to the end of time."[459] Not in vain had the Holy Spirit said through Isaiah, "Behold a virgin will conceive in her womb and will give birth to a son, and they will call him Emmanuel, which means 'God with us.'"[460] Jesus therefore fulfills the unique character of his name. He who ascended into heaven does not desert his adopted children. He who sits at the right hand of the Father dwells in his entire body. He himself strengthens to endurance those here below while inviting them to glory up above.

4. We must not act foolishly in trifling matters, nor be fearful in adversities. Falsehoods lure us in the former, trials become a burden in the latter. Because "the earth is full of the Lord's mercy,"[461] however, Christ's victory remains present to us everywhere, so as to fulfill the word that says: "Do not be afraid, because I have overcome the world."[462] Consequently, whether we fight against the ambition of the world, against the desires of flesh, or against the darts of heretics, we are always armed with the Lord's Cross. We never retreat from the Paschal Feast if we "abstain from the yeast of that old malice."[463]

(2) Among all the vicissitudes of this life, which is filled with different kinds of troubles, we ought to remember the encouragement of the Apostle where he instructs us by saying: "Perceive this also in yourselves, just as in Christ Jesus. Being in the form of God, he did not think it robbery to be equal to God. Yet he emptied himself, accepting the form of a servant, made in the likeness of human beings, and found to be a man according to what had been taken on. He humbled himself, having been made obedient unto death, even to death on the cross. On this account, God exalted him as well, giving him a name

---

458. Col 3.1–4.
460. Mt 1.23 and cf. Is 7.14.
462. Jn 16.33.

459. Mt 28.20.
461. Ps 32(33).5.
463. Cf. 1 Cor 5.8.

above every other name. At the name of Jesus, therefore, every knee should bend, of those in heaven, on earth, and under the earth. Every tongue should confess that the Lord Jesus Christ is in the glory of God the Father."[464]

He means this for those who understand the "mystery of great compassion,"[465] for those who take note of what the only Son of God has done for the salvation of human kind. He says that such people should "perceive this" in themselves "just as in Christ Jesus." No rich person can reject his humility, no noble person can scorn it. Indeed, no human good fortune whatsoever can be brought to such a height that people might consider as shameful for themselves something which he, remaining as God "in the form of God,"[466] did not consider to be such.

5. Imitate what he did. Love what he loved. Since you have discovered the grace of God in yourselves, respond by loving your own nature in him. As he did not lose riches in his poverty, nor diminish glory in his humility, nor lose eternity in his Death, so you, following in his footsteps to the same degree, scorn earthly things in order that you might attain to heavenly ones. Taking up the cross means the extermination of lusts, the death of vices, the renunciation of frivolity, and the disowning of all error.

Although the shameless, the wanton, the proud, and the avaricious do not celebrate the Lord's Passover, none at any rate are as separated from this feast as heretics, especially those who think erroneously about the Incarnation of the Word—either by diminishing what belongs to the divinity, or by hollowing out what belongs to the flesh.

(2) For the Son of God is true God, having from the Father all that the Father is. He is not temporal in his beginning, not changeable in his movements, not divided from the One, not different in omnipotence. He is, rather, the eternal Only-Begotten of the eternal Father. Faithful minds, believing in the Father and the Son and the Holy Spirit, neither divide the unity within the single essence of the one divinity by degrees of rank,

---

464. Phil 2.5–11.
466. Cf. Phil 2.6.
465. Cf. 1 Tm 3.16.

nor jumble the Trinity into one. It is not enough to know the Son of God only in the nature of the Father if we do not recognize him in ours (though he did not withdraw from his own).

This "emptying" of himself [467]—the price he paid for human restoration—was an act of mercy, not a deprivation of power. From the eternal wisdom of God, "there is no other name under heaven given to human beings, in which it is necessary to be saved."[468] Invisible, he has made his substance visible. Eternal, he has made it temporal. Beyond suffering, he has made it subject to suffering—not that strength might fail in weakness, but so that weakness could become incorruptible strength.

6. That is why the Hebrews, while we call this festival the Pasch, call it the Phase, that is, Passover, as the Evangelist witnesses by saying, "Before the feast day of the Pasch, Jesus knew that his hour had come to pass over from this world to the Father."[469] Of whose nature was this passage to be if not of ours, since the Father is inseparably in the Son and the Son inseparably in the Father? Yet because Word and flesh constitute a single Person, the one taken does not become separated from the one taking, and the honor of the one to be exalted does not get called an increase for the one exalting.

For the Apostle says in a passage quoted earlier: "Wherefore God both exalted him and gave him a name above every other name."[470] Undoubtedly, reference was being made to the exaltation of his assumed manhood in him. While he continues to be co-eternal in the glory of divinity, the divinity remains undivided in his sufferings. In order that his faithful might participate in this ineffable gift, the Lord himself was preparing a blessed passage for them when, his impending Passion being close at hand, he prayed not only for his apostles and disciples, but also for the entire Church, saying: "I pray not only for these, but also for those who are going to believe in me through their word, that all may be one. As you, Father, in me and I in you, may they also be one in us."[471]

467. Cf. Phil 2.7.
469. Jn 13.1.
471. Jn 17.20–21.

468. Acts 4.12.
470. Phil 2.9.

7. Those who deny that the human nature remains in the Son of God, true God, will not be able to have any fellowship in this unity, since they assail the mystery of salvation and have thereby been exiled from the Paschal Feast. Because they gainsay the Gospel and contradict the Creed, they cannot celebrate with us. Although they presume to arrogate for themselves the name of Christian, they are repelled by every creature which has Christ for its Head.[472]

As you exult properly in this solemnity and rejoice with holiness, accept no falsehood in place of truth. Do not doubt the Birth of Christ according to the flesh, nor his Passion and Death, nor his bodily Resurrection. Recognize the real Christ coming from the Virgin's womb without any separation from the divinity, real on the wood of the cross, real in the burial of his body, real in the glory of his Resurrection, real at the right hand of the Father's majesty. So, as the Apostle says, "It is from heaven also that we await our Lord Jesus Christ the Savior. He has transformed the body of our lowliness, so that it might be conformed to the body of his glory,"[473] who lives and reigns with the Father and with the Holy Spirit for ever and ever. Amen.

472. Cf. Eph 4.15 and Col 1.18.
473. Phil 3.20–21.

ASCENSION

Two sermons for the Feast of the Ascension, dated to the years 444 and 445, deal predominantly with faith. As the Gospels relate, the apostles doubted the Resurrection. According to Leo, it is from their wavering that subsequent believers receive assurance (*Serm.* 73.1). Those forty days after the Resurrection were given for further proofs of that event (*Serm.* 73.2). When the Lord ascended, human nature ascended with him (*Serm.* 73.4).

Sermon 73

1 June 444

AFTER THE blessed and glorious Resurrection of our Lord Jesus Christ, when the divine power, "in three days, raised" the true "temple" of God which Jewish wickedness had "destroyed,"[1] on this day, dearly beloved, the number of the forty holy days is completed.[2] While the Lord draws out the time of his bodily presence, our faith in his Resurrection is being strengthened by the necessary signs. All this has been planned by the sacred dispensation and made useful for our instruction.

(2) The Death of Christ had greatly disturbed the hearts of the disciples. A certain numbness of distrust had stolen upon their minds, weighed down with sorrow, at the suffering on the cross, at his last breath, at the burial of his lifeless body. When the holy women, as the Gospel story has told us, proclaimed that the stone had been rolled away from the tomb, the sepulcher was empty of the body, and that angels were witnesses of the living Lord,[3] their "words seemed" to the apostles and other disciples as pure "nonsense."[4]

---

1. Cf. Jn 2.19. Cf. Acts 2.24 and 3.15.
2. Cf. Acts 1.3.   3. Cf. Lk 24.1–11.
4. Cf. Lk 24.11.

The Spirit of Truth would by no means have permitted this hesitation, wavering in human weakness, to enter the hearts of his preachers, if their trembling anxiety and questioning delay were not to have established the foundations of our faith. Consequently, it was our doubts, our danger, that was being considered in the apostles. We, in the guise of the apostles, were being instructed against the slanders of the wicked and the proofs of earthly wisdom. Their "seeing" instructed us, their "hearing" informed us, their "touching" strengthened us.[5] Let us give thanks for the divine plan and the necessary "slowness" of the Holy Fathers.[6] They "doubted" so that we need not doubt.[7]

2. These days, dearly beloved, between the Resurrection of the Lord and his Ascension, did not pass by in useless flow. They provided the opportunity to confirm great mysteries, to reveal great secrets. In these days the fear of dreaded death was removed and the immortality not only of the soul but also of the flesh is assured. In these days the "Holy Spirit" was poured into all the apostles by the "breath" of the Lord;[8] and to blessed Peter above all the others, after the "keys of the kingdom,"[9] the care of the Lord's sheep is entrusted.[10]

In these days the Lord is joined to the two disciples on the road as a third companion,[11] and, to wipe out all the mist of our doubt, he rebukes the "slowness" of these frightened and trembling men.[12] Their illuminated hearts received the flame of faith, and these, who were lukewarm, became fervent when the Lord "opened the Scriptures."[13] Also, in the "breaking" of the bread, the eyes of those at supper "are opened."[14] The eyes of these men were opened far more happily when the glorification of their own nature was revealed to them, than the eyes of those first parents of our race on whom the confusion of their own lying was inflicted.

3. Among these other wonders, when the disciples were burning with anxious thoughts, the Lord appeared in their

5. Cf. 1 Jn 1.1–3.
6. Cf. Lk 24.25.
7. Cf. Mt 28.17.
8. Cf. Jn 20.22.
9. Cf. Mt 16.19.
10. Cf. Jn 21.15–17.
11. Cf. Lk 24.15.
12. Cf. Lk 24.25.
13. Cf. Lk 24.26–27 and 32.
14. Cf. Lk 24.30–31.

midst and said: "Peace be with you." So that what they were turning over in their hearts would not remain in their thoughts (for they thought they "saw a spirit" and not flesh), he proved that their "sentiments" were wrong.[15] He pressed on their doubting sight the signs of the cross still showing in his hands and feet, and asked them to touch him for proof. He had preserved the wounds of the nails and the lance[16] as signs, to heal the hearts of unbelievers, so that, with a very constant knowledge, not a hesitant faith, they would understand that this nature which had lain in the tomb was to take its place on the throne of God the Father.

4. Through all this time, dearly beloved, which went by between the Resurrection of the Lord and his Ascension, the providence of God took thought for this, taught this, and penetrated their eyes and heart with this: that they should recognize the Lord Jesus Christ as truly risen, who was truly born, truly suffered, and truly died. The blessed apostles and all the disciples who had been frightened by his Death on the cross and were doubtful with respect to faith in his Resurrection, were strengthened by the manifest truth. The result was that not only were they not afflicted with sadness but were filled with "great joy"[17] when the Lord went into the heights of heaven.

Truly it was a great and indescribable source of rejoicing when, in the sight of the heavenly multitudes, the nature of our human race ascended over the dignity of all heavenly creatures, to pass the angelic orders and to be raised beyond the heights of archangels.[18] In its ascension it did not stop at any other height until this same nature was received at the seat of the eternal Father, to be associated on the throne of the glory of that One to whose nature it was joined in the Son.

Since the Ascension of Christ is our elevation, and since, where the glory of the Head has preceded us, there hope for the body is also invited, let us exult, dearly beloved, with worthy joy and be glad with a holy thanksgiving. Today we are established not only as possessors of Paradise, but we have even pen-

15. Cf. Lk 24.36–38.
17. Cf. Lk 24.52.
16. Cf. Lk 24.39 and Jn 20.25–27.
18. Cf. Eph 1.20–21.

etrated the heights of the heavens in Christ, prepared more fully for it through the indescribable grace of Christ which we had lost through the "ill will of the devil."[19] Those whom the violent enemy threw down from the happiness of our first dwelling, the Son of God has placed, incorporated within himself, at the right hand of the Father, the Son of God who lives and reigns with God the Father Almighty and with the Holy Spirit forever and ever. Amen.

Sermon 74

17 May 445

The mystery of our salvation, dearly beloved, which the Creator of the universe thought worth the price of his blood, has, from the day of his bodily birth to the end of his suffering, been carried to completion through the condition of his humility. Although many signs of the divinity in the "form of a servant"[20] have been evident, strictly speaking, the action of that time pertained to demonstrating the truth of the humanity he assumed. After his Passion, when the chains were broken of that death which had destroyed its own strength by proceeding against one who "had no acquaintance with sin,"[21] then weakness was turned to strength, mortality to eternity, disgrace to glory. The Lord Jesus made this obvious in the sight of all "by many" and clear "signs,"[22] until he carried the triumph of victory that he had brought back from death up into heaven.

(2) As the Resurrection of the Lord was a cause of rejoicing for us in the Paschal liturgy, so his Ascension into heaven is a matter of present delight for us. We recall and rightly venerate that day when our lowly nature was carried in Christ above all the hosts of heaven, over all the angelic orders and beyond the height of all powers, to the seat of God the Father.[23] We have been established, we have been built in this order of divine works, that the grace of God becomes the more wonderful

---

19. Cf. Wis 2.24.
21. Cf. 2 Cor 5.21.
23. Cf. Eph 1.20–21.

20. Cf. Phil 2.7.
22. Cf. Acts 1.3.

when those things which are felt to invite proper reverence are removed from the sight of human beings and still faith does not weaken, hope does not waver, love does not grow cold.

This is the strength of great souls, and it is the light of intensely faithful spirits to believe unhesitatingly what is not seen by bodily perception, and to fix their desire where they cannot fix their sight. From where would this devotion be born in our hearts; or how would anyone be "justified through faith,"[24] if our salvation consisted only in those things that lie under our eyes? For this reason the Lord even said to that one who seemed to doubt the Resurrection of Christ unless, by sight and touch, he tested the marks of the Passion in his very flesh: "Because you have seen me, you have believed; blessed are those who have not seen and yet believe."[25]

2. So then, that we can be fit for this blessedness, dearly beloved, after all had been fulfilled that belonged to the preaching of the Gospel and the mysteries of the New Testament, our Lord Jesus Christ was raised to heaven. He made an end to his bodily presence in the sight of his disciples on the fortieth day after the Resurrection. He was to remain at the Father's right hand until the time predetermined by God for filling the number of the children of the Church should come, and he would return to judge the living and the dead in the same flesh with which he ascended. What was to be seen of our Redeemer has passed over into the Sacraments. In order that faith might be more perfect and more firm, teaching has taken the place of sight, and to this authority the hearts of believers, illumined by heavenly rays, have conformed.

3. This faith, reinforced by the Ascension of the Lord and strengthened by the gift of the Holy Spirit, has not been terrified by chains, by prison, by exile, by hunger, by fire, by the mangling of wild beasts, nor by sharp suffering from the cruelty of persecutors. Throughout the world, not only men but also women, not just immature boys but also tender virgins, have struggled on behalf of this faith even to the shedding of

---

24. Cf. Rom 5.1 and Gal 3.24.
25. Jn 20.29.

their blood. This faith has cast out demons, driven away sicknesses, and raised the dead.

Those blessed apostles, strengthened as they were by so many miracles, taught by so many sermons, although they had been terrified at the Lord's Passion and had not accepted the truth of his Resurrection without hesitation, advanced so much at the Lord's Ascension that whatever had brought fear to them before was turned into joy. They had raised the whole gaze of their souls to the divinity of the one sitting at the right hand of the Father. No longer are they held back by any use of bodily sight which would prevent them from looking with sharpness of soul on that one who had neither been absent from the Father by his coming down, nor had departed from the disciples by his Ascension.

4. Then, dearly beloved, the son of a human being became known more eminently and more sacredly as the Son of God when he entered into the glory of his Father's majesty. In an ineffable way, he began to be more present in the divinity as he became more remote from our humanity. Then, by a spiritual step, a more instructed faith began to give assent to the Son equal to the Father, and it did not need the touch of the bodily substance in Christ, by which he is less than the Father,[26] because, with the nature of the glorified body remaining, the faith of believers was drawn there where the Only-Begotten Son equal to the Father might be touched not by fleshly hand but by the spiritual intellect.

Hence it is that after his Resurrection, when Mary Magdalene, manifesting the person of the Church, was hastening to approach to touch him, he said to her: "Do not touch me because I have not yet ascended to my Father."[27] He was in fact saying, I do not want you to come to me bodily, nor to acknowledge me with the perception of your flesh. I am taking you to higher things. I am preparing greater things for you. When I have ascended to my Father, then you will feel me more perfectly and more truly. You will embrace what you do not touch

26. Cf. Jn 14.28.
27. Jn 20.17.

and believe what you do not see. When the searching eyes of the disciples were following the Lord with keen wonder as he ascended into heaven, two angels stood before them shining in marvelously radiant clothing[28] and said: "Men of Galilee, why do you stand looking up into the sky? This Jesus, who was taken up from you, will so come as you have seen him going into heaven."[29]

(2) By these words all the children of the Church are taught that we believe Jesus Christ is going to come, visible, in the same flesh in which he ascended. No one can doubt that "all things have been made subject to him,"[30] whom, from the very beginning of his natural Birth, the angelic household had served. Just as the angel announced to the Blessed Virgin that Christ would be conceived through the Holy Spirit,[31] so the voice of the heavenly choir sang to the shepherds that he was born from the Virgin.[32] As the first witness of the heavenly messengers told that he had risen from the dead,[33] so the service of the angels was to announce that he would come to judge the world[34] in the very same flesh. In this way we might understand how many powers there will be with him when he comes to judge, to whom such a great number "ministered" even when he was about to be judged.[35]

5. Let us exult, therefore, with a spiritual gladness, dearly beloved, and joyfully, with fitting gratitude to God, let us freely raise the eyes of our hearts to that height where Christ is.[36] Let not earthly desires hold down the souls called upwards. Let perishable things not hold those ordained for eternity. Let false pleasures not delay those who have entered the "way of truth."[37] Let the faithful so travel over these temporal things that they may realize they are pilgrims in this valley of the world, where, even though certain pleasures attract, these are not to be vainly embraced, but must be passed over bravely. The blessed apostle Peter urges us to this devotion, and, ac-

---

28. Cf. Acts 1.10.
29. Acts 1.11.
30. Cf. 1 Cor 15.27–28.
31. Cf. Lk 1.28–38.
32. Cf. Lk 2.8–15.
33. Cf. Mt 28.1–7.
34. Cf. Mt 24.31.
35. Cf. Mt 4.11.
36. Cf. the Preface of the Mass.
37. Cf. Ps 118(119).30.

cording to that desire for "feeding the sheep of Christ" which he conceived at the threefold avowal of his love to the Lord,[38] he begged them saying: "I urge you, my dear people, just as visitors and pilgrims, to keep yourselves free from the selfish passions that attack the soul."[39]

For whom, if not for the devil, do the worldly pleasures make war? Who is it that delights in hindering, by the pleasures of corruptible goods, the souls reaching for heaven, and in leading them away from that home from which he himself fell? Against his snares all faithful souls ought wisely to keep watch, so that, from that which is made a temptation against them, they might be able to crush this enemy.

(2) Nothing is stronger, dearly beloved, against the wiles of the devil than the kindness of mercy and the generosity of love, through which "every sin" is either avoided or conquered.[40] But the sublimity of this virtue is not gained until what is contrary to it has been broken down. What is so inimical to the works of mercy and charity as greed, from which "root" the seed of "all evil" comes?[41] Unless this be cut down in its first growth, it is certain that in the field of that heart in which the plants of this evil become strong, spines and thorns of sins will rise, rather than any seed of true virtue. Let us resist then, dearly beloved, this rankling evil, and "strive after" charity,[42] without which no virtue can shine. Through this way of love, by which Christ descended to us, we also can ascend to him, to whom are honor and glory with God the Father and with the Holy Spirit forever and ever. Amen.

38. Cf. Jn 21.15–17.
39. 1 Pt 2.11.
40. Cf. 1 Pt 4.8.
41. Cf. 1 Tm 6.10.
42. Cf. 1 Cor 14.1.

PENTECOST

As far as can be determined,[1] Leo delivered these sermons on Pentecost Sunday, with the exception of *Serm.* 80, which he gave on one of the fast days. *Serms.* 75–77, while barely mentioning the fast, emphasize the Feast of Pentecost, where Leo describes the coming of the Holy Spirit upon the apostles (*Serm.* 77.1).

As usual, Leo denounces the relevant heresies. Macedonianism, while holding the Father and the Son to be equal, considered the Holy Spirit to have an inferior nature (*Serm.* 75.4), thus undermining the Trinity, for "by no reckoning is that truly one which is different by any inequality" (*Serm.* 77.3). Leo decries the claim that the Manichaeans make concerning Mani and the Holy Spirit (*Serm.* 76.6). He lists the marks of the Holy Spirit (*Serm.* 75.5) and the benefits of the Holy Spirit (*Serm.* 76.4), underscoring the fact that the Holy Spirit differs in no way from the Father and the Son (*Serm.* 76.2).

Serms. 78–81 emphasize the fast. Leo urges his flock to recognize the value of fasting, which must be done with love (*Serm.* 79.3) and with prompt faith (*Serm.* 79.4). As with the other fasts, he urges people to "withhold some small portions of food, so that what is not spent on our tables might benefit alms" (*Serm.* 80.1).

Sermon 75

23 May 443

THE HEARTS of all Catholics know well, dearly beloved, that today's solemnity ought to be honored among the special feasts. No one doubts how much reverence is owed to this day which the Holy Spirit has consecrated by the wonderful miracle of his own gift. For, from that day on which the Lord ascended over all the heights of heaven to sit at the right hand of God the Father, this day is the tenth. It is likewise the fiftieth from the Resurrection of that same Lord who enlightened us about him from whom light began. It contains

---

1. Cf. CCL 138.cxci.

great mysteries in itself of both the old and the new dispensations, by which it is very clearly shown that grace was foretold by the old law and that the law was fulfilled by grace.

As once to the Hebrew people, freed from Egypt, the law was given on Mt. Sinai on the fiftieth day after the sacrifice of the lamb, so after the Passion of Christ when the true Lamb of God was killed, on the fiftieth day from his Resurrection, the Holy Spirit came down on the apostles and the community of believers. The attentive Christian can easily know that the beginnings of the Old Testament had ministered to the principles of the Gospel, and that the Second Covenant was established by the same Spirit who had set up the first.

2. As the history of the apostles shows us, "When the fifty days were completed and they were all together in the same place, suddenly a sound was made from heaven as of a violent wind approaching, and it filled the whole house where they were. And there appeared to them parted tongues as if of fire, and these rested on each of them. And they were all filled with the Holy Spirit, and began to speak in other tongues, just as the Holy Spirit was giving them to speak."[2] O how swift is that speech of wisdom! Where God is the teacher, how quickly is that learned which is being taught! No interpretation is used in order to understand, no practice is needed in order to use it. No time is needed to study, but, with the "Spirit" of Truth "blowing wherever he pleases,"[3] the particular voices of each distinct people become familiar in the mouth of the Church.

From this day the trumpet of the Gospel teaching resounds. From this day showers of graces, streams of benedictions, water all the desert and every wasteland, since to "renew the face of the earth,"[4] "God's Spirit hovered over the water."[5] To take away the old darkness, beams of new light flash out, when by the splendor of those glowing tongues, the Word of the Lord becomes "clear"[6] and "speech takes fire."[7] Both the force of giving light and the power for burning were present for this reason, to create knowledge and to destroy sin.

2. Acts 2.1–4.
3. Cf. Jn 3.8.
4. Cf. Ps 103(104).30.
5. Gn 1.2.
6. Cf. Ps 18(19).9.
7. Cf. Ps 118(119).140.

3. Although, dearly beloved, the very appearance of this event was especially awesome, and there is no doubt that, in the exultant harmony of all the languages of the world, the majesty of the Holy Spirit was present, still no one should think that the divine substance had appeared in these things which were seen with bodily eyes. The invisible nature, also common to Father and Son, showed by means of the sign he wished, the quality of his gift and work, but in his divinity he held the distinctiveness of his own essence. As human sight cannot touch the Father or the Son, neither can it touch the Holy Spirit. In the divine Trinity nothing is dissimilar, nothing is unequal. All that can be thought of in that substance have not been separated in strength nor in glory nor in eternity. Although, in the qualities of the Persons, one is Father, the other is Son, and the other is Holy Spirit, nevertheless there is not another divinity nor is there a diverse nature.

If indeed the Son is the Only-Begotten from the Father, and the Holy Spirit is the Spirit of the Father and the Son, he is not like any created being which belongs to the Father and the Son, but is with each, living and powerful, and subsisting eternally from that which is the Father and the Son. Thus, when the Lord before the day of his Passion promised to his disciples that the Holy Spirit would come, he said: "I still have many things to say to you but you are not able to bear them now. But when the Spirit of Truth comes he will lead you to the complete truth. For he will not be speaking from himself but will say whatever he has heard; and he will tell you the things to come. All the things which the Father has are mine, and on that account did I say that he will receive from mine and will announce to you."[8]

(2) Consequently, there are not some things that belong to the Father, some to the Son, and others to the Holy Spirit, but everything the Father has, the Son also has, and the Holy Spirit also has. Never was there not this fellowship in that Trinity, because to have all things is to exist always. No times, no gradations, no differences should be imagined there. If no one can

---

8. Jn 16.12–13 and 15.

explain about God what he is, let no one dare to affirm what he is not. It is more excusable not to speak words worthy of the indescribable nature than to define what is contrary. Whatever devout hearts can conceive about the eternal and unchangeable glory of the Father, they understand also of the Son and of the Holy Spirit inseparably and without distinction. Hence we confess this Blessed Trinity as one God, because in these three Persons there is no diversity of substance, nor of power, nor of will, nor of operation.

4. Just as we shun the Arians who want some separation between the Father and the Son, so we equally shun the Macedonians who, although they attribute equality to the Father and the Son, think the Holy Spirit to be of an inferior nature. They do not realize that they fall into that blasphemy which is to be forgiven neither in this age nor in the future judgment, as the Lord says: "Whoever speaks a word against the Son of Man will be forgiven; but whoever speaks against the Holy Spirit will not be forgiven either in this age or in the one to come."[9]

Those remaining in this rebellion are without pardon, because they shut off from themselves the one through whom they would be able to confess. These can never come to the healing of mercy when they have no advocate to plead for them. For from that very one is the appeal to the Father, from that very one are the tears of penitence, from him are the cries of suppliants; and "no one can say 'Jesus is Lord' except in the Holy Spirit."[10] His equal omnipotence and single divinity with the Father and the Son, the apostle very clearly preaches saying: "There is a variety of gifts but the same Spirit; there are different kinds of services, but the same Lord; and there are different kinds of labors, but the same God who manages all things in all of them."[11]

5. With these and with other proofs without number, dearly beloved, with which the authority of the divine words shine out, let us rouse ourselves with one mind to the celebration of Pente-

9. Mt 12.32.   10. 1 Cor 12.3.
11. 1 Cor 12.4–6.

cost. Let us rejoice in honor of the Holy Spirit through whom the whole Catholic Church is sanctified and every rational soul is filled. He is the inspiration of faith, the teacher of knowledge, the fountain of love, the sign of chastity, and the cause of all virtue. Let the spirits of all the faithful rejoice that in the whole world one God, Father, Son, and Holy Spirit, is extolled by the praise of all languages, and that this sign, which appeared as fire, perseveres in both its work and its gift. This Spirit of Truth makes the home of his glory shine with the glow of his own light, and in his temple wishes that nothing be dark, nothing be lukewarm.

From this strength and this teaching also has come for us the cleansing of fasts and alms. A custom of healthful observance follows this honorable day, that all holy people have always found useful for themselves. It is one which, with pastoral care, we urge you to celebrate earnestly, so that if unguarded carelessness has produced any spot in recent days, the reproof of fasting might atone for it, and a holy devotion amend it. Let us fast on Wednesday and Friday. On Saturday, however, in this very place, let us celebrate the vigil with customary devotion, through Christ our Lord.

Sermon 76

2 June 444 (Recension A)[12]

The text of the divine reading, dearly beloved, has shown us fully the cause and meaning of today's solemnity. Here we recognized that the Holy Spirit was infused into the disciples of Christ, in the long-awaited promise on the fiftieth day after the Lord's Resurrection, which is the tenth from his Ascension.

---

12. This sermon comes down to us in two recensions. Recension A had been composed in 444. Recension B appears to represent a revision made by Leo himself at some later date. Material found in both recensions will appear in normal text. Material found only in Recension A will appear in **bold**. Material found only in Recension B will appear in *italics*. Some material found in both recensions but in a different order will be reproduced in both bold and italics in their proper order. Some material that does not coincide between the two versions of the Latin text but does not affect the English translation (such as word order or certain syntactical variants) will not be indicated.

But, in order to instruct the new children of the Church, we must add the duty of our sermon. We are not afraid that the spiritual and learned people will scorn hearing the things they know, because for their own good, they should want to have made known to as many as possible the things they have learned to their great profit. May the generosity of the divine gifts come to all hearts, and may the learned and the uninstructed not spurn the service of our lips. *Let the former prove that they love what they know and the latter show they are eager for what they do not know.* May there be present to your preparation the generosity of him about whose grandeur we attempt to speak, so that, toward the progress of his whole Church, he may make you receptive, and us bountiful.

2. When we turn the eyes of our mind to understand the dignity of the Holy Spirit, let us picture to ourselves nothing different in the excellence of the Father and the Son, for the essence of the Divine Trinity differs in no way from its unity. It belongs eternally to the Father to be the begetter of his Son, co-eternal with himself. It belongs eternally to the Son to be the begotten of the Father, outside of time. It belongs eternally to the Holy Spirit to be the Spirit of the Father and of the Son, for the Father was never without the Son, the Father and the Son were never without the Holy Spirit.

All gradations of existence are excluded, and no Person there is first, none is last. The unchangeable divinity of this Blessed Trinity is one in substance, undivided in work, united in will, the same in power, equal in glory. When Holy Scripture speaks of it thus and gives in deeds or in words anything that seems to belong to separate Persons, Catholic Faith is not disturbed but instructed. Through the proper signification of either the word or the action, the truth of the Trinity is brought home to us, and the mind does not divide what the hearing establishes.

Certain things come to us under the name of the Father or the Son or the Holy Spirit, so that the acknowledgment of the faithful in the Trinity might not err. Although it is inseparable, it will never be known to be a Trinity if it is always mentioned without differentiation. This difficulty in expressing clearly by speech draws our hearts to the power of discerning, and, through our weakness, the heavenly doctrine helps us, that, because in the divinity of Father, Son, and Holy Spirit, neither singularity nor diversity is to be considered. The true unity and true Trinity can be apprehended "at the same time" by the mind, but cannot be produced at the same time by the lips.

3. By this faith established in our hearts, dearly beloved, we believe beneficially that at the same time the whole Trinity is one perfection, one majesty, one substance, undivided in work, inseparable in love, without difference in power, at the same time filling and containing all things. What the Father is, this also is the Son, this also is the Holy Spirit; and the true divinity is in no thing greater or less than itself. It is acknowledged to be in Three Persons in such a way that the Trinity allows no solitariness and the equality preserves the unity.

(2) If this faith is firmly held, I say, let us not doubt that, when on the day of Pentecost the Holy Spirit filled the disciples, it was not the beginning of the gift but an addition to his generosity. The patriarchs, the prophets, the priests, and all the saints who lived in former times were invigorated by the sanctifying of the same Spirit. Without this grace no mysteries were ever instituted, no rites celebrated, for there was always the same strength of grace although there was not the same measure of the gifts.

4. The blessed apostles themselves did not lack the Holy Spirit before the Passion of the Lord, nor was the power of his strength absent from the Savior's works. When the Lord "gave" to the disciples "the power of healing and the power to cast out demons,"[13] he was bestowing the effects of the Spirit. But the wickedness of the Jews denied that he ruled over "unclean spirits,"[14] and credited the divine benefits to the devil.[15] Blaspheming in this manner, they rightly heard the judgment of the Lord when he said: "Every sin and blasphemy will be forgiven to human beings, but blasphemy against the Spirit will not be forgiven to human beings. And anyone who has said a word

---

13. Mk 3.15.
15. Cf. Mk 3.22 and Lk 11.15.

14. Cf. Mk 1.27 and Lk 4.36.

against the Son of Man will be forgiven, but the one who has spoken against the Holy Spirit will not be forgiven in this age nor in the one to come."[16]

It is clear, then, that remission of sin does not happen without the aid of the Holy Spirit, nor can any lament as they should or pray as they ought without him. As the Apostle says, "We do not know what to pray for as we ought, but the Spirit himself makes intercession for us with sounds that cannot be expressed,"[17] and, "No one can say 'Jesus is Lord' except in the Spirit."[18] To be without him is exceedingly destructive and exceedingly deadly, because those who are deserted by their intercessor never deserve pardon. All, therefore, dearly beloved, who have believed in the Lord Jesus have the Holy Spirit infused into them. The apostles at that time also received the power of forgiving sins when after his Resurrection the Lord breathed on them and said, "Receive the Holy Spirit. Whose sins you forgive, they will be forgiven; whose sins you retain, they will be retained."[19]

(2) To this perfection to be conferred on the disciples, a greater grace and more abundant inspiration was reserved. Through this, they would both take on even what they had not yet received and would be better able to hold what they had taken on. It was for this the Lord said: "I still have many things to say to you, but you cannot bear them now. But, when the Spirit of Truth comes, he will lead you to the complete truth. For he will not be speaking from himself but will say only what he has learned; and he will make known to you things that are going to be, since he will receive from me what is mine and will make it known to you."[20]

5. What did the Lord mean, promising the Holy Spirit to the disciples, when he had already said, "I have made known to you everything I have learned from my Father,"[21] but added, "I still have many things to say to you, but you cannot bear them now. But, when the Spirit of Truth comes, he will lead you to

---

16. Mt 12.31–32.
17. Rom 8.26.
18. 1 Cor 12.3.
19. Jn 20.22–23.
20. Jn 16.12–14.
21. Jn 15.15.

the complete truth"?[22] Did the Lord want himself to be considered as of inferior knowledge or to have learned something less from the Father than the Holy Spirit learned? Since he himself is Truth, and the Father cannot say, nor the Spirit teach, anything without the Word. For this reason it was said, "He will receive from what is mine,"[23] seeing that, with the Father giving, the Son gives what the Spirit receives.

No other truth was to creep in, no other doctrine was to be preached. It was necessary, though, to increase the capacity of those who were being taught, and to multiply the constancy of that "love" that "drives out all fear"[24] not dreading the rage of persecutors. The apostles, after they were filled with the new abundance of the Holy Spirit, began to will more ardently and to work more efficiently, profiting from the knowledge of their teachers to bear suffering.[25] Trembling under no storms, by their surpassing faith, they trod underfoot the vicissitudes of the age and the pride of the world. Despising death, they carried the Gospel of truth to all nations.

6. As to what the Lord added, saying, "He will say only what he has learned, and he will tell you things that are going to be,"[26] we are not to receive it with a lazy mind, dearly beloved, or with a cursory hearing. Besides other sayings of the Truth by which the wickedness of the Manichaeans is refuted, this phrase quite openly overthrows their whole dogma of sacrilege and falsehood.

So that they might seem to follow a certain great and sublime founder, his disciples believed that the Holy Spirit appeared in their teacher Manes. They believed that the Paraclete promised by the Lord did not come before this deceiver of unfortunate people arose. They believed that in him the Spirit of God so lived that Manes himself was no other than the Spirit who by the ministry of an embodied voice and tongue would lead his disciples into all truth and would disclose secrets never known to former ages. The authority of the Gospel teaching

---

22. Jn 16.12–13.
24. Cf. 1 Jn 4.18.
26. Jn 16.13.

23. Jn 16.15.
25. Cf. 2 Cor 1.6.

itself shows how false and empty this is. *It is wearisome to show how ridiculous and how vain this is, except that up to this time it did not shame some people to believe it.*

Manes, therefore, who must be condemned as a lackey of the devil's falsehood and a founder of filthy superstition, became known at that time when after the Resurrection of the Lord the two hundred and sixtieth year was fulfilled.[27] At this time, when Probus and Paulinus were consuls,[28] when the eighth persecution against Christians was raging,[29] and uncounted thousands of martyrs had proved by their own victories that what the Lord had promised was fulfilled, saying, "When they hand you over, do not worry about how to speak or what to say. What you are to say will be given to you in that hour, because it is not you who speak, but the Spirit of your Father who speaks in you."[30]

7. The promise of the Lord could not be put off for such a long interval. And that Spirit of Truth, whom the "world" of wicked men "has not accepted,"[31] could not hold back the sevenfold bounty of his gifts in such a way as to deprive so many generations of the Church **of his inspiration, until the monstrous leader of shameful lies should be born.** *of "wisdom and understanding, counsel and fortitude, knowledge and piety, and the" very "fear of God"*[32] *until that monstrous standard-bearer of shameful lies should be born. It cannot be attributed to him that he received even a minimal portion of divine inspiration, since he is also from that part of the "world" which is "not able to receive the Spirit of Truth."*[33]

That same one, filled with the spirit of the devil, "resists the Spirit" of Christ,[34] and, when the teaching of the Paraclete al-

27. Manes began to preach about A.D. 240 and was put to death by the Persians about 274–277.
28. Imperator Caesar M. Aurelius Probus Augustus and Paulinus were consuls in 277 A.D.
29. Although persecutions were probably being endured in different areas at different times, there is a traditional list of ten, ending with that of Diocletian (303–313). Leo is probably referring to that of Aurelian who reigned from 270 to 276.
30. Mt 10.19–20.   31. Cf. Jn 14.17.
32. Is 11.2–3.   33. Cf. Jn 14.17.
34. Cf. Acts 7.51.

lowed the saints of God to predict the future,³⁵ he turned the **ignorance** *shamelessness* of his scandalous stories on past ages, lest the very course of events should prove his falsehoods. As if the holy law and divinely inspired prophecies had taught us nothing about the eternity of the Creator, nothing about the order of creation, which is "good as a whole,"³⁶ **he wove conflicting marvels of lies which insulted God and injured all well-founded natures.³⁷ With these, he was at last about to introduce his madness only to the very foolish and to those turned off from the light of truth.** *he wove monsters of inexplicable lies which insulted God and injured all nature. With these, he was at last about to introduce his madness only to the sluggish and those very turned off from the light of holiness.* Such people, either from the blindness of ignorance or from delight in shamefulness, come to these things, not sacred but sacrilegious, which from common reticence ought not to be expressed in our sermon, although now they are fully exposed by their own confession.

8. May none of you, dearly beloved, be persuaded that the Holy Spirit has in any way approved the author of such wickedness. Nothing certainly has come to him from that strength which Christ both promised and sent to his Church. The blessed apostle John said: "The Spirit had not yet been given, because Jesus had not yet been glorified."³⁸ The Ascension of the Lord was the cause of the giving of the Spirit, but Manes must deny that the Spirit was given when he denies that the true man in Christ was carried to his seat at the right hand of the Father.

But let us, dearly beloved, adopted into the blessed eternity of both soul and body through the regeneration of the Holy Spirit,³⁹ celebrate the sacred feast of this day with the proper worship⁴⁰ *and pure joy.* Let us confess with the blessed apostle Paul that the Lord Jesus Christ, "when he ascended to the height, took captivity captive and gave gifts to men."⁴¹ In this way, through every utterance of the human voice, the Gospel

---

35. Cf. Jn 16.13.
36. Sir 39.21.
37. Cf. Gn 1.31.
38. Jn 7.39.
39. Cf. Ti 3.5.
40. Cf. Rom 12.1.
41. Eph 4.8. Cf. Ps 67(68).19.

of God may be preached, "so every tongue might confess that the Lord Jesus is in the glory of God the Father."[42]

9. To the present solemnity, dearly beloved, we must also add that devotion, so that we might celebrate *with holy observance* the fast which conforms to the apostolic tradition. This ought to be numbered among the great gifts of the Holy Spirit, that, against the desires of the flesh and the snares of the devil, the protection of the fasts has been set up for us. By these we may overcome all temptations with the help of God.

Let us fast on Wednesday and Friday. On Saturday, however, let us celebrate the vigil with the blessed apostle Peter as advocate for our prayers, that we might deserve to obtain the mercy of God in all things through our Lord Jesus Christ, *who lives and reigns with the Father and with the Holy Spirit for ever and ever. Amen.*

Sermon 77

(31 May 442)?

That coming of the Holy Spirit, dearly beloved, has consecrated this day's feast as worthy of reverence in all the world. He, on the fiftieth day after the Resurrection of the Lord, came down on the apostles and the crowd of believers, as they hoped. They hoped, indeed, because the Lord Jesus had promised the Spirit would come, not that then for the first time he should begin to live in the saints, but that he might inflame even more fervently the hearts consecrated to himself and might flow over them more abundantly. He was increasing his gifts, not simply beginning them. Because he was richer in his generosity does not mean that he was a novice in giving.

The majesty of the Holy Spirit is never separated from the omnipotence of the Father and the Son. Whatever the divine government does in managing all things, it comes from the providence of the whole Trinity. In the Trinity, the kindness of mercy is one, the application of justice is one, and there is no division in action where there is no difference in will. What

---

42. Phil 2.11.

the Father illumines, the Son illumines, and the Holy Spirit illumines. Although the Person of the one sent is one, of the one sending is another, of the one promising is another, at the same time there is made clear for us both unity and Trinity, so that the essence, having equality yet not allowing solitariness, is understood to be of the same substance yet not of the same Person.

2. By the saving cooperation of the indivisible divinity, whatever the Father, whatever the Son, whatever the Holy Spirit accomplishes in his particular way, is the plan of our Redemption. It is the order of our salvation. For, if human beings, made in the image and likeness of God, had remained in the honor of their own nature and, undeceived by the devil's lies, had not deviated from the law placed over them for their lusts, the Creator of the world would not have become a creature, the eternal would not have undergone temporality, and God the Son, equal to God the Father, would not have assumed the "form of a servant"[43] and the "likeness of sinful flesh."[44]

Since, however, "by the ill will of the devil, death entered the world,"[45] and because captive humanity could only be freed in one way, namely, if that one would undertake our cause who, without the loss of his majesty would become true man, and who alone had no contagion of sin.[46] The mercy of the Trinity divided for itself the work of our restoration so that the Father was appeased, the Son was the appeaser, and the Holy Spirit enkindled the process. It was right that those to be saved should do something for themselves, and, when their hearts were turned to the Redeemer, that they should cut themselves off from the domination of the enemy. In regard to this, the Apostle says: "God has sent the Spirit of his Son into our hearts crying, 'Abba, Father.' "[47] "Where the Spirit of the Lord is, there is freedom."[48] "No one can say 'Jesus is Lord' except in the Holy Spirit."[49]

43. Cf. Phil 2.7. 44. Cf. Rom 8.3.
45. Wis 2.24.
46. Cf. Jn 8.46, 2 Cor 5.21, and Heb 4.15.
47. Gal 4.6. 48. 2 Cor 3.17.
49. 1 Cor 12.3.

3. If, then, led by grace, dearly beloved, we would know with faith and wisdom what belongs to the Father, what to the Son, and what to the Holy Spirit in our Restoration, and what is common to them, we will accept without any doubt those things which have been done for us in lowliness and in the flesh. In this way we would feel nothing unworthy about one and the same glory of the Trinity. Although no mind is adequate to think about God, no tongue to speak of him, nevertheless, whatever human intelligence touches on concerning the essence of the Fatherhood of God, unless it is one and the same when either his Only-Begotten Son or the Holy Spirit is considered, the thinking is not done in a worthy manner but is too much darkened in a carnal way. That very thing which seems to be understood consistently about the Father is lost, because it withdraws from the whole Trinity, if the unity is not held fast in it. By no reckoning is that truly one which is different by any inequality.

4. When we direct the keenness of our mind to praise the Father and the Son and the Holy Spirit, let us dispel far from our soul the forms of visible things and the ages of natures in time. Let us place far off the structures of places and the conditions of bodies. Let there depart from the heart what has extension in space, what is limited by boundaries, and whatever is not always everywhere, and what is not whole. Let any thought conceived about the divinity of the Trinity not take into consideration anything about difference, anything about degrees. If it understands something worthy about God, let it not dare to deny this to any Person in the Trinity, as if it would ascribe something of more honor to the Father that it does not attribute to the Son and to the Holy Spirit. It is not reverent to put the Father before the Son. Abuse of the Son is an injury to the Father. What is taken away from one is subtracted from both. With them, both eternity and divinity are common. And the Father can not be thought omnipotent or unchangeable if he either begot one less than himself or if he derives advantage by having him whom he did not have before.

5. The Lord Jesus does indeed say to his disciples, as it was read in the Gospel, "If you loved me you would rejoice that I

am going to the Father, because the Father is greater than I."[50] But those ears which more often heard, "I and the Father are one,"[51] and "Who sees me sees the Father also,"[52] receive it without any variation of the divinity, nor do they understand this concerning that essence which they know to be eternal with the Father and of the same nature. The elevation of humanity by the Incarnation of the Word is entrusted to the apostles, and those who were distressed at the departure of the Lord when it was told them are encouraged to eternal joy by the increase of their honor. "If you loved me," he said, "you would rejoice that I am going to the Father."[53]

If in perfect knowledge you saw what glory is added to you in this, that, begotten from God the Father, I was also born of a Mother from the human race; that, though the Lord of eternity, I wanted to be one of the mortals; though invisible, I presented myself as visible; though eternal in the "form of God," I took the "form of a servant,"[54] "you would rejoice that I am going to the Father."[55] For, to you this Ascension is important, and your lowliness is raised in me above all the heavens and placed at the right hand of the Father. But I who, with the Father, am that which the Father is, remain with the Father, inseparable, and thus I do not leave him in coming to you, just as I do not leave you in returning to him.

Rejoice, therefore, "that I am going to the Father, because the Father is greater than I."[56] I have united you to myself, and I have become the son of a human being so that you can be children of God. Granted that I am one in both, nevertheless, where I am conformed to you, I am less than the Father; but, in that I am not divided from the Father, I am also greater than myself. And so, let the nature that is less than the Father go to the Father, and let the flesh be where the Word always is. Let the one faith of the Catholic Church believe that according to his divinity, he is equal, whom, according to his humanity, it does not deny that he is less.

50. Jn 14.28.
51. Jn 10.30.
52. Jn 14.9.
53. Jn 14.28.
54. Cf. Phil 2.6–7.
55. Jn 14.28.
56. Jn 14.28.

6. As a result, dearly beloved, let us despise the empty and blind crafts of the wickedness of heretics who flatter themselves with a perverse interpretation of these words. When the Lord says, "All things which the Father has are mine,"[57] heretics do not understand that they take from the Father whatever they dare to deny the Son. They so miss the mark in those things which are human that they therefore think the qualities of the Father are lacking to the Only-Begotten because he has taken on our qualities.

(2) Mercy in God has not lessened his power, nor is the reconciliation of the beloved creature a defect in eternal glory. What the Father has, the Son also has, and what the Father and the Son have, the Holy Spirit also has, because the whole Trinity is one God. Earthly wisdom has not invented this faith, nor has human opinion fixed it, but the only Son has taught it himself, and the Holy Spirit established it. Nothing different must be believed about him than about the Father and the Son. Although he is not the Father, and he is not the Son, yet he is not divided from the Father and the Son. As he has his own Person in the Trinity, so he has one substance in the divinity of the Father and the Son, filling all things, containing all things, and governing the universe with the Father and the Son.

Sermon 78

(2 May 441)?

As you know, dearly beloved, a solemn fast, advantageously instituted for the care of souls and bodies, follows today's feast, consecrated by the descent of the Holy Spirit. And we ought to celebrate this fast with devout observance. When the apostles had been filled with the promised power, and the Spirit of Truth had entered their hearts, we have no doubt that, among other mysteries of heavenly doctrine, this discipline of spiritual self-denial was first brought them by the agency of the Paraclete. This would make their souls, sanctified by the fast, more open to the graces conferred.

---

57. Jn 16.15.

Indeed, the protection of omnipotent help was with the disciples of Christ, and the whole divinity of the Father and the Son in the presence of the Holy Spirit guarded the leaders of the young Church. But they could not fight, either by means of physical strength or with the satisfaction of the flesh, against the pressing attacks of persecutors and the strident threats of the wicked, for what delights the exterior man greatly corrupts the interior. The more the bodily flesh is chastised, so much the more the rational soul is purified.

2. And so these teachers, who have filled all the children of the Church with their examples and traditions, began their first attempts at Christian warfare with holy fasts. In this way, when about to fight against spiritual evils, they would take up the weapon of abstinence with which to cut off the enticements of sin. The invisible adversaries and spiritual enemies will have no strength against us, if we have not been swallowed up by any bodily desires. The will to harm is everlasting in the devil, but he will be disarmed and helpless if he finds nothing in us from which he might give battle against us.

Are there any, enclosed in this fragile flesh and set up in this very body of death, who, even if they have accomplished much of value, would now be so secure in their own stability that they would believe themselves free from the danger of all enticements? Although divine grace may give daily victories to his saints, it does not take away the matter of the struggle. Indeed this is another gift from the mercy of our protector, who wanted something to be left for our changeable nature to overcome, lest it should be proud concerning the completed battle.

3. Consequently, after the days of holy joy which we have spent in honor of the Lord, risen from the dead and then ascended into heaven, and after the reception of the gift of the Holy Spirit, the custom of a fast has been advantageously and needfully ordained. If a careless freedom of uncontrolled license should put anything in the way of the real joys of the feast, the discipline of a devout abstinence will correct it. This result must be earnestly sought for, so that those things which have been given to the Church by divine grace on this day might remain in us. Since we have become the "temple of the

Holy Spirit"[58] and are flooded by a greater flow than ever of the divine outpouring, we ought not to be overcome by any evil desires. We ought not to be possessed by any vices, so that the home of virtue will not be stained with any pollution.

4. It is possible for us all to achieve this, God ruling and helping us, if through the purification of the fast and the generosity of mercy, we wish earnestly to be "freed" from the stain of our "sins"[59] and to be rich in the fruits of charity. Whatever we spend on food for the poor, on the care of the weak, on the ransom of captives, and on any other work of mercy, is not lost but increased. What had been expended in kind-hearted faith never perishes before the Lord, for whatever it has paid out will be kept as a reward. "Blessed are the merciful, for God will be merciful to them,"[60] nor will there be any memory of faults where there is the witness of compassion.

(2) Let us fast, therefore, on Wednesday and Friday. On Saturday, however, let us celebrate the vigil with the blessed apostle Peter, by whose prayers we hope to be freed from spiritual enemies and from bodily adversaries, through Christ our Lord.

Sermon 79

31 May 453

We must not doubt, dearly beloved, that every Christian observance comes from the divine teaching, and whatever has been received by the Church into its customs of worship arises from the apostolic tradition and the teaching of the Holy Spirit. He now protects the hearts of the faithful by his instructions, to the end that all may obediently guard these things and intelligently understand them. On the day of Pentecost, which we celebrate fifty days after the Passover of the Lord, the Holy Spirit, promised by the Lord, had filled the hearts of those waiting for him with a greater abundance than ever and with a clearer presence of his majesty. It is certainly obvious that,

---

58. Cf. 1 Cor 6.19.   59. Cf. Tb 4.11.
60. Mt 5.7.

among other gifts of God, the grace of the fast also, which follows close on today's feast, was then ordained. As self-indulgence was the beginning of sins, so self-control is the source of virtue.

2. In applying this gift of God, we ought not to be too slothful, because Jews and heretics often refrain from the freedom in eating. Even with pagans themselves, there are certain meaningless fasts. Reason directs one in truth, deception the other in falsehood. With us, faith sanctifies even the one eating; with them, their unbelief mars even the one fasting. From this, that outside the Catholic Church nothing is holy, nothing pure, and, as the Apostle says, "Everything which is not from faith is a sin,"[61] the fast is assuredly especially healthful and of the greatest importance for us. We are not united in any way with those who are separated from the unity of the body of Christ. We are not engaged with them in any communion.

Nothing brings us sooner to the virtue of self-restraint than abstinence from sins, for then at last we are walking surely when we walk in the "way of truth."[62] Those who avoid "narrow and difficult" roads[63] by following a sloping and broad way, they come quickly to destruction. It is better to walk more slowly along a direct route, than to hasten quickly on an unfrequented by-way.

3. Let the Catholic Christian, therefore, recognize the fruit of his fast, because even with great almsgiving it will be sterile unless it has come forth under the outpouring of the Holy Spirit. Since the Apostle says that no virtues "benefit him without love,"[64] and, when the same one says that "the love of God is spread through our hearts by the Holy Spirit who has been given to us,"[65] we must beware lest we lose by pride the good things that we cannot do without his goodness.

Those who, from the zeal of their own activity, "glory" in themselves more than "in the Lord,"[66] rightly strip themselves of all praise, for blessed David shows that God is to be praised

---

61. Rom 14.23.
63. Cf. Mt 7.14.
65. Rom 5.5.
62. Cf. Ps 118(119).30.
64. Cf. 1 Cor 13.3.
66. Cf. 1 Cor 1.31 and 2 Cor 10.17.

in the works of the saints. He says, "Wonderful is God in his saints, the God of Israel himself will give strength and courage to his people."[67] At another point, he says: "Lord, they were walking in the light of your countenance; in your name they will rejoice all day, and they will be exalted in your justice because you are the glory of their strength."[68]

4. As a result, dearly beloved, according to the teaching of the Holy Spirit, through whom the gifts of all the virtues have been bestowed upon the Church of God, let us undertake the solemn fast with prompt faith. In his commands, as far as we can, let us guard ourselves from the puffing up of pride, referring everything to the glory of God who is both the inspirer of good will and the author of good deeds. The Lord says, "So let your light shine before men, that they might see your good works and glorify your Father who is in heaven,"[69] who lives and reigns with the Son and with the Holy Spirit forever and ever. Amen.

Sermon 80

(June 442)?

The order of the holy feasts has been performed, dearly beloved, and the devotion of spiritual joy is fulfilled. Now it is right to come back to the healthy practice of frugality and to provide the remedy of a fast, both for training our souls and for subduing our bodies. Since divine instruction and our own experiences have taught us well on this subject, let us first give thanks to the divine compassion for the course of these holy days. Then, when we earnestly strive for the holy pleasures of self-control, we might withhold some small portion of the abundance of the food of the earth, so that what is not spent on our tables might benefit alms. Truly indeed, the medicine of the fast accomplishes the cure of souls when the abstinence of the one fasting refreshes the hunger of the needy.

2. We know that, before the merciful God, the generosity of

---

67. Ps 67(68).36.
68. Ps 88(89).16–18.
69. Mt 5.16.

alms exceeds fasts, as the Lord says: "Give alms, and all things will be clean for you."[70] If we want our souls to be cleansed from the sordidness of our sins, let us not deny alms to the poor, so that on the day of retribution, in order to gain the mercy of God, we might be helped by our works of mercy.[71]

Sermon 81

(27 May 445)?

Among all the precepts of the apostles' teaching, dearly beloved, which have come to us from the fountain of divine knowledge, there is no doubt that, with the Holy Spirit rushing onto the leaders of the Church, they received this discipline first of all. They were to lay the foundations of all virtues by the observance of a holy fast. It would benefit them much for following the commands of God, if the Christian soldiers would fortify themselves against all the allurements of sin by the sanctification of self-restraint.

Since the first cause of sin crept in from the enjoyment of food, what more salutary gift of God does our redeemed liberty use than that it, which did not know how to restrain itself from forbidden things, now knows how to restrain itself from lawful things? "Every creature of God is good, and nothing ought to be rejected, which is received with the giving of thanks."[72] We were not created to seek out all the riches of the world with a foul and shameless greed, as if what we may have, we must not refrain from.

2. May God be praised, who gave so much to the use of human beings; but let the rational soul realize that greater delights have been given to the spirit than to the flesh. When any hear it said to them by the Spirit, "Do not go after your own lusts, restrain yourself from your own will,"[73] they must understand that they are to pursue the virtue of moderation against everything that entices the bodily senses. It is through virtue that the wisdom of the interior human being is increased while

70. Lk 11.41.
72. 1 Tm 4.4.
71. Cf. Mt 25.34–40.
73. Sir 18.30.

the pleasure of the exterior is lessened. There is not the same energy in the heart under the burden of food as under the light weight of the fast, nor can satiety create the same feeling that moderation does. When the flesh, "tempting the spirit,"[74] is overcome by spiritual desire, our health becomes free and our freedom healthy, so that the flesh is ruled by the judgment of the spirit and the spirit by the help of God.

3. From the Resurrection of the Lord to the coming of the Holy Spirit, fifty days have been completed which were spent in the joy of this special feast. The present time invites us, dearly beloved, to this service, that we should return to the remedy of the fasts. It could happen, by chance, from the opportunity for more pleasant relaxations, that the habit of an agreeable life should fall into some faults of negligence. The dust of our flesh, unless it undergoes constant cultivation, from sloth and ease quickly brings forth thorns and briars, and in a worthless harvest will give fruit not to be put into the barn but to be burned by fire.

As the Lord says, "Any plant which my Father has not planted will be pulled up by the roots."[75] We must guard the goodness of every sprout and seed that we receive from the planting of the Supreme Gardener. We must watch with the greatest care that no gifts of God be damaged by the deceit of a jealous enemy, and that no forest of sins should grow in the garden of virtues.

4. Nothing is stronger for avoiding this evil than almsgiving and fasting. Self-restraint kills off the desires of the flesh, and the practice of mercy multiplies the fruits of spiritual desires. For this reason we give solemn warning to your kind hearts that we should fast on Wednesday and Friday, wishing to be cleansed from the sordidness of our sins through discipline of the body and works of mercy. On Saturday, however, let us celebrate the vigil with blessed Peter the apostle. By his merits and prayers we believe that we shall be helped in such a way that the mercy of God may be with your fasts and your prayers, through Christ our Lord. Amen.

74. Cf. Gal 5.17.
75. Mt 15.13.

FEAST OF STS. PETER AND PAUL

Serms. 82–83, written in 441 and 443 respectively for the Feast of Sts. Peter and Paul, instruct the flock by emphasizing the fact that all the might and secular glory of Rome cannot compare with the Rome blessed by the presence of Christ in his two apostles (*Serm.* 82.1). Their courage, in entering the city to claim it for Christ, remained undaunted by the cruelty of Nero's persecution, which actually increased the number of faithful Christians (*Serm.* 82.6). *Serm.* 83, taken largely *verbatim* from *Serm.* 1, focuses on our Lord's preferential treatment of Peter, particularly noted in the section of the Gospel of Matthew 16.16–19. Leo offers a meditation on the bond between Christ and Peter, on Christ giving Peter primacy and the power of the keys.

Sermon 82

29 June 441 (Recension A)[1]

THE WHOLE WORLD has a part in all the holy ceremonies, dearly beloved, and the holiness of our one faith demands that, whatever is recalled to mind as done for the world's salvation, it should be celebrated everywhere with like festivity. Yet today's feast must be revered with a special celebration of its own for our city, beyond the respect it deserves from the rest of the world. Where the death of the leaders of the apostles has been covered with glory, there should be the chief place of joy on the day of their martyrdom.

---

1. This sermon comes down to us in two recensions. Recension A had been composed in 441. Recension B appears to represent a revision made by Leo himself at some later date. Material found in both recensions will appear in normal text. Material found only in Recension A will appear in **bold**. Material found only in Recension B will appear in *italics*. Some material found in both recensions but in a different order will be reproduced in both bold and italics in their proper order. Some material that does not coincide between the two versions of the Latin text but does not affect the English translation (such as word order or certain syntactical variants) will not be indicated. Some lines may also have been added by a third recension, but these have been ignored for the purposes of this translation.

These are the men through whom the Gospel of Christ enlightened you, o Rome, and you who were the **mother** *teacher* of error were made the **daughter** *disciple* of truth. These selfsame men are your holy fathers and true shepherds, who built you up to be a part of the heavenly kingdom better by far and much more favorably **than those twins quarreling to the point of murder,** *than those of whom the one, who gave you your name, defiled you with the murder of his twin brother.*[2] Yet these are the men who raised you to this glory, that, as "a holy nation, a people set apart, a priestly and royal city,"[3] you might be made head of the world through the sacred throne of blessed Peter. You hold eminence more widely by your reverence for God than in earthly rule. Although grown larger by many victories, you have spread out the law of your empire on land and sea, nevertheless what the labors of war have subjected to you is less than what the peace of Christ has subdued.

2. The good and just and omnipotent God, who has never refused his mercy to the human race, has, by his overflowing kindnesses,[4] taught all mortals in common the knowledge of himself. He has taken pity, in his very mysterious wisdom and deep compassion, on the willful blindness of those in error and their bad mortal quality prone to worse things, by sending his Word, equal to himself and co-eternal. And this "Word made flesh,"[5] **associated** *united* the divine nature to the human in such a way that his abasement to the lowest depths, became our ascent to the heights.

So that the effect of this inexpressible grace might be spread throughout the whole world, divine Providence prepared the Roman Empire with such growth to its boundaries, that the whole population was neighbor to and bordering upon all peoples everywhere. The work, divinely planned, was especially suitable to the incorporation of many kingdoms under one rule. A general proclamation would quickly reach all the people whom the government of one city was protecting. But this city, unmindful of the Author of its dignity, although it ruled almost

---

2. The reference is to Romulus, traditional founder of Rome, who killed his brother Remus in order to become ruler.
3. 1 Pt 2.9.   4. Cf. Acts 14.17.
5. Cf. Jn 1.14.

all nations, succumbed to the errors of all nations. It seemed to have taken to itself a great religion because it did not repudiate any falsehood. Thus as much as it had been bound more tightly by the decrees of the devil, by so much has it been more wonderfully loosened by Christ.

3. When the twelve apostles, in receiving the speech of all languages from the Holy Spirit, had undertaken to fill the world with the Gospel, and the territories of the earth were distributed to them, blessed Peter, chief of the order of the apostles, was assigned to the citadel of the Roman Empire. The light of truth, which was revealed for the salvation of all nations, would then pour itself out more effectively from the head itself through the whole body of the world.

Was there any nation whose people were not in this city then? Were there any people anywhere who did not know what Rome had learned? In this place the opinions of philosophy were about to be trampled on, in this place the emptiness of earthly wisdom was to be dissolved, here the worship of demons was to be overthrown, here the wickedness of all profanation was to be destroyed, where whatever had been established anywhere was enclosed, gathered together by a very diligent superstition.

4. It is to this city that you, most blessed apostle Peter, were not afraid to come. While the apostle Paul, companion of your glory, was still engaged in the founding of other churches, you walked into this forest of wild beasts and to this **deep ocean of wicked superstition** *ocean of stormy depths* more readily than when you walked on water.[6] And you did not fear Rome, the mistress of the world, though you feared the maid in the house of Caiaphas, the high priest.[7] Was the power of Claudius or the cruelty of Nero less than the judgment of Pilate or the cruelty of the Jews?

The strength of love overcame the object of fear. You did not consider that those ought to be feared whom you had accepted to love. You had already conceived this disposition of intrepid charity when the profession of your love for the Lord

---

6. Cf. Mt 14.30.
7. Cf. Mt 26.69–70.

was firmly established by the mystery of his three-fold questioning.[8] He did not seek anything from this probing of your spirit except that in feeding the sheep of him whom you love, you should provide the food of **heavenly nourishment** *with which you yourself were endowed.*

5. How many miraculous signs, how many gifts of grace, how many proofs of virtue have increased your faith! At one time you had taught those people who from the circumcision had believed; at another you had filled very many peoples with the laws of Gospel holiness. *At yet another, you founded the Church in Antioch where the dignity of the name Christians first arose;*[9] *then you filled Pontus, Galatia, Cappadocia, Asia, and Bithynia with the laws of the Gospel preaching.* With no fears for the outcome of your work, and fully aware of the limit of your age, you bore the trophy of the Cross of Christ in the Roman citadel, where by the divine plan the honor of his power and the glory of his suffering had gone before you.

6. Your blessed co-apostle, Paul, "vessel of election" and special teacher of the nations,[10] coming to this city, was your associate at that time when all innocence, all honor, all liberty was suffering under the will of Nero, whose rage, inflamed by an excess of all vices, in this time drove him up to such a flood of insanity that he was the first to bring on the horror of a general persecution for the name of Christian. **He seemed to think that the grace of God might be cut off through the slaughter of his holy ones. He did not know that the religion founded on the mystery of the Cross cannot be extinguished by any kind of cruelty, since "precious in the sight of the Lord is the death of his holy ones."**[11] **This does not diminish, but it increases, the Church.** *As if the grace of God could be blotted out by the slaughter of his holy ones, for whom it was the greatest profit that the contempt of this failing life brought the knowledge of eternal happiness. Therefore "precious in the sight of the Lord is the death of his holy ones."*[12] *Not by any kind of cruelty can the religion founded in the mystery of the*

---

8. Cf. Jn 21.15–17.
9. Cf. Acts 11.26.
10. Cf. Acts 9.15.
11. Ps 115(116).15.
12. Ps 115(116).15.

Cross of Christ be destroyed. The Church is not diminished by persecutions but increased, and always the Lord's field is clothed with richer crops, while the grains, falling singly, are born many times as numerous. Thus thousands of blessed martyrs give witness to how great a progeny these two illustrious shoots of the divine seed proliferated. The followers of the triumphs of the apostles have encircled our city with an ennobled populace, shining to far distances, and they have crowned it as if with a diadem fitted with the beauty of many gems.

7. From this guardianship, dearly beloved, divinely prepared for us as an example of patience and a confirmation of faith, we should rejoice everywhere in the memory of all the saints, but in the pre-eminence of these fathers we must surely exult with greater joy. The grace of God has raised them to such a height among all the children of the Church that he has made them as it were twin lights of the eyes in the body of which Christ is the Head.[13] We ought to think nothing divisive, nothing disruptive in their merits and virtues, for they surpass every means of description. They were on a par in election, alike in their work, and their martyrdom made them equal.

As we ourselves have experienced and as our ancestors have learned, we believe and trust that, in all the labor of this life, we are to be aided always by the prayers of these special patrons to attain the mercy of God. As we are hindered by our own sins, so we are encouraged by the apostles' merits, *through our Lord Jesus Christ, to whom, with the Father and with the Holy Spirit is equal glory, the same power, one divinity, forever and ever. Amen.*

Sermon 83

29 June 443

Let us rejoice in the Lord, dearly beloved, let us be glad with spiritual delight. The Only-Begotten Son of the Father, our Lord Jesus Christ, that he might initiate us into the mysteries of his teaching and his divinity, was pleased to choose beforehand for this city blessed Peter, the chief of the apostolic order.

---

13. Cf. Eph 1.22–23 and Col 1.18.

His feast today, when the triumph of his martyrdom comes around, offers his example and his glory to the world. That confession, dearly beloved, which was inspired by God the Father in the apostle's heart, brought this about; it transcended all the uncertainties of human opinions, and it received the solidity of rock which no blows can shake.

In the Gospel story,[14] the Lord asked all the apostles what people thought about him. But, when the Lord wanted to know what the disciples felt, the first in dignity among the apostles was the first to confess the Lord. When he had said, "You are Christ, Son of the living God,"[15] Jesus replied to him, "Blessed are you, Simon, son of John, since flesh and blood have not revealed this to you, but my Father who is in heaven,"[16] that is to say, for this reason are you blessed, since my Father taught you; since earthly opinion did not deceive you, but heavenly inspiration instructed you; since neither flesh nor blood but he, whose only Son am I, made me known to you.

"And I," he said, "tell you,"[17] that is to say, just as my Father has manifested my divinity to you, so I make known to you your own prominence. "That you are Peter,"[18] that is to say, although I am the indestructible rock, I "the cornerstone who make both things one,"[19] I "the foundation on which no one can lay another,"[20] you also are rock because you are made firm in my strength. What belongs properly to my own power you share with me by participation.

2. "And on this rock I shall build my Church, and the gates of hell will not prevail against it."[21] "On this" strength, he means, I shall raise up an eternal temple, and the loftiness of my Church, piercing into heaven, will rise up on the firmness of this faith. This confession will not be restrained by the gates of hell. It will not be bound by the chains of death. For that declaration is indeed a declaration of life. While it lifts those who confess it up to heaven, no less does it sink down to hell those who deny it.

It was with this in view that the most blessed Peter was told:

---

14. Cf. Mt 16.12–19.
15. Mt 16.16.
16. Mt 16.17.
17. Mt 16.18.
18. Mt 16.18.
19. Cf. Eph 2.20 and 14.
20. 1 Cor 3.11.
21. Mt 16.18.

"I shall give you the keys to the kingdom of heaven. Whatever you bind on earth will be bound also in heaven, and whatever you loose on earth will be loosed also in heaven."[22] Certainly, the right to use this power was conveyed to the other apostles as well. What was laid down by this decree went for all the leaders of the Church. Yet not without purpose is it handed over to one, though made known to all. It is entrusted in a unique way to Peter because the figure of Peter is set before all the rulers of the Church. Therefore, this privilege of Peter resides wherever judgment has been passed in accordance with his fairness. There cannot be too much severity or too much lenience where nothing is bound or loosed outside of that which blessed Peter has loosed or bound.

3. When the Passion of the Lord was drawing near, an event that was going to shake the constancy of his disciples, he said: "Simon, Simon. Behold, Satan has obtained his request to sift you (all) like wheat. I, however, have begged for you that your faith not fail. Once you have converted, strengthen your brethren, lest you (all) enter into temptation."[23] Each apostle encountered the same danger through temptation from fear. All equally needed the help of divine protection, since the devil wanted to harass them all and to crush them all. Still, the Lord took special care of Peter and prayed especially for Peter. It was as if the condition of the others would be more secure if the mind of their leader were not overcome.

(2) In Peter, therefore, the fortitude of all is reinforced, for the aid of divine grace is ordered in such a way that the firmness given to Peter through Christ is conferred upon the apostles through Peter. After his Resurrection and after entrusting the keys of the kingdom to the blessed apostle Peter, the Lord said by a mystical suggestion (three times in answer to his threefold profession of unending love): "Feed my sheep."[24] Doubtless he now does that. As a dedicated shepherd, he carries out the mandate from the Lord.

He strengthens us with his exhortations and never stops

22. Mt 16.19.
24. Jn 21.17.
23. Lk 22.31–32 and 40.

praying for us that we might not be overcome by any trial. If, moreover, he extends this devoted concern to all the people of God everywhere—as indeed it has to be believed—how much more is he willing to lavish his assistance upon us, his adopted children? Among us does he rest on the sacred bed of blessed sleep, with the same flesh in which he presided [over the Church].

(3) As a result, dearly beloved, since we see so great a protection divinely established for us, let us rightly and properly rejoice in the merits and worth of our leader, and give thanks to the eternal King, our Redeemer and Lord, Jesus Christ, because he gave such power to the one whom he made head of the entire Church, to the glory and praise of his name.

COMMEMORATING ALARIC'S INVASION OF ROME

After the fall of Carthage (19 October 439), the Vandals severely threatened the whole Mediterranean area, particularly Italy and Rome. They reached Sicily but did not enter Italy. In 442 Valentinian III was obliged to accept the treaty offered by Gaiseric, the Vandal leader.

Alaric had sacked Rome on 28 August 410, and a commemoration of gratitude for Rome's deliverance had been held annually ever since. During the years immediately preceding the treaty with Gaiseric (441–442), the first years of Leo's pontificate, people attended the anniversary celebration in great numbers as the Vandals were threatening. After the treaty had been concluded, however, their relief led to anniversary celebrations that were—on this particular occasion at least—very sparsely attended.

"More effort is spent on demons than on the apostles, and the wild entertainments draw greater crowds than the shrines of martyrs. Who restored this city to safety? Who snatched it from captivity? Who protected it from slaughter? Was it the games of the circus, or the watchful care of saints?" (*Serm.* 84.1) "Let us attribute our deliverance not, as the pagans think, to the effects of stars, but to the inexpressible mercy of almighty God, who willed to soften the hearts of raging barbarians" (*Serm.* 84.2).

Sermon 84

30 August or 6 September 442

WHAT RELIGIOUS DEVOTION, dearly beloved, with which the whole body of the faithful used to come together to give thanks to God for the day of our chastisement and of our liberation, has recently been neglected by almost everyone, as the very scarcity of the few who were present has shown. It brings much sadness to my heart and produces very great anxiety. There is serious danger in being ungrateful to God and, through forgetfulness of his benefits, feeling neither remorse after his correction nor joy in his pardon.

I fear then, dearly beloved, that the voice of the prophet

seems to have reproached just such people in saying: "You have scourged them, and they have not felt pain. You have punished them, and they have refused to accept the discipline."[1] What correction does one see in them when such great rejection is found? It shames me to say it, but one must not keep silent. More effort is spent on demons than on the apostles, and the wild entertainments draw greater crowds than the shrines of martyrs.

Who restored this city to safety? Who snatched it from captivity? Who protected it from slaughter? Was it the games of the circus, or the watchful care of saints? Assuredly, it was by their prayers that the sentence of divine judgment was appeased, so that we who deserved wrath might be saved for forgiveness.

2. I beg, dearly beloved, that your hearts may be touched by that statement of our Savior, who, when he had cleansed the "ten lepers" by the power of his mercy, said that only "one of them returned to give thanks."[2] He clearly pointed out about the ungrateful ones that, even if they had attained bodily health, they did not have spiritual health because they were lacking in this duty of reciprocity. Lest this mark of the ungrateful be attributed to you, dearly beloved, return to the Lord and realize the wonderful things he has been willing to do for us. Let us attribute our deliverance not, as the pagans think, to the effects of stars, but to the inexpressible mercy of Almighty God, who willed to soften the hearts of raging barbarians.

(2) Therefore, devote yourselves to the memory of such great kindness with the whole energy of your faith. Greater penance must be used to cure a serious negligence. For our correction, let us make use of the gentleness of one who spares us, that blessed Peter and all the saints who have been with us in many difficulties may be willing to help our prayers for you to the merciful God, through Christ our Lord. Amen.

1. Jer 5.3.
2. Cf. Lk 17.15–18.

MARTYRDOM OF THE MACCABEES

It is not known exactly when this sermon was composed. Most likely, however, Leo delivered it on 1 August (the Feast of the Maccabees) any year between 446 and 461. Leo expresses gratitude that his flock appreciates this feast and that they especially appreciate the mother of the Maccabees (*Serm.* 84B.1). He cautions them not to become complacent in the absence of government persecution, but to probe the depths of the heart, where the devil's persecutors (i.e., vices) constantly lurk (*Serm.* 84B.2). With regard to these temptations which attack everyone (and these are enumerated), Leo explains: "When you see that you are waging a battle on many fronts, then must you also, in imitation of the martyrs, pursue a many-sided victory" (*Serm.* 84B.2). In urging practice of the virtues which counteract vices, he employs yet another one of his aphoristic "one-liners": "Things that have been heard become tiresome if they are not taken up to be imitated" (*Serm.* 84B.2).

Sermon 84B

1 August (446–461?)

WE GIVE THANKS, dearly beloved, to the Lord our God that, even if I should be silent, your assembly here shows how great is the solemnity of this day. You have come together with such single-minded enthusiasm and such a devout spirit that the meeting itself bears witness to the splendor of the feast, and rightly so, even if the sermon did not mention it. We have a twofold cause for joy, in that we both celebrate the Church's birthday and rejoice in the suffering of martyrs. It is proper for the Church to exult in their martyrdom—and not inappropriate—for it is adorned by their example.

You have learned the reason for today's feast very clearly, dearly beloved, from the reading of the sacred story.[1] No, you

---

1. Cf. 2 Mc 7.

could not have failed to understand the instruction which you received in so great a series of events when, with your exultant and clamorous affection, you gave honor to the glorious mother of the seven martyrs, who suffered indeed with each single son but was crowned in all of them. She followed in her happy departure those she had sent ahead with her unconquered encouragement.

Blessed mother, blessed offspring! Those who went first showed a memorable devotion, those who came after, a marvelous fortitude. In that series of deaths and in that arrangement of punishments, the most savage king in his godlessness had devised the following scheme. He banked on victory, both from the first brothers whom he tortured without precedent, as well as from the later ones whom he tormented through his punishment of the others. As a result, the palms of the martyrs are multiplied. While each conquers in them all, all have earned the seven crowns in addition to their own.

2. But are these things to be reflected on for an unfruitful pleasure of the ears? "Knowledge puffs up" unless obedience "erects" the building.[2] Things that have been heard become tiresome if they are not taken up to be imitated. Though persecution and torture have ceased, though all forces now fight for God, Christians do not for that reason lack sufferings to overcome. "Child, as you come to the Lord's service, stand in justice and in fear, and prepare your soul for testing."[3] As the Apostle says, "whoever wishes to live devoutly in Christ suffers persecution on account of justice."[4]

If you think that persecution has relaxed and that you have no quarrel with the enemy, look closely at the hidden center of your heart. As a diligent inspector, enter all the recesses of your soul. Then see if no opposition confronts you, if no tyrant wants to rule in the citadel of your spirit. Do not make peace with avarice, and despise the rewards of unjust dealings. Refuse to make an accord with pride, and fear more to be raised up in glory than to be trampled on in humiliation.[5] Restrain

2. Cf. 1 Cor 8.1.
3. Sir 2.1.
4. 2 Tm 3.12 and cf. Mt 5.10.
5. Cf. Sir 24.11.

yourself from anger, and do not let the desire for vengeance inflame the resentment of ill will. Renounce pleasure, turn away from uncleanness, dispel luxury, flee unrighteousness, resist falsehood. When you see that you are waging a battle on many fronts, then must you also, in imitation of the martyrs, pursue a many-sided victory. Every time we die to sins, the sins die in us, and this "death of his holy ones is precious in the sight of the Lord,"[6] because a "human being" dies "to the world"[7] not by the destruction of senses, but by the death of vices.[8]

3. If then, "dearest friends, you do not take up the yoke with unbelievers,"[9] if you cease to be sinners and yield to no temptations of bodily desires, you legitimately celebrate this solemn day. Venerate not only the martyrs and the mother of the martyrs, but also, with due honor, the memory of that one who on this day redoubled the ancient feast by the consecration of this place, the magnificent builder of walls, but even more magnificent architect of souls. He extended works of piety well beyond the bounds of his own lifetime, so that a devout posterity would enjoy also in this very place the benefits of his institutions, both by inhabiting what he built and by doing what he taught.

4. Accept then, dearly beloved, all the things that you see with your eyes and remember in your mind. Accept them for the advancement of your own building up. Let each one of you so use the dwelling place prepared by your ancestors that you might recall that the temple of God is built in yourselves.[10] May you add nothing weak to the structure, nothing unstable, but in the joining of "living" and chosen "stones,"[11] may it "grow"[12] by an imperishable "bond"[13] into the unity of the Lord's body,[14] with the help of that "cornerstone,"[15] our God and Lord Jesus Christ who, with the Father and the Holy Spirit, reigns forever and ever. Amen.

6. Cf. Ps 115(116).15.
7. Cf. Gal 6.14.
8. Cf. Gal 5.24.
9. Cf. 2 Cor 6.14.
10. Cf. 1 Cor 3.16–17 and 2 Cor 6.16.
11. Cf. 1 Pt 2.5.
12. Cf. Eph 2.12 and 4.15.
13. Cf. Eph 4.16.
14. Cf. Eph 4.3–6.
15. Cf. Eph 2.20 and 1 Pt 2.6.

FEAST OF ST. LAWRENCE

Martyrs eminently put into practice the essence of Christ's message, love of God and love of neighbor. Their examples are more powerful than words (*Serm.* 85.1). Leo tells the story of Lawrence's sufferings: "... that fire was less effective which burned on the outside than the one which burned within" (*Serm.* 84.4); "... even the instruments of torture were transformed into the honor of his triumph" (*Serm.* 84.4), and he went, despite the cruelty of his executioner, to the embrace of his God.

Sermon 85

10 August (446–461?)

INCE, dearly beloved, the peak of all virtues and the fullness of complete justice is born of that love directed toward God and one's neighbor, this love stands out more sublimely and shines more clearly in the blessed martyrs than in anyone else. By the imitation of his charity and by the likeness to his suffering, they are near to our Lord Jesus Christ, who died for all. It is true that no kindness of anyone at all is able to equal that love by which the Lord redeemed us,[1] because it is one thing for someone to die for the just when it will necessary to die any way, but another to die for the wicked when no debt is owed to death.

Nevertheless, the martyrs also have offered much to all people. The Lord used their courage—which he had given them—in such a way that he wished to make the penalty of death and the torment of the cross not a source of dread to any of his own, but a pattern to be imitated by many. No good people are good only for themselves, and wisdom does not benefit only the person who has it. True virtues have this nature, that they lead

---

1. Cf. Eph 5.2.

many away from shadowy error (which becomes clear by their light). If this is so, then no instance of any such virtue has more usefulness for instructing the people of God than martyrdom. Eloquence may be suitable for exhortation, reason may be effective in persuasion, but examples are more forceful than words, and it is better to teach by deeds than by words.

2. Lawrence, the blessed martyr, whose suffering makes this day illustrious, was renowned with great honor in this preeminent kind of teaching. Even his persecutors could feel this, when that marvelous courage of soul, born chiefly from the love of Christ, not only did not yield itself, but even strengthened others by the example of its endurance. When the fury of pagan powers raged against some of the most chosen members of Christ and especially sought out those who were of priestly rank, the wicked persecutor was inflamed against the deacon Lawrence, who stood out not only in the ministry of the Sacraments. but also in the administration of ecclesiastical goods.

This agent banked on a double reward from the arrest of one man, for if he could make him an embezzler of the Church's money, he would also make him a traitor to the true religion. This man, therefore, desirous of money and hostile to the truth, is armed with a double motive: with avarice (to seize the money) and with wickedness (to destroy Christ). He insists that the ecclesiastical wealth he so avidly desired be brought to him by the untarnished keeper of the treasury. This most virtuous deacon, showing him where he kept them hidden, presented the countless flocks of the holy poor. It was for their food and clothing that he had secured resources that could not be lost. He took care of these resources all the more carefully, since the expenditures had been approved for so holy a purpose.

3. So the frustrated robber protested and, burning with hatred for the religion that claimed such use of wealth, undertook the plundering of the even more desirable treasure. Where he found no real money, he wanted to steal away that deposit according to which [Lawrence] was rich in a holier way. He ordered [him] to renounce Christ and prepared to oppress the remarkably firm courage of the deacon's soul with dire cruel-

ties. When the first attempt obtained nothing, worse followed. He ordered the limbs, mangled and torn with the many cuts of lashes, to be burned over a fire on an iron grate—which by now, from the steady heat, had on its own the ability to burn. This way, as his limbs were being turned over and over, he might be tortured more fiercely and the punishment might be drawn out.

4. You gain nothing, you accomplish nothing, O cruel savagery! The mortal body is removed from your schemes, and Lawrence escapes you as he goes to heaven. The flame of love for Christ cannot be overcome by your flame, and that fire was less effective which burned on the outside than the one which burned within. You, o persecutor, helped the martyr in being harsh; you increased his victory when you added to his punishment. What did your skill not invent for the glory of the victor, when even the instruments of torture were transformed into the honor of his triumph?

(2) Let us then take joy, dearly beloved, with a spiritual joy, in the most blessed end of this celebrated man. Let us glory in the Lord who is "wonderful in his saints,"[2] in whom he established a protection and an example for us. He has so illumined his own glory through the whole world that, from east to west, where the brilliance of the lights of his deacons shines, as Jerusalem has become renowned for Stephen, so Rome has become as renowned for Lawrence. We believe that we are helped by his prayer and his patronage without ceasing. Since the Apostle says, "All who wish to live devoutly in Christ suffer persecution,"[3] we are strengthened by the spirit of love and fortified to overcome all temptations by the perseverance of a steady faith, through our Lord Jesus Christ, living and reigning with the Father and the Holy Spirit for ever and ever. Amen.

2. Cf. Ps 67(68).36.
3. 2 Tm 3.12.

DAYS OF FAST IN SEPTEMBER

Leo placed great confidence in the spiritual efficacy of fasting. "Although any time is suitable for restraint, this time is most fit because we see it as chosen by the appointment of the apostles and the laws, that, as in other days of the year, so in September, we should cleanse ourselves by spiritual purification" (*Serm.* 93.3). The sermons for the four seasonal fasts have slightly different emphases. This group highlights the benefits of the corporateness of the act. Leo praises unity of worship and action as a protection against temptations. "A general fast ought to be celebrated on certain days by all together, for then devotion is more efficacious and more holy when ... the understanding of the whole Church is one" (*Serm.* 89.2), and "the people of God become more powerful when the hearts of all the faithful come together in the unity of holy obedience" (*Serm.* 88.2). Nevertheless, with sensitivity, he realizes that each one's capacity is different and so "the infirm may be released from the labor that is beyond the powers of the body by the outlay of their resources" (*Serm.* 87.3).

Serm. 89.1, given in 444, refers again to the Manichaeans and their customs, "the barefoot processions, the sad-faced fasts, the disreputable clothing," warning the audience and urging that "many fighting together against an enemy are in less danger than one fighting alone" (*Serm.* 89.2).

Years later, in 453 (*Serm.* 91.2), Leo is still fighting heresy. This time he condemns the Nestorians who damage the unity of Christ by "separating the human from the divine" in him, and the Eutychians who "obliterate the human in the divine." Faith and participation in the Blessed Eucharist provide a remedy against all errors (*Serm.* 91.3).

Sermon 86

441

WE KNOW your observance, dearly beloved, to be so devoted that you exercise your souls not only in the prescribed fasts, but in voluntary fasts as well. Still, to your eagerness we must add the encouragement of a reminder. In this way, if any are too irresolute in the practice of fasting, at least they will join us obediently for common abstinence on these days when it is our duty to celebrate the holy custom more carefully. We hope that we may deserve divine help against all our enemies through the humility of a fast. This matter has a special importance, as we show from authority and encourage from love. When we restrain our freedom in eating, we can concentrate on disciplining the body and giving alms to nourish the poor. In nourishing the poor, we refresh our own souls and change our worldly feasts into eternal delight.

2. Let the growth of holy desires succeed into the place of evil lusts. Let iniquity cease, but let justice never stop working. If no one has suffered wrong at your hands, let someone experience your assistance. It is a very small thing not to take others' goods unless you are generous with your own. We are under the eyes of a just judge who knows how much and to whom he has given the means for good works. He does not wish his gifts to be idle, for he so distributes the measure of mystical "talents" to his servants that those who have liberally invested their loan will increase it, while those who preserved it unused will lose it.[1]

(2) Now, dearly beloved, since it is time to celebrate the fast of September, let us remind you in your holiness that we fast on Wednesday and Friday. On Saturday, however, let us together keep the vigil of blessed Peter the apostle. By his prayers and merits, may we deserve to be delivered from all trials, through Christ our Lord.

Sermon 87

442

God created and redeemed the human race. He wishes us to walk along the "paths of justice"[2] toward the promises of eternal life. Since temptations will always be present to oppose us in the way of virtue (as treacherous obstacles), he has endowed us with many defenses, dearly beloved, with which to trample

1. Cf. Mt 25.20–29.
2. Cf. Ps 22(23).3.

the "devil's snares."[3] Among these defenses, God provided this most salutary means for his servants, that they arm themselves against all the enemy's wiles with the courage of self-restraint and with works of mercy.

That one who, from the beginning, instilled an appetite for forbidden food into the first human beings, and, through the pleasure of eating, poured the poison of all excessive desires into those of weak faith,[4] does not cease to use again these same deceits. In the nature that he knows to be corrupted by his seeds, he seeks a crop of his own planting, that, by weakening the zeal for virtue, he might inflame the desire for sensuality. But he cannot harm in any way the souls of those who know how, with the help of God, to rule their own bodies. So the growth of Christianity serves as his punishment.

(2) Rebellious desires must be reined in with a reasonable moderation and with a holy resolution. Bodily lusts cannot be allowed to oppose chaste and spiritual desires. Interior human beings should realize that they rule over their exterior behavior, and the mind, governed by divine mastery, should constrain the earthly substance into a kindly-disposed obedience. Our merciful King does not fail to help us preserve this state, for it is he who informed us with an understanding of a very salutary discipline. He prescribed for us certain days of fast through the course of the seasons, days in which the strength of our souls may be confirmed by the chastisement of our bodies.

2. A duty to apply this remedy, dearly beloved, has also been laid down for this month of September, which calls us to undertake it with a willing energy. In addition to that abstinence in which some discipline themselves individually and privately, according to the degree of their own ability, this abstinence (which has been appointed for us all) should be celebrated more devoutly. In every contest of the Christian struggle, the use of self-restraint has very great value.

On occasion, certain spirits of fierce demons have not been driven out of possessed bodies by any commands from the ex-

3. Cf. 1 Tm 3.7 and 2 Tm 2.6.
4. Cf. Gn 3.5–6.

orcists, but have been expelled only through the power of fasting and prayers, as the Lord said: "As for this kind of demon, it is cast out only by prayer and fasting."[5] The prayer of someone fasting pleases God and terrifies the devil. All know how much it adds to their own salvation when it is so important to another's.

3. Certainly, in this observance, dearly beloved, it is right for us all to be of one mind in devotion. If there are any whose infirmity prevents this good will, they may be released from a labor that is beyond the body's powers by the outlay of their resources. There are many works of mercy which may lend aid to this unavoidable need of eating with greater benefit if, in a zeal for goodness, they add to the purification of those fasting. For it happens that those who omit nothing from the humiliation of fasting, exert themselves with meaningless fatigue—unless they sanctify themselves with the distribution of as much alms as they can.

It is fitting that those who have less strength to fast should show greater generosity in giving alms to the poor. What some in their weakness do not deny themselves, let it be generously spent on another's need. Let them share what they need for themselves with the poor. Those who relax their fast out of weakness are not blameworthy—if they give food to a hungry person in need. Nor do any become defiled by taking food when they have been cleansed by the distribution of alms, as the Lord said: "Give alms, and then indeed all things are clean for you."[6]

4. In this practice, dearly beloved, even those who restrain themselves from the pleasure of food ought to prepare the fruits of mercy for themselves, so that the more they have sown, the more they will reap. This crop never fails its cultivator, nor does the practice of the work of mercy hold any uncertain hope. The heat will not burn, nor the flood wash away, nor will the hail flatten, that which has been scattered in this way by the hand of the sower. All the expenses of mercy are always safe.

---

5. Mt 17.21 and Mk 9.29.
6. Lk 11.41.

Not only do they remain intact, but they are increased in amount and are transformed in quality. Heavenly things come forth from earthly, great things grow from small, and a temporal gift turns into an eternal reward.

(2) Each of you who loves riches, each of you who is anxious to multiply what you possess, arouse yourself toward these rewards, aspire to these increases of your goods, from which no "thief" steals, no "moth destroys," no rust consumes.[7] Do not despair of interest. Do not distrust your receipts. "What you have done to one of these, you have done to me."[8] Realize who says this, and, free from anxiety, recognize with the clear eyes of faith into whose hands you are placing your wealth. If Christ owes a debt to someone, that person need not doubt its repayment. Let your generosity not be anxious, nor your fasting sad. "God loves a cheerful giver."[9] He is faithful to his word and abundantly restores the gifts which he gave to be kindly shared.

Sermon 88

443

Devout fasting has a very great value for gaining the mercy of God and for strengthening human frailty. We know this from the teaching of holy prophets, dearly beloved. They insist that the arousal of divine justice—which the people of Israel frequently brought upon themselves in punishment for their wickedness—could not be placated except by fasting. Joel the prophet warns us in saying: "The Lord God says these things: 'Turn to me with all your heart, in fasting, in weeping, and in mourning. Rend your hearts, and not your garments. Be converted to the Lord your God, because he is merciful and patient and magnanimous and rich in mercy.'"[10] At another point, the same prophet says: "Make holy a fast, preach healing, call together the people, make holy the assembly."[11] This exhortation, dearly beloved, is what we must embrace in our

---

7. Cf. Lk 12.33 and Mt 6.20.
8. Mt 25.40.
9. 2 Cor 9.7.
10. Jl 2.12–13.
11. Jl 2.15–16.

times also. We must of necessity preach the remedy of this healing, so that Christian devotion in the observance of that ancient means for sanctification might acquire what the Jewish transgression lost.

2. Among all the zeal for voluntary observances, reverence for the divine ordinances always has a privileged place. What is celebrated, then, by public regulation would be done in a holier way than what is dependent on private initiative. The exercise of self-restraint, which some decide for themselves by their own judgment, pertains to the benefit of certain individuals; but a fast undertaken by the whole Church leaves no one out from the general purification. It is then that the people of God become most powerful, when the hearts of all the faithful come together in the unity of holy obedience, because, in the camp of the Christian fighters, there is similar preparation all around, and the fortification is the same everywhere. Although the watchful fury of the cruel enemy rages and spreads out hidden snares everywhere, he can take no one, he can wound no one, if he finds everyone armed, everyone active, everyone sharing in the works of mercy.

3. This solemn fast of September also invites us, dearly beloved, to the power of this unconquered unity, so that we may raise up our hearts to the Lord, free from the cares of the world and earthly interests. We cannot all hold on to this intention for long (though it is always necessary), and, through human frailty, we fall back from the heights rather frequently. At least during these days, assigned to us for a most healthy cure, let us withdraw ourselves from worldly occupations and steal some time for the benefit of eternal goods. "We all offend in many respects,"[12] as it has been written.

We are all cleansed by the daily gift of God from various contaminations. In unwary souls, however, many gross spots adhere that ought to be washed out with greater care and cleansed with more effort. The fullest remission of sin is obtained when there is one prayer and one confession of the whole Church. If the Lord promises that all things asked for will be granted

---

12. Jas 3.2.

to the holy and devout "consent of two or three,"[13] what will be denied to many thousands of the people of the Church following one devotion together and praying in harmony through the one Spirit?

4. It is great in the sight of the Lord, dearly beloved, and very precious when the whole people of Christ at the same time press on in the same duties, and all ranks and all orders of each sex cooperate in the same good will. In thwarting evil and practicing good, there is one equal feeling in all, since God is glorified in the works of his servants, and he is blessed "in the many acts of gratitude"[14] to the Author of all goodness. The hungry are fed, the naked clothed, the sick visited, and "none looks to their own advantage but to another's."[15] What one has is sufficient to relieve another's suffering. It is easy to find a "cheerful giver"[16] where understanding of one's ability regulates the due measure of action.

Through this grace of God, "which works all things in all people,"[17] comes the common fruit of the faithful and the common merit. The souls of those people can be equal though their possessions are not. As one rejoices in the generosity of another whose expenditures they could not equal, they are on a par in good will. In such a community, there is nothing unmannerly and nothing divisive, where all the members of the whole body work together for a single strength of holiness. [One member] is not embarrassed by its own insignificance when it can glory in the abundance of others. The excellence of a part serves as an ornament of the whole. Since "we" all "live in the Spirit of God,"[18] not only those things that we ourselves do are ours, but also those from which we take pleasure in the actions of others.

5. Let us embrace that blessed solidarity of most holy unity, dearly beloved. Let us enter the solemn fast with harmonious resolution of good will. We ask nothing difficult of anyone, nothing harsh, nor, as far as we are concerned, do we suggest anything that exceeds your powers, either in the discipline of

13. Cf. Mt 18.19–20.
15. 1 Cor 10.24.
17. 1 Cor 12.6.
14. Cf. 2 Cor 9.11–12.
16. Cf. 2 Cor 9.7.
18. Cf. Rom 8.14.

abstinence or in the generosity of alms. You all know what you can do and what you cannot. Some may spend a small amount, others will assess themselves with a just and reasonable appraisal, so that the "sacrifice of mercy"[19] may not be offered with gloominess, nor be numbered among one's losses. Spend on this work of mercy what justifies your heart, what cleanses your conscience, what, in short, benefits the receiver and the giver.

Happy are those souls and very remarkable who, in the love of doing good, do not fear the loss of their means. They are sure that the one from whom they received what they have already spent will give the means to spend again. But such magnanimity is characteristic of few. It is the fullness of compassion not to desert the care of one's own, so we, without injuring those more perfect, encourage you in general with this rule, to carry out the command of God according to the measure of your "ability."[20] Benevolence should be "cheerful,"[21] and it should temper its own generosity so that through it both the refreshment of the poor may bring rejoicing and one's own supplies will not suffer. "The one who provides seed for the sower and bread for eating will also multiply your seed and will enlarge the growth of the fruits of your justice."[22]

(2) Let us fast, therefore, on Wednesday and Friday. On Saturday, however let us celebrate the vigil together with blessed Peter the apostle. By his merits and prayers we trust that the mercy of God will protect us in all things, through Christ our Lord.

Sermon 89

444

The custom well-known to you, dearly beloved, helps me in preaching, and the course of the season sets off to advantage the duty of the priest, so that what the word of the law demands and the devotion of good will suggests do not seem burden-

---

19. Cf. Sir 35.4.   20. Cf. Tb 4.8.
21. Cf. 2 Cor 9.7.   22. 2 Cor 9.10.

some and hard. When these things come together into one, with the help of God's grace, "the letter" does not "bring death, but the spirit gives life."[23] "Where the Spirit of God is, there is freedom,"[24] for freedom follows the law, not from fear but from love. Obedience softens the command, and we are not driven by a harsh compulsion when we love what is ordered.

When, therefore, dearly beloved, we encourage you on to certain matters set out even in the Old Testament, we are not subjecting you to the yoke of Jewish observance, nor are we suggesting to you the custom of a worldly people. Christian self-denial surpasses their fasts, and, if there is anything in common between us and them in circumstances, there are great differences in our character. Let them have their barefoot processions, and let their pointless fasts show in the sadness of their faces. We, however, show no change in the respectability of our clothes. We do not refrain from any right and necessary work. Instead, we control our freedom in eating by simple frugality, limiting the quantity of our food, but not condemning what God has created.

2. Though all are free to discipline their own bodies by voluntary penances, and to control, at times rather easily and at times more strictly, the bodily lusts which are opposed to the spirit. There ought, nevertheless, on certain days, to be a general fast celebrated together by everyone. Devotion is then more efficacious and more holy when, in the works of mercy, the soul and the understanding of the whole Church is one. Public devotion must be put before one's own, and a special kind of value must be recognized where the common care watches over us.

Let the worship of each single one, therefore, preserve carefully its own diligence, and let each one, asking the help of divine protection, seize the heavenly weapons against the plots of "spiritual wickedness."[25] Soldiers of the Church, even if they can act bravely in private struggles, will fight more safely and successfully if they stand up against the enemy openly in battle formation. Here they not only enter the strife with their own

23. 2 Cor 3.6.
24. 2 Cor 3.17.
25. Cf. Eph 6.12.

strength, but come victorious through the overall war, under the command of the unconquered King in company with the armies of his brothers. Many, fighting together against an enemy are in less danger than one alone. Those are less liable to be wounded whom not only their own courage, but that of others as well, defend with the protecting shield of faith. Where the cause belongs to all, so does the victory.

3. Our adversary incessantly ensnares us with various arts of temptation. The one purpose of his schemes is to be able to draw away from the commands of God those redeemed by the blood of Christ. For this reason, we are bound to take the greatest care not to be wounded by any darts of the enemy. His weapons are not harsh to the senses of the body. In fact, they are all too pleasant to the flesh, in order to harm the soul. For the sense of sight, they draw the eyes to various desires so that, from the beauty of the world, the flames of lust might be kindled, or the errors of superstition might be born. The sense of hearing, through treacherous sounds, is touched with gentle rhythms, so that the stability of the soul might be undermined by enticing music.

In these ways, unsuspecting and ill-prepared hearts may be captivated by the use of fatal sweetness. The protection of divine grace and the teaching of the Gospel doctrine make these wiles of the devil ineffective and harmless. Those who have received the Holy Spirit and in whom the fear of the Lord has been roused, not from dread of punishment but from the love of God, have broken the snares of such deceptions with the unharmed strength of their faith. They use the beauty of all creatures to the glory and praise of their Creator, and love above all things him "through whom all things were made."[26]

4. Let the affection of all the faithful strive to admire him, dearly beloved. From him, let a wise self-restraint seek for itself the delights that are not perishable but eternal. Let unstained chastity burn toward the love of that good without which nothing is good. It is for this reason that the Christian practices have been handed down to us, so that with all unlawful pleasure cut

26. Jn 1.3.

off, we might be ardent for the holy and spiritual delights. Since we ought always to be eager for virtues, certain days have been consecrated to the exercise of common observance, that the soul still bound in earthly desires and hindered by worldly cares might, at least for a short while, be refreshed among divine things. Because this is a portion of the divine field, it may bring forth fruits worthy of the heavenly barns. There is hope of a harvesting where there is care in sowing.

5. Having briefly said all this for your progress at this convenient time, dearly beloved, we call your attention to the fast of September. We remind you not only about abstinence from food but also about the works of mercy. What you give up in your daily life in devout frugality may you pass on as alms for the poor and food for the sick. Be mindful of all the needy in general good will, but "especially" be mindful of those who are members of the body of Christ and who are joined to us in the unity of the Catholic Faith.[27] We owe more to our own in the fellowship of grace than to outsiders in the mutual participation of nature.

6. Let Christian kindness overflow in you, dearly beloved. As you desire the recurring seasons of the year to be filled with fruit, so let your hearts be generous in feeding the poor. Assuredly, God himself could produce the necessary materials for them, since all things are his. He could distribute so much goods to them that they would need nothing from your generosity. Much of the matter of virtue would be lacking to them and to you, if their want did not drive them to the crown of patience nor your abundance lead you to the glory of compassion. Divine Providence has wonderfully arranged it that there should be in the Church both holy poor and good rich people, who in turn benefit each other from their very diversity. In order for the eternal and incorruptible rewards to be gained, those receiving give thanks to God, and those distributing give thanks to God, for as it is written, both "the patience of the poor will not perish forever,"[28] and "God loves a cheerful giver."[29]

27. Cf. Gal 6.10.
28. Ps 9.19.
29. 2 Cor 9.7.

(2) Let us fast, therefore, on Wednesday and Friday. On Saturday, however, let us celebrate the vigil with the blessed apostle Peter, hoping that we shall be so helped by his prayers that the God of mercies, pleased by the sacrifice of the fast, will hear us, through Christ our Lord. Amen.

Sermon 90

445 (Recension A)[30]

Confidently encouraging you with fatherly counsels, dearly beloved, we preach the fast dedicated in September to the exercises of common devotion, sure that what was first the Jewish fast will become Christian by your observance.[31] It is fitting at any time and approved by both Testaments that we should look for divine mercy through the discipline of both mind and body. Nothing is more effective in praying to God than that human beings should judge themselves and never cease from begging for forgiveness, for they knows they are never without sin.[32]

Human nature has this fault in itself, not placed there by the Creator, that from a corruptible body there arises also what can corrupt the soul. This fault was contracted from the one who tried to deceive and it was handed on to posterity by the law of generation. Hence the interior human being, even if already reborn in Christ *and rescued from the chains of captivity*, has constant conflicts with the flesh. As long as people live through **their growing years** *concupiscences*, they suffer in fighting against them. In this struggle there is not easily obtained a victory so perfect that the things which should be broken may not still bind, and the things which ought to be slain may not continue to wound.

---

30. This sermon comes down to us in two recensions. Recension A had been composed in 445. Recension B appears to represent a revision made by Leo himself at some later date. Material found in both recensions will appear in normal text. Material found only in Recension A will appear in **bold**. Material found only in Recension B will appear in *italics*. Some material found in both recensions but in a different order will be reproduced in both bold and italics in their proper order. Some material that does not coincide between the two versions of the Latin text but does not affect the English translation (such as word order or certain syntactical variants) will not be indicated.

31. Cf. Zec 8.19.   32. Cf. Prv 20.9 and 1 Jn 1.8.

However wisely and prudently the spirit may sit as judge over the external senses, temptation is always too near a neighbor to it, even among those very cares and judgments in subduing or nourishing the flesh. Who are able to separate themselves from the pleasure of the body or from pain in such a way that whatever pleases or torments the exterior does not pertain also to the very soul? Joy is undivided, sorrow is inseparable. There is nothing in human beings that anger does not inflame, nothing that happiness does not relax, nothing that grief does not affect. What avoidance of sin can be there where the one passion belongs to both ruler and ruled? Rightly does the Lord say that "the spirit is willing but the flesh is weak."[33]

2. So that despair might not lead us to passive inactivity, the Lord also promises that the things which are impossible to human beings from their own feebleness are possible from divine strength. For "narrow and strait is the road which leads to life,"[34] and none put their foot on it, none make a step toward it, unless Christ himself restores the difficult approach by making himself the Way. The Builder of the road becomes the power of the one walking it, for he both begins the labor and brings it to rest.

In him therefore is our hope of eternal life, and in him also is the pattern of our patience. "If we suffer with him, we shall also reign with him,"[35] since, as the Apostle says, "those who claim that they remain in Christ ought themselves to walk just as Christ walked."[36] Otherwise we are using the likeness of a false profession if we do not follow the commands of him in whose name we glory. And these would indeed not be burdensome to us, and would free us from all dangers, if we would love only what he commands us to love.

3. There are two loves from which all wills proceed, as different in kind as they are separated in their sources. The rational soul, which cannot live without love, is a lover either of God or of the world. In the love for God there can never be an excess; in love for the world, however, everything is potentially harmful.

33. Mt 26.41.
34. Mt 7.14.
35. Rom 8.17 and 2 Tm 2.12.
36. 1 Jn 2.6.

It is therefore necessary to cling steadily to eternal good, but to use temporal things cursorily. We are travelers, hastening to go back to our own country. Whatever happens to us in the good fortune of this world should be only a refreshment on the journey, not the luxury of a home. The Apostle is telling us this when he says: "Time is short. It remains that those who have wives should be as not having them, and those who weep, as though not weeping; those who rejoice, as though not rejoicing; those who buy, as not possessing; and those who enjoy this world, as though not enjoying it. For the figure of this world is passing away."[37]

But we do not easily set aside what pleases us in appearance, in abundance, in variety, unless in the very beauty of visible things we love their Creator rather than the creature. When God says, "You shall love the Lord your God with your whole heart, with your whole mind, and with your whole strength,"[38] he wants us in no way to be released from the chains of his love. When he joins to this command the love of neighbor also,[39] he requires us to imitate his own goodness. We should love what he loves and act as he acts.

Although "we are God's cultivation, we are God's edifice,"[40] and, "neither the one who plants is anything, nor the one who waters, but it is God who gives the growth,"[41] he asks the service of our ministry in all things and wants us to be stewards of his good things, that those who bear the "image of God"[42] should do the will of God. It is for this that we very devoutly say in the Lord's prayer: "Your kingdom come, your will be done as in heaven so also on earth."[43] With these words, what else do we ask than that God should subdue the one whom he has not yet subjected to himself and that, as the angels in heaven, so also on earth he would make human beings the ministers of his will. When we ask this, we love God and love our neighbor. There is one love in us, not diverse loves, when we want the servant to serve and the master to rule.

37. 1 Cor 7.29–31.
38. Mk 12.30.
39. Cf. Mk 12.31.
40. 1 Cor 3.9.
41. 1 Cor 3.7.
42. Cf. Gn 1.27.
43. Mt 6.10.

4. This love then, dearly beloved, from which earthly love is excluded, is strengthened by the habit of good works, because it is inevitable that conscience be pleased by right action, and freely approve what it rejoices in having done. We undertake fasts for this reason, we protect chastity, we increase **alms** *generosity*, we pray often, and it comes about that the desire of each is the prayer of all. Labor nourishes patience, mildness quenches wrath, kindness spurns envy, unclean desires are killed by holy desires, avarice is driven out by generosity, and the burdens of the rich become instruments of virtues.

The devil, however, even in the midst of our efforts, does not relax his schemes. **We, then, must take care, at certain periods of time, of the re-energizing of our strength. At a time when the mind, concerned with the goods of the present, can rejoice in the temperate weather and the fertile fields, and when the fruits are gathered into great barns and it can say to its soul, "You have many good things, eat,"**[44] **it may receive a kind of rebuke from the divine voice, and may hear it saying, "Fool, this very night they demand your soul from you. The things you have prepared, whose will they be?"**[45]

This should be the careful consideration of wise people, that since the days of this life are short and the time uncertain, death should never be unexpected for those who are to die. Those who know that they are mortal should not come to an unprepared end. *Therefore this, which has been proclaimed by the voice of the prophet, should be taken up in the hearts of those praying, so that it may be said, not with the lips only but with the heart: "Guard me, o Lord, as the pupil of your eye; under the shadow of your wings, protect me."*[46] *For we are always in need of divine help. This is the unconquerable courage of human devotion, that we always have a protector without whom we are not able to be brave.*

(2) And so it benefits both the sanctification of the body and the restoration of the soul that we should fast on Wednesday and Friday. On Saturday, however, let us celebrate the vigil with the blessed apostle Peter, **to be aided by his prayers so**

---

44. Lk 12.19. 45. Lk 12.20.
46. Ps 16(17).8.

that we may attain the result of holy desires, through Christ our Lord. Amen. *with the blessed apostle Peter, that the prayer of the most glorious shepherd may support the intercessions of the good sheep, through our Lord Jesus Christ reigning with the Father and with the Holy Spirit forever and ever. Amen.*

Sermon 91

453

There is nothing, dearly beloved, in which divine providence may not aid the devotion of the faithful, for even the elements of the world themselves serve to train souls and bodies to holiness. As the distinctly varied recurrence of days and months reveals certain pages of its rules to us, even the seasons are expressing clearly in a certain way what the sacred laws advise. When the return of the year has brought September back to us, I recognize that your devotion is spiritually aroused to celebrate a solemn fast. You have learned by experience how much this preparation purifies both the exterior and the interior human being, for when you abstain from permitted things, you more easily resist those not permitted. The reason for abstinence, dearly beloved, is not only in disciplining the body, nor in lessening the food. The greater good of this virtue comes from that purity of the soul which not only wears down the desires of the flesh, but also scorns the emptiness of worldly wisdom. As the Apostle says, "Make sure that no one deceives you by philosophy and empty falsehood, according to the tradition of human beings."[47]

2. We must refrain from food, but much more, we must fast from errors. In this way, the mind, not given to any carnal pleasure, will not be the captive of any deception. As in the past, so even in our own day, the "enemies" of the truth[48] are not lacking who dare to incite civil wars within the Catholic Church. They boast that, by inducing inexperienced people to agree with the evil teaching, they have increased the numbers whom

---

47. Col 2.8.
48. Cf. Phil 3.18.

they have been able to separate from the body of Christ. What is so opposed to the prophets, what is so repugnant to the Gospels, what is so antagonistic to apostolic doctrine, as to preach that, in the Lord Jesus Christ, born of the Virgin Mary, and coeternal with the eternal Father beyond time, there is one single nature? If this nature is to be understood as human nature, where is the God who redeems? If this is to be understood only as the nature of God, where is the humanity that is redeemed?

(2) Catholic Faith, resisting all errors, at the same time refutes these evils also, condemning Nestorius, who separates the divine from the human, and repudiating Eutyches, who obliterates the human in the divine. The Son, true God of true God, having unity and equality with the Father and with the Holy Spirit, condescended to be likewise true man, not separated from the flesh either by the conception of his Virgin Mother or by his birth. He united humanity to himself in such a way that he remained God, unchangeable. He imparted divinity to human beings in such a way that he did not destroy, but enriched them, by the glorification. He who was made in the "form of a servant" did not cease to be in the "form of God,"[49] nor is one simply with the other, but he is one in both. From the fact that "the Word was made flesh"[50] our faith need in no way be disturbed by the kinds of appearances, whether in the miracles of virtues or in the insults of the Passion. Let us believe God who is man, and the man who is God.

3. As you profess this confidence with full heart, dearly beloved, cast off the wicked words of the heretics, so that your fasts and alms may not be disfigured by the contagion of any falsehood. For the oblation of the sacrifice is pure and the generosity of mercy is holy when those who bestow it understand what they are doing. Since the Lord said, "If you do not eat the flesh of the Son of Man and drink his blood, you will not have life in you,"[51] you ought to participate in the holy table in such a way that you do not doubt henceforth of the truth of the body and blood of Christ. Faith believes in what the mouth is receiv-

---

49. Cf. Phil 2.6–7.   50. Jn 1.14.
51. Jn 6.53–54.

ing. In vain do they respond "Amen" who argue against what they receive.

(2) As the prophet says, "Blessed is the one who cares for the needy and the poor."[52] Those who distribute clothing and food among the poor are worthy of praise, for they realize that they are clothing and feeding Christ in the needy. Christ himself said: "In so far as you did it to one of my brethren, you did it to me."[53] And so the one Christ is true God and true man, rich in his own,[54] poor in ours. He receives gifts and distributes gifts,[55] sharing mortality and giving life to the dead, "so that at the name of Jesus Christ every knee should bend, of those in the heavens, on earth, and under the earth, and every tongue should confess that the Lord Jesus is in the glory of God the Father,"[56] living and reigning with the Father and with the Holy Spirit forever and ever. Amen.

Sermon 92

454

The Apostles distinguished the Old Testament decrees, dearly beloved, in such a way that they might extract some of them, just as they had been composed, to benefit the teaching of the Gospel. What had for a long time been Jewish custom could become Christian observance, for the Apostles understood that the Lord Jesus Christ had come into the world, "not to destroy the law but to fulfill it."[57] Although the kinds of sacrifices, the differences in baptisms, and the Sabbath rest all ceased when circumcision of the flesh ceased, nevertheless, in these very books, many moral precepts remain for us also.

When it is stated there, "You will love the Lord your God with all your heart," etc. and "You will love your neighbor as yourself,"[58] we know, with Christ the Lord teaching us, that "on these two commandments the whole law depends, and the

52. Ps 40(41).2.
53. Mt 25.40.
54. Cf. 2 Cor 8.9.
55. Cf. Eph 4.8 and 2 Pt 1.17.
56. Phil 2.10–11.
57. Mt 5.17.
58. Dt 6.5. Mt 22.37 and 39.

prophets also."⁵⁹ So great is the union of both Testaments under the mandate of this double charity that, without the binding together of these virtues, neither law nor grace is found to have justified anyone. Also, those parts of the legal commands, by which some things are ordered to be done and some are forbidden to be done, retain the strength of their ancient authority.

(2) On this account, Gospel perfection must not be thought opposed to these, because both the desires for virtues are aroused to greater lengths, and the avenging of crimes is softened by the balm of penitence. The Lord says: "If your justice is not richer than that of the scribes and Pharisees, you will not enter the kingdom of heaven."⁶⁰ How indeed will your justice be richer, unless mercy is "even more so?"⁶¹ What is so "just" and what so "worthy"⁶² as that the creature made "in the image and likeness of God"⁶³ should imitate its Creator? He has determined the "restoration" and sanctification of believers by the "forgiveness of sins,"⁶⁴ so that, when the severity of vengeance is withdrawn and all punishment ceases, the guilty might be returned to innocence and the end of wrongdoing might become the beginning of virtue.

2. When, from the teaching of ancient doctrine, dearly beloved, we undertake the fast of September to purify our souls and bodies, we are not subjecting ourselves to legal burdens. We are embracing the good use of self-restraint that serves the Gospel of Christ. In this too, Christian virtue can "exceed that of the scribes and Pharisees,"⁶⁵ not by making void the law, but by rejecting worldly wisdom. Our fasts ought not to be such as were those about which Isaiah the prophet, with the Holy Spirit speaking in him, said: "Your new moons, and Sabbaths, and great day I do not endure; the fast and free days and festivals my soul hates."⁶⁶

When the Lord gave a form of fasting to his disciples, he said:

---

59. Mt 22.40.
60. Mt 5.20.
61. Cf. Jas 2.13.
62. Cf. the first words of the Preface of the Mass.
63. Cf. Gn 1.26.
64. Cf. Acts 10.43.
65. Cf. Mt 5.20.
66. Is 1.13–14.

"When you fast, do not become sad as the hypocrites do. For they destroy their appearance, to let people know that they are fasting. Amen I tell you, they have had their reward."[67] What reward, if not that of human praise? It is because of their desire for this that they put forward the appearance of justice. Where there is no concern for conscience, they embrace fame with a falsehood, with the result that wickedness, proven by its concealment, enjoys its reputation in a lie.

3. Do not defile your reasonable and holy fast by the boasting of praise and ostentation. May none of the faithful be willing to let their own good depend on human judgments. For those who love God, it is enough to please the one whom they love, for no greater reward can be sought than this love. To this extent is "love from God," that "God" himself "is love."[68] A holy and pure soul is so overjoyed "to be filled with him,"[69] that it wishes "to be pleased" by nothing outside of God.[70] What the Lord says is most surely true: "Where your treasure is, there will your heart be also."[71] What is a person's treasure but a certain harvest of fruits and the completion of labors? "What people sow, this they also reap,"[72] and as their work is, so is their reward. Where there is the delight of enjoyment, there the care of the heart is fixed.

(2) But, since there are many kinds of treasures and different grounds for joy, each one's treasure corresponds to the movement of their desire. If it is an appetite for earthly things, it makes those who share in it not happy but wretched. Those who "savor the things above, not what is on earth,"[73] and are not eager for what perishes but for what is eternal, have hidden, incorruptible resources, in that about which the prophet says: "In your treasure is our salvation. There wisdom and knowledge and holiness are from the Lord. These are the treasures of his justice."[74]

Through them, with God's grace helping us, even earthly goods are transformed into heavenly, as long as many use their

---

67. Mt 6.16.
68. Cf. 1 Jn 4.7 and 8.
69. Cf. Eph 3.19.
70. Cf. Ps 91(92).5.
71. Mt 6.21.
72. Gal 6.8.
73. Cf. Col 3.2.
74. Is 33.6.

wealth, either left them by law or otherwise acquired, as instruments of goodness. When they distribute, from what they can count as overabundance, to the support of the poor, they collect for themselves riches which cannot be lost, so that what they have withdrawn for alms cannot be credited to expense, and they properly keep their heart where they have "their treasure."[75] It is most blessed to use wealth of this kind that it may grow, and not fear lest it be destroyed.

4. Therefore, dearly beloved, we must "do good to all, especially however to those who belong to the household of the faith."[76] Let us set aside September (the seventh month) for the fruits of self-restraint. It has represented from the beginning the mystical sevenfold Spirit and is made holy by its very number in order.

Let us keep the fast, in the custom of the Sabbath, on Wednesday and Friday of the week. On Saturday, however, let us celebrate the vigil with blessed Peter. His prayers and merits will be helping us, so that all may be granted to be able to do as much good as they "wish,"[77] through our Lord Jesus Christ who, with the Father and with the Holy Spirit, lives and reigns forever and ever. Amen.

Sermon 93

(457)?

Every teaching of the divine commandments, dearly beloved, greatly emphasizes this fact in the hearts of the faithful: that honest love may overcome a perverse love, and the delight in justice may destroy the desire for sin. Scripture says: "Do not follow your lusts, but turn yourself away from your own will."[78] But, since in the souls of our people there are many good desires and praiseworthy inclinations, what does it mean to be commanded not to give in to our feelings? It means that, by following this command, we are kept from that lust and recalled from that will, the source of which resides in ourselves.

75. Cf. Mt 6.21.
77. Cf. Phil 2.13.
76. Gal 6.10.
78. Sir 18.30.

For this reason it is called hurtful, because it is clearly shown to be ours.

To distinguish the desires that come from God, it has been well said to us, "Do not follow your lusts,"[79] so that we might know that we should avoid what we recognize as our own. The Lord then, quite rightly, in the prayer he gave us, did not want us to say to God, "Our will be done," but "Your will be done;"[80] that is, not what the flesh arouses but what the Spirit inspires. Those who know themselves to be children of Adam easily understand where this self-indulgence originated, and they should always fight against it. They recognize that, when the father of the human race sinned, what was corrupted in the root was corrupted in the offspring. Although through the grace of our Lord Jesus Christ we have passed "from the old into a new creature"[81] and the "heavenly" human being has lifted us "from the image of the earthly one,"[82] nevertheless, while we bear a mortal body, it is necessary to fight against self-indulgence. It is good for a soul devoted to God to be afraid of "falling,"[83] and to have something to overcome, since "power is made perfect in weakness,"[84] and what trains us in self-control brings us to glory.

2. We must abstain, dearly beloved, from those pleasant things that harm us. The "law of sin which is in our members,"[85] must be superseded by the law of God. Many attractions slip in through all the senses of the body, but the soul for whom God is the highest good and true joy, will live in the breadth of his wisdom and in the light of his truth, among pure and spiritual delights. When human beings of reason compare themselves to themselves and judge all the quality of their acts with a true perception, they will, in the depths of their conscience, never find as much pleasure from a wrong they have committed as from the uprightness they have preserved. Will the pleasure of human enjoyment accomplish for anyone as much as spiritual longing does? Those who prefer to sink into uncleanness rather

79. Sir 18.30.
80. Mt 6.10.
81. Cf. 2 Cor 5.17.
82. Cf. 1 Cor 15.49.
83. Cf. 1 Cor 10.12.
84. 2 Cor 12.9.
85. Rom 7.23.

than to shine in what is holy have known nothing of the good in virtue. They have tasted nothing from the sweetness of holiness.

(2) To hearts not altogether imprisoned, it is against reason that glutted anger should be as pleasing as vengeance which has been relinquished. Things wrongly taken from another do not give as much joy as those properly taken from one's own goods. Frugal moderation is always more fruitful than profuse luxury. There is greater "rest for the humble" than for the proud.[86] That spirit is more exalted which, in the face of prohibitions and promises, considers it more certain to hope for heavenly things than to love worldly things.

That the devout soul might excel in this process and obtain the right of mastering itself, the discipline of fasting must be applied to subdue the body. Although a fast in general seems to apply to all self-restraint, it refers especially to a diminishment in eating. For this reason, it is advantageous now voluntarily not to take the thing whose enjoyment, forbidden in the beginning, brought disaster.[87] As in the former incident, desire resulted in wounding, so here, restraint results in salvation.

3. Although any time is suitable for this remedy, dearly beloved, still we hold this time most fit. We see that it was chosen by the appointment of the apostles and of the laws, that, as in other times of the year, so in September, we should cleanse ourselves by spiritual purification. When our three devotions come together into one design, that is, "prayer, alms, and fasting,"[88] the grace of God furnishes us with a restraint in desires, the granting of our prayers, and forgiveness of sins, through our Lord Jesus Christ, who, with the Father and with the Holy Spirit, lives and reigns for ever and ever. Amen.

Sermon 94

(458)?

I know quite well, dearly beloved, that most of you are so devoted to our Christian observances that you do not need my

---

86. Cf. Mt 11.29.
88. Cf. Tb 12.8.
87. Cf. Gn 2.17 and 3.17–19.

exhortations about them. What tradition long ago settled and custom has established, your learning does not ignore, nor does your goodness omit. The priestly order has the duty, nevertheless, toward all the children of the Church, to have an unbiased care for everything that benefits both unlearned and learned. These whom we love at the same time, we must equally encourage, to celebrate with eager faith, by discipline of soul and body, this fast which September brings back yearly. Although to take a smaller portion of food seems properly to affect the flesh, nevertheless, anything which is either granted or denied to the bodily senses concerns the commanding spirit as much as it does the obeying. Since all people have a twofold law of restraint within themselves, and since nothing we do ought to be referred to the body only, but many things to the soul alone, we ought carefully to notice how improper and how unjust it is if an inferior neglects what a superior imposes. As the rational spirit corrects external things for the soul's health, it ought also to carry out its personal fasts, because it is right to give resistance not only to the desires of flesh, but to the ambitions of the spirit also, as Scripture says: "Do not follow your lusts, turn yourself away from your desires."[89]

(2) Let the one fasting from these things which the flesh seeks fast also from these things which the inner being wrongly desires. The worst food of the soul is to wish for what is not allowed, and a poison of the heart is the delight that feeds on dishonest wealth, or is exalted in pride, or takes pleasure in revenge. Although the motions of the body contribute also to these feelings, all things nevertheless look to their own origin, and there the quality of the action is assessed, where the beginning of the desire is found. To recall the soul from its ill desires is the best and greatest fast, for then abstinence from food is most fruitful when the exterior restraint proceeds from the interior discipline.

2. Since therefore, dearly beloved, we are going to celebrate the true and spiritual fast that sanctifies body and soul with its purity, let us search into the secrets of our hearts and, whether

89. Sir 18.30.

they make us sad or joyful, let us consider them with a careful examination. If there is present any love of vainglory or any root of avarice or germ of hatred, let the soul take nothing of such food, but, intent on the delights of virtues, let it place heavenly feasts before earthly pleasure. People should acknowledge their own dignity, and see themselves as "made in the image and likeness of" their Creator;[90] they should not become so terrified from the sufferings which they meet through that great common sin[91] that they do not bring themselves to the mercy of their Redeemer.

He himself says: "Be holy, for I am holy,"[92] that is to say, choose me and keep from what displeases me. Do what I love, love what I do. If what I order seems difficult, come back to me who order it, so that, from where the command was given, help might be offered. I who furnished the desire will not refuse support. Fast from contradiction, abstain from opposition. Let me be your food and drink. None desire in vain what is mine, for those who stretch out towards me seek me because I first sought them.

3. All the pages of divine Scripture, dearly beloved, are full of these exhortations by which God invites you to unchanging goods and to eternal joys. The teaching of each Testament directs us to this, that we should cling to the truth and hold back from falsehood. We cannot lay hold on what has been promised, unless we have guarded what was ordered. But what is better than that human beings should do the will of God whose "image" they bear,[93] and by abstaining from food should also abstain from the law of sin?

The four seasons of the year have their allotted time for that same observance of restraint. We continue to know, as the course of the whole year returns, that we are unceasingly in need of purification. While we are tossed about in the vicissitudes of this life, we must always struggle, by fasts and alms, to destroy the sin which is caused by the weakness of the flesh and the uncleanness of our desires.

90. Cf. Gn 1.26.
92. Lv 11.44 and 19.2.
91. Cf. Gn 3.17–19.
93. Cf. Gn 1.26 and 27.

4. Let us be a little bit hungry, dearly beloved, and put aside something from our daily custom for better use in helping the poor. Let a sense of good deeds be happy with the fruits of generosity. While giving joy, you will receive what will give you pleasure too. The love of your neighbor is the love of God, who has determined the fulfillment of "the law and the prophets" in this unity of the double charity.[94] None doubt that they offer to God whatever they distribute to human beings, as our Lord and Savior said when he spoke about nourishing and helping the poor: "What you did to one of these, you did to me."[95]

(2) Let us fast, therefore, on Wednesday and Friday. On Saturday, however, let us celebrate the vigil with the blessed apostle Peter, by whose merits and prayers we know we are helped, that by the devotion of our fast we may please the merciful God, through our Lord Jesus Christ, who with the Father and with the Holy Spirit lives and reigns for ever and ever. Amen.

94. Cf. Mt 22.40.
95. Mt 25.40.

ON THE BEATITUDES

Leo introduces the Beatitudes by reminding his audience that, while the Lord effected many bodily cures, he gave special instructions for interior health in the Beatitudes. His meditation on "most happy poverty" is somewhat more detailed than any of the others. By using the last thought on one Beatitude as the first thought on the next Beatitude, Leo links the virtues into a whole, ending with peace and adherence to the will of God.

Sermon 95
(446–461)?

READING FROM THE Holy Gospel according to Matthew. "At that time, Jesus, seeing the crowds, went up onto the mountain and, when he sat down, his disciples came to him," etc.[1]

When our Lord Jesus Christ was "preaching the Gospel of his kingdom," dearly beloved, he was curing different kinds of "illnesses in the whole of Galilee."[2] The reputation of his power was spread through all of "Syria," and "great crowds from all Judea" flocked to the heavenly Healer.[3] The faith of human ignorance is slow in believing what it does not see and in hoping for what it does not know. By physical cures and visible wonders, therefore, divine instruction must stimulate those who need encouragement. In this way, they do not doubt the efficacy of that instruction whose gentle power they were experiencing. Thus the Lord transferred physical benefits into spiritual healing and, after the healing of bodies, he worked also the cure of souls.

Then, going apart from the crowds around him, he went up to the solitude of a nearby mountain. Having summoned his

---

1. Mt 5.1.
2. Cf. Mt 4.23.
3. Cf. Mt 4.24–25.

apostles, he wished to instruct them in the more sublime doctrines. From the height of the mystical place, he showed them, from the very quality of this place and of his work, that it was he himself who had once honored Moses by speaking to him on that mountain, indeed, with a more fearful justice—but on this mountain, with a holier mercy. This was to fulfill what had been promised when Jeremiah the prophet said: "See, the days are coming, says the Lord, and I shall set in order the house of Israel. After those days, says the Lord, I shall give my laws in their minds and in their hearts I shall write them."[4] What he said to Moses he said also to the apostles, and the swift hand of the Word, writing in the hearts of the disciples, established the precepts of the New Testament.

The thickness of cloud did not surround them here as in that earlier time, nor were the people frightened away from the approach to the mountain by terrifying sounds of thunder and flashes of lightning. The gentleness of his message filled the ears of those standing around. The tranquillity of grace smoothed away the sharpness of the law, while the spirit of adoption swept away the fear of servitude.[5]

2. His own sacred expressions, then, tell what is the nature of Christ's teaching, so that those who wish to reach eternal blessedness may recognize the stages which approach to that happy goal. He said: "Blessed are the poor in spirit, for the kingdom of heaven is theirs."[6] It might be doubtful indeed which poor he, as Truth, was speaking about when saying, "Blessed are the poor," if he had added nothing about the kind of "poor" to be understood. It might seem that this neediness alone, which many suffer in heavy and hard necessity, were enough to deserve the kingdom of heaven. But when he said, "Blessed are the poor in spirit," he showed that the kingdom of heaven is to be given to those whom humility of soul commends rather than lack of means. We cannot doubt that the poor attain the virtue of this humility more easily than the rich, as long as in the former mildness is a companion in their need, and in the

---

4. Heb 8.8 and 10. Cf. Jer 31.31 and 33.
5. Cf. Rom 8.15.   6. Mt. 5.3.

latter pride is a companion to their wealth. Nevertheless, even in many of the wealthy is found this spirit that uses its abundance not for the swelling of pride, but for works of kindness. This same spirit names as its greatest riches what it spends on relieving the misery of another's suffering.

To every race and level of mankind it is given to be a partaker of this virtue, for people can be equal in purpose and unequal in property. It does not matter how much they are different in earthly possessions when people are known to be equal in spiritual goods. That poverty is blessed which is not obsessed by the love of temporal things, nor longs to be enriched in the resources of the world, but strives to grow rich in heavenly goods.

3. After the Lord, the first disciples offered us an example of this magnanimous poverty. Having left behind everything of their own without distinction, they were changed by an instant conversion, at the voice of their heavenly teacher, from being catchers of fish, to being "fishers of human beings."[7] They made many to be like themselves by imitating this faith, at the time when among those first-born of the Church there was "one heart and one soul of all the faithful."[8] When all their goods and possessions were dispersed, the people were enriched in eternal goods through this most holy poverty. Because of the apostles' teaching, they were glad "to have nothing" in this world but to "possess all things with Christ."[9]

Thus, "when a lame man requested alms from Peter as he was going up into the temple," the Apostle said, "Silver and gold I do not have, but what I have I give you. In the name of Jesus Christ the Nazarene, get up and walk."[10] What is higher than this lowliness? What is richer than this poverty? It has no resource in money, but it has gifts of nature. The man's mother bore him disabled from her womb. Peter made him whole by a word. He who did not give the image of Caesar on the coin restored the image of Christ in the man. By the riches of this treasure, Peter helped not only the one whose walking was re-

7. Mt 4.19.
9. Cf. 2 Cor. 6.10.
8. Cf. Acts 4.32.
10. Acts 3.1, 3.3, and 3.6.

stored, but also "five thousand men." They then "believed" in the preaching of the Apostle because of the miracle of this cure and its wonder.[11] The poor Apostle who had nothing to give to the petitioner gave such abundance of divine grace that, just as he had set one man on his feet again, so he healed many thousands of the faithful in their hearts. He made eager in Christ those whom he had found limping in Jewish unbelief.

4. After the preaching of this very fruitful poverty, the Lord spoke again, saying: "Blessed are those who mourn, for they will be comforted."[12] These mourners, dearly beloved, to whom eternal consolation is promised, do not share in the feelings of this world. Those laments which are poured out by the weeping of the whole human race do not make anyone blessed. The groans of the holy are of another kind. There is another cause of consecrated tears. Devout sorrow grieves at the sin of another or its own, not at what divine justice does. Religious sorrow grieves at what is committed by human iniquity, where the one doing the evil ought to be more wept for than the one suffering it. Their own malice directs the unjust to their penalty, but patience leads the just to glory.

5. Then the Lord said: "Blessed are the gentle, for they will possess the earth."[13] It is to the gentle and the mild, the humble and the unassuming, and to those prepared to bear all injuries that the possession of the earth is promised. This must not be considered a small or contemptible inheritance, as if it were separated from the heavenly home, for these are the very ones who are understood to enter the kingdom of heaven. The earth promised to the mild, to be given into the possession of the gentle, is the very flesh of the saints. This will be changed by a happy resurrection because of the merit of humility, and will be clothed in the glory of immortality. It will no longer be in any way contrary to the spirit, and will have the harmony of perfect unity with the will of the soul.

Then the exterior person will be the quiet and undisturbed possession of the interior. No obstacles of bodily weakness will

11. Cf. Acts 4.4
12. Mt 5.5
13. Mt 5.4.

hinder the mind intent on seeing God. It will no longer be necessary to say, "A perishable body presses down the soul, and this tent of clay weighs down the mind thinking about many things."[14] The earth will no longer struggle against the one who dwells on it, nor dare anything in excess contrary to the command of its Ruler. The gentle will possess that earth in eternal peace. Nothing will ever be diminished from their rights, because "this corruptible nature will have put on incorruptibility and this mortal nature put on immortality,"[15] so that the risk is transformed into reward, and the burden into a bounty.

6. After this the Lord added: "Blessed are those who hunger and thirst for what is right, for they will be satisfied."[16] This is not bodily hunger. This thirst seeks nothing earthly, but longs to be filled with the good of justice. When it is brought into the hidden place of all mysteries, it hopes "to be filled with the Lord himself."[17] Happy is the soul that wants this food and burns for such a drink, which assuredly it would not be seeking if it had not already tasted something of its sweetness. When it hears the spirit of the prophet saying to it, "Taste and see that the Lord is sweet,"[18] it has received a certain portion of heavenly sweetness and is ardent in love of the purest delight.

The soul then spurns all temporal things and is inflamed to eat and drink justice with all its good will. It comprehends the truth of that first commandment which says, "You shall love the Lord your God with your whole heart, with your whole mind, with all your strength,"[19] since to love God is nothing else than to love justice. Finally, as in that place the care of the neighbor is joined to the love of God, so here the virtue of mercy is united to the desire for justice, and it is said:

7. "Blessed are the merciful, for God will have mercy on them."[20] Realize, o Christian, the dignity of your wisdom, and understand to what rewards you are called by the practice of such teaching. Mercy wants you to be merciful; justice wants you to be just. In this way the Creator will appear in his own

---

14. Wis 9.15.
15. 1 Cor 15.53.
16. Mt 5.6.
17. Cf. Eph 3.19.
18. Ps 33(34).9.
19. Mk 12.30.
20. Mt 5.7.

creature, and "the image of God,"[21] expressed through the paths of imitation, may shine in the mirror of the human heart. Let the faith of those laboring be firm. Your desires will sustain you, and you will possess without end those things you love. Since "all things are clean" for you through your "alms,"[22] you will also come to that beatitude which has been promised in consequence, with the Lord saying:

8. "Blessed are those with a clean heart, for they will see God."[23] What great happiness, dearly beloved, for whom such a reward is prepared! What does it mean to have a clean heart except to be zealous for those virtues spoken of above? What mind can conceive, what tongue can explain the great blessedness it would be to see God? Yet this will be accomplished when human nature is transformed, and then not in a mirror nor in a dim reflection. "Face to face"[24] each one will see that divinity which "no human being can see" as it is.[25] "What the eye has not seen and the ear has not heard, what has not entered the human heart,"[26] each one will obtain through the indescribable joy of eternal contemplation.

Well is this blessedness promised to the clean of heart. Unclean eyesight will not be able to see the splendor of the true light, and what will be true bliss to glowing hearts will indeed be punishment to the tainted. Let the clouds of earthly frivolities be turned away. Let the inner eye be cleansed from all the filth of sin, so that a serene contemplation may be nurtured with the indescribable vision of God. To gain this, we understand that what follows is applicable.

9. "Blessed are the peacemakers, for they will be called children of God."[27] This blessedness, dearly beloved, does not come from any sort of fellowship or some agreement. It is that concerning which the Apostle said, "Have peace with God."[28] It is that about which the prophet David said, "Great peace for those who love your name, and for them there is no stumbling

21. Cf. Gn 1.27.
22. Cf. Lk 11.41.
23. Mt 5.8.
24. Cf. 1 Cor 13.12.
25. Cf. 1 Tm 6.16.
26. 1 Cor 2.9.
27. Mt 5.9.
28. Rom 5.1.

block."[29] The most binding ties of friendship and the most inseparably united similarities of souls do not in reality claim this peace for themselves if they are not in accord with the will of God. Equality in desiring evil acts, treaties of crime, and compacts of wickedness are outside the worthiness of peace.

Love of the world is not in agreement with the love of God. Those who have not separated themselves from a carnal age will not come to the society of the children of God. But those who "are careful to preserve the unity of the Spirit in the bond of peace,"[30] are always in union with the mind of God. They never depart from the eternal law, saying with sincere prayer: "Your will be done, as in heaven, so also on earth."[31]

These are the peacemakers. These are truly of one soul, united in holiness. These will be called eternally by the name of "children of God, co-heirs with Christ."[32] Love of God and love of neighbor will obtain this: that one will feel no adversities, fear no stumbling block, but, when the struggle with all temptations is over, will rest in the quiet peace of God, through our Lord Jesus Christ, who with the Father and with the Holy Spirit lives and reigns forever and ever. Amen.

29. Ps 118(119).165.
31. Mt 6.10.
30. Eph 4.3.
32. Rom 8.17.

AGAINST EUTYCHES

Leo himself clearly indicates how he means to be the prudent physician using preventative remedies for his people. Agents from Alexandria had brought with them the monophysite doctrine that only the nature of the divinity was in Christ, and the real nature of human flesh which he took from Mary was not in him. These newcomers peddled their doctrine in the *Velabrum*, the commercial quarter of Rome near the Tiber, and it was to the Roman workers there, in the Basilica of St. Anastasia, that Leo once again clearly states the doctrine of the Incarnation, inveighing against the heresies of Eutyches, of Photinus, of the Manichaeans, and of Apollinaris.

Sermon 96

25 December 457

UST AS IT IS the duty of skilled and prudent physicians both to prevent by remedies the sufferings of human weakness, and to teach how to avoid things contrary to good health, dearly beloved, so it is the duty of the pastor to take care that the evil of heresy does not harm the flock of the Lord, and to demonstrate how to avoid the wickedness of those wolves and robbers.

Our Holy Fathers have always discovered and rightly condemned the evil of heresy no matter how cleverly it concealed itself. And so it was not able to conceal from our solicitude, which we owe to your affection, the fact that certain Egyptians, principally traders, had come to the City. They were supporting those statements detestably admitted by heretics at Alexandria. These asserted that, in Christ, there was only the nature of the divinity; that he did not have, in his innermost depths, the real nature of human flesh which he took from the Blessed Virgin Mary. What wickedness to say that Christ's manhood was false and that God is able to suffer. We cannot have any doubt about the spirit or the plan by which they dare to do this.

They themselves have withdrawn from the truth of the Gospel. They have followed the lies of the devil, and they wish to make others partners in their perdition.

For this reason we are warning you with the concern of a father and a brother. Do not, in any mood of sympathy, accept the enemies of the Catholic Faith, the enemies of the Church. They deny the Incarnation of the Lord, and they object to the Creed set up by the holy apostles. As the Apostle says, "Avoid heretics after one and a second correction, knowing that people of this kind are perverse and have been condemned by their own judgment."[1]

2. By their own obstinacy have those people been lost, and by their own mindlessness have those gone away from Christ who follow that wickedness through which they know that many before them have perished. They suppose to themselves that that is religious and Catholic which everyone knows the holy Fathers have condemned—in the treachery of Photinus, in the madness of the Manichaeans, and in the insanity of Apollinaris—so that those who deny the Mystery of the Incarnation of the Lord take part in the depravity, for the destruction of their own souls, as if it were still new and not yet condemned.

(2) As if, in the whole Gospel reading, we would be taught something other than that, by this one mystery of divine mercy, the human race is saved in those who believe:[2] that the Only-Begotten Son of God, in all things equal to the Father, by the taking up of our flesh, remaining what he was, deigned to be what he was not, clearly true man, true God, who without the uncleanness of any sin whatsoever, united to himself our nature whole and perfect in the reality both of soul and flesh. Conceived within the womb of the Blessed Virgin Mother by the power of the Holy Spirit, he did not shrink from being brought forth in birth nor from the first beginnings of infancy, so that the Word of God the Father clearly expressed that human substance belonged to himself both in the power of the divinity and in the weakness of humanity, having from his human body bodily actions, from his divinity spiritual powers.

1. Ti 3.10–11.
2. Cf. Rom 1.16.

(3) Surely it is human to be hungry, to be thirsty, to sleep; human it is to fear, to weep, to be sad; finally it is human to be crucified, to die, and to be buried. But it is divine to walk on water, to change water into wine, to raise the dead, to make the world tremble at one's own death, and to ascend, with flesh restored to life, over all the height of heaven. Those who believe this cannot doubt what they ought to ascribe to humanity, what they ought to assign to divinity, because Christ is one in both, who did not lose the power of his divinity and, by being born, undertook the reality of a perfect human being.

3. Consequently, dearly beloved, run away from those about whom we are speaking as if from "fatal poison."[3] Detest, turn aside, and keep away from their conversations, if, having been rebuked, they do not wish to be corrected by you, since, as it has been written: "Their speech crawls like a crab."[4] No communion ought to be granted to those removed by just judgment from the unity of the Church, for they have squandered this, not by our ill will, but by their own crimes. You, therefore, "beloved by God,"[5] and crowned with apostolic testimony, to whom the blessed apostle Paul, teacher of the Gentiles, said: "Because your faith is being proclaimed in the whole world,"[6] protect in yourselves what you know such a great preacher has felt about you.

(2) None of you should be proven a stranger to this praise, so that the infection even of Eutyches would not be able to stain you, whom, with the Holy Spirit teaching, no heresy has violated throughout so many ages. And indeed we trust that the protection of God may guard your hearts and your faith, so that, by keeping the Catholic Faith with constancy into eternity, you might be pleasing to him, whom you have thus far "obeyed" faithfully,[7] through Christ our Lord.

3. Cf. Jas 3.8.
4. 2 Tm 2.17.
5. Cf. Rom 1.7.
6. Rom 1.8.
7. Cf. Rom 16.19.

INDICES

GENERAL INDEX

Numerical References to Leo Indicate Sermon.Section(Subsection)

Aaron, 3.1; 5.3.
Abba, Father, 77.2.
Abel, 60.3.
Abraham, 24.1(3); 26.2(2); 30.4; 30.7; 33.2,3,5; 53.3; 60.3; 63.2,6; 66.2.
abstinence, 13.1; 16.2; 19.2; 20.2,3; 31.3(2); 39.5; 40.4; 42.2,4,5,6; 50.2; 78.2,3; 79.2; 80.1; 86.1; 87.2,3; 88.5; 89.5; 91.1; 94.1(2).
Adam (the first), 12.1; 25.5; 27.6; 28.3,5,6; 30.4; 45.1; 52.1; 59.8; 64.2; 65.4; 69.3(2),5; 93.1.
Adam (the Second), 12.1; 69.3(2),5.
adoption, 26.2(2),3,5; 27.2(2); 29.3,3(2); 30.3,7; 35.2(2),3; 44.1; 49.3; 51.6; 61.5(3); 63.6; 66.2; 72.3; 76.8; 95.1.
Adoptionists, 28.4n.
Alexandria, 96.1.
alms, 8.2; 9.3; 10.3; 11.1; 12.4; 15.2; 16.6; 18.3(2); 19.4; 20.3(2); 41.3; 44.2(2); 45.3,4; 46.4; 48.5; 49.6; 50.3; 71.1; 75.5; 80.1; 87.3; 88.5; 89.5; 90.4; 91.3; 92.3,3; 94.3; 95.7.
almsgiving, 6.1; 9.4; 15.1; 16.2; 17.1; 44.2(2); 49.6; 79.3; 81.3; has a certain strength of baptism, 20.3(2); obliterates sins, 12.4; 49.6; removes faults, 7.1; a work of love, 7.1.
altar, of the cross, 64.3; of the heart, 4.1; of the world, 59.5.
angel(s), 2.2; 4.2; 9.2; 21.2(2); 22.5; 25.5; 26.1,3; 29.1(2); 32.1,3; 35.1(2); 40.3; 44.2(2); 46.2(2); 54.4; 55.5; 57.1; 69.4; 71.3; 73.1(2),4; 74.1(2),4,4(2); the devil and his, 9.2; 26.4(2); of light, 27.3.
anger, 12.1; 18.2; 19.3; 42.6; 42.6; 48.2; 59.3; 60.2; 67.3; 84B.2; 90.1; 93.2(2).
Anna, 30.4.
Annas, 59.2.
Antichrist 34.5.
Antioch, 82.5.
Apollinarianism, 28.4n.; 30.2n.
Apollinaris, 24.5; 47.2; 96.2.
Apostle(s), 3.2,3,4(2); 4.1,2,3; 5.4; 9.3(2); 10.3; 12.1,2,4; 16.3; 17.1; 18.1,3; 19.1,3; 20.1; 23.4,5; 25.1(2),4,4(2),6; 26.3,5(2); 27.6; 29.2(2); 30.1,5,7; 31.3(2); 33.5; 34.4(2); 35.3,4(2); 36.2,4; 38.2,3; 39.4; 40.1; 42.1,2,4; 43.1,3; 45.2; 46.1,2(2),3; 47.1; 49.2; 51.2(2),4,8; 52.4; 59.5; 60.2,3(2),4,4(2); 63.1,2,3,7; 64.3; 65.3,4,5; 66.2; 67.2,3,3(2),4; 68.2; 69.1,4,5; 70.4,5,6; 71.2,3,5(2); 72.3,4(2),6,7; 73.1(2),2,4; 74.3; 75.1,2; 76.4,5; 77.1,2,5; 78.1; 79.2,3; 81.1; 82.1,2,6; 83.1,2,3(2); 84.1; 84B.2; 85.4(2); 90.2; 91.1; 92.1; 93.3; 95.1; 96.1; Creed of, 34.4(2); key of, 49.3; custom of, 9.3; dignity of, 83.1; doctrine of, 91.2; 10.3; 11.1; 44.2; faith of, 51.2; pity of, 34.5(2); precept of, 28.7; 42.2; tradition of, 8.1; 10.1; 12.4; 76.9; 79.1; 96.3.
archangel, 22.2; 30.4; 73.4.
Arianism, 23.2; 28.4n.
Arians, 75.4.

407

Arius, 16.3; 24.5.
Ascension, 26.2; 70.1(2); 73.2,4; 74.1(2); 74.3; 76.1,8; 77.5.
Asia, 82.5.
Augustine, Saint, 32.2n.; 76.2n.
author, of death, 68.2; of good works, 63.7; of life, 55.4; 61.2(2); of their crimes, 67.3(2).
authority, 35.3; 52.1; 57.2; 71.3; 74.2; 75.5; 86.1; 92.1; of the apostolic institutions, 62.2; of the Fathers, 10.1; of the law, 36.1; of Peter, 3.3,4; 4.3; of the prophets, 34.2; of the Redeemer, 40.4; of the Scriptures, 28.2.
avarice, 36.3(2); 40.4; 45.4; 60.4; 67.4; 69.5; 84B.2; 85.2; 90.4; 94.2.

Balaam, 34.2.
Baptism, 18.1; 21.3; 24.3,6(2); 25.5; 34.4(2); 36.3; 41.2; 43.3; 44.1; 60.3,4(2); 63.6; 66.2,5; 67.3; 92.1; differences in baptisms, 15.2; 20.1; of the Holy Spirit, 45.1; of the Lord, 41.2; of regeneration, 7.1; 9.4; renews our nature, 18.1; strength of, 20.3(2); unity of, 4.1; water of, 49.6; 67.3; 69.5; 70.4.
Barabbas 54.5(2); 59.3; 61.2(2).
barbarians, 84.2.
Barnabas, 12.2.
basilica, 27.4.
Basilides, 16.3.
Beatitudes, 95.
belt of continence, 57.2.
Bethlehem, 31.2,3; 32.3; 33.4; 34.1(2),2(2),3; 35.2; 37.4(2).
Birth (of the Lord), 35.1(2); 46.1,2(2); 48.1; 52.1; 67.5; 72.3,7; 74.1,4(2); 91.2(2); 96.2(2).
birthday, 26.2,5(2); 28.2; 29.2; of our submission, 4.4.
bishop(s), 3.4; 5.1,1(2),2,3; 48.1; 72.1; chief office of, 2.1; Pope as Primate of all, 3.4; a Manichaean, 16.4.
Bithynia, 82.5.
blasphemer, 55.1.
blood, 42.5; 57.3,3(2); 58.1(2); 59.2,3; 60.3(2); 62.3; 66.1(2); 70.1(2); 74.3; drink his, 91.3; innocent, 64.3; blood money, 57.3; of the Passion, 69.5; price of his, 74.1; the Savior's, 67.3.
Blood of Christ, 21.3; 35.2(2); 41.3; 48.4; 51.7; 53.3; 54.3; 55.3,5(2); 59.7; 63.7; 65.2; 66.3(2); 68.3; 89.3; 91.3.
body, 58.4(2); 71.2,5(2); 72.7; the Church, 4.1; Peter's, 4.4.
Body of Christ, 2.2; 18.2; 25.5; 28.2,7; 30.7; 42.5; 51.3; 54.3; 59.7; 63.7; 65.5; 69.5; 70.6,6(2); 71.4; 89.5; 91.2,3; Church as, 46.3.
Boy Christ, 35.1(2).
bread, dipped in wine, 58.4; of life, 33.4(2).
breastplate of decision, 57.2.

Caesar, 59.2; 61.1; 61.2(2); 95.3.
Caiaphas, 57.2; 59.2; 82.4.
Cain, 60.3.
Canaan, seed of, 67.4.
Cappadocia, 82.5.
Catholic(s), 26.5(2); 28.5; 42.5; 65.1; Church, 75.5; 77.5; faith, 24.5; 25.3(2),5; 28.4; 30.3; 34.5; 54.1(2); 64.4; 69.5; 96.1,3(2); lapsed from faith, 16.3.
centurion, 68.3(2).
Cerinthus, 28.4n.
Chair of Peter, 2.2.
charity, 2.2; 9.2(2); 14.2; 18.3(2); 19.4; 26.5(2); 28.5; 35.3,4(2); 36.2; 38.4; 43.3; 44.2(2); 45.2; 48.1,3; 49.6; 52.2; 55.5; 58.4(2); 60.4(2); 62.3; 64.5; 66.4(2); 74.5(2); 78.4; 82.4; 85.1; 92.1; 94.4.
chastity, 22.2(2); 39.4,5; 40.5; 55.5; 75.5; 89.4; 90.4.
child (childhood), 22.4; 34.3,3(3); 37.1,2,3(2),4; 46.2(2); 59.4.
child-bearing, 23.1(2); 28.2; 29.2(2); 30.4.
children, 4.4; 33.4; of the Church, 50.2; 76.1; 82.7; of the devil, 42.6; of God, 49.6; 95.9; of the promise, 66.2; of truth, 42.6.
Christ, 3.1; 3.4(2); 4.1; 5.4; 6.2;

GENERAL INDEX

9.2(2); 10.3; 11.1; 12.3; 13.2; 14.2; 17.5; 21.3; 22.1(2),3,6,6(3); 23.4; 24.1,3,4,5,6; 25.3,3(2),6; 26.2,4; 27.1,6; 28.2,4,6; 29.1(2),2(2); 30.2,6,7; 31.2(2),3; 32.1,2,3,4; 33.1,3,4,5(2); 34.2,2(2),5; 35.1(2),2(2); 36.1(2),3; 37.3(2),4(2); 38.2;40.2,3; 42.1,3; 44.3; 45.1,2; 46.1,3,4; 47.1,2; 48.2,5; 49.3; 50.1; 51.1,3,7; 52.2,5; 53.2,3; 54.5(2),5(3); 56.1,3,3(2); 57.4; 58.1,1(2),2,3; 59.3; 60.2,3(2); 61.4; 62.2,4,5; 63.1,2,3,4,6,7; 65.2,3,6; 66.4(2),5; 67.1(2),2,3,6; 68.2,2(2); 69.2,3,3(2),4; 70.1(2),3; 71.4,6; 72.3,4,7; 73.4; 74.1(2),4(2),5(2); 76.7; 82.2; 85.2; 87.4(2); 88.5(2); 90.1,2; 92.2; 95.3; 96.2(3); birth of, 9.4; 22.6; 26.2; 32.1; 33.3; blood of, 21.3; co-heirs with, 41.3; crucified for the world, 54.1; death of, 73.1(2); family of, 26.4; fellowship with, 3.3; hand of, 52.4; has spent himself, 4.2; ineffable kindness of, 9.2; in God, 72.3; in the poor, 6.1; Jesus, 59.8; 64.3; 72.4(2); the Lord, 6.2; 13.2; 17.5; 29.1(2); 39.6; 42.5,5(2); 78.4(2); 81.4; 86.2(2); 92.1; the love of, 36.2; 55.5(2); the man, 30.5; members of, 41.2,3; 69.5; mercy and justice of, 9.1; name of, 16.3; 72.1(2); our Passover, 59.5; 61.5(3); the power of God and the wisdom of God, 21.2(2); reborn in, 4.1; rules as head, 4.2; Savior of the world, 36.1; Son of the living God, 3.2,3; 4.2; 29.1.

Christian(s), 4.1; 8.1; 14.2; 16.1; 16.3; 17.2; 18.2; 20.1; 21.3; 22.4(2),6; 25.6; 26.2; 27.4; 28.5(2); 29.1(2); 30.7; 34.5; 35.4(2); 36.3,3(2); 37.3,4; 38.1; 39.4,5; 40.1,4,5(2); 41.1,2; 44.2(2),7; 45.1; 46.2(2); 47.2; 48.1,2; 49.3,5; 57.5; 60.2,3; 63.2,5; 64.1; 65.4; 66.2,3,3(2); 69.1,5; 70.4,5; 71.4; 72.7; 75.1; 78.2; 79.1,3; 81.1; 82.5; 87.2; 88.2; 89.4; 90.1; 92.1; 94.1; 95.7.

Christianity, 87.1.

Church, 2.2; 3.1,2,3,4(2); 4.1,2,3,4; 5.4; 8.2; 9.3,4; 10.2; 11.2; 16.7; 18.2; 18.3(2); 19.1; 20.1,2; 25.1,5; 26.2; 28.6(2),7; 29.1(2),3; 30.5(2); 33.5(2); 34.4(2),5,5(2); 36.3; 42.5(2),6; 44.1; 46.1; 47.1; 49.5; 51.1,3,8; 58.4(2); 62.2; 63.3,6,7; 66.1,3(2); 68.2,3(2); 72.6; 76.1,7; 78.3; 79.1; 81.1; 82.6; 83.2; 84B.1; 88.2,3; 89.2,6; 95.3; 96.1; body of the, 4.1; 48.1; catholic, 75.5; 79.2; 91.2; chief of the whole, 4.4; 83.3(2); children of the, 58.5; 70.4; 74.2; 74.4(2); 78.2; 79.2; 94.1; holy, 8.2; mouth of the, 75.2; of God, 16.7; 25.1; 36.3; 79.4; prince of the, 60.4(2); universal, 5.2,3; 30.5(2); 64.1; whole as the Body of Christ, 46.3.

circumcision, 22.4; 33.3; 45.2; 59.5; 63.2,5; 66.2; 69.2; 82.5; 92.1; uncircumcision, 45.2; 59.5; 63.2.

city, 59.5; 67.2; 82.1,2,4,6; 83.1; 96.1; of God, 35.4(2); holy city as the Church of God, 66.3(2); priestly and royal, 82.1; royal, 82.1.

Claudius, 84.2.

co-equal, 52.1,2.

co-eternal, 52.1,2.

Collections, 6.2; 7.1; 8.2; 9.3; 10.3; 11.2; 16.1.

command(s), 49.4; 51.8; 67.4; 79.4; 81.1; divine, 49.4; 50.3; God's, 63.2; 88.5; 89.3; of the law, 51.4; 92.1.

Commandments of God 57.5; 66.4(2); 92.1; of circumcision, 69.2; divine, 93.1; first, 95.6;.

constancy, 12.3; 18.3(2); 20.3; 51.7; 60.1,4(2); 68.4; 70.3; 76.5.

Cornerstone, 4.2; 84B.4.

courage, 49.3; 62.4; 63.6; 85.1,2,3; 87.1; 89.2.

covenant, 29.3; 57.2; 75.1.

crab, 16.3; 96.3.

creation, new, 71.6; second, 66.1(2).

Creator, 2.2; 6.1; 11.1; 12.2,3; 16.1;

(Creator *continued*)
19.2; 20.2; 22.5; 23.1,1(2),2,2(2); 24.2,3; 25.4,4(2),5,; 26.1,3,4; 27.4,5; 28.1,2,5; 33.3; 37.1; 38.3; 40.3; 42.3,4,5; 43.1,4(2); 44.1; 54.3; 56.1; 57.4; 62.1(2),2(2); 63.1; 66.1; 70.3; 74.1; 77.2; 87.1; 90.1,3; 92.1(2).

creed, 62.2; 72.7; 96.1; Catholic and Apostolic, 24.6; 46.3.

cross, 25.5; 30.2; 48.1; 49.3; 52.3,5; 53.1(2); 54.5(2); 55.2; 57.4; 59.4; 60.1; 61.3,5; 62.5; 63.4; 65.3; 66.3,3(2); 67.1; 68.2; 70.6(2); 72.5; 73.3; acceptance of, 51.2(2); of Christ, 9.4; 45.4; 46.1; 47.1; 51.8; 55.3; 56.1,2; 58.4(2); 59.5; 60.2; 62.5; 61.5; 64.1; 65.1; 66.3; 67.7; 68.1,3(2); 70.3,4,5; 71.1; 82.5; enemies of Christ's, 42.6; fount of all benediction, cause of all graces, 59.7; a mystery and a sign, 72.1(2); one's own, 47.1; 56.2(2); 70.4; penalty of, 51.7; 59.3; 85.1; power of, 59.7; scandal of, 51.3; sign of, 4.1; 33.4; 55.5; triumph of, 52.4; wood of, 72.7.

crucified, 28.6(2); 30.5(2); 34.4(2); 35.2(2); 46.3; 53.1(2); 54.1; 55.1,2; 57.4; 58.4(2); 59.5,7; 60.3(2); 61.5; 62.2,5; 63.6; 64.1; 65.3,5; 66.5; 67.1(2),3,5; 68.2; 69.4; 70.5,5(2); 71.4; 72.1; crucified in Christ, crowned in Christ, 69.5; crucify!, 61.2(2); Jesus, 66.3(2); Lord, 68.1; thieves with Christ, 55.3.

darkness, 35.2; 42.6; 57.4; 66.3(2); 70.51; children of, 59.1; of ignorance, 61.5(3); of lying, 39.5; powers of, 57.5; 63.7.

David, 3.1; 17.2,3; 24.1(3),3; 25.1(2),4; 28.2,3; 29.1(2),2,2(2),3; 33.5(2); 34.3(2); 35.4; 43.2; 45.2; 55.2; 67.1(2); 79.3; 95.9; Psalms of, 9.4; root of, 21.1(2).

day, the Lord's, 6.2; the first, second, third, 71.2; daylight, 50.2; 53.2.

deacon, 85.2,3,4(2).

deaconries, 8.2.

death, 4.3; 9.2; 15.1; 21.1(2),2; 22.1(2),2,4(2); 24.2,3,4; 25.2,3(2),5; 27.2; 28.3; 29.3; 30.2,3,5; 31.2,2(2); 33.5; 35.4; 36.2,3(2),4; 37.3; 40.2; 42.4; 46.1,2(2); 47.2; 49.2,3; 51.2(2); 52.1; 54.1(2),3,4,5(2); 56.2; 59.8; 60.2; 61.1,2(2),3,4; 63.4; 66.5; 67.7; 68.1; 69.3; 70.1(2),3,4; 72.2,5; 74.1; 76.5; 77.2; 82.6; 83.2; 85.1,2; 90.4; author of, 37.3; 61.4; 68.2; of Christ, 46.1; 51.5; on the cross, 37.3; 72.4(2); 73.4; gates of, 62.2(2); and resurrection of Christ, 66.1(2),5; of the sinner, 50.1; laws of, 51.1; snares of, 57.5; through death to life, 51.8; 71.1(2).

deceit, 9.1; 41.2; 42.4; 46.2(2),3; 51.7; 62.3,4; 63.4; 66.1(2); 80.5; 81.3; 87.1.

deity, 22.4,6,6(3); 25.3,3(2),4,4(2); 28.2,3,4,6,6(2); 30.2,5; 38.2; 42.6; 46.1,2(2); 47.2; 48.1; 51.2(2),6; 52.2; 56.1(2); 59.8; 62.1(2); 64.3,4; 65.1,5; 66.4(2); 67.5; 68.1; 70.3; 71.2; 74.1,4; 76.2; 77.2,4; 91.2,2(2); 96.1,2(2); of the Father, Son, and Holy Spirit as one, 64.2; in Christ, 51.2; in the flesh and the flesh in, 46.2; inviolable, 53.1(2); one in both, 51.6; power of, 65.2; of the Word, 69.5.

deluge, 30.7.

descent, 23.1n.; 29.1n.; 30.1n.

devil, 3.3; 4.3; 8.2; 9.1,2,4; 11.1; 13.1; 15.1; 16.4,5,6; 18.1,3; 20.1(2); 21.1(2),3; 22.1(2),3,4; 23.3; 24.2,6(2); 25.5; 26.4(2); 27.2,3; 35.2; 36.2; 37.2; 39.4; 40.3; 41.2; 42.3,4,6; 44.1; 47.2; 48.2; 49.3; 51.7; 52.1,4; 54.3; 55.3; 56.1(2); 57.5,5(2); 58.3,4,4(2); 59.1; 60.2,3(2); 61.4; 62.3,4; 63.1,6; 64.2; 66.1(2); 67.4; 69.3,4,5; 71.1(2); 72.2; 73.4; 74.5,5(2); 76.4; 76.6,9; 77.2; 82.2; 83.3; 87.1,2; 89.3; 90.4; 90.4; 96.1.

GENERAL INDEX 411

devotion, 2.2(2); 3.4,4(2); 4.1,4;
8.1,2; 9.1,4; 11.2; 12.2,3; 13.1;
15.1; 16.6; 17.1; 18.2,3; 31.3(2);
33.2,4; 34.1; 36.1; 40.4; 41.2,3;
42.6; 44.2(2); 45.1,3; 46.1; 47.1;
48.2; 49.4; 57.1; 60.4(2); 67.5;
69.5; 70.5,5(2); 71.1; 74.1(2),5;
75.5; 76.9; 80.1; 84.1; 85.4(2);
87.3; 88.1,3; 89.2; 90.1; 90.4;
91.1.
disciple(s), 19.1; 26.5(2); 31.3(2);
34.4(2); 37.3(2); 38.3; 47.1;
48.2,3; 51.1,2(2),6; 54.5; 57.1;
60.1,2,4(2); 62.2; 65.4; 67.3(2);
70.1(2),5(2); 71.2,3; 72.6;
73.1(2),2,4; 74.2,4; 75.3;
76.1,3(2),4; 78.1.
discipline, 42.4; 45.4; 49.5; 53.3;
78.1,3; 81.1; 83.1; 87.1(2); 88.5;
89.2; 94.1(2); of the body, 18.3(2);
81.4; 86.1; 91.1; of the Church,
50.2; of fasting, 93.2(2); of the
forty days, 41.2; 42.1; of mind
and body, 90.1; 94.1; of truth,
46.2(2).
divinity, 5.2; 23.2,2(2); 24.1,5; 25.2;
27.1,3; 28.1,4; 29.2(2),3(2);
34.1,3(3); 36.3(2); 38.2,3; 40.3;
51.1,6; 55.1; 68.1,2(2); 69.3;
72.2,5,5(2),6,7; 74.3; 75.3; 76.3;
77.4,5; 83.1; 95.8; 96.2(3).
Docetism (Docetists), 28.4n.; 30.2n.
doctors, blind, 35.2.
drachma, double, 61.1.
dream, 33.4.
dust, 24.2; 25.5; 26.2(2); 28.6; 42.1;
43.3; 46.2(2); 49.2; 53.3.
Dweller, undivided in his own temple, 63.3.

East, 85.4(2); kingdoms of, 32.1; nations of, 32.3.
Egypt, 31.3; 32.1; 33.4(2); 60.2;
64.4; 75.1.
Egyptian(s), 33.4(2); 53.3; 96.1;
plagues, 55.5.
elements (of nature), 4.2; 12.2; 16.1;
18.2,3(2); 44.1; 46.2(2); 53.2;
55.4; 57.4,5(2); 59.7; 61.5;
68.3(2); 91.1.
Elijah, 42.2(3); 51.4,5.

Elizabeth, 21.1(2); 30.4; 35.1(2).
Emmanuel, 23.1(2); 24.1(3);
29.2(2); 72.3.
envy, 18.2; 41.3; 48.2; 49.3,4; 55.2;
57.2; 59.3; 61.1; 77.2; 84B.2;
90.4.
Epiphany (Manifestation), 31.1;
32.1,2; 34.6; 38.2.
episcopate, 4.1.
essence, 24.3; 25.1(2),2,3; 27.1(3),2;
28.4; 29.1; 34.3(3); 51.6; 63.1;
64.2,4; 69.3; 70.3; 71.4; 72.2(2);
75.3; 76.2; 77.1,5.
eternal, 68.1; 69.3; 71.5; 72.5(2);
77.2; 87.4; 89.4; 90.2; 92.3.
eternity, 3.4; 21.1,2; 23.2(2);
35.2(2),3; 70.3; 72.5; 74.1,5; 75.3;
76.7,8; 77.4; 96.3(2); Lord of,
77.5.
Eunomius, 16.3.
Eutyches, 28.5; 91.2(2); 96; 96.3(2).
evangelist, 34.3; 37.3(2); 63.1; 72.6.
Eve, 30.4.
Exodus, 28.6.
expectation, of the nations, 35.2.

faith, 1.1; 2.2(2); 3.2,3,4(2); 4.1,2,3;
5.2,4; 9.1,2,4; 10.1,2,3; 12.1,4;
16.1,5; 18.3(2); 21.1(2);
22.4(2),5,6; 23.3,4;
24.1(2),4,5,6(2); 25.1,1(2),3,4(2);
26.2(2),3,5(2); 27.1,3,6; 28.5(2);
29.1; 30.1; 31.1,2(2); 32.4;
33.2,3,5; 34.1,1(2),2,3;
35.2,2(2),3; 36.1,1(2),2,3,3(2),4;
37.1; 38.2,3; 39.3,4; 40.4; 41.3;
42.1,2(3),4; 44.2(2); 45.3;
46.2,2(2),3; 47.2; 48.3; 49.2;
51.1,3,5,6,8; 52.1; 53.1(2);
55.1,3,5; 56.2; 57.1; 58.4(2);
59.5,6,8(2); 60.1,4(2); 61.5(3);
63.2,6; 64.1,3,5; 66.1,1(2),2;
68.2(2); 69.2,5; 70.1,2,5; 71.4;
73.1,1(2),2,3,4; 74.1(2),2,3,4;
75.5; 76.3; 77.5,6(2); 78.4; 79.2,4;
82.1,5,7; 83.3; 84.2(2); 85.4(2);
87.4(2); 89.2,3; 91.2(2); 94.1;
95.1,3; 96.3(2); bad, 46.1; Catholic, 76.2; 89.5; 91.2; Christian,
57.5; 62.2(2); 65.1; eyes of, 71.4;
household of, 41.3; 92.3; integrity

GENERAL INDEX

(faith *continued*)
of, 63.2; liberty of, 68.3; rule of, 62.2; as the strength of love, 45.2; of the thief, 66.3(2); unity of, 4.1.

faithful, 18.1; 27.5; 43.2; 44.1,2(2); 46.3; 47.1; 48.1; 54.5; 58.5; 59.4; 62.1,6; 63.2; 66.3(2),5; 67.1; 68.4; 70.5(2); 72.6; 74.1(2),5; 75.5; 76.2; 91.1; 92.2; 95.3; unfaithfulness, 46.1.

faithlessness, 33.3; 70.2.

fast(s), 13.1; 14.2; 15.2; 16.2,6; 17.1; 18.2,3(2); 19.2,3,4; 20.1,2,3(2); 39.1,6; 40.4; 41.3; 42.1,2,3,4,6; 46.1,3; 47.1,3; 48.5; 49.1,6; 50.2; 68.4; 71.1; 75.5; 76.9; 78.1,2,3,4; 79.1,2,3,4; 80.1,2; 81.1,2,3,4; 86.2(2); 87.1(2),3; 88.1,3,5(2); 89.5; 90.1,4,4(2); 91.1,2,3; 92.2; 93.3; 94.1,2,3; of forty days, 41.2; 42.3; 43.3; 44.2; 45.1; 46.4; 48.1; 50.1; general, 89.2; 93.2(2); of heretics, 24.6; 34.5; 42.5; 79.2; in honor of the sun and moon, 42.5; meaningless, 79.2; pointless, 89.1; prescribed, 86.1; of September, 86.2(2); 88.3; 89.5; 90.1; 91.1; 92.2; 93.3; 94.1; voluntary, 86.1; 94.1.

fasting, 13.1; 14.1; 15.1; 17.1; 39.1,5; 42.2,4; 44.2; 64.4; 87.3,4(2); 92.2; 94.1(2),2; as act of worship, 12.4; discipline of, 93.2(2); from sin, 50.3; great protection of, 19.2; power of, 87.2; prayer of, 87.2.

father, God the, 1.2; 3.2; 4.2; 5.3; 9.3(2); 17.1; 18.3; 22.2,5; 23.1(2),2(2); 24.3,5,6(2); 25.1(2),2,3,3(2),4(2),5; 26.1,2,3,4,4(2),5,5(2); 27.1,1(3),2; 28.1,3,4,6,6(2); 29.2(2),3; 30.1,5(2),6; 34.1,4(2); 35.4(2); 36.1(2); 38.2,3; 39.5(2)B; 41.3; 43.4(2); 44.3; 45.3; 46.3; 49.6; 50.3; 51.1,3,6,8; 52.1,2,5; 54.2,4; 55.1,5(2); 56.2(2); 58.3,4,4(2),5; 59.5,6; 60.2; 61.3; 62.1(2),2,3; 63.1; 64.2,4; 66.4(2),5; 67.7; 68.1,2,4; 69.3; 70.3; 72.3,4(2),5(2),6,7; 73.3,4; 74.1(2),2,3,4; 75.1,3,3(2),4,5; 76.2,3,5,8; 77.1,2,3,4,5,6,6(2); 78.1; 83.1; 91.2(2); 96.2(2); with Son and Holy Spirit, 12.4; 18.3(2); 19.4; 22.6(3); 27.6(2); 28.7; 29.3(2); 30.7(2); 33.5(2); 34.5(2); 36.4(2); 38.4; 39.6; 40.5(2); 44.3; 45.4; 46.4; 48.5; 49.6; 50.3; 51.8; 62.6; 63.7; 64.5; 65.5; 66.5; 69.5; 70.6(2); 79.4; 82.7; 84.4; 85.4(2); 90.4(2); 91.3(2); 92.4; 93.3; 94.4(2); 95.9; of the Church, 4.2; 9.2,3; 10.1; 11.2; 16.2; 96.2; holy, 7.1; 11.2; 25.4; 66.1(2); 73.1(2); 82.1,7; 96.1; of lies, 46.1; of the nations (Abraham), 26.2(2); 33.2,5; 60.3; father(s) 5.1; 26.4; 28.2; 35.3; 63.2; 66.1.

fear, 3.4; 4.3; 5.2; 20.1; 27.3; 34.4(2); 38.3; 47.1; 51.6; 54.4; 58.5; 60.3(2),4(2); 61.3; 70.5; 73.2; 74.3; 82.4; 89.3; to, 36.4(2); 42.3; 51.7,8; 62.2(2); 70.5(2).

fellowship, 3.3; 4.1,2; 8.1; 9.1,2(2),3(2); 14.2; 15.2; 30.7; 35.4(2); 39.6; 48.1; 49.6; 50.1; 63.1; 69.4; 72.7; 89.5; fellow-disciples, 58.3; with the wicked, 42.6.

festival(s), 5.1; 44.3; 47.1; 48.1; 50.1; 58.2; 60.2; 61.5(3); 68.4; 72.5,6; 76.8; 77.1; 92.2; Jewish, 54.5(2); 58.2.

fig tree, 18.3.

fire, 9.2; 10.2; 18.3; 45.4; 49.6,7; 85.3,4; of God's love, 12.1; 50.2; of holy charity, 52.4.

flesh, 1.2; 4.2; 5.1(2),2; 15.1; 19.1; 20.1; 21.3; 22.1,2,2(2),3,5,6(3); 23.5; 24.2(2),3,5,6; 25.2,4,5; 26.1,2(2),3; 27.2,2(2); 28.4,5,7; 29.1(2),2(2); 30.2,3,4,4(2); 31.2(2); 34.4,5; 54.2; 55.1; 69.3,3(2),4,5; 70.3,4,5; 71.2,3,4,5(2),6(2); 72.2,3,4,5,7; 73.2,3; 74.1(2),2,4,4(2); 76.9; 77.2,5; 78.1,2; 81.2; 83.1; 89.3; 90.1; 91.1,3; 93.1; 94.1; 96.2; lusts of, 69.5.

GENERAL INDEX

food, 9.2(2); 14.2(2); 19.1; 20.1,3(2); 44.2; 45.3; 50.2; 58.3; 64.4; 66.4(2); 69.2; 78.4; 80.1; 81.1,2; 85.2; 87.3,4; 89.1,5; 91.1,2,3(2); 94.1; 95.6; of wrong, 46.1; worst of the soul, 94.1(2).
foreigner(s), 12.2; 27.2(3); 32.2; 33.2.
forgive (forgiveness), 15.1; 33.1(3); 39.5(2); 39.6; 40.5(2); 43.4; 44.3; 45.1; 46.4; 48.4; 49.5; 50.2,3; 52.5; 55.1; 62.3,4,6; 65.3; 70.2; 76.4; 84.1; 90.1; 92.1(2); 93.3.
form, of glory, 51.6; of God, 23.2(2); 30.5(2),6; 34.1; 53.1(2); 63.4; 64.2; 69.3,5; 72.4(2); 77.5; 91.2(2); of the Lord, 46.2; of man, 31.2(2); 72.2; of a servant, 23.2(2); 30.5(2),6; 34.1; 46.2(2); 51.6; 53.1(2); 65.3; 69.3,5; 72.4(2); 74.1; 77.5; 91.2(2); of sinful flesh, 63.4; of a slave, 46.1.
Fotinus, see Photinus.
frankincense, 33.2; 34.3; 36.1(2).
Friday, 12.4; 13.2; 15.3; 16.7; 17.5; 18.3; 19.4; 42.6; 75.5; 76.9; 78.4(2); 81.4; 86.2(2); 88.5(2); 89.6(2); 90.4; 92.4; 94.4.
friend (friendship), 12.1; 16.1; 26.3,5(2); 46.2(2); with the holy angels, 35.4(2).
fruit(s), 13.1; 16.1; 17.1; 18.3; 19.2; 35.4; 90.4; of charity, 17.1; of devotion, 18.3; of mercy, 87.4; forbidden, 87.1; as reward, 9.1; 10.3; 14.1; 18.3(2); 20.3(2); 40.4; 50.3; 60.4; 66.3.

Gabriel, 26.1; 29.1(2).
Galatia, 82.5.
Galilee, 74.4; 95.1.
games, of the Circus, 84.1.
Gardener, Supreme, 81.3.
garments (priestly), 57.2.
genealogy, 3.1.
generosity, 6.1; 8.2; 10.1,2; 14.2; 15.2; 16.2; 17.1,4; 19.4; 26.3; 32.4(2); 40.4; 43.4; 45.4; 47.1; 48.5; 50.3; 67.8; 69.1; 76.1,3(2); 80.2; 86.2(2); 87.3; 88.4,5; 89.6; 90.4; 94.4; abolishes greed, 18.2; of the divine goodness, 16.1, 17.1; of grace, 49.3; of love, 74.5(2); of mercy, 87.4;
generous, 42.2; 86.2.
Gentile(s), 8.1; 26.5(2); 32.2; 35.1(2),4(2); 38.1; 56.1; 70.2; 71.4.
gift(s), 2.1; 3.1; 5.1; 10.3; 11.2; 12.3; 22.1(2); 23.4,5; 24.1; 26.3,4; 30.1; 31.2(2),4; 33.2; 34.2,3; 36.1,1(2); 38.1,3; 39.2,6; 40.4; 42.1,3; 44.2(2); 45.1; 49.1; 53.1(2); 61.5(3); 63.7; 67.1,3,6; 72.6; 75.1,4,5; 76.1,3(2),8; 77.1; 79.1,2,4; 81.1,3; 87.4; 91.3(2); of the Holy Spirit, named, 76.7; 88.3.
glory, 3.1,4(2); 4.2; 9.3(2); 10.2; 19.3; 21.2; 22.2; 23.2,5; 24.2(2); 25.5,6; 27.1,1(2-3),6; 29.1(2),2; 32.3; 33.4,5; 35.4; 36.3; 37.3(2),4(2); 44.2(2); 45.2,4; 46.1,2(2),3; 50.1; 51.2(2),3,4; 53.3; 55.1; 56.2; 59.5,6,7; 61.3; 66.4,4(2); 67.6; 69.1,4; 70.3; 72.1,2,6,7; 74.1,4; 76.2; 77.3,5; 79.3,4; 85.4; of God the Father, 12.2; 29.2; 38.2; 66.5; 72.4(2); 91.3(2); to glory, 22.5; 29.3(2); 38.4; 48.2; 85.4(2); 88.4; 90.2; of martyrdom, 36.2; of the Passion, 59.7.
God, 1.1,2; 2.1; 3.3,4,4(2); 4.1,4; 5.3,4,5; 8.1; 9.1,2(2),4; 10.1,2,3; 11.2; 12.1,2,3; 13.1; 14.2; 15.1; 16.1,3,6; 17.2,3,4; 18.1; 19.2,3; 20.1,2,3; 21.2,3; 22.1(2),2,6(2); 23.1(2),2(2),4,5; 24.1,1(3),2,3,5; 25.4,4(2),5; 26.1,2(2),3,4,5; 27.1(2),2(2),4,5,6; 28.1,4; 29.1(2),2(2); 30.2,3; 31.1; 32.4; 33.1(2),3,5; 34.3(3),5; 35.1,3,4,4(2); 36.1,4,4(2); 37.1,2,3; 38.3,4; 39.2,3,4; 40.3; 41.3; 42.1,2; 43.3,4(2); 44.1; 45.1,2; 46.2(2),3,4; 47.3; 48.3,4; 49.4; 50.1,3; 51.1,2(2); 52.1,5; 53.3; 54.4; 55.5; 56.1(2),2(2),3(3); 57.2,5(2); 58.4(2); 60.2; 61.1;

(God *continued*)
  62.1,2; 63.1,6; 64.3; 65.1,2,3,5;
  66.1(2),3; 67.2,5,7,8; 68.1,2(2);
  69.1,3,4,5; 70.2,3; 71.1(2); 72.2,3;
  73.3,4; 74.1,5(2); 75.1,2; 76.8;
  77.3; 82.2; 87.4(2); 89.6;
  91.2(2),3,(2); 92.3, 93.1.
gold, 33.2; 34.3; 36.1(2).
Golgatha, 57.4.
Good News, 26.1; 35.1(2); 46.1.
Gospel, 3.2,4(2); 9.1; 17.1; 18.3;
  19.2; 20.1; 23.4; 24.1(2); 27.1(2);
  28.4,5; 29.1(2),2(2); 30.3; 31.2(2);
  33.1; 34.4(2); 35.1; 36.1; 38.1;
  40.3; 41.3; 42.3; 46.2,2(2); 48.3;
  51.1,4; 52.1; 56.1; 58.1; 59.7;
  60.1; 62.6; 63.5; 64.1; 65.1;
  66.1,2; 69.1,3; 70.1; 72.1,7;
  73.1(2); 74.2; 75.1; 76.5,6,8; 77.5;
  82.1,3,5; 83.1; 91.2; 92.1,1(2),2;
  96.2(2); light of, 35.2; of peace,
  39.4; teaching of, 51.8; 75.2; 89.3;
  truth of, 47.2; 67.1; 96.1.
government, of the Church, 2.2(2);
  3.3; divine, 77.1.
grace(s), 2.1,2,2(2); 3.1; 4.1,2,3,4;
  9.2(2),4; 12.1; 16.1; 18.2; 22.5,6;
  23.4; 25.4(2); 26.2(2),4(2),5;
  27.2(2),6; 28.3; 29.3; 31.2; 32.1;
  33.1(3),5; 34.1(2); 35.1(2), 35.2,3;
  37.1; 38.1,3; 41.3; 42.1; 48.1,2,4;
  49.3; 51.4; 58.5; 61.5(2); 63.5;
  66.2; 67.1; 69.2; 70.5(2); 73.4;
  75.1; 82.4; 92.1; 93.1; 95.1,3; divine, 36.1; 67.5; 78.2,3; 83.3(2);
  of the fast, 79.1; of God, 35.3;
  39.1,6; 43.1,4(2); 51.1; 55.5; 57.1;
  58.1,5; 59.1; 60.1; 62.6; 66.5;
  67.3,6; 68.4; 70.6(2); 71.1; 72.5;
  74.1(2); 82.6,7; 89.1; 92.3; 93.3;
  Gospel of, 20.1.
greed, 9.1; 10.2; 18.2; 32.4(2); 36.3;
  40.2; 41.1; 42.4; 47.1; 74.5; 81.1.
Greek, 63.2.

handicapped (by various disabilities), 48.5.
hate (hatred), 16.3; 19.3; 32.4;
  36.3(2); 37.4(2); 38.3; 40.2,5;
  41.2,3; 42.6; 42.6; 43.1; 45.4;
  47.1; 48.2; 49.6; 58.2,4,5; 59.2,3;
  62.3; 66.3; 73.4; 85.3; 94.2; of the devil, 70.5(2); 71.1.
headdress, 57.2.
heart(s), 2.1; 3.3; 9.1; 11.1; 12.2,3;
  14.2; 16.1; 17.1,4; 18.2; 19.1;
  22.6; 23.1,5; 24.2,6; 26.5(2);
  27.5,6; 28.6,7; 30.1,4; 31.3(2);
  32.2,3,4; 34.1; 35.3; 36.1,4; 37.1;
  38.3,4; 39.1,2; 42.1,5(2);
  43.1,2,3,4; 44.1; 46.1,3; 47.1,3;
  48.3; 49.2,3,4; 50.1,2; 51.2(2),3;
  52.1; 54.3,5; 57.3,3(2); 58.3; 60.4;
  61.2,5; 62.2,3; 65.3; 66.3(2),4;
  67.1,1(2); 74.1(2),5,5(2);
  75.1,3(2); 78.1; 79.1,3; 84.1;
  84B.2; 89.6; 90.4; 91.1,3;
  94.1(2),2; 95.1,3,8; 96.3(2); altar
  of, 4.1; evil, 62.4; hardness of,
  68.2(2); inner ear of, 45.1; of the
  Jews, 67.3.
heaven(s), 3.2; 3.3,4(2); 4.2,3; 6.1;
  9.2(2); 10.2; 12.2; 19.2; 21.2(2);
  26.1,5(2); 27.2(2); 32.1,3,4; 33.2;
  34.1(2); 35.2; 37.1; 39.2,3; 42.4;
  44.1; 45.3; 46.2(2); 51.7; 53.2;
  57.4; 58.4(2); 65.5; 66.4(2);
  72.3,7; 73.4; 74.2; 75.2; 85.4;
  92.1(2); citizens of, 46.4; illumination of, 69.1; lights of, 59.7.
Hebrew, leaders, 34.2(2); 59.5; 72.6;
  people, 33.4(2); 39.1; 75.1.
hell, 4.2; 35.4; 57.4; fire of, 45.4;
  gates of, 3.3; 4.3; 51.1.
heresy (heresies), 16.4; 24.5; 30.3.
heretic(s), 16.3; 25.3(2); 26.5; 28.4;
  36.2; 46.3; 65.3,4; 69.5; 72.4,5;
  77.6; 79.2; 91.3; 96.1.
heretical, 30.5; evil, 96.1; madness,
  3.3; man, 96.1; ungodliness, 96.1.
Herod, 31.2(2),3; 32.1,3; 33.2,3,4;
  34.2(2); 35.2; 36.2; 38.1; 64.4;
  67.2.
hierarchy, 5.1.(2).
holiness, 37.1; 43.2; 50.2; 63.2;
  72.7.
Holy of Holies, 59.7; 61.5; 68.3.
Holy Spirit, 3.1; 4.4; 9.4; 12.4;
  18.3(2); 19.2,4; 21.1(2),3;
  22.2,3(2),6(3); 23.5; 24.1(3),3,5,6;
  25.1(2),2,5; 26.1,3,5(2);
  27.1(2),2,6; 28.1,4,7; 29.1(2),3(2);

30.3,7(2); 33.5(2); 34.3,4,4(2);
35.1(2); 35.2; 36.4(2); 38.1,4;
39.6; 40.5(2); 42.6; 43.1; 44.3;
45.4; 46.2; 47.1; 48.5; 50.2,3;
51.8; 55.5(2); 57.5(2); 62.2,6;
63.6,7; 67.1(2); 68.2(2),4; 69.4,5;
70.4,6(2); 71.3,6(2); 72.3,5(2),7;
73.2; 73.4; 74(2),5(2);
75.1,2,3,4,5;
76.1,2,3,3(2),4,5,6,8,9; 77.1,
2,3,4,6(2); 78.1,3; 79.3,4; 81.1,3;
82.3; 82.7; 84B.4; 85.4(2); 89.3;
90.4(2); 91.2(2),3(2); dwelling
places of, 42.6; gift(s) of, 67.3;
74.3; 76.9; teaching of, 41.2; 79.1;
unction of, 4.1.
homoousios, 30.6.
honor, 1.1; 2.1,2; 5.5; 9.3(2); 16.4,5;
21.1(2); 22.1(2),6; 24.2(2),4; 25.5;
26.4; 34.3; 35.4(2); 42.2(2); 47.2;
48.1; 51.3; 53.3; 55.5(2); 56.3;
74.5(2); 77.2; 85.2; of the apostolic order, 58.3; priestly, 57.2.
hope, 3.4(2); 11.1; 18.3(2); 22.6;
26.5(2); 27.6; 29.2(2); 32.4; 33.4;
34.4(2); 46.4; 49.2; 51.3; 53.2;
55.5; 63.2; 66.4; 69.5; 74.1(2);
87.4; Christian, 56.1; 65.5; pattern of all, 71.4; to hope, 38.4;
45.2; 95.1.
Hosea, 59.8.
human being(s), 4.2; 5.2,3; 8.2;
9.1,2(2),4; 10.1; 11.1; 12.1;
14.2(2); 16.4,5; 18.2; 20.2; 21.2;
22.1(2),3(2); 24.2,3,6(2);
25.2,3,4(2),5; 26.1,2,4;
27.2(2),5,5(2); 28.1,2,3,4,5,6(2);
29.1(2),2,2(2); 30.4,5(2),6,7(2);
31.1,2(2); 33.1(3); 34.1,2,3(3),4,5;
35.1,4(2); 36.1,4,4(2); 37.2,3;
38.2,3; 39.5(2); 40.3,4; 41.3;
42.3,4,5; 43.1,2,4(2); 44.2(2);
45.3; 46.2(2),4; 48.2; 50.3; 51.4;
52.1,2,5(2); 54.1(2); 58.4(2); 62.2;
64.4; 67.3; 68.1; 69.5; 70.3; 71.2;
72.4(2),3; 74.1(2); 76.8; 77.2;
85.4(2); 91.2(2); 95.3; new,
22.3(3); 56.1(2).
humanity, 16.1; 22.2; 31.1; 33.1(3);
40.2; 70.5(2); 96.1; assumed,
72.6; 74.1; true, 69.3.

humeral (of strength), 57.2.
humility, 3.4; 9.3(2); 20.1(2);
21.1(2),2; 23.2(2),5; 25.1,2,3,5,6;
26.2; 28.3; 29.2,3; 31.3(2); 32.4
(2); 37.2,3,3(2),4(2); 38.2,3; 39.5;
41.2; 42.6; 47.2; 51.3,7; 52.2,3;
53.3; 54.4; 55.3; 58.1; 61.1;
62.1(2),3; 66.4(2); 67.6; 68.1;
69.3(2); 72.4(2),5; 74.1,1(2); 77.3;
84B.2; 86.1; 87.3; 95.2,3,5; casts
out arrogance, 18.2; of the Divinity, 52.2; love of, 44.3; of the man,
70.3; mystery of, 63.1; toward,
2.2(2).
hypocrisy (hypocrites), 9.1; 36.2;
57.3; 92.2.

image, of Christ, 95.3; of God, 41.3;
43.3; 49.4; 90.3; 95.7; and likeness, 45.2; 77.2; 92.1(2); 94.2; of
mercy, 44.2; 65.2.
immortality, 22.1(2); of the flesh,
73.2; of the soul, 73.2.
Incarnation, 22.5; 23.4; 27.1;
28.4,5(2); 46.3; 47.3; 64.1;
66.1(2),5; 68.1; 69.5; 72.5; 77.5;
96.1,2.
incense (frankincense), 33.2;
34.3(2),3(3),5; 36.1(2).
indwelling, 30.3(2).
infancy, 34.3(2),3(3),5; 35.2; 37.2,4;
38.2.
infant, 37.1.
Isaiah, 12.1; 23.1(2); 24.1(3),3; 28.6;
29.2(2),3; 33.5; 36.1; 45.1; 55.2;
58.4(2); 59.4; 65.3; 72.3; 92.2.
Israel,5.2; 26.3; 29.2,2(2); 31.3;
32.3; 33.1,3; 34.1(2),2,2(2); 35.2;
55.2; 60.2; 61.5(3); 66.2; 67.2;
68.2; 70.2; 79.3; 88.1; 95.1.
Israelite(s), 26.2; 30.7; 32.2; 35.1(2);
39.1; 59.5; 66.2; 70.3; priests,
68.3(2).

Jacob, 30.4; 34.2; 35.2.
James, Apostle, 49.4; 51.2(2).
Jeremiah, 30.4; 95.1.
Jerusalem, 21.2(2); 31.2; 32.2; 34.2;
51.2; 85.4(2); daughters of, 61.3;
people of, 21.2(2).
Jesse, 24.1(3); 30.4.

Jesus, 22.2; 24.6(2); 25.5, 26.2; 29.1,2; 30.2,4; 31.3,3(2); 34.3,5; 36.1; 37.2; 44.2(2); 46.2; 51.2,2(2),4,5; 52.3; 53.1(2); 54.4,5(2); 55.1; 56.2; 57.1,2,3,4; 58.2,3; 59.2,3,6; 63.2; 65.4; 66.3; 67.2,5; 68.2,2(2); 69.2; 72.1,2,3; 74.4,4(2); 76.8; 83.1; Christ our Lord, 25.1; 40.3; 53.3; as Lord, 75.4; 76.4; name of, 72.4(2); 91.3; of Nazareth, 65.2; 95.3; put to death, 35.2; works of, 61.2.

Jews, 26.5; 28.2; 29.2(2); 31.2(2); 32.2,3,4; 33.2; 34.2; 35.2; 36.2; 52.5; 53.2; 54.5(2); 55.1,2,4; 56.1; 57.3,4; 59.1,5; 60.2,3,3(2); 61.1,2(2); 62.3,5; 63.2; 65.3; 66.2; 67.2; 68.2(2),3(2),4; 70.1(2),3; 79.2; angry, 70.1(2); blinded, 65.3; blindness of, 35.1(2); 56.2; 57.1; chiefs of, 60.2; 61.2(2),5; crime of, 59.2,7; 70.2; false, 59.3; hostile, 53.1(2); malice of, 60.2; 67.2; sacrilegious chiefs of, 58.1; 59.3; savagery of, 82.4; three thousand baptized, 62.3; unhappy, 59.4; violence of, 72.2; wickedness of, 76.4; worldly, 16.4; 29.3; 60.2; wrath of, 65.2.

Jewish, 5.3; 33.3; 34.2(2); 92.1; disbelief, 95.3; fast, 90.1; observances, 89.1; offenses, 56.1; transgressions, 88.1; wickedness, 61.1; 66.4; 73.1.

Job, 27.5; 47.1.

Joel, Prophet, 88.1.

John, Apostle, 12.1; 26.4(2); 27.1(2); 30.3,5(2); 34.5; 37.3; 41.1; 48.1; 51.2(2),4; 52.3; 58.4,4(2); 63.5; 64.4; 70.2; 76.8; Gospel of, 48.3.

John, Baptizer, 30.4; 35.1; 45.1.

Jonah, son of, 3.2.

Joseph, the true, 33.4(2); Saint, 35.1(2).

joy, 3.4,4(2); 4.1,2; 5.1,5; 9.3(2); 17.4; 20.1; 21.1; 22.6; 23.1,5; 26.5(2); 27.3; 29.1(2); 30.4; 31.1; 33.5; 35.4(2); 36.1; 42.2,5; 49.1; 50.2; 51.1,5; 60.2; 62.1; 73.4; 74.3; 77.5; 78.3; 81.3; 84.1; 90.1; 92.3; 93.2; 94.4;; dangerous, 35.4 spiritual, 74.5; 80.1; 85.4(2).

Judah, 32.3; 33.2; 34.2(2),3(2); 35.2; 67.4.

Judas Iscariot, 52.3,5; 53.1(2); 54.2; 56.3; 58.3,4,4(2); 60.3(2),4; 62.4.

Judea, 33.3; 34.2(2); 35.1(2); 95.1; temple in, 59.7.

judge, 1.2; 2.1; 5.4; 8.2; 9.2,(2); 14.2; 18.3; 43.3,4; 49.4; 54.5(2); 59.2; 62.4; 86.2; 90.1; to judge, 11.1; 30.5(2); 31.2; 35.3; 39.1; 42.2(3); 46.3; 48.3; 57.3; 63.4; 74.2,4(2); 90.4.

judgment, 1.1,2; 9.1; 10.2; 12.2,3; 22.5,6(3); 26.4(2); 28.3; 35.3; 39.6; 41.1; 42.5; 43.3; 47.3; 49.5; 50.3; 52.3; 54.5(2); 55.4; 72.1; 75.4; 76.4; 81.2; 92.2; 96.1; of God, 45.4; 70.4; of Peter, 3.3; 51.1 of philosophy, 82.3.

justice, 2.1; 4.3; 5.2; 9.2; 12.2; 17.1; 18.2; 20.2,3; 22.1(2),3; 24.2,2(2),3,6(2); 25.5; 28.3; 29.3; 33.1(3),5(2); 37.3; 40.4; 42.2(2),6; 43.2,4; 51.1,8; 52.2,5; 58.2; 60.4; 67.6; 69.3; 70.2,5; 71.1(2); 77.1; 85.1; 86.2; 87.1; 92.1(2),2; 93.1; 95.1,6; divine, 35.3; 41.1; 70.5(2); 88.1; 95.4,6; of God, 9.1; 50.2; 79.3; of reason, 64.2; patterns of, 62.6; supreme, 67.2.

kindness, 6.1; 9.3(2); 10.2; 12.2,3; 15.2; 17.3; 23.4; 24.1; 35.3,4; 38.3; 40.4; 42.2(3),6; 43.4,4(2); 44.1; 45.3,4; 46.2(2); 48.5; 49.5; 50.1; 56.1; 58.3; 62.4; 67.3(2); 69.4; 74.5(2); 77.1; 82.2; 85.1; 87.3; 89.6; 90.4; 95.2; abolishes envy, 18.2; 20.3.

king, 9.3(2); 15.1; 26.4(2); 29.2(2); 31.2; 32.1; 33.2,3,4,5(2); 35.2; 36.1(2),2,3; 43.2; 45.3; 48.1; 53.1(2); 61.1; 67.6; 87.1(2); 89.2; highway of, 53.3; threats of, 5.4.

kingdom, 35.2; 37.3(2); 51.2(2); 53.1(2); 54.5(2); 59.7; 68.3; 95.1; of the devil, 60.3(2); of God, 19.1; 21.3; 31.2(2); 33.5(2); 38.4; of heaven, 3.3; 22.5; 32.4; 35.3;

GENERAL INDEX 417

37.3(2); 45.4; 61.5(3); 92.1(2); 95.2,5; Jewish, 33.3; keys of the, 3.2; 4.3; 73.2; 83.2,3(2); prepared, 45.3; of wickedness, 35.2; of the world, 42.3.

lamb, 33.4(2); 59.5; 60.2; sacrifice of, 75.1.

Lamb of God, 35.1(2); 56.3(2); 59.7; 64.4; 70.2; 75.1; blood of the Spotless, 55.3,5; Immaculate, 66.3; Paschal, 69.2; True, 58.1(2); 68.3.

lamps, of your spirit, 35.4(2).

law, 9.4; 20.1,3; 22.4; 23.2(2); 24.2(2); 25.4; 26.2(2); 27.1(2); 30.3; 33.1(2); 34.3(2),4(2); 39.3; 47.2; 57.3; 58.1(2),2; 59.7; 61.5(2); 63.5; 66.2; 68.3(2); 70.2; 75.1; 91.1; 92.1,2,3; 93.3; 94.4; 95.1,9; of death, 69.3; doctors of, 61.5; of equity, 21.1(2); given through Moses, 51.4; of God, 22.3(2); 93.2; knowledge of, 36.2; and the prophets, 54.5(2); of restraint, 94.1; of the (Roman) Empire, 82.1; of the spirit, of the body, 70.5(2); tyranical, 40.2; word of, 89.1.

Lawrence, Saint, 85.2,4(2).

Lent, 39.2(2),3,3n.; 42.6; fast of, 40.1; observance of, 71.1(2); 73.1.

Levites, a higher order of, 59.7.

life, 1.2; 2.1; 3.4; 10.3; 12.1,4; 15.2; 16.1; 18.1; 19.1; 21.1; 23.5; 24.2(2),6,6(2); 25.1(2),5,6; 26.4; 27.1(3),6; 30.5(2); 31.3(2); 33.5(2); 35.4(2); 37.1; 39.6; 45.1; 46.4; 47.2; 48.3; 49.2,4; 51.1,7; 53.1(2); 54.4; 58.3; 59.6,8(2); 63.3; 66.4; 68.2; 70.3; 71.6; 90.4; author of, 54.5(2),4; end of this, 35.4; eternal, 57.5; 58.4(2); 63.3; 87.1; of the faithful, 45.2; hidden, 50.1; 51.3; of the holy ones, 35.3; human, 47.1; newness of, 66.5; stages of, 66.4(2).

light, 3.4(2); 12.1; 16.3,5; 22.6; 23.1; 24.5; 25.1(2),2,3(2),4; 26.1,4,4(2); 27.1,4,5(2),6; 28.4; 29.3; 30.1; 31.3(2); 32.4; 33.2,5,5(2); 34.4; 35.1(2),2,3,4(2);

37.2; 38.2,3; 42.6; 43.4(2); 45.3; 47.2; 48.1; 51.2; 52.3; 54.5(2); 59.1,7; 63.7; 66.3(2); 68.4; 69.4; 70.2,5; 71.3; 74.1(2); 75.1,2,5; 76.7; 79.3; 82.3; 93.2; 95.8; enemy of the true, 16.3.

Lord, 1.1,2; 2.1,2; 3.1,2,3,4(2); 4.1,2,3,4; 5.1,2,3; 8.1; 9.1,2(2),3(2),4; 12.2,3,4; 14.1,2; 15.2; 16.1,4,7; 17.1,3,4; 18.1; 19.2,3,4; 20.1; 21.1(2); 22.1,2(2),6(3); 23.1(2),5; 24.1(3),6,6(2); 25.1(2),4,4(2),5,6; 26.1,3,4,5(2); 27.1,2(2),5; 28.1,2,3,4,6; 29.1(2),2(2),3; 30.1,4,5; 31.2(2),3(2); 32.1,2,4; 33.1,4(2),5; 34.1,5(2); 35.1,1(2),2(2),3,4(2),5(2); 36.1,4(2); 37.1; 38.3,4; 39.3; 40.3; 41.2,3; 42.2(3),3; 43.1,2; 44.1,2(2),3; 45.1,2,3; 46.1,2(2),3; 47.1; 48.2; 49.6; 50.2,3; 51.3,4,5; 52.3,4,5; 53.1(2); 54.3,5,5(2,3); 55.2,4; 56.1,2,3; 57.2,4; 58.1,3,4,4(2); 59.1,7; 60.2; 61.3,5; 62.1,2(2),3,4,6; 63.7; 64.3; 65.3; 66.2; 67.1(2),2,3,4,6; 68.3(2); 69.5; 70.4; 71.6; 72.3,6; 73.1,1(2),2; 75.1,3; 76.4,6; 79.3; 83.1; 84B.1; 91.3; 95.5,6; birth of, 23.5; day of, 6.2; 42.5; of the great harvest, 12.3; Jesus, 33.4; 34.1,3(3),4(2); 35.1(2); 38.4; 44.3; 52.1,3; 55.1; 58.4(2); 60.3(2),4(2); 61.1,2(2),3; 65.3; 72.1; Jesus Christ, 3.4(2); 36.4(2); 37.3(2); 38.2; 40.3,5(2); 45.4; 46.2; 47.2; 50.3; 51.1; 52.1; 53.3; 56.1(2); 57.1; 60.4(2); 62.2,2(2),5; 64.3,4,5; 65.1,5; 66.2; 67.3(2),7; 68.4; 69.3,5; 72.4(2),7; 73.1,4; 74.1,2; 76.8; 77.1; 82.7; 83.1; 84B.4; 85.1,4(2); 90.4(2); 91.2; 92.4; 93.1,3; 94.4(2); 95.1,9; of majesty, 59.3; 60.3(2); and Master, 60.4; 69.4; mercy of, 34.5; prayer of, 39.5(2); 49.5; 50.2; of the universe, 22.2; 23.2; 59.4; of the world, 54.5(2); 61.1; lords of this world, 36.3.

love, 1.1; 2.1,2,2(2); 3.4(2); 4.4; 5.2;

GENERAL INDEX

(love *continued*)
7.1,2; 8.2; 9.1,2,2(2); 10.2,3; 11.1(2); 12.1,2,3; 15.2; 19.3,4; 22.1(2); 26.4; 35.4; 38.4; 40.4,5; 41.3; 44.2(2); 48.1,3; 51.8; 57.4; 60.4; 74.1(2),5; 75.5; 76.3; 79.3; 82.4; 85.1; 86.1; 89.1; 90.3; 92.3; 93.1; 94.2; of Christ, 55.5(2); 70.5; 85.2,4; distorted, 26.5(2); of God, 50.2; 79.3; 89.3; 95.9; of God and neighbor, 38.4; 45.1; 85.1; 94.4; 95.6,9; of holiness, 59.8(2); of money, 60.4; as the power of faith, 45.2; of revenge, 49.5; spirit of, 85.4(2); that drives out all fear, 76.5; to love, 26.5(2); 31.3(2); 41.3; 42.6; 48.1,2; 49.2; 52.5; 66.1; 70.5(2); 72.5.

Luke, 30.7.

luxury, 46.1; 48.2; 49.1; 69.5; 84B.2; 87.1; 90.3; 93.2(2).

Lyconians, 12.2.

Maccabees, 84B.1; mother of, 84B.1.

Macedonius, 24.5; 28.4n.; 75.4.

Manichaeans, 9.4; 16.4; 24.4,5,6; 34.4,4(2); 42.5; 47.2; 76.6,8; 96.2.

Marcion, 16.3.

martyr(s), (martyrdom), 5.4; 31.3; 32.3; 35.4(2); 36.2,3; 37.4(2); 38.1; 58.5; 63.6; 70.5; 76.6; 82.1; 83.1; 84.1; 84B.1,2,3; 85.1,4.

Mary, Blessed Virgin, 22.2; 23.1(2); 24.1(3); 25.5; 26.1; 28.5; 29.1(2); 34.3; 35.1(2); 96.1.

Mary Magdalene, 74.4.

Matthew, Saint, 30.7.

Mediator, 21.2; 31.2; 64.3; 69.5.

Melchisedech, the order of, 3.1; 5.3.

mercy (of God), 3.1,3,4(2); 8.2; 9.1; 11.1; 12.1; 15.3; 17.1; 20.1; 21.3; 22.1(2); 24.2; 27.3; 30.5(2),6; 33.1; 35.4; 37.3; 39.5(2),6; 40.5; 41.3; 42.1,6; 43.4; 45.2; 46.1; 47.3; 48.2; 49.1,6; 50.1,2; 52.2; 54.1,1(2); 55.5; 57.5(2); 59.8; 62.3; 63.2,7; 66.2,4; 68.2,4; 69.4; 70.2,3; 72.2; 76.9; 77.2,6; 80.2; 82.7; 84.2(2); 88.1; 90.1; 94.2; 94.4(2); 95.7; as the Architect, 49.4; ineffable, 33.2; of the Lord, 2.1; 68.3; 70.2; 72.4; 71.2; Mercy Itself, 24.1; mystery of divine, 47.1; 66.1(2); works of divine, 34.1; 44.3.

mercy, 2.1; 7.1; 8.2; 9.2,2(2),3(2); 10.1,1(2),2; 11.1(2); 12.3; 13.1(2); 16.1.2; 17.1,2; 18.3; 19.4; 20.2,3; 21.3; 22.3; 23.2(2),5; 25.2; 28.3; 29.1,3(2); 33.1(2-3),2; 34.5,5(2); 35.3; 36.4,4(2); 40.4; 43.2,4(2); 44.2(2),3; 48.4; 49.3,4,5; 55.5; 58.4(2); 60.2; 61.3; 62.5; 66.1; 67.3; 69.3; 70.1(2); 72.5(2); 75.4; 78.2; 81.4; 84.2(2); 92.1(2); 95.6; caricature of, 57.3; discipline of, 20.3; duties of, 16.6; effects of, 42.2(3); expenses of, 87.4; image of, 44.2(2); measure of, 72.2; sacrifice of, 20.1; 88.5; works of, detailed, 10.1; 11.1(2); 13.1(2); 16.1; 40.4; 43.3; 45.3; 47.3; 86.2; 88.4.

ministry, 4.1; 5.5; 6.1.

miracle(s), 21.1(2); 23.4; 25.4; 28.3,6(2); 31.2(2); 32.3; 34.1(2),3(3); 37.1,2; 46.2; 51.4; 53.1(2); 54.2,3,4; 58.4,4(2); 60.1; 67.5; 74.3; 75.1; 91.2(2); 95.3.

mirror, 24.2(2); 49.4; of the heart, 43.3; of the mind, 41.1.

mission, 25.4(2).

moderation, 15.1; 49.2,5; 81.2; 87.1(2); 93.2(2).

Monday, 7.2; 42.5,6.

moon, 22.6(2); 27.5; 34.4(2); 42.5; 92.2.

Moses, 9.4; 34.4(2); 51.4,5; 58.1; 59.6; 61.5(2); 63.5; 69.2; 95.1.

mother, 22.3(2); 24.3; 25.3,5; 28.2,5; 30.2; 31.1; 35.1(2); 37.2,3(2); 48.1; 62.2(2); 64.4; 77.5; 95.3; of God, 21.1(2); of the seven martyrs (Maccabees), 84B.1; virginity of God's, 46.2(2); of virtues, 50.3.

myrrh, 33.2; 34.3; 36.1(2).

mystery (mysteries), 4.2; 5.3; 22.1(2),6(3); 23.1,1(2),3,4; 24.1(2),4; 25.1,2,5,6; 26.1,4; 27.1,2,2(2),6; 28.1; 29.1; 30.1,7; 31.1,2(2),3(2); 32.3; 33.2; 34.4(2);

GENERAL INDEX 419

37.4(2); 38.1,4; 39.6; 41.1,3; 42.5; 48.1,4; 49.1; 51.1,4; 52.2; 54.1(2); 55.3,4; 56.1; 57.5; 58.3,4; 59.4,5,7; 60.2; 63.4,5; 64.1; 66.2; 67.3(2),7; 69.1,2; 70.2,4; 72.1(2); 73.2; 74.2; 75.1; 76.3(2); 78.1; 82.4; 95.6; of the true and prophesied altar, 55.3; of the ancient sacrifices, 59.5; of his calling, 3.3; of Christ, 37.1; 66.2; of the Cross of Christ, 82.6; of the Death and Resurrection, 43.3; 54.2; of divine goodness, 34.4(2); of the divine mercy, 47.1,2; 49.4; 56.1; 66.1(2); of divine priesthood, 3.1; of the episcopate 4.1; of faith, 34.3(3); of forgiveness, 33.1(3); of great holiness, 56.3; 69.4; 72.2,4; of human nature, 65.2; of his humility, 9.3(2); 40.3; 63.1; of the inferior substance, 51.2; of the law, 51.7; 55.2; Paschal, 45.2; 47.1; 50.3; 65.2; 66.4; 70.6(2); 72.1; of his Passion, 42.1; 69.2; of the past, 53.2; 54.1; of redemption, 43.3; 52.4; 62.4; of restoration, 50.1; of salvation, 35.1; 41.1; 46.1; 55.1; 58.1; 70.2; 72.7; 74.1; of the saving Passover, 53.3; veil of, 51.4; of wonderful patience, 68.2(2); of worship, 46.1.

nation(s), 4.1,2; 9.2; 10.2; 21.2(2); 24.6; 26.2(2); 29.3; 32.1,2,4; 33.5; 34.2; 35.2,2(2); 36.1,2; 40.2; 53.2; 59.5,7; 63.6; 66.2; 67.2; 82.1,2,6.
Nativity, 21.2; 23.4; 24.4; 25.1; 26.1,2,3; 29.1(2); 34.1(2).
nature, divine, 21.3; 22.1,2; 23.1; 24.5; 25.2,5; 26.3; 27.2; 28.1,2,4,6,6(2); 29.3(2); 30.2; 46.1; 52.2; 64.4; 67.5; 72.2,5(2); 74.4; 75.3; 82.2; human, 9.2(2); 10.2; 11.1(2); 12.2; 18.1; 20.3; 21.1(2); 22.2,2(2),3,3(2),4(2),5; 23.3; 24.1,2,2(2),3,5; 25.1,3,4,5; 26.1; 27.6; 28.6,6(2); 29.2(2); 30.3,3(2); 31.1; 32.1; 34.1,3(3),4,4(2),5; 35.1(2); 36.1(2); 38.2,3; 40.1,3; 41.2,3; 42.4; 45.3; 46.1,2(2); 47.3; 50.2,3; 51.2,2(2); 52.2; 53.1; 54.2; 55.3; 56.1(2); 57.4; 58.5; 60.2; 61.3,4; 63.3; 64.1,2,4; 65.4; 66.1,2,4(2); 69.3; 70.5; 71.4,5(2); 72.2,5,6,7; 73.2,3,4; 74.1(2); 77.2,5; 78.2; 82.2; 87.1; 89.5; 90.1; 95.5,8; 96.1,2(2); both, 21.2; 23.1(2),2(2); 27.1(3); 28.1,3,5(2); 40.3; 46.1,2; 47.2; 52.2; 54.1(2); 56.2(2); 59.1; 68.1; 70.3; 71.3; 75.3.
nature, 16.1; 19.2; 20.2; 38.3; 39.5; 42.3; 44.1; 48.2; 51.6; 53.2; 68.3(2); 69.3(2); 70.3; 76.7; 91.2; of evil, 42.2; figures of, 8.2; 10.3; 12.3; 14.1; 17.1; 18.3,3(2); 20.2; 27.6; 35.3; 39.5; 43.1; 45.1; 71.6; 72.1; 74.5(2); 75.2; 81.3; 82.6; 87.1,4; 89.4; 90.3.
neighbor, 12.2,4; 19.3; 20.3; 92.1; 95.6.
Nero, 82.4,6.
Nestorius, 28.5; 91.2(2).
Noah, ark of, 60.3.

oath, 5.3.
obedience(s), 1.1; 10.1; 33.5(2); 35.3; 37.3; 40.3; 43.1; 61.1; 67.6; 88.2; 89.1.
office, papal, 3.1,2,4; priestly, 4.1; 5.4.
olive, sign of peace, 12.2; trees, 16.1.
Only-Begotten, 23.2; 28.6; 30.6; 36.1(2); 37.2; 51.6; 52.2; 58.4(2); 63.1; 66.4(2); 68.1; 69.3; 72.5(2); 74.4; 75.3; 77.3,6; 83.1; 96.2(2).
oracles, ancient, 32.2; divine, 34.2(2); of the prophets, 34.4(2).
order(s), 4.1; 22.2,6; of Melchisedech, 3.1; 5.3.
Orient, 33.2; 34.1(2); 36.1.

pagan(s), 9.3; 16.4; 20.1; 22.6; 26.5(2); 27.4; 33.3; 34.2; 36.2; 66.2; 67.2; 79.2; 85.2; blindness, 8.1; 21.1; derision, 56.1; falsehood, 3.3.
palm, as reward, 9.4; 45.1.
Paraclete, 76.6,7; 78.1.
paradise, 16.5; 22.5; 53.1(2); 55.3; 61.5,5(3); 66.3; 73.4; of the Church, 70.4.

paralytic, 62.4.
Paschal, Feast, 40.1; 41.2; 42.1; 44.1; 45.1,4; 46.1; 47.3; 48.1; 49.1; 58.2; 69.5; 70.4; 72.4,6,7; Liturgy, 74.1(2); Meal, 54.3; Mystery, 50.3; 55.5; 58.1; 70.6(2); 71.1; Solemnity, 50.1; 58.1(2); 60.2; Observance, 55.2; Paschaltide, 71.6(2); Pasch, 72.6.
Passion, 23.3; 24.4; 26.2,5(2); 37.2,4(2); 40.5(2); 45.4; 48.1; 49.3; 50.1; 51.2,2(2); 52.2,3; 53.1; 54.1(2),4,5,5(3); 55.1; 56.1; 57.1; 58.1(2),4(2); 59.1,6; 60.1,2,4(2); 62.1,6; 63.1; 65.1,2; 66.1,3(2); 67.1,2; 68.1,2; 69.1,3,4; 70.1,1(2),4,5,6; 71.2; 72.6; 74.1,3; 75.1,3; 76.4; 91.2(2); and Death, 72.7; marks of, 74.1(2); and Resurrection, 74.5; 90.1.
passion, selfish, 74.5; 90.1.
Passover, 33.4(2); 39.2,6; 40.5; 41.2; 43.4; 44.3; 46.1; 48.1,4; 53.3; 55.5(2); 58.3; 60.2; 64.1; 66.3; 70.2,6; 72.5,6; 79.1.
patience, 18.1; 31.3(2); 35.3; 42.3(2); 53.3; 58.5; 64.3; 65.2; 67.2,6; 69.4; 70.5(2); 82,7; 85.2; 89.6; 90.2,4; 95.4; of Christ, 51.2(2); 57.1; of the Crucified, 70.1(2); of God, 36.4; 43.3; 50.1; 57.4; of the Lord, 58.3; 60.3(2).
patriarch(s), 33.3; 35.4(2); 52.1; 55.5; 63.6; 76.3(2).
Paul, Saint, 12.2; 30.3(2); 37.4; 42.5(2); 48.5; 49.2; 50.1; 51.3; 58.4(2); 59.8,8(2); 66.5; 70.2; 71.4; 76.8; 82.4,6; 96.3; Peter and, 9.4.
Paulinus, Consul, 76.6.
peace, 1.2n.; 2.2(2); 5.5; 13.1(2); 18.1; 21.2(2); 26.1,3-4,5; 37.4; 39.2; 40.5; 42.2(2),6; 44.2(2),4; 45.4; 47.1,3; 55.5(2); 66.3; 70.5; 73.3; 84B. 2; 95.5,9; appearance of, 52.3; cords of, 39.4; enemy of, 48.2; gospel of, 39.4; keep at, 70.5(2); kiss of, 54.3; peacemakers, 41.3; 49.6; 95.9; rebuild fraternal, 49.6; that Christ gives, 41.1; 82.1.

Pentecost, 75.5; 76.3(2); 79.1.
People of God, 3.1; 4.2,4; 8.1; 36.3; 47.3; 48.3; 50.2; 71.6; 83.3(2); 88.2.
persecution(s), 36.2,3(2); 37.2; 47.1; 67.6; 69.5; 70.5; 72.2; 76.6; 82.6; 84B.2; 85.4(2); of Christ, 67.2;
persecutor(s), 32.1; 36.3; 37.3; 52.4,5; 54.2,4; 58.5; 60.2; 62.3; 65.3; 68.2; 69.3; 70.2; 74.3; 76.5; 84B.2; 85.2,4.
person(s), 23.1(2),2; 25.1(2); 28.6(2); 47.1; 92.4; both, 51.6; of the Church, 74.4; not doubled in Christ, 69.3; one of the divinity and the humanity, 72.2; one of God and man, 47.2; one and the same, 37.1; 46.2; one of the twofold nature, 46.1; one of the Word of God and the flesh, 64.4; 68.1; poor, 42.2(2); unity of, 30.5(2).
Peter, Apostle, 2.2; 3.2,3,4(2); 4.1,2; 5.2,4,5; 12.4; 13.2; 15.3; 16.7; 17.5; 18.3(2); 19.4; 24.6; 27.4; 42.6; 51.1n.,2,2(2),5; 52.4; 54.5; 57.1; 58.4(2); 60.4(2); 62.2; 63.4,6; 67.3; 73.2; 74.5; 76.9; 78.4(2); 81.4; 82.1,3,4; 83.1,2,3,3(2); 84.2(2); 86.2(2); 88.5(2); 90.4(2); 92.4; 94.4(2); 95.3; Chair of, 2.2; glory of, 4.2; privilege of, 4.3.
Pharaoh, 60.2.
Pharisees, 59.3; 60.3(2); 65.2; 92.1(2); 92.2.
Phase, 72.6.
Philistines, 39.1.
philosophers, 70.3; philosophy, 28.7; 30.3(2); 91.1.
Photinus, 16.3; 24.5; 28.4n.; 30.2n.; 96.2.
Physician, Omnipotent, 67.5.
Pilate, 54.5(2); 55.1; 57.3,3(2),4; 59.2,3; 61.1,2(2); 67.2; 82.4.
Pontus, 82.5.
poor, the, 6.1; 7.1; 8.2; 9.2,2(2),3(2); 10.1,1(2),3; 11.1,2,2(2); 13.1(2); 15.2;16.2; 17.2; 18.3; 19.4; 20.3; 39.5(2); 40.4; 45.3; 48.5; 49.6; 85.2; 87.3; 88.5; 89.6; 91.3; 92.3;

GENERAL INDEX

94.4; 95.2; in spirit, 95.2; poverty, 3.1; 44.2(2); 49.1; 61.1; 72.5; 95.2,3.
pray, to, 12.3; 35.2(2); 50.2; 56.2(2); 62.3; 65.3; 70.2; 72.6; 76.4; 90.1,4.
prayer(s), 1.2; 2.2(2); 5.5; 8.1; 12.4; 13.2; 15.1,3; 16.2,6; 17.1,5; 19.4; 35.2,4(2); 36.4(2); 42.6; 43.4; 53.1; 54.5(3); 55.1; 56.3(3); 58.1,5; 59.1; 62.3,6; 67.8; 71.1; 76.9; 81.4; 82.7; 84.2(2); 85.4(2); 86.2(2); 87.2; 88.3,5(2); 92.4; 93.3; 94.4(2); act of worship, 12.4; of Christ, 66.3; constant, 56.2; daily, 3.3; of fasting, 87.2; house of, 41.1; the Lord's, 39.5.
preaching, 25.4(2); 31.2(2); 36.1; 45.1; 51.7; 62.3; 63.2; 67.3; 69.1; 70.3,5; 71.3; 73.1(2); 74.2; 89.1; 95.4; of the Apostles, 40.1; 95.3.
Preface of the Mass, 67.1(2)n; 92.1(2)n.
presbyters, 16.4.
pride, 3.4(2); 9.1; 19.2,3; 22.1(2); 25.5; 32.4(2); 36.2; 37.4(2); 38.3; 39.5; 41.1,2; 42.3; 45.4; 47.1; 49.1; 50.2; 55.3; 67.6; 69.3(2),5; 76.5; 79.3,4; 84B.2; 94.1(2); 95.2; of the devil, 69.4; spirit of, 44.3.
priest(s), 4.1,2; 5.1(2),4; 9.4; 32.2; 59.7; 62.1; 66.2; 76.3(2); 89.1; 94.1; chief, 51.2; 54.5; 55.2; 58.2; 60.3(2); 65.2; Eternal, 3.2; 5.4; fellow, 1.1; 2.2; 3.1,4; High, 68.3; high, 57.1; 61.2(2),5; 64.3; holy, royal, divine, 4.1; 5.3; 24.6; Jewish, 33.2; 34.2(2); 54.5(2); 56.3(2); 59.1; 70.1(2); the order of, 35.2; 57.2; priesthood, 1.2; 3.1; 61.5; of the second order, 48.1; servant girl of, 60.4(2); unjust, 61.1; unworthy, 59.7; wicked, 58.1(2); 62.5; 68.2(2).
prince, of life, 62.4; of the world, 70.4.
Probus, the Consul, 76.6.
prophet(s), 3.1; 8.1; 9.4; 12.1; 19.2; 20.3; 23.4; 25.4; 27.1(2); 28.1(2); 29.1,1(2),2(2),3; 30.3; 32.2; 33.2; 35.4(2); 36.4; 42.2(3); 43.1,2; 44.1; 45.1; 47.2; 50.2; 51.7; 52.1; 54.5(2); 55.2; 56.3; 60.1; 62.1; 63.2; 66.2; 67.1(2); 69.2; 70.2,4; 76.3(2); 76.7; 88.1; 90.4; 91.2,3(2); 92.1; 92.3; 94.4.
providence, 16.1; 17.1; 18.2; 24.1; 33.1,4(2); 35.3; divine, 34.1; 43.2; 89.6; 91.1.
Psalms (of David), 3.1; 9.4; 33.5(2).

Redeemer, 4.4; 9.1; 25.6; 29.2; 35.2; 40.4; 52.5; 53.1(2); 54.1(2); 55.1; 58.4(2); 61.4; 62.3; 64.3; 65.2; 66.3(2),4; 67.2,4,7; 68.2,4; 70.1(2); 72.2; 74.2; 77.2; 83.3(3); 87.1; 94.2.
redemption, 23.3; 30.7; 31.3,3(2); 33.4(2); 34.4(2); 41.1; 44.1; 46.1; 49.3,4; 52.1; 54.2; 56.1(2); 58.4; 59.1,8(2); 61.3; 66.1(2); 67.5; 69.5; 72.1(2).
Remus, 82.1n.
repentance, 5.3; 35.4; 56.3.
restraint, (moderation, temperance), 18.2; 44.2; 45.4; 46.1,3; 50.3.
resurrection, 4.4; 9.4; 26.2; 28.5(2); 34.3(2); 40.5(2); 42.5; 46.1; 47.2; 48.1; 50.1; 53.3; 56.2; 59.8(2); 65.4; 66.1(2),3(2),5; 70.1(2),6(2); 71.1(2),3,4,6(2); 72.7; 73.1,2,4; 74.1(2),2,3; 75.1; 76.1,4,6; 77.1; 81.3; 95.5; eternity of, 69.4; from the dead, 52.1.
reverence, 1.1.
rock(s), 60.4(2); 61.5; 63.6; 66.3(2); 83.1,2; apostolic, 3.4(2); firmness of, 53.2; indestructible, 4.2; inviolable, 51.1; strength of, 3.3; unassailable, 62.2(2); upon this, 3.2,3; 5.4.
Roman, citadel, 82.5; Empire, 32.1; 82.2,3; laws, 59.2; 61.1; soldiers, 68.3(2); world, 40.5(2).
Romulus, 82.1n.
ruler, of the world, 37.1.

Sabbath, 69.2; 92.1,2,4.
Sabellius, 16.3; 24.5; 28.4n.
Sacrament(s), 21.3; 42.5; 58.3,4(2); 59.5,7; 67.5; 74.2; 76.3(2); 85.2.
sacrifice(s), 5.3; 20.1; 26.1; 35.2;

GENERAL INDEX

(sacrifice(s) *continued*)
59.5; 61.5(3); 64.3; 66.3; 68.3(2); 69.2; 91.3; 92.1; of almsgiving, 9.4; of animals, 36.3(2); 59.7; 60.2; of devotion, 4.1; to God, 45.2; of the Mass, 26.1; of mercy, 48.4; 88.5; of praise to the Lord, 1.1; spiritual, 4.1; mystery of ancient, 59.5; Manichaean, 16.4.

saints, 2.2; 23.4; 30.7; 33.5; 34.1; 38.3; 45.4; 48.2; 52.1; 53.2; 63.3; 64.2,3; 69.3(2); 70.5,5(2); 76.3(2),7; 77.1; 78.2; 79.3; 82.7; 84.1,2(2); 85.4(2).

salvation, 1.2; 22.1,3,4; 24.6; 26.4(2); 27.1(3); 28.5; 29.1,2,3; 30.1,7; 31.1,2(2),3(2); 32.1,4; 34.1,4(2); 35.2(2),3; 36.1; 38.3; 39.3,4; 40.2,3; 41.1; 42.5; 46.1; 47.1; 48.1; 49.2; 51.1; 52.1,5; 54.1; 55.1,5(2); 56.1; 57.4; 58.3,4(2); 59.1; 60.1,3; 61.3; 66.4,4(2); 67.3,6; 68.3; 69.2; 70.1(2); 71.5(2),6; 72.4(2); 74.1(2); 77.2; 82.1,3; 84.1; 87.2; 92.3; 93.2(2); adoption to, 35.3; day of, 42.1; of all nations, 33.1(2),5(2); of souls, 1.1.

Samuel, 30.4.

Sarah, 30.4.

Satan, 4.3; 83.3.

Saturday, 3.2; 11.2; 12.4; 16.7; 17.5; 18.3(2); 19.4; 42.6; 58.5(2); 70.6(2); 75.5; 76.9; 78.4(2); 81.4; 86.2; 88.5(2); 89.6(2); 90.4(2); 92.4; 94.4.

Savior, 9.1; 12.1; 16.3; 17.1; 19.1; 20.1; 21.1; 22.2,4; 23.1,2(2),4; 24.3,6; 25.5; 26.1,2,3; 28.2; 29.1(2); 30.1,5(2),7; 31.1; 32.1,2; 34.1,4(2),5; 37.2,4(2); 38.1,2; 40.3; 41.2; 42.3; 45.2; 51.2; 54.5(2); 55.2; 59.5; 60.2,3(2); 61.3; 62.4; 63.4,5; 65.5; 66.1(2); 67.1(2),3; 68.2,2(2); 72.7; 76.4; 84.2; of the human race, 37.1; 51.1; Passion of the, 62.1(2); enemy of the, 35.2; 52.1.

scribes, 32.2; 34.2; 51.2; 57.2; 59.3; 60.3(2); 68.2(2); 92.1(2),2.

Scriptures, 6.1; 27.5; 28.2,3; 30.7; 32.2,3,4; 33.3; 34.2,4(2); 35.2; 43.2; 49.6; 55.4; 64.5; 66.1,2; 67.3; 71.3; 73.2; 76.2; 93.1; 94.1,3.

season(s), 11.2; 19.2; 27.5(2); 34.1; 43.3; 47.3; 87.1(2); 89.1,6; 91.1; 94.3.

self-control, 79.1; 80.1; 93.1.

self-denial, 13.1; 68.4; 78.1; 89.1.

self-indulgence, 79.1; 93.1.

self-restraint, 19.2; 79.2; 81.1,4; 87.1,2; 88.2; 89.4; 92.2,3; 93.2(2).

serpent, 16.3; 22.1(2); 40.3; 42.2.

servant(s), 2.2; 21.2; 22.3(3); 23.2(2); 28.1,3; 30.5(2),6; 35.3,4(2); 40.5; 42.6; 43.4(2); 44.2(2); 50.3; 66.4(2); 77.2,5; fellow, 9.2(2); 45.1; 50.3; of God, 48.2; of the high priest, 52.4; to the king, 36.2.

service, 1.2; 2.2(2); 4.1; 19.2; 33.5(2); 34.2(2),3(2); 39.3; 40.5; 48.1; 53.3; 75.4; 90.3.

shepherd, 2.2; 3.4,4(2); 4.1,2,4; 5.2,4,5; 26.1; 29.1(2); 30.5; 32.1,3; 35.1(2); 60.2,3; 63.6; 74.4(2); 82.1; 83.3(2); 90.4(2).

sick, the, 44.2; 49.6; 67.4; cures of, 53.1(2); medicine for the, 56.1(2).

sickness, 49.1; 71.6(2), 74.3.

sign, 1.1; 9.1; 17.1; 24.1(2); 25.4; 26.2(2); 30.4; 31.1,1(2); 32.1,3; 33.4(2); 34.1(2),2; 35.1(2),4(2); 38.2; 40.3; 42.5; 51.4; 52.1; 54.1; 60.1; 63.2,5; 66.2; 67.3(2); 68.1; 71.3; 72.1(2); 73.1; 74.1; 75.3,5; 82.4; of the Cross, 4.1; 73.3; of divine power, 42.3.

Simon, 4.3; 83.3; a certain Cyrenian, 59.5; son of John, 4.2; son of Jonah, 3.2; 83.1.

sin, 3.4(2); 11.1; 19.2; 20.3(2); 21.1(2); 22.1(2),3(2); 23.5; 24.2,3; 25.5; 26.4(2); 27.2(2); 33.1(2); 35.4,4(2); 36.4; 37.3; 39.1,2; 41.1,3; 43.2; 44.1,3; 46.1; 48.1; 49.2; 50.1,2; 52.1,3; 58.4(2); 61.4; 63.4; 64.3; 66.1(2),2,5; 67.4,5; 68.2(2); 69.3; 70.4,5; 71.1(2);

GENERAL INDEX

74.1,5(2); 75.2; 76.4; 78.4; 79.2; 81.4; 82.7; 84B.2; 88.3; 90.1; 93.1; 94.2; 95.8; attractions of, 36.4; author of, 48.2; cause of, 10.1; contagion of, 72.2; deadly, 45.1; debt of, 51.7; dominion of, 46.1; multitude of, 6.1; Original, 46.2(2); 49.3; remedy of, 11.1; remission of, 50.3; sinner(s), 35.2(2); 40.5; 43.3; 46.4; 48.2; 54.3; 56.2(1); 61.3; 62.2(2),4; 66.1(2); 67.3; 68.2; slave of, 56.1(2); snares of, 41.2; stain of, 18.1; 42.6; unpunished, 43.3; washed away, 7.1; of the world, 35.1(2).

Sinai, Mount, 75.1.
slave, 12.2; 19.2.
solicitude, 1.1; 28.5.
Solomon, 10.3; 39.3.
Son, Beloved, 33.5; 51.6; of God, 12.1; 20.1(2); 21.1(2),2,3; 22.2; 23.1(2),2; 24.3,5; 25.1(2),2,3,3(2),4,4(2); 26.1,5(2); 27.1(3),2,2(2); 28.1,2,3,4,5,6(2); 29.1,1(2),2(2); 30.4,5(2); 31.3(2); 34.1,3(3),4; 37.1,2; 38.2;40.3; 42.6; 46.1,3; 47.2; 48.1; 51.1,2; 52.1,5; 55.1,2,3; 56.2,3(2); 57.2,5(2); 58.5; 60.4(2); 62.2,3; 63.1,3,4,6,7; 64.2,4; 65.1,2; 67.5; 68.1,2,3(2); 69.3; 70.3; 71.3; 72.4(2),5(2),7; 73.4; 74.4; 75.3,4,5; 76.2,3; 77.1,2,3,4,5,6; 78.1; 79.4; 91.2(2); of Man, 10.2; 28.5; 30.2,5(2); 38.2; 46.1; 47.2; 51.1,2(2); 52.1; 54.2; 56.2(2); 57.2; 59.6; 62.4; 64.4; 65.2; 66.4(2); 67.5; 74.4; 75.4; 76.4; My, 29.3; Only, 4.2.
son(s), child(ren), of Adam, 28.3; of God, 22.5; 26.3; 30.7; 41.3; 49.3; of man, 5.1; 62.3; 69.3(2); of peace, 26.5.
soul(s), 1.2; 2.2; 4.1; 5.2; 6.1; 10.3; 11.1(2); 12.2,3; 14.2(2); 15.2; 16.3,6; 17.3; 19.2; 20.3; 22.6; 24.2,4,6; 26.1,5; 28.2,4; 31.3(2); 34.4,5; 36.1,4; 38.2; 39.1,2,5; 40.1; 41.1; 42.1,2; 43.2,4(2); 45.4; 46.1; 48.3; 49.1,2,4; 50.1,2; 51.1; 54.4,5(2); 56.1; 57.5; 58.4(2); 59.6; 60.2,4; 61.3; 62.4; 64.1; 67.1,3; 68.4; 70.4; 71.2,5(2),6(2); 74.3,5; 78.1; 80.1; 81.2; 87.1; 89.3; 90.4; 91.1; 93.1; 94.1; 95.1,5; and body, 70.4; integrity of, 44.2; strength of, 74.1(2).

Spirit (of God), 16.5; 22.2(2),3,5; 23.5; 25.1(2); 26.3,5(2); 27.6; 34.2(2); 38.3,4; 41.3; 42.5; 45.4; 66.2,4,4(2); 67.2; 69.5; 76.7; 81.2; 88.4; 89.1; 93.1; of the Father, 62.2; 76.6; gifts of, named, 76.7; of grace, 1.2; 48.1; palace of, 19.1; of peace, 26.5(2); sevenfold, 92.4; sword of, 39.4; temple of, 23.5; of truth, 18.2; 59.6; 73.1(2); 75.2,3,5; 76.4(2),5,7; 78.1.

spirit, 1.1; 3.4; 4.2; 8.2; 12.1,3; 13.1; 14.2(2); 15.2; 19.2; 24.2(2),6(2); 25.3; 26.5(2); 28.2,7; 29.2(2),3; 34.3(2); 41.1; 42.2; 44.2(2); 45.2; 47.1; 55.4; 60.4(2); 73.3; 81.2; 90.1; evil, 70.5(2); hard and ungrateful, 35.4; joyful, 41.1; nobility of, 35.3; of Peter, 4.4; prophetic, 54.4; troubled,71.2; unclean, 8.1.

star(s), 22.6(2); 27.3; 31.1(2); 32.1,2,3; 33.2,5(2); 34.1(2),2,3; 35.1,1(2),2,4(2); 36.1; 37.2; 38.1,2; 42.5; 61.5; 64.4; movement of, 57.5(2); 84.2; power of, 43.2.

Stephen, Saint, 85.4(2).
stone(s), 4.1; 40.3; 48.1; 66.2; 68.3; 84B.4; rolled away 71.3; 73.1(2); of the sepulchre, 70.4.
substance, 23.1(2),2,2(2); 24.2(2),3,5; 25.2,3,4; 26.1; 28.4,6(2),7; 30.2,3,6; 34.4; 57.4; 63.1; 66.3(2),4(2); 69.3; 71.2,4; 72.2,5(2); 76.2,3; 77.1,6(2); bodily, 24.3; 56.3(2); 74.4; divine, 65.3; 75.3; divine and human, 56.1(2); 65.1; of the flesh, 22.3(3); 24.3(2); 39.5; of flesh and blood, 51.1; of flesh and spirit, 42.2; of God as incorporeal, 65.5; human,

(substance *continued*)
22.2; 64.3; no diversity of, 75.3(2); no evil, 42.2; properties of each, 62.1(2); of the Savior, 65.4; of true man, 70.3; unity of, 24.5; of weakness, 46.1.

suffering, 16.1; 22.2; 25.1(2),6; 28.3; 30.2; 35.3; 36.3(2); 37.2; 39.3; 40.3,4; 42.2(3),5; 43.3(2); 45.4; 46.1,2; 47.1,2; 49.1; 51.2,3,5,7,8; 52.3; 54.1(2),2; 56.3(2); 57.4; 58.4(2); 59.1,5; 60.2,4(2); 62.1(2),2; 63.4; 66.3,4; 67.3(2),7; 68.1; 69.3,5; 70.3,5; 72.2; 73.1(2); 74.1,3; 84B.2; 85.1; 95.2; 96.1; of Christ, 51.2(2); God cannot suffer, 51.2; of the Lord, 58.5(2); voluntary, 44.2; 51.3; 55.2.

sun, 27.4; 32.1; 34.4,4(2); 41.3; 42.5; 51.3; 53.2; 57.4; 61.5; glory of the, 51.3; new, 22.6,6(2).

superstition(s), 8.1; 9.1; 32.1.

swaddling clothes, 22.4; 46.2(2).

symbol, 35.2.

synagogue, 29.3; 68.3(2).

Syria, 95.1.

tabernacle(s), 2.2.

teacher(s), 44.1; 54.5; divine teaching, 49.2; mad, 35.2.

temple, 57.3(2); 58.2; 59.5; 61.5; 68.3; 95.3; and the altars, 54.5(2); of his body, 65.2; Christians that of God, 43.1; the Church, 42.6; 45.2; eternal, 4.2; 83.2; of God, 27.6; 28.2; 41.1; 48.1; 73.1; 84B.4; honor of, 66.2; of the Spirit of God, 69.5; 75.5; veil of, 53.2; 57.2; 59.7; 68.3(2).

temptation, 41.1,2; 43.1; 44.1; 49.1,5; 50.2; 55.5(2); 56.2(2); 58.5; 60.1; 69.5; 76.9; 83.3; 85.4(2); 87.1; 89.3; 90.1; 95.9.

Testament, New, 15.2; 17.1; 29.2(2); 33.3; 34.4(2); 51.4; 60.1; 61.5(2-3); 68.3; 74.2; 90.1; 94.3; 95.1; dispensations of, 75.1.

Testament, Old, 3.1; 15.2; 17.1; 20.1; 29.2(2); 34.4(2); 47.2; 51.4; 58.3; 60.1,2; 61.5(2); 66.2; 69.2; 89.1; 90.1; 92.1; 94.3; dispensations of, 75.1.

thanksgiving, 5.1(2); 74.5; give, 12.3; 36.4; 81.1; 84.1,2; 89.6; gratitude, 48.5; 50.3; 73.4; ingratitude, 84.1,2.

thief, converted, 6.1,5; two thieves, 55.1,3.

Thomas, Apostle, 34.3(2).

Tobias, 10.3.

Tradition, Apostolic, 8.1; 10.1.

Transfiguration, of the Lord, 51.1,3.

tree(s), 35.3; barren, 18.3; fig, 18.3,3(2).

Trinity, 4.2; 23.2(2); 24.5; 30.7(2); 36.3(2); 68.1; 72.5(2); 75.3; 76.2,3; 77.1,2,3,4,6(2); eternal, 64.2.

Truth Itself, 17.1; 23.5; 24.1; 32.1; 33.3; 40.4; 43.2; 45.1; 51.7; 54.5; 58.1(2),3; 61.5(2); 71.2; 76.6; Spirit of, 73.1(2); 75.3; 76.4(2).

truth, 3.3; 9.1; 12.1,3; 16.3; 19.2; 21.3; 22.2(2); 23.3,5; 24.3,5,6; 25.2,4; 27.1,1(3); 28.5; 29.1,2(2); 30.1; 31.2,3(2); 32.1,2,4; 34.3,4(2); 35.2; 37.3; 38.2; 39.6; 41.1; 45.1,2; 46.3; 47.1,2; 48.2; 51.4; 54.1(2); 59.7,8(2); 60.1; 63.5; 64.4; 66.5; 68.3(2); 69.2,3,4,5; 70.1,2,5; 73.4; 74.5; 76.2,5; 79.2; 93.2; 94.2; of baptism, 66.2; children of, 42.6; disciples of, 8.1; enemies of, 91.2; of humanity, 66.4(2); ignorance of, 9.1; lack of, 33.4(2); school of, 42.5.

Tuesday, 8.2.

unanimity, 1.2; 42.6.

unity, 23.2,2(2); 24.1,5,6(2); 27.2; 28.4,6(2); 30.5(2),6; 31.2(2); 41.3; 42.6; 51.6; 54.1(2); 62.2; 68.1; 69.5; 70.3; 72.5(2),7; 76.2,3; 77.1; 88.2,3,5; 91.2(2); 94.4; 95.5; apostolic, 58.4(2); of the body of Christ, 79.2; 84B.4; of the Catholic Faith, 89.5; 96.3; Christian, 4.1; of the Church, 16.3; of the Divinity, 66.4(2); of faith, 4.1; of the

GENERAL INDEX

Lord, 21.2; of person, 30.6; of the Spirit, 95.9; of the Word and flesh, 46.2.
usury, art of, 17.2; evil of, 17.3; system of, 17.3.

victim(s), 23.3; 54.1; 55.3; 56.3(2); 58.1(2),2,3; 59.7; 63.5; 68.3,3(2); Jewish, 5.3; Lord as, 58.1(2); manifold, 58.1(2); new, 59.5; unique, 33.4(2).
Victor, over the devil, 59.4; 85.4.
vine, spurious, 55.4.
vinegar, 55.4.
vineyard, 55.4.
Virgin, (Blessed Virgin Mary), 21.1(2),2; 22.1(2),2,3,6(3); 23.1(2); 24.1(3),3,4; 25.2,4,5; 26.2; 27.2; 28.2,5; 29.2(2); 30.2,4; 32.1; 34.1; 35.1(2); 47.2; 52.1; 54.1(2); 56.1; 62.2; 70.3; 72.3,4; 74.3; 91.2; 96.1; Mother, 25.3; 26.1,2; 27.1; 29.1(2); 30.2; 37.1; 63.6; 64.2,4; Son of, 62.2(2); womb of, 46.2(2); 48.1; 64.1; 65.1; 67.5; 72.7; 96.2(2).
virginity, 23.1(2); 27.2; 28.2; 31.1; 46.2(2); maternal, 66.4(2); virginal fertility of the Church, 49.3; virgin birth, 24.1(3).
virtue(s), 3.4(2); 10.1,2; 12.4; 13.1; 14.1; 15.2; 16.4; 17.1; 18.2; 19.2; 23.5; 25.1(2); 38.3; 40.1,5; 41.1; 42.2(2),3; 43.1; 45.2; 48.2,3,4; 49.1,2,4; 50.2; 55.5; 74.5(2); 75.5; 78.3; 79.3; 85.1; 87.1; 89.4,6; 90.4; 91.1; 92.1,1(2); 93.2; 94.2; 95.2,6; Christian, 92.2; foundations of, 44.2; seeds of, 39.5.

Way, the, 25.6; 69.3(2),6; 72.1(2); 90.2.
wealth, 10.1; 11.2(2); 17.2; 19.3; 40.4; 49.1; 67.4; 85.2; 95.2,3; Christian poverty as, 42.2(2); dishonest, 94.1(2); of divine bounty, 23.5; less, 44.2(2); of Paradise, 66.3(2).
Wednesday, 9.3(2); 12.4; 13.2; 15.3; 16.7; 17.5; 18.3(2); 19.4; 42.6; 52.5(2); 54.5(3); 56.3(3); 58.5(2); 62.6; 64.5; 67.8; 75.5; 76.9; 78.4(2); 81.4; 86.2(2); 88.5(2); 89.6(2); 90.4; 92.4; 94.4(2).
wickedness, 35.2(2),3; 36.3(2); 37.4; 44.2; 51.1; 52.2,5; 54.3; 55.2,3,4; 56.1; 57.1,3; 58.4; 61.2(2),3,5; 63.1; 67.1(2),2,3; 70.2,5(2); 72.1; 76.8; 78.2; 82.3; 84.2; 85.2; 92.2; 96.2; fast from, 50.2; of the Jews, 68.3(2); 69.4; 73.1; spiritual, 41.2; 89.2.
widow, loneliness of, 40.4; of Sarepta, 42.2(3); two coins of, 20.3; 42.2(3); 44.2(2); vessel of, 12.3.
wife, wives, 49.2.
will, 9.3(2); 10.1; 12.1; 26.4(2); 27.2(2); 28.3; 29.3(2); 41.1; 48.1; 49.4; 50.3; 67.2; 71.5; of the devil, 22.3(2); 78.2; evil, 86.2; of the Father and the Son, 58.4(2); 68.2; of God, 5.3; 12.1,2,3; 22.1(2); 26.4(2),5; 27.3; 29.1(2); 52.5; 54.2; 56.1(2); 58.4,5; 62.3,5; 63.1; 66.2; 67.2,5; 70.5(2); 75.3(2); 76.2; 77.1; 93.1; 95.9; good, 1.2; 6.2; 7.1; 10.1; 11.2(2); 15.2; 21.2(2); 29.1(2); 37.4,4(2); 40.4; 42.3; 44.2(2); 45.4; 70.5(2); 79.4; 87.1(2); 88.4,5; 89.1,5; 93.1; 95.5; ill, 39.2(2); 52.2; of the mob, 59.2; 61.2(2); to will, 6.1; 22.2(2); 26.3; 37.2; 38.3; 51.7; 56.2; 57.3,3(2); 67.7; unjust, 44.2.
wisdom, 4.2; 12.1; 21.1(2); 22.3,6; 23.4; 24.2; 25.2,4(2); 30.3,5(2); 31.2(2); 49.4; 51.7; 60.3(2); 82.2; 93.2; 95.7; Christian, 37.3; 45.1; divine, 19.1; 52.3; 70.3; earthly (worldly), 26.2(2); 27.1; 28.4; 34.3; 36.1; 37.4; 46.3; 48.2; 72.1(2); 73.1(2); 82.3; 91.1; 92.2; eternal, 29.2; 30.5; of the Gentiles, 56.1(2); of God, 39.3; 42.3; 52.1; 53.3; 67.3; 72.5(2); human, 25.2; of God's mercy, 46.1; 48.1; speech of, 75.2; of truth, 69.4.
Wise Men, 31.(2),3; 32.1,2,3,4; 33.2,3,4,5(2); 34.1(2),2,2(2),3; 35.1,1(2),2,2(2),4(2); 36.1; 37.2,4(2); 38.1.
woman, women, 16.2; 23.2(2); 25.4;

34.3(2),4; 46.2(2); 61.3; 71.3; 73.1(2); 74.3.
wonder(s), 36.1; 73.3; 95.3.
Word, the, 21.2; 23.3; 25.3,5; 26.1; 27.1(2),2; 28.2,4,5; 29.1(2),2(2); 30.2,3(2),5; 31.2(2); 32.1; 35.3; 39.4; 40.4; 46.1; 50.3; 52.2; 54.2; 64.4; 65.3; 69.3; 70.3; 71.3; 76.5; 77.5; 82.2; co-eternal with and equal to the Father, 24.1; and flesh as one Person, 72.6; Incarnation of, 23.4; inviolable, 46.2; made flesh, 4.2; 23.1; 24.3; 25.4,5; 27.1(2),2; 29.1(2); 30.3,5; 32.1; 47.2; 52.1; 54.1(2); 56.1(2); 63.1; 64.1; 66.4; 67.4; 91.2(2); power of, 32.3; 56.1.
word, of life, 4.3; 83.2; of the Lord, 65.2; 75.2; and signs, 52.1; of truth, 49.1; of truth and mercy, 58.3.
works, of the devil's deception, 42.3; of devotion, 16.3; divine, 29.1; 30.4; 43.4(2); 58.1; 62.1; 63.1; 65.1; 67.1; 68.2(2); 74.1(2); 76.2,3; earthly, 45.3; of faith, 16.6; of God, 27.6; 45.2; 62.2; of God's; design, 67.7; good, 14.2, 20.3; 40.1; 42.2(3); 59.8; 63.7; 90.4; of grace, 49.1; heavenly, 45.3; of love, 10.3; of mercy, 9.2; 15.2; 17.1; 20.3; 38.3; 42.2(2),6; 44.2(2); 46.3,4; 47.3; 48.3; 54.1; 59.8(2); 68.4; 74.5(2); 78.4; 81.4; 87.1; 88.2,5; 89.2,5; of peace, 26.3; of piety, 8.1; 9.2(2); 10.1; 84B.3; of virtue, 39.3.
world, 15.1; 17.2; 18.1; 19.1; 22.1(2),2; 23.4; 24.1(2); 25.2; 26.2(2); 27.6; 31.1; 32.1; 33.1(3); 35.1(2),2(2),4(2); 36.2; 37.2; 40.2,5(2); 43.2; 48.1; 49.2; 51.4; 54.4; 57.4; 58.4(2); 60.2; 61.5; 65.2; 66.3; 69.3,3(2),4; 70.5; 72.4; 74.3,4(2); 82.1; 90.3; 95.3,9; end of, 66.1(2); lower, 3.2.

Zachariah, 30.4.
zeal, 33.5(2); 41.3.

INDEX OF HOLY SCRIPTURE

Numerical References to Leo Indicate Sermon.Section(Subsection)

Old Testament

Genesis
1.2: 75.2.
1.14-15: 27.5(2).
1.18: 27.6(2).
1.26: 20.2; 24.2(2);
 27.6; 45.2; 64.2;
 92.1(2); 94.2;
 94.3.
1.27: 9.1; 28.3;
 41.3; 43.3; 49.4;
 72.2; 90.3; 94.3;
 95.7.
1.31: 76.7.
2.1: 27.6(2).
2.7: 24.2(2); 30.4.
2.17: 22.1(2);
 93.2(2).
2.21-22: 30.4.
3.1: 16.3.
3.3-4: 42.4.
3.5-6: 87.1.
3.15: 22.1(2);
 24.1(2).
3.17-19: 93.2(2);
 94.2.
3.19: 22.5; 24.2(2);
 25.5; 28.6; 42.4.
3.23-24: 22.5.
3.24: 66.3(2).
17.4: 26.2(2).
21.2: 30.4.
22.18: 24.1(3);
 26.2(2).
25.23: 33.3.
25.25: 30.4.
49.10: 33.2; 35.2.

Exodus
15.6: 28.6.
15.16: 55.5.
28: 57.2.
29.14: 59.5.
31.18: 69.3.

Leviticus
10.6: 57.2.
11.44: 45.2; 94.2.
19.2: 45.2; 94.2.
21.10: 57.2.

Numbers
24.17: 34.2.

Deuteronomy
6.5: 92.1.
9.10: 69.3.
19.15: 51.4.
28.66: 59.6.

1 Samuel
1.11-20: 30.4.
7.6-11: 39.1.

1 Kings
17.9-16: 12.3;
 42.2(3).

Tobias
4.7: 10.3; 17.1.
4.8: 6.2; 7.1; 9.3(2);
 10.1; 88.5.
4.9: 8.2; 10.3; 40.4.
4.11: 6.1; 10.3; 78.4.

12.8: 12.4; 93.3.
12.9: 10.3.

Job
1.8: 27.5.
7.1: 2.1; 41.1; 47.1;
 50.2.
14.4: 28.3.
14.4-5: 21.1(2).
31.26-28: 27.5.

Psalms
2.7-8: 29.3.
4.9: 26.3.
6.6: 35.4; 36.4.
7.12: 8.2.
9.19: 89.6.
10.3: 24.6.
14.1: 17.3.
14.5: 17.3.
16.8: 90.4.
18.2: 32.1.
18.2-3: 19.2.
18.5: 32.1.
18.9: 75.2.
18.13-14: 44.1.
21: 67.1(2).
21.2: 67.7; 68.1;
 68.2.
21.13: 54.5(2); 60.2.
21.17: 54.5(2).
21.17-19: 55.2.
22.3: 87.1.
23.8: 18.1.
23.10: 62.2(2); 67.6.
24.10: 43.2; 45.2.

26.1: 26.4(2).
27.8: 31.3(2).
29.6: 12.1.
32.5: 44.1; 72.4.
33.4: 2.2.
33.6: 27.6.
33.9: 50.2; 95.6.
34.1: 2.3.
36.23-24: 71.6.
40.2: 6.2; 9.3(2); 91.3(2).
41.8: 60.1.
42.3: 25.4.
45.8: 62.2(2).
48.17-18: 17.2.
49.1: 32.1
49.14: 1.1.
50.17: 58.1.
54.22: 24.6.
54.23: 43.1.
56.5: 59.3.
66.7: 20.2.
67.19: 5.2; 76.8.
67.36: 38.3; 79.3; 85.4(2).
68.22: 55.2.
68.35: 44.1.
72.2-3: 43.2.
75.2: 33.3.
76.11: 18.2; 27.2(2); 63.7.
77.39: 54.3.
80.11: 58.1.
84.12: 24.3.
85.9: 33.5(2).
85.15: 8.2; 22.3; 22.3(3).
88.16-18: 79.3.
91.5: 92.3.
93.12: 25.1(2).
95.10: 55.2.
95.13: 21.3.
97.2: 29.3; 33.5(2).
99.3: 5.1.
103.30: 75.2.
104.4: 62.1.
106.8: 24.2.
106.22: 1.1.
108.6: 54.3; 62.4.
108.7: 56.3.
109.1: 5.3; 25.5; 28.6; 29.2(2).
109.4: 3.1; 5.3.
113.1: 60.2.
113.20: 1.1.
114.5: 50.3.
115.12: 1.1.
115.15: 64.3; 82.6; 84B.2.
118.5: 70.5.
118.30: 74.5; 79.2.
118.120: 45.4; 47.1; 70.4.
118.140: 75.2.
118.155: 61.3.
118.165: 95.9.
119.2: 16.3.
120.3-4: 5.2.
129.3: 2.1.
131.11: 24.1(3).
135.4: 1.1.
135.11-12: 55.5.
135.12: 53.3.
135.23: 1.1.
144.14: 36.4(2).
144.19: 36.4(2).
144.21: 1.1.
145.6: 42.4; 44.1.
145.7-8: 34.5(2).

Proverbs
9.1: 25.2; 30.3.
10.12: 7.1; 10.3; 48.4.
11.17: 6.1; 16.2.
15.27: 10.3.
16.6: 10.3.
20.9: 11.1; 37.3; 43.2; 44.1; 50.1; 90.1.
21.13: 10.3.
29.27: 48.2.

Wisdom
1.11: 39.5.
1.13: 25.2.
2.24: 9.1; 21.1(2); 40.2; 49.3; 73.4; 77.2.
9.15: 45.2; 95.5.

Sirach
2.1: 39.3; 84B.2.
3.33: 10.3; 20.3(2); 49.6.
13.1: 49.2.
18.30: 70.5(2); 81.2; 93.1; 94.1.
23.27-29: 43.3.
24.11: 84B.2.
29.15: 10.3.
35.4: 9.3; 9.4; 13.1(2); 20.2; 88.5.
39.21: 76.7.
42.20: 43.3.

Isaiah
1.2-3: 26.3.
1.13-14: 92.2.
1.16: 20.3(2).
4.2: 28.3.
7.14: 23.1(2); 24.1(3); 29.2(2); 72.3.
9.2: 25.3(2); 29.3; 33.5.
9.6: 59.4.
11.1: 24.1(3).
11.2-3: 76.7.
33.6: 92.3(2).
35.5-6: 54.4.
40.3: 45.1; 45.3.
40.4: 45.1.
42.16: 12.1.
45.8: 14.1; 24.3.
50.6: 55.2; 65.3.
52.5: 35.4.
52.10: 36.1.
52.11: 8.1.
52.15: 36.1.
53.1: 28.6.
53.4-5: 58.4(2).
53.5-6: 56.3(2).
53.8: 3.1; 23.1; 29.1; 30.1.
53.11-12: 56.3(2).
55.5: 29.3; 33.5.
55.7: 9.2(2).
65.1: 12.1.
65.2: 59.7.

INDEX OF HOLY SCRIPTURE 429

Jeremiah
1.5: 30.4.
2.21: 55.4.
5.3: 84.1.
23.5: 28.3.
31.31: 95.1.
31.33: 95.1.

Lamentations
4.13: 64.3.

Ezekiel
18.22-23: 22.1(2).
33.11: 22.1(2);
50.1.

Daniel
4.24: 10.3; 11.1;
12.4.
13.56: 67.4.

Hosea
4.7: 59.4.
12.3: 30.4.
13.14: 59.8.

Joel
2.12-13: 88.1.
2.15-16: 88.1.

Micah
5.2: 32.3; 34.2(2).

Habakkuk
2.4: 5.2; 10.3;
22.4(2); 23.3;
24.6(2).
3.2: 3.1.

Zechariah
8.19: 12.4; 90.1.

Malachi
1.2: 30.4.

2 Maccabees
7: 84B.1.
7.28: 22.6(2).

New Testament

Matthew
1.1: 29.2(2).
1.1-16: 30.7.
1.22-23: 23.1(2).
1.23: 24.1(3);
29.2(2); 72.3.
2.2: 46.2(2).
2.4: 32.2; 32.3.
2.5-6: 32.3.
2.6: 34.2(2).
2.7: 46.2(2).
2.9-11: 46.2(2).
2.10-11: 34.3.
2.11: 46.2(2); 64.4.
2.13: 64.4.
3.9: 66.2.
3.17: 64.4.
4.1-11: 39.3; 40.3;
42.3.
4.2: 64.4.
4.3: 40.3.
4.10: 15.2; 27.5.
4.11: 40.3; 74.4(2).
4.16: 25.3(2); 29.3;
33.5.
4.19: 95.3.
4.23: 95.1.
4.24-25: 95.1.
5.1: 95.1.
5.3: 95.2.
5.4: 95.5.

5.5: 95.4.
5.6: 40.4; 50.2;
95.6.
5.7: 8.2; 10.2; 11.1;
16.2; 47.3; 49.5;
78.4; 95.7.
5.8: 50.1; 51.2(2);
95.8.
5.9: 26.3; 41.3; 49.6;
95.9.
5.10: 84B.2.
5.16: 26.4; 35.4;
38.3; 43.4; 45.3;
79.4.
5.17: 17.1; 20.1;
34.3(2); 66.2;
92.1.
5.20: 92.1(2); 92.2.
5.44: 12.2; 35.3.
5.45: 38.3; 41.3.
6.10: 26.4(2); 90.3;
93.1; 95.9.
6.12: 39.5(2); 43.4;
44.3; 46.4; 48.4;
49.5; 50.2.
6.13: 46.4.
6.14: 41.3; 43.4.
6.14-15: 39.5(2);
50.3.
6.16: 92.2.
6.20: 6.1; 87.4(2).

6.21: 26.5(2); 92.3;
92.3(2).
6.23: 35.4.
6.24: 71.1(2).
7.2: 47.3.
7.14: 25.1(2); 45.1;
49.2; 79.2; 90.2.
7.15: 16.3; 52.3.
8.24: 46.2(2); 64.4;
66.4(2).
9.2: 62.4.
9.13: 35.2(2); 48.2;
62.4.
10.19-20: 76.6.
10.22: 24.6(2).
10.32: 66.4(2).
10.38: 47.1; 59.4;
70.4.
10.42: 42.2(3);
44.2(2).
11.19: 66.4.
11.28-29: 23.5.
11.28-30: 35.3.
11.29: 93.2(2).
12.29: 22.4(2); 40.2;
51.7; 70.4.
12.31-32: 76.4.
12.32: 75.4.
13.30: 10.3.
13.39: 10.3.
13.43: 51.3.

430 INDEX OF HOLY SCRIPTURE

14.15-21: 48.5.
14.17: 46.2(2).
14.20-21: 46.2(2).
14.30: 82.4.
15.13: 39.5; 81.3.
15.30: 64.4.
15.36: 48.5.
16.12-19: 83.1.
16.16: 3.3; 4.2; 62.2; 83.1.
16.16-19: 3.2.
16.17: 4.2; 83.1.
16.18: 4.2; 5.4; 62.2; 83.1; 83.2.
16.19: 4.3; 73.2; 83.2.
16.21: 51.2.
16.22-23: 51.2.
16.24-25: 51.2.
16.28: 51.2(2).
17.1-9: 51.1.
17.1: 51.2(2).
17.2: 51.3.
17.4: 51.5.
17.5: 51.6; 51.8.
17.21: 87.2.
17.24-25: 61.1.
18.1-4: 37.3(2).
18.11: 62.4.
18.16: 51.4.
18.19-20: 88.3.
19.14: 32.3.
19.21: 6.1.
19.29: 7.2.
21.19: 18.3.
22.9: 50.1.
22.11-12: 50.1.
22.21: 61.1.
22.37: 12.2; 15.2; 92.1.
22.39: 12.2; 15.2; 92.1.
22.40: 20.3; 92.1; 94.4.
22.43-44: 28.2; 29.2(2).
22.45: 29.2(2).
23.12: 31.3(2).
24.13: 24.6(2).
24.31: 74.4(2).
25.20-29: 86.2.

25.27: 69.1.
25.31-46: 9.2; 10.2.
25.34-40: 80.2.
25.34-46: 45.3.
25.35-40: 6.2.
25.37: 6.1; 12.3.
25.40: 6.1; 45.3; 87.4(2); 91.3(2); 94.4.
25.41-42: 18.3.
26.5: 58.2.
26.15-16: 60.4.
26.20-21: 58.3.
26.21: 58.3.
26.22: 58.3.
26.23: 58.3.
26.37: 66.4(2).
26.38: 54.4; 60.2.
26.39: 54.4; 56.2(2); 58.4(2); 58.5; 67.7.
26.41: 90.1.
26.42: 58.5; 67.7.
26.45-46: 56.2(2).
26.47: 65.2.
26.51-52: 52.4.
26.52: 57.1.
26.53: 54.4.
26.57-62: 59.2.
26.63: 57.2.
26.64: 57.2.
26.65: 57.2.
26.67: 59.2.
26.69-70: 82.4.
27.1-2: 59.2.
27.1: 54.5(2).
27.2: 59.2.
27.4: 52.5.
27.19: 59.2.
27.21: 59.3.
27.22-23: 59.3.
27.24: 59.2.
27.25: 35.2(2); 53.2; 59.3; 62.3.
27.30: 59.2.
27.32: 59.5.
27.38: 55.1.
27.42: 55.2; 61.5; 68.2(2).
27.45: 57.4; 61.5.

27.46: 67.7; 68.1; 68.2.
27.50: 55.4; 68.3(2).
27.50-53: 53.2.
27.51: 57.4; 61.5; 68.3(2).
27.51-52: 57.4; 61.5.
27.53: 66.3(2).
27.54: 68.3(2).
28.1-7: 74.4(2).
28.2: 71.3.
28.17: 73.1(2).
28.20: 5.2; 30.5(2); 63.3; 72.3.

Mark
1.27: 76.4.
3.15: 76.4.
3.22: 76.4.
3.27: 40.2.
4.38: 46.2(2).
6.41: 48.5.
8.6-7: 46.2(2).
9.29: 87.2.
12.30: 90.3; 95.6.
12.31: 90.3.
12.41-44: 20.3; 42.2(3); 44.2(2).
14.19: 58.3.
14.35: 58.4(2); 58.5.
14.36: 54.4.
15.34: 67.7; 68.1; 68.2.

Luke
1.15: 30.4.
1.24: 30.4.
1.28-38: 74.4(2).
1.35: 22.2(2); 25.5; 29.1(2); 30.4; 66.4(2).
1.41: 30.4.
1.46: 1.2.
2.7: 46.2(2); 64.4.
2.8-15: 46.2(2); 74.4(2).
2.10: 29.1(2); 32.3.
2.11: 26.1.
2.12: 22.4.
2.13: 30.5.

INDEX OF HOLY SCRIPTURE

2.14: 21.2(2); 26.1; 29.1(2); 44.2(2).
2.18: 32.3.
2.21: 22.4.
2.22-24: 22.4.
2.40: 22.4; 66.4(2).
2.52: 22.4; 66.4(2).
3.4: 45.1.
3.5: 45.1.
3.23-38: 30.7.
4.4: 40.4.
4.36: 76.4.
6.36: 17.1; 41.3; 45.2; 48.5.
6.37: 17.1; 39.6.
6.38: 17.1; 17.2.
7.11-15: 64.4.
7.47: 2.1.
8.23: 46.2(2).
8.24: 46.2(2).
9.16: 48.5.
9.62: 71.6.
10.42: 70.5(2).
11.15: 76.4.
11.22: 40.2.
11.34-35: 35.4.
11.41: 10.3; 18.3(2); 20.3(2); 46.4; 80.2; 87.3; 95.7.
12.19: 90.4.
12.20: 90.4.
12.33: 87.4(2).
12.35: 35.4.
12.49: 50.2.
14.11: 31.3(2); 37.4(2); 45.1.
15.13: 22.5.
15.18: 22.5.
17.15-18: 84.2.
17.21: 38.4.
18.16: 32.3.
19.10: 52.1; 54.2; 62.4.
19.23: 69.1.
21.2-4: 20.3; 42.2(3).
21.19: 31.3(2).
21.34: 19.1.
22.31-32: 4.3; 83.3.
22.32: 4.4.
22.33: 60.4(2).
22.40: 4.3; 83.3.

22.51: 52.4.
22.61: 54.5; 60.4(2).
22.62: 60.4(2).
23.27: 61.3.
23.28-29: 61.3.
23.33: 55.1.
23.34: 35.2(2); 52.5; 55.1; 62.3; 65.3; 67.3.
23.39-43: 55.1.
23.42: 53.1(2).
23.43: 53.1(2); 55.3; 61.5; 66.3(2).
23.44-45: 61.5.
24.1-11: 73.1(2).
24.11: 73.1(2).
24.12: 71.3.
24.15: 73.2.
24.25: 73.1(2); 73.2.
24.26-27: 73.2.
24.27: 71.3.
24.30-31: 73.2.
24.32: 73.2.
24.36-38: 73.3.
24.39: 71.3; 73.3.
24.45-46: 71.3.
24.52: 73.4.

John
1.1: 25.3.
1.1-3: 21.2; 27.1(2).
1.3: 23.2(2); 46.3; 51.6; 64.2; 68.1; 89.3.
1.5: 69.4.
1.9: 27.6; 63.7.
1.12: 22.5; 64.3.
1.13: 26.5; 27.2(2); 63.6.
1.14: 4.2; 23.1; 24.3; 25.5; 27.1(2); 27.2; 29.1(2); 29.2(2); 30.3; 47.2; 52.1; 54.1(2); 63.1; 64.1; 65.1; 67.5; 70.3; 82.2; 91.2(2).
1.17: 34.4(2); 51.4; 63.5; 69.2.

1.29: 35.1(2); 56.3(2); 59.7; 64.4; 70.2.
1.47: 30.6.
2.1-10: 40.3.
2.2: 46.2(2).
2.9: 12.3; 46.2(2).
2.19: 73.1.
2.21: 28.2; 65.2.
3.3: 24.3.
3.5: 22.5; 24.3; 24.6; 41.3; 66.2; 66.4(2).
3.8: 75.2.
3.16: 58.4(2).
5.17: 51.6.
5.19: 51.6.
5.25-27: 30.5(2).
5.46: 61.5.
6.9: 12.3.
6.38: 26.5.
6.51: 33.4(2).
6.53-54: 91.3.
7.39: 76.8.
8.11: 62.4.
8.34: 56.1(2).
8.44: 9.1; 46.1; 48.2; 57.5(2).
8.46: 62.2(2); 77.2.
8.56: 33.5.
9.6: 46.2(2).
10.15: 63.6.
10.16: 63.6.
10.17-18: 31.2(2); 68.2.
10.30: 23.1(2); 23.2; 27.1(3); 64.4; 77.5.
10.38: 51.6.
11: 64.4.
11.35-36: 46.2(2); 66.4(2).
11.39: 46.2(2).
11.43-44: 46.2(2).
11.47-53: 58.3.
12.23: 59.6.
12.25: 70.5(2).
12.27: 59.6.
12.28: 59.6.
12.30-32: 59.6.
12.31: 22.4(2); 70.4.

12.32: 52.1; 57.4; 64.3; 66.2; 67.7.
12.47: 31.2.
13.1: 72.6.
13.2: 58.3.
13.26-27: 58.4.
13.27: 58.4.
13.35: 48.3.
14.6: 24.1; 26.1; 35.3; 51.7; 67.6; 69.3(2); 69.5; 72.1(2).
14.9: 25.3(2); 77.5.
14.17: 76.7.
14.27: 26.5(2); 41.1.
14.28: 23.1(2); 23.2; 27.1(3); 64.4; 74.4; 77.5.
15.5: 5.4; 38.3; 49.4.
15.9: 51.8.
15.15: 76.5.
15.20: 54.5.
16.12-13: 75.3; 76.5.
16.12-14: 76.4(2).
16.13: 76.6; 76.7.
16.15: 75.3; 76.5; 77.6.
16.33: 18.1; 70.6; 72.4.
17.1: 58.4(2).
17.3: 24.6(2).
17.6: 58.4(2).
17.11: 1.2; 58.4(2).
17.12: 58.4(2); 62.4; 67.4.
17.20-21: 72.6.
17.21: 58.4(2).
17.22-23: 58.4(2).
18.3: 59.1; 65.2.
18.4-5: 52.3; 65.2.
18.6: 65.2.
18.11: 58.4(2).
18.13: 59.2.
18.24: 59.2.
18.38: 59.2.
18.40: 59.3.
19.1-5: 59.3.
19.3: 59.2.
19.6: 57.3; 59.2; 59.3; 61.2.
19.12: 61.1.

19.15: 59.2; 59.4.
19.17: 59.4.
19.30: 55.4.
20.5-6: 71.3.
20.17: 74.4.
20.19: 71.3.
20.19-27: 65.4.
20.20: 71.3.
20.22: 71.3; 73.2.
20.22-23: 76.4.
20.25-27: 71.3; 73.3.
20.27: 71.3.
20.29: 74.1(2).
21.1: 14; 71.3.
21.15-17: 73.2; 74.5; 82.4.
21.17: 4.4; 63.6; 83.3(2).
21.22: 54.5.

Acts

1.3: 73.1; 74.1.
1.3-4: 71.3.
1.10: 74.4.
1.11: 74.4.
2.1-4: 75.2.
2.5: 63.6.
2.24: 73.1.
2.37: 67.3.
2.37-39: 67.3.
2.41: 62.3; 67.3.
3.1: 95.3.
3.3: 95.3.
3.6: 95.3.
3.15: 54.5(2); 61.2; 62.4; 73.1.
4.4: 95.3.
4.12: 30.7(2); 72.5(2).
4.24: 67.2.
4.27-28: 67.2.
4.28: 52.5.
4.32: 62.3; 95.3.
7.51: 68.2(2); 76.7.
9.15: 67.4; 82.6.
10.43: 92.1(2).
11.26: 82.5.
14.15: 42.4; 44.1.
14.15-16: 12.2.
14.17: 82.2.
20.35: 10.1.

Romans

1.3: 29.2(2); 34.3(2); 46.3; 67.1(2).
1.7: 96.3.
1.8: 3.4; 96.3.
1.16: 46.1; 96.2(2).
1.17: 5.2; 10.3; 22.4(2); 23.3; 24.6(2); 64.3.
1.20: 19.2.
1.20-21: 44.1.
1.25: 42.5.
2.4: 35.3; 43.3; 50.1.
2.24: 35.4.
2.25: 33.3.
3.24: 58.5.
3.27: 33.3.
4.3: 26.2(2).
4.5: 34.1; 35.2(2); 51.1; 64.3.
4.12-18: 63.6.
4.17: 51.1.
4.18: 33.5.
4.20-21: 26.2(2); 33.5.
4.25: 30.5(2).
5.1: 74.1(2).
5.1: 26.3; 26.4(2); 95.9.
5.5: 79.3.
5.6: 59.8.
5.12: 24.2; 52.1.
5.14: 25.5.
5.18: 24.2.
5.20: 64.3.
6.3-8: 66.5.
6.4: 39.6; 63.7.
6.5: 63.6.
6.5-6: 50.1.
6.12: 39.2.
6.14: 25.5.
7.23: 93.2.
8.3: 25.2; 29.3(2); 62.2(2); 63.4; 67.6; 69.3; 77.2.
8.9: 42.6; 71.5.
8.14: 26.5(2); 38.4; 88.4.
8.15: 22.5; 29.3; 95.1.
8.17: 25.6; 29.3;

INDEX OF HOLY SCRIPTURE 433

35.3; 41.3; 47.1;
  59.5; 66.2; 69.5;
  70.4; 90.2; 95.9.
8.18: 51.3.
8.24: 49.2; 71.5.
8.26: 56.2(2); 76.4.
8.29: 26.5.
8.31-32: 57.5(2).
8.32: 52.5; 60.2;
  68.2.
8.35: 55.5(2).
8.35-37: 36.2.
9.8: 33.3; 66.2.
9.13: 30.4.
10.1: 57.4.
10.4: 63.5.
10.9: 72.3.
10.10: 72.3.
10.12: 63.2.
11.11: 35.3; 70.2.
11.11-12: 67.3.
11.17: 12.2.
11.25: 33.3; 53.2;
  66.2.
11.31: 70.2.
11.32: 33.1(2); 66.2;
  70.2.
11.33: 21.1(2); 67.3.
12.1: 1.2; 76.8.
12.10: 42.6.
12.15: 11.1(2);
  34.5(2).
12.16: 41.1.
12.17: 37.4; 38.3;
  44.3; 48.2.
13.12: 32.4(2).
13.14: 71.5(2).
14.11: 3.3.
14.23: 46.1; 79.2.
15.21: 36.1.
16.17-18: 42.5(2).
16.19: 96.3(2).

1 Corinthians
1.8: 24.6(2).
1.10: 69.1.
1.17: 46.1.
1.19-20: 42.3; 70.3.
1.21: 25.4(2); 70.3.
1.23: 25.3; 25.4(2).
1.23-24: 53.3; 56.1.

1.24: 21.2(2); 51.7.
1.30: 31.3(2).
1.31: 5.1; 38.4; 42.3;
  45.4; 55.5; 79.3.
2.4: 25.2.
2.4-5: 34.3.
2.8: 54.5(2); 60.2;
  60.3(2); 65.3;
  67.2; 69.4.
2.9: 65.3; 95.8.
2.12: 25.1(2); 26.3.
3.7: 90.3.
3.9: 23.5; 26.4(2);
  35.3; 69.1; 90.3.
3.11: 4.2; 83.1.
3.16: 27.6; 42.6;
  43.1; 48.1.
3.16-17: 84B.4.
4.7: 17.2; 67.6.
5.7: 53.3; 55.5(2);
  58.2; 59.5;
  61.5(2).
5.8: 39.6; 59.8(2);
  63.7; 69.5; 72.4.
6.15: 21.3; 23.5;
  41.2; 41.3; 69.5.
6.17: 30.5.
6.19: 21.3; 23.5;
  69.5; 78.3.
6.20: 21.3; 23.5;
  35.4; 41.3; 52.2;
  53.3; 55.5; 57.5;
  58.5.
7.19: 63.2.
7.23: 21.3; 52.2.
7.29-31: 49.2; 90.3.
8.1: 36.2; 84B.2.
9.27: 70.6.
10.4: 63.6.
10.11: 23.2(2);
  26.2(2); 30.1.
10.12: 43.3; 93.1.
10.13: 18.1.
10.24: 37.4(2); 88.4.
11.1: 25.6.
12.3: 75.4; 76.4;
  77.2.
12.4-6: 75.4.
12.6: 3.1; 35.3; 38.4;
  45.3; 63.7; 69.5;
  88.4.

13.2: 45.2.
13.3: 79.3.
13.12: 95.8.
14.1: 24.6(2);
  74.5(2).
14.20: 31.3(2);
  37.4.
15.20: 65.4; 66.3.
15.21: 52.1.
15.22: 25.5; 59.8;
  65.4; 69.3(2).
15.23: 66.3.
15.27-28: 74.4(2).
15.28: 63.3.
15.47-49: 71.2.
15.48: 24.2(2).
15.48-49: 55.5.
15.49: 27.2(2); 63.6;
  93.1.
15.53: 95.5.
16.2: 7.1; 7.2; 8.2;
  9.3(2); 10.3.

2 Corinthians
1.6: 58.5; 76.5.
2.16: 25.1(2).
3.6: 89.1.
3.12: 22.6.
3.17: 77.2; 89.1.
4.16: 43.1; 59.8(2).
4.18: 27.6(2);
  49.2.
5.10: 35.3.
5.15: 59.8(2).
5.16: 71.4.
5.17: 21.3; 26.5;
  27.2(2); 40.2;
  41.2; 59.8(2);
  63.7; 69.4; 71.6;
  93.1.
5.19: 54.4; 63.1;
  65.2; 67.7; 69.4.
5.21: 62.2(2); 74.1;
  77.2.
6.2: 40.2; 42.1.
6.3: 42.2.
6.7: 42.2(2).
6.8: 42.2(2).
6.10: 42.2(3); 95.3.
6.14: 8.1; 42.6; 47.1;
  70.5; 84B.3.

6.16: 42.6; 43.1;
  48.1; 84B.4.
6.17: 8.1.
7.1: 42.2.
8.9: 9.3(2); 68.4;
  91.3(2).
8.11-12: 8.2.
8.15: 10.3.
9.6: 10.3;10.3.
9.7: 7.1.
9.7: 11.2; 48.5;
  87.4(2); 88.4;
  88.5; 89.6.
9.8: 10.3.
9.10: 48.5; 88.5.
9.11-12: 48.5; 88.4.
10.17: 5.1; 38.4;
  42.3; 45.4; 55.5;
  79.3.
11.14: 16.3; 27.3.
11.29: 34.5(2).
12.9: 93.1.
13.1: 51.4.

Galatians
1.9: 24.6.
3.7: 63.2.
3.7-9: 60.3.
3.11: 5.2; 10.3;
  22.4(2); 23.3;
  24.6(2).
3.16: 30.7; 33.5.
3.22: 33.1(2); 66.2.
3.24: 74.1(2).
3.27-29: 63.2.
3.28: 4.1.
4.4: 21.1(2); 23.2(2);
  25.4; 25.5;
  34.3(2).
4.6: 77.2.
4.7: 66.2.
4.31: 53.3.
5.6: 45.2.
5.17: 39.2; 41.1;
  42.2; 47.1; 81.2.
5.19: 21.3.
5.24: 84B.2.
6.8: 92.3.
6.9: 10.3.
6.10: 10.3; 41.3;
  89.5; 92.4.

6.14: 70.5; 84B.2.
6.15: 21.3; 26.5;
  40.2; 41.2; 63.7.

Ephesians
1.4: 23.4; 24.1(2).
1.6: 60.1.
1.10: 21.1(2).
1.13: 39.4.
1.18: 27.1.
1.20-21: 46.3; 73.4;
  74.1(2).
1.22-23: 46.3; 82.7.
2.4-5: 21.3.
2.7: 2.3.
2.14: 4.2; 26.5(2);
  83.1.
2.15-16: 64.3.
2.15-17: 66.3.
2.18: 26.5(2).
2.20: 4.2; 83.1;
  84B.4.
2.21: 84B.4.
2.22: 48.1.
3.19: 92.3; 95.6.
3.20: 3.1; 35.3;
  45.3.
4.2: 23.5; 25.6.
4.3: 26.3; 95.9.
4.3-6: 84B.4.
4.4-5: 41.3.
4.5-6: 24.6(2).
4.8: 5.2; 76.8;
  91.3(2).
4.15: 72.7; 84B.4.
4.16: 84B.4.
4.24: 44.1.
5.1: 45.2.
5.2: 52.5; 58.4(2);
  64.3; 85.1.
5.8-9: 33.5(2).
5.8: 35.4.
5.25-26: 68.2.
5.27: 41.1; 65.1.
5.29: 71.5(2).
6.9: 11.2(2).
6.11: 22.5.
6.12: 39.4.
6.12: 39.2; 40.2;
  89.2.
6.14-17: 39.4.

Philippians
2.2: 26.5; 26.5(2).
2.5-11: 72.4(2).
2.6: 23.2(2); 28.1;
  34.1; 46.2(2);
  51.6; 52.2; 63.4;
  64.2; 72.4(2).
2.6-7: 21.2; 27.1(3);
  30.5(2); 30.6;
  46.1; 53.1(2);
  54.2; 69.3; 69.5;
  77.5; 91.2(2).
2.7: 22.2; 22.3(3);
  23.2; 23.2(2);
  24.2; 25.2; 28.1;
  31.2; 34.1(2);
  46.2(2); 51.6;
  59.1; 62.1(2);
  63.4; 65.3;
  66.4(2); 67.6;
  72.5(2); 74.1;
  77.2.
2.8: 25.5.
2.9: 72.6.
2.10-11: 12.2; 29.2;
  91.3.
2.11: 38.2; 76.8.
2.12-13: 38.3.
2.13: 3.1; 19.3;
  26.4(2); 35.3;
  45.3; 49.4; 92.4.
2.15: 35.4.
3.3: 64.3; 66.2.
3.18: 42.6; 65.1;
  66.5; 91.2.
3.20: 46.4.
3.20-21: 65.5; 72.7.
4.1: 1.2; 3.4.
4.4: 32.1.

Colossians
1.5: 39.4.
1.12: 21.3.
1.12-13: 33.5.
1.13: 21.3; 57.5;
  63.7.
1.15: 26.5; 63.3.
1.18: 28.5(2); 72.7;
  82.7.
1.18-20: 63.3.
1.20: 55.5(2).

INDEX OF HOLY SCRIPTURE

1.23: 22.6; 24.6.
2.2: 66.1.
2.8: 91.1.
2.8-10: 28.7; 30.3(2).
2.9-10: 65.5.
2.10: 30.3(2).
2.14: 22.4; 51.7; 53.1(2); 61.4.
2.15: 59.4; 61.4; 67.7.
3.1-2: 26.5(2).
3.1-4: 46.3; 72.3.
3.2: 31.3(2); 33.5(2); 92.3(2).
3.3-4: 27.6(2); 50.1; 51.3; 63.7; 69.4.
3.8-9: 21.3; 43.1.
3.10: 26.2; 44.1; 63.4.
3.12: 31.3(2).
3.13: 44.3.
3.25: 11.2(2).

1 Thessalonians
2.19-20: 1.2; 3.4.
5.5: 33.5(2).
5.6: 32.4.
5.9: 64.3.
5.16-18: 12.3.
5.22: 32.4(2).

1 Timothy
1.10: 37.3.
1.15: 59.8; 67.3.
1.19: 30.1.
2.4: 38.3.
2.5: 21.2; 31.1; 63.2; 64.3; 69.5.
2.15: 3.4.
3.7: 87.1.
3.16: 23.4; 25.2; 30.1; 34.4(2); 47.2; 56.3(2); 57.5; 66.1(2); 72.2; 72.4(2).
4.4: 42.4; 81.1.
4.14: 67.6.
5.6: 24.6(2).
6.10: 45.4; 60.4; 74.5(2).
6.12: 24.6.
6.16: 95.8.
6.18: 6.1; 9.2(2).
6.20: 23.3.

2 Timothy
1.9: 60.1.
2.6: 87.1.
2.12: 25.6; 59.5; 69.5; 70.4; 90.2.
2.17: 16.3; 96.3.
3.12: 47.1; 69.5; 70.5; 84B.2; 85.4(2).
4.18: 32.4(2).

Titus
1.2: 26.2(2); 30.1; 60.1.
1.15: 42.4.
1.16: 9.1; 36.4.
2.11: 23.5.
3.4: 23.4; 23.5.
3.5: 76.8.
3.10-11: 96.1.

Hebrews
1.1: 24.1; 25.4.
2.14: 37.3.
2.18: 58.5.
4.13: 43.3.
4.15: 62.2(2); 63.4; 77.2.
5.2: 5.1.
5.3: 5.1.
5.6: 3.1.
5.9: 23.4.
6.20: 3.1; 5.3.
7: 5.3.
7.11: 3.1; 5.3.
7.27: 5.1.
8.8: 95.1.
8.10: 95.1.
9.14: 68.3.
10.12: 56.3(2); 68.3(2).
10.14: 68.3(2).
10.19: 46.4.
10.20: 68.3.
10.22: 22.5; 66.1.
10.23: 46.4.
10.36: 22.5.
10.38: 5.2; 10.3; 22.4(2); 23.3; 24.6(2).
11.1: 45.2
11.2: 69.2.
11.6: 24.6(2); 45.2.
11.16: 35.4.
12.1: 39.5.
12.14: 24.6(2).
13.11-12: 59.5.
13.16: 48.4.
13.17: 5.2.

James
1.3: 39.3.
1.5: 49.4.
1.17: 5.1.
2.13: 11.1; 92.1(2).
2.17: 10.3.
2.20: 10.3.
2.26: 10.3.
3.2: 49.5; 88.3.
3.8: 96.3.
5.8: 34.5.

1 Peter
1.7: 39.3.
1.13: 3.4.
1.20: 24.1; 33.1(2); 34.1; 52.1; 66.1(2).
2.5: 4.1; 43.1; 84B.4.
2.6: 84B.4.
2.9: 3.1; 4.1; 24.6; 26.3; 82.1.
2.11: 31.3(2); 74.5.
2.12: 63.7.
2.21-24: 63.4.
3.2: 3.4.
3.14: 51.8.
3.20-21: 60.3.
3.22: 69.4.
4.5: 46.3.
4.8: 6.1; 7.1; 10.3; 48.4; 74.5(2).

2 Peter
1.4: 21.3; 25.5.
1.12: 34.5.
1.17: 91.3(2).

2.20: 27.3.
3.9: 22.1(2).

1 John
1.1: 26.1; 64.1.
1.1-3: 73.1(2).
1.8: 37.3; 41.1; 90.1.
2.6: 90.2.
3.8: 22.3; 22.3(3);
27.2(2); 44.1; 66.1(2); 69.3.
3.24: 1.2.
4.2: 22.1(2).
4.2-3: 34.5.
4.4: 26.4(2); 39.3.
4.7-8: 48.3; 92.3.
4.10: 12.1.
4.16: 38.4; 48.3.
4.18: 76.5.
4.19: 12.1; 48.1.
5.3: 23.5.
5.19: 15.1; 26.4(2).
5.20: 12.1.

Jude
1.12: 18.3.

Revelation
5.9: 51.7.

www.ingramcontent.com/pod-product-compliance
Lightning Source LLC
Chambersburg PA
CBHW032022290426
44110CB00012B/636